THE PILLOW BOOK OF
SEI SHŌNAGON

TRANSLATIONS FROM
THE ASIAN CLASSICS

THE PILLOW BOOK OF
SEI SHŌNAGON

TRANSLATED AND EDITED BY IVAN MORRIS

COLUMBIA UNIVERSITY PRESS
NEW YORK

Columbia University Press
New York   Chichester, West Sussex
Copyright © 1991 Columbia University Press
All rights reserved

Library of Congress Cataloging-in-Publication Data

Sei Shōnagon, db. ca. 967.
   [Makura no sōshi. English]
   The pillow book of Sei Shōnagon
translated and edited by Ivan Morris.
      p. cm.—(Translations from the Asian Classics)
   Translation of : Makura no sōshi.
   ISBN 0-231-07336-4.
   ISBN 0-231-07337-2 (pbk.)
   I. Morris, Ivan I.
   II. Title.
   III. Series.
PL788.6.M3E56   1991
895.6'8107—dc20   91-15757
                          CIP

∞

Casebound editions of Columbia University Press books are printed on permanent and durable acid-free paper.

Printed in the United States of America
c 10 9 8 7 6 5 4 3 2
p 10

This translation is dedicated to my friend and colleague Professor Donald Keene

CONTENTS

INTRODUCTION

Sei Shōnagon is among the greatest writers of prose in the long history of Japanese literature; *The Pillow Book* is an exceedingly rich source of information concerning the halcyon period in which she lived. Yet about her own life we have almost no definite facts. She was born approximately a thousand years ago (965 is a likely date) and served as lady-in-waiting to Empress Sadako during the last decade of the tenth century. Her father, whether real or adoptive, was Motosuke, a member of the Kiyowara clan, who worked as a provincial official but was best known as a scholar and a poet. It is possible, though I think unlikely, that Shōnagon was briefly married to a government official called Tachibana no Norimitsu, by whom she may have had a son. Her life after her service ended is totally obscure. There is a tradition that she died in lonely poverty; but this may be the invention of moralists who, shocked by her worldly approach and promiscuous doings, ascribed to her last years a type of retribution that occurs more often in fiction than in reality.

Of Shōnagon's relations with her family nothing is known, and she mentions her father only once; we have no idea where or how she lived when not at Court, nor when or where she died. Even her name is uncertain: in the palace she was called Shōnagon ('Minor Counsellor'), but recent research suggests that her real name may have been Nagiko; *Sei* refers to the Kiyowara family.

There is an acidulous reference to Sei Shōnagon in the diary of her great contemporary, Murasaki Shikibu, the author of *The Tale of Genji*:

Sei Shōnagon has the most extraordinary air of self-satisfaction. Yet, if we stop to examine those Chinese writings of hers that she so presumptuously scatters about the place, we find that they are full of imperfections. Someone who makes such an effort to be different from others is bound to fall in people's esteem, and I can only think that her future will be a hard one. She is a gifted woman, to be sure. Yet, if one gives free rein to one's emotions even under the most inappropriate circumstances, if one has to sample each interesting thing that comes along, people are bound to regard one as frivolous. And how can things turn out well for such a woman?

This is almost our only information about Sei Shōnagon except what is revealed by *The Pillow Book* itself. A vast collection of personal notes, her book covers the ten-odd years during which she served at Court, and reveals a complicated, intelligent, well-informed woman who was quick, impatient, keenly observant of detail, high-spirited, witty, emulative, sensitive to the charms and beauties of the world and to the pathos of things, yet intolerant and callous about people whom she regarded as her social or intellectual inferiors.

Shōnagon wrote during the great mid-Heian period of feminine vernacular literature that produced not only the world's first psychological novel, *The Tale of Genji*, but vast quantities of poetry and a series of diaries, mostly by Court ladies, which enable us to imagine what life was like for upper-class Japanese women a thousand years ago. In many ways, such as her love of pageantry and colour, her delight in poetry, her mixture of naïvety and sophistication, she resembled the other women writers we know. But *The Pillow Book* also suggests some notable differences. Shōnagon's scorn for the lower orders, which has moved one indignant Japanese critic to describe her as a 'spiritual cripple', and her adoration of the Imperial family were so pronounced as to seem almost pathological. Her attitude to men, even to those of a somewhat higher class than hers, was competitive to the point of overt hostility. And, partly owing to this combative spirit, her writing is free of the whining, querulous tone that often marks the work of her female contemporaries when they describe their relations with men.

In a section of *The Pillow Book* that can be dated about 994 Shōnagon writes:

One day Lord Korechika, the Minister of the Centre, brought the Empress a bundle of notebooks. 'What shall we do with them?'

10

Her Majesty asked me. 'The Emperor has already made arrangements for copying the "Records of the Historian".'

'Let me make them into a pillow,' I said.

'Very well,' said Her Majesty. 'You may have them.'

I now had a vast quantity of paper at my disposal, and I set about filling the notebooks with odd facts, stories from the past, and all sorts of other things, often including the most trivial material. On the whole I concentrated on things and people that I found charming and splendid; my notes are also full of poems and observations on trees and plants, birds and insects.

It is uncertain whether this passage is authentic; yet no doubt Shōnagon started her book while still serving in the Court whose life she describes with such minute detail. We know that some of the sections were written many years later than the events they record, and the work was not completed until well after Shōnagon's retirement following the Empress's death in 1000.

Though this is the only collection of its type to have survived from the Heian period, it is possible that many others were written. Of the dozen or so works of prose fiction she lists in her book only one has come down to us; Heian miscellanies like *The Pillow Book* may have had an equally poor rate of survival. The title, *Makura no Sōshi* ('notes of the pillow'), whether or not Shōnagon actually used it herself, was probably a generic term to describe a type of informal book of notes which men and women composed when they retired to their rooms in the evening and which they kept near their sleeping place, possibly in the drawers of their wooden pillows, so that they might record stray impressions. This form of *belles-lettres* appears to have been indigenous to Japan. *The Pillow Book* is the precursor of a typically Japanese genre known as *zuihitsu* ('occasional writings', 'random notes') which has lasted until the present day and which includes some of the most valued works in the country's literature.

Apart from the 164 lists, which are perhaps its most striking feature, Shōnagon's collection contains nature descriptions, diary entries, character sketches, and anecdotes, and provides such a detailed picture of upper-class Heian life that Arthur Waley has described it as 'the most important document of the period that we possess'. Its title, suggesting something rather light and casual, belies the length and variety of the book. The main edition that I have followed has 1,098 closely printed pages; admittedly much of it consists of annotation and commentary, but even the less encumbered texts consist of several hundred pages.

The arrangement of the book in the main versions that we know is desultory and confusing. The datable sections are not in chronological order, and the lists have been placed with little attempt at logical sequence. It is of course possible that the book Shōnagon actually wrote may have been organized in an entirely different way from the existing texts. The earliest extant manuscripts of *The Pillow Book* were produced some 500 years after she wrote, and there was no printed version until the seventeenth century. During the hundreds of intervening years scholars and scribes freely edited the manuscripts that came into their hands, often moving passages from one part of the book to another, incorporating glosses into the body of the text, omitting words or sentences they believed to be spurious; and they made mistakes in copying. All this has led to considerable differences among the texts, sometimes involving an almost total rearrangement of the sections.

The eminent classicist, Professor Ikeda Kikan, established four main textual traditions: (i) *Den Nōin Hōshi Shojihon* (the earliest extant copy is the sixteenth-century *Sanjōnishikebon*); the *Shunsho Shōhon* version, on which Kaneko Motoomi's monumental text is based, was produced by Kitamura Kigin in 1674, (ii) *Antei Ninen Okugakibon* (usually known as the *Sankanbon*; the earliest extant copy is dated 1475), (iii) *Maedabon* (this is the oldest extant version of *The Pillow Book*, the earliest manuscript dating from the mid thirteenth century), (iv) *Sakaibon* (earliest copy: 1570). Of these traditions (i) and (ii) are usually described as *zassanteki* ('miscellaneous', 'mixed'), (iii) and (iv) as *bunruiteki* ('classified', 'grouped'). My own translation is based on (i) and (ii); in (iii) and (iv) Shōnagon's sections on nature, people, things, etc. are rearranged under topic headings.

The original text of *The Pillow Book* had disappeared well before the end of the Heian period, and by the beginning of the Kamakura period (twelfth century) numerous variants were already in circulation. Except in the unlikely event that a Heian manuscript of *The Pillow Book* is discovered, we shall never be sure which version is closest to the original. My own impression is that the book actually written by Shōnagon was at least as unsystematic and disordered as the *Shunsho Shōhon* and *Sangenbon* texts. Much depends on whether Shōnagon was, as she protests, writing only for herself, or whether she had other readers in mind. It is possible that *The Pillow Book* was begun casually as a sort of private notebook *cum* diary (the numerous lists of place-names can hardly have been intended for anyone but herself); according to this theory, it was only after 996, when its existence became known at Court, that it developed into a more deliberate and literary work. In this case Shōnagon may herself have rearranged some of the sections in her book in order to make it more coherent and readable.

The structural confusion of *The Pillow Book* is generally regarded as its main stylistic weakness; yet surely part of its charm lies precisely in its rather bizarre, haphazard arrangement in which a list of 'awkward things', for example, is followed by an account of the Emperor's return from a shrine, after which comes a totally unrelated incident about the Chancellor that occurred a year or two earlier and then a short, lyrical description of the dew on a clear autumn morning.

About the extraordinary beauty and evocative power of Shōnagon's language Japanese readers have always agreed. School-children are still introduced to *The Pillow Book* as a model of linguistic purity; for, apart from proper names, titles, and quotations, there is hardly a single Chinese word or locution in the entire book. The language, rhythmic, quick-moving, varied, and compressed, is far clearer than that of *The Tale of Genji* with its long sentences and huge networks of dependent

13

clauses; for this reason many Japanese consider Shōnagon's book to be a greater work of literature. In his scintillating volume, *The Pillow Book of Sei Shōnagon*, which contains translated extracts totalling about a quarter of the original work, Arthur Waley says:

As a writer she is incomparably the best poet of her time, a fact which is apparent only in her prose and not at all in the conventional *uta* [31-syllable poems] for which she is also famous. Passages such as that about the stormy lake or the few lines about crossing a moonlit river show a beauty of phrasing that Murasaki, a much more deliberate writer, certainly never surpassed.

It is true that Shōnagon revels in repeating certain words and phrases. Adjectives like *okashi* ('charming') and *medetashi* ('splendid') recur in nearly every sentence, almost invariably accompanied by the ubiquitous and virtually meaningless adverb *ito* ('very'); and often a single word will reappear in a sentence with a somewhat different meaning. This love of repetition, which most Western readers are bound to find tiresome, cannot simply be explained by the paucity of adjectives and adverbs in classical Japanese. In both Chinese and Japanese literature repetition was a deliberate stylistic device; and even as careful a craftsman as Murasaki Shikibu uses the same adjective again and again in consecutive sentences. In the writing of Sei Shōnagon the reiteration of a word like *okashi* or a phrase like *ito medetashi* often serves as a sort of poetic refrain, giving a particular rhythm or mood to a passage rather than contributing specifically to its sense.

This is one of the insuperable difficulties that confront the translator when he tries to convey the beauty of Shōnagon's prose in a language as remote from Heian Japanese as modern English. Should he reproduce each *okashi* and each *ito* by a given English equivalent, however monotonous and banal the result may be for Western readers? Or should he conceal the repetitiveness of Shōnagon's style by searching for synonyms or even by leaving out some of her favourite words when they seem

to add little to the meaning? In broader terms, should he reproduce her sentences with the greatest possible mechanical
accuracy, or try to suggest the poetic quality of her language at
the cost of obscuring certain characteristic elements of her style?
One possibility would be to produce both a literal and a literary
version; but even the most long-suffering publisher could hardly
welcome that solution.

As usual in translation, one must compromise between the two
extremes. When in doubt, I have tended to be 'free'. This is
partly because the language of *The Pillow Book*, in which the most
laconic phrasing is often combined with seeming redundancy, is
peculiarly resistant to literalism. Any 'accurate' translation
would impose terrible ordeals on all but the most determined.
Since Shōnagon's book is noted for the limpid beauty of its
language, a translation that adhered to the exact wording of the
original, faithfully reproducing each particle, each repetition,
each apparent ambiguity, would from a literary point of view be
totally inaccurate. A language that afforded as little pleasure to
the Japanese as the following passage does to English readers
would hardly have preserved *The Pillow Book* from oblivion for a
thousand years:

the manner in which [they] did such things as deliver [honourable]
letters and move about and behave was not awkward-seeming and
[they] conversed and laughed[.] even wondering indeed when in the
world [I] would mix thus was awkward[.]

While I have not aspired to convey the beauty of Shōnagon's
prose, I have at least tried not to obscure it entirely by the stark,
graceless literalism and the 'rebarbative barricades of square
brackets' that Mr Vladimir Nabokov, for one, appears to recommend. When the need to put Shōnagon's sentences into readable
English has obliged me to take unusual liberties with her text,
I have appended a more or less literal translation in the notes.
Students and other readers who require a close translation of the
entire book should refer to *Les Notes de chevet de Sei Shōnagon* (Paris, 1934), in which Docteur André Beaujard has

conscientiously retained everything that was possible from the original and indicated necessary additions by a liberal, though not always consistent, use of brackets.

In translating the quoted and original poems from *The Pillow Book*, I have abandoned all attempts to be literal and have tried instead to give their general meaning and to suggest a certain poetic rhythm. I have not preserved the line or word patterns of the poems unless they seemed to lend themselves naturally to those forms in English. There can be no literature in the world less suited to translation than classic Japanese poetry; and it is only because verse is such an integral part of *The Pillow Book* that I have ventured on an undertaking that is unlikely ever to succeed. Docteur Beaujard has provided *ad verbum*, prosaic versions, arranging them all, line by line, in the forms of the original poems.

My complete translation (Oxford University Press and Columbia University Press, 1967) is based primarily on the *Shunsho Shōhon* version as edited by Kaneko Motoomi in 1927 and on the Nihon Koten Bungaku Taikei edition of the *Sankanbon* version edited by Ikeda Kikan and Kishigami Shinji in 1953. Publication in a single volume necessitated certain cuts. As a devotee of Sei Shōnagon I found it hard to excise passages of her book; but in the hope that this new edition would make her work available to many more readers I removed the necessary number of pages from my original translation and from the accompanying notes. Most of the cuts are lists, especially lists of place names, words, titles, and the like that are interesting mainly to the specialist. Though Sei Shōnagon would certainly have disapproved of such tampering with her text, which she might well have included in her list of Presumptuous Things, I am confident that I have not jettisoned a single passage of outstanding interest or beauty.

With a few exceptions I have avoided making any additions to the text. Japanese authors, especially those writing in the classical language, omit personal names and pronouns as much as·possible; in direct quotations the identity of the speakers is usually left to the reader's imagination. All this has to be supplied if the text is to be comprehensible in English. When Shōnagon does identify her characters, she usually refers to them by their titles or offices. This helps to date the sections, but can result in great confusion since people frequently changed their posts; a gentleman who appears in one section as a Chamberlain, for example, may be described a few pages later as an Imperial Adviser and 'Chamberlain' may now refer to an entirely different person. In my translation I normally identify men by their given names (e.g. Korechika) rather than by their titles (e.g. Major Counsellor).

I have headed each of the sections with a title. In the lists these are the first words given by Shōnagon herself (e.g. 'Hateful Things'); in the other sections they are the first words of my translation (e.g. 'Once during a Long Spell of Rainy Weather'). I have also added my own numbers for each section. I have not indicated these various additions by square brackets; if brackets were used consistently, that is, if they enclosed every single word and punctuation mark not in the original, almost each sentence would have a dozen or more pairs and to read the text would be a suffering for all but the most resolute students.

In translating titles, government offices, and the like I have normally followed the nomenclature in R. K. Reischauer's *Early Japanese History*, but I have occasionally altered his terms when they seemed cumbersome or misleading. Except when it was essential for clarifying puns, I have usually not translated proper names. This is not a result of 'Translator's Despair' but because I wished to avoid the type of false exoticism that can result from identifying the Emperor's residence, for example, as 'the Pure and Fresh Palace'. Names should not be made to sound more colourful in translation than they do to the reader of the original Japanese. For the same reason months are identified by their numbers (e.g. Fifth Month), which are clearer, though admittedly less poetic, than literalisms like 'Rice-sprouting Month'. I have, however, given direct translations of the hours ('Hour of the Monkey', 'Hour of the Sheep', etc.) since there is no simple Western equivalent for the zodiacal system of time-keeping. My translations of trees, flowers, birds, and the like are often approximations; I have preferred to use words that correspond more or less to the Japanese original and that have a similar degree of familiarity (e.g. 'cypress' for *hinoki* and 'maple' for *kae no ki*) rather than technically exact equivalents (*Chamaecyparis obtusa* and *Acer pictum*), which would be meaningless to most non-specialists.

Some fifty sections of *The Pillow Book*, representing about two fifths of its total length, can be dated by methods that are on the whole reliable. It would have been a simple matter to rearrange these sections in chronological order, possibly putting them all together in the first part of the book, which would then become a sort of diary. I have, however, preferred to retain the confused time-sequence of the traditional texts, not because this was necessarily the order in which Shōnagon arranged her book, but because any systematic reorganization would be arbitrary and possibly misleading. If one thing is clear about the writing of *The Pillow Book*, it is that Shōnagon was not keeping a daily, or even a monthly, record of events. To suggest that this was her intention would falsify the spirit of her work. Readers who wish to peruse the datable sections in chronological sequence can do so by consulting Appendix 5 (Chronology).

The notes are numbered consecutively from 1 to 584 and have been placed separately, in order to avoid encumbering the text. Shōnagon and her courtly contemporaries, who expected their world and its customs to continue as long as civilized society lasted, would no doubt have been shocked to find that such a large quantity of annotation and scholarly accessories was necessary to explain an informal, seemingly simple collection of lists, descriptions, and anecdotes; but without supplementary material of this kind much of *The Pillow Book* is obscure, even incomprehensible, not only to Westerners, but to modern Japanese readers as well.

Any book from a civilization as remote in time, space, and almost every other respect as Heian Japan would normally require far more extensive annotation and introductory material than are provided here. Most of the lacunae are filled by my study of Court life in ancient Japan entitled *The World of the Shining Prince* (Penguin Books, 1969), which contains general background information about Sei Shōnagon's society. The five appendices to the present edition give details about certain subjects that are particularly useful for understanding her book: (1) The Calendar; (2) The Government; (3) Places; (4) Clothes, Houses, etc.; (5) Chronology.

In addition to the scholars already mentioned, I should like to thank my friends in England, America, Japan, and Norway for all their help and encouragement during the five years spent with *The Pillow Book*. I am also most grateful to Professor Hans Bielenstein and to Fang Chao-ying for checking the Chinese quotations and references, to Dr Hakeda Yoshito for his advice on Sanskrit terms, and to Mrs Shirley Bridgwater and Mrs Karen Brazell for proof-reading a most complicated manuscript. Finally I am indebted to Professor Edwin Cranston for the many valuable suggestions and corrections contained in his review article on my *Pillow Book of Sei Shōnagon* published by the *Harvard Journal of Asiatic Studies*, vol. xxix, 1969.

1. *In Spring It Is the Dawn*

In spring it is the dawn that is most beautiful.[1] As the light creeps over the hills, their outlines are dyed a faint red and wisps of purplish cloud trail over them.

In summer the nights. Not only when the moon shines, but on dark nights too, as the fireflies flit to and fro, and even when it rains, how beautiful it is!

In autumn the evenings, when the glittering sun sinks close to the edge of the hills and the crows fly back to their nests in threes and fours and twos; more charming still is a file of wild geese, like specks in the distant sky. When the sun has set, one's heart is moved by the sound of the wind and the hum of the insects.

In winter the early mornings. It is beautiful indeed when snow has fallen during the night, but splendid too when the ground is white with frost; or even when there is no snow or frost, but it is simply very cold and the attendants hurry from room to room stirring up the fires and bringing charcoal, how well this fits the season's mood! But as noon approaches and the cold wears off, no one bothers to keep the braziers alight, and soon nothing remains but piles of white ashes.

2. *Especially Delightful Is the First Day*

Especially delightful is the first day of the First Month, when the mists so often shroud the sky. Everyone pays great attention to his appearance and dresses with the utmost care. What a pleasure it is to see them all offer their congratulations to the Emperor and celebrate their own new year![2]

I also enjoy the seventh day, when people pluck the young herbs that have sprouted fresh and green beneath the snow.[3] It is amusing to see their excitement when they find such plants growing near the Palace, by no means a spot where one might expect them.[4]

This is the day when members of the nobility who live outside the Palace arrive in their magnificently decorated carriages to admire the blue horses.[5] As the carriages are drawn over the ground-beam of the Central Gate,[6] there is always a tremendous bump, and the heads of the women passengers are knocked together; the combs fall out of their hair, and may be smashed to pieces if the owners are not careful. I enjoy the way everyone laughs when this happens.

I remember one occasion when I visited the Palace to see the procession of blue horses. Several senior courtiers[7] were standing outside the guard-house of the Left Division; they had borrowed bows from the escorts, and, with much laughter, were twanging them to make the blue horses prance. Looking through one of the gates of the Palace enclosure, I could dimly make out a garden fence, near which a number of ladies, several of them from the Office of Grounds, went to and fro. What lucky women, I thought, who could walk about the Nine-Fold Enclosure as though they had lived there all their lives! Just then the escorts passed close to my carriage – remarkably close, in fact, considering the vastness of the Palace grounds – and I could actually see the texture of their faces. Some of them were not properly powdered; here and there their skin showed through unpleasantly like the dark patches of earth in a garden where the snow has begun to melt. When the horses in the procession reared wildly, I shrank into the back of my carriage and could no longer see what was happening.

On the eighth day[8] there is great excitement in the Palace as people hurry to express their gratitude, and the clatter of carriages is louder than ever – all very fascinating.

The fifteenth day is the festival of the full-moon gruel,[9] when a bowl of gruel is presented to His Majesty. On this day all the women of the house carry gruel-sticks, which they hide carefully from each other. It is most amusing to see them walking about, as they await an opportunity to hit their companions. Each one is careful not to be struck herself and is constantly looking over her shoulder to make sure that no one is stealing up on her. Yet the precautions are useless, for before long one of the women manages to score a hit. She is extremely pleased with herself and laughs merrily. Everyone finds this delightful – except, of course, the victim, who looks very put out.

In a certain household a young gentleman had been married during the previous year to one of the girls in the family.[10] Having spent the night with her, he was now, on the morning of the fifteenth, about to set off for the Palace. There was a woman[11] in the house who was in the habit of lording it over everyone. On this occasion she was standing in the back of the room, impatiently awaiting an opportunity to hit the man with her gruel-stick as he left. One of the other women realized what she had in mind and burst out laughing. The woman with the stick signalled excitedly that she should be quiet. Fortunately the young man did not notice what was afoot and he stood there unconcernedly.

'I have to pick up something over there,' said the woman with the stick, approaching the man. Suddenly she darted forward, gave him a great whack, and made her escape. Everyone in the room burst out laughing; even the young man smiled pleasantly, not in the least annoyed. He was not too startled; but he did blush a little, which was charming.

Sometimes when the women are hitting each other the men also join in the fun. The strange thing is that, when a woman is hit, she often gets angry and bursts into tears; then she will upbraid her assailant and say the most awful things about him – most amusing. Even in the Palace, where the atmosphere is usually so solemn, everything is in confusion on this day, and no one stands on ceremony.

It is fascinating to see what happens during the period of appointments. However snowy and icy it may be, candidates of the Fourth and Fifth Ranks come to the Palace with their official requests. Those who are still young and merry seem full of confidence. For the candidates who are old and white-haired things do not go so smoothly. Such men have to apply for help from people with influence at Court; some of them even visit ladies-in-waiting in their quarters and go to great lengths in pointing out their own merits. If young women happen to be present, they are greatly amused. As soon as the candidates have left, they mimic and deride them – something that the old men cannot possibly suspect as they scurry from one part of the Palace to another, begging everyone, 'Please present my petition favourably to the Emperor' and 'Pray inform Her Majesty about me.' It is not so bad if they finally succeed, but it really is rather pathetic when all their efforts prove in vain.

3. *On the Third Day of the Third Month*

On the third day of the Third Month I like to see the sun shining bright and calm in the spring sky. Now is the time when the peach trees come into bloom, and what a sight it is! The willows too are most charming at this season, with the buds still enclosed like silkworms in their cocoons. After the leaves have spread out, I find them unattractive; in fact all trees lose their charm once the blossoms have begun to scatter.

It is a great pleasure to break off a long, beautifully flowering branch from a cherry tree and to arrange it in a large vase. What a delightful task to perform when a visitor is seated nearby conversing! It may be an ordinary guest, or possibly one of Their Highnesses, the Empress's [12] elder brothers; but in any case the visitor will wear a cherry-coloured [13] Court cloak, from the bottom of which his under-robe emerges. I am even happier if a butterfly or a small bird flutters prettily near the flowers and I can see its face.

4. *How Delightful Everything Is!*

How delightful everything is at the time of the Festival! [14] The leaves, which still do not cover the trees too thickly, are green and fresh. In the daytime there is no mist to hide the sky and, glancing up, one is overcome by its beauty. On a slightly cloudy evening, or again at night, it is moving to hear in the distance the song of a *hototogisu*[15] – so faint that one doubts one's own ears.

When the Festival approaches, I enjoy seeing the men go to and fro with rolls of yellowish green and deep violet material which they have loosely wrapped in paper and placed in the lids of long boxes. At this time of the year, border shading, uneven shading, and rolled dyeing all seem more attractive than usual.[16] The young girls who are to take part in the procession have had their hair washed and arranged; but they are still wearing their everyday clothes, which sometimes are in a great mess, wrinkled and coming apart at the seams. How excited they are as they run about the house, impatiently awaiting the great day, and rapping out orders to the maids: 'Fit the cords on my clogs' or 'See that the soles of my sandals are all right.' Once they have put on their Festival costumes, these same young girls, instead of prancing about the rooms, become extremely demure and walk along solemnly like priests at the head of a procession. I also enjoy seeing how their mothers, aunts, and elder sisters, dressed according to their ranks, accompany the girls and help keep their costumes in order.

5. *Different Ways of Speaking*

A priest's language.
The speech of men and of women.[17]
The common people always tend to add extra syllables to their words.

6. *That Parents Should Bring Up Some Beloved Son*

That parents should bring up some beloved son of theirs to be a priest is really distressing. No doubt it is an auspicious[18] thing to do; but unfortunately most people are convinced that a priest is as unimportant as a piece of wood, and they treat him accordingly. A priest lives poorly on meagre food, and cannot even sleep without being criticized. While he is young, it is only natural that he should be curious about all sorts of things, and, if there are women about, he will probably peep in their direction (though, to be sure, with a look of aversion on his face). What is wrong about that? Yet people immediately find fault with him for even so small a lapse.

The lot of an exorcist is still more painful. On his pilgrimages to Mitake, Kumano, and all the other sacred mountains he often undergoes the greatest hardships. When people come to hear that his prayers are effective, they summon him here and there to perform services of exorcism: the more popular he becomes, the less peace he enjoys. Sometimes he will be called to see a patient who is seriously ill and he has to exert all his powers to cast out the spirit that is causing the affliction. But if he dozes off, exhausted by his efforts, people say reproachfully, 'Really, this priest does nothing but sleep.' Such comments are most embarrassing for the exorcist, and I can imagine how he feel must.

That is how things used to be; nowadays priests have a somewhat easier life.

7. *When the Empress Moved*

When the Empress moved into the house of the Senior Steward, Narimasa, the east gate of his courtyard had been made into a four-pillared structure,[19] and it was here that Her Majesty's palanquin entered. The carriages in which I and the other ladies-in-waiting were travelling arrived at the north gate. As there was no one in the guard-house, we decided to enter just as we were, without troubling to tidy ourselves; many of the women had let their hair become disordered during the journey, but they did not bother to rearrange it, since they assumed that the carriages would be pulled directly up to the veranda of the house. Unfortunately the gate was too narrow for our palm-leaf carriages. The attendants laid down mats for us from the gate to the house, and we had to get out and walk. It was extremely annoying and we were all very cross; but what could we do about it? To make matters worse, there was a group of men, including senior courtiers and even some of lower rank, standing next to the guard-house and staring at us in a most irritating fashion.

When I entered the house and saw Her Majesty, I told her what had happened. 'Do you suppose it is only people outside the house who can see what a state you are in?' she said. 'I wonder what has made you all so careless today.'

'But, Your Majesty,' I replied, 'the people here are all used to us, and it would surprise them if we suddenly took great trouble over our appearance. In any case, it does seem rather strange that the gates of a house like this should be too small for a carriage. I shall have to tease your steward about it when I see him.'

At that very moment Narimasa arrived with an inkstone and other writing implements, which he thrust under the screen, saying, 'Pray give these to Her Majesty.'

'Well, well,' said I, 'you really are a disgraceful man! Why do you live in a house with such narrow gates?'

'I have built my house to suit my station in life,' he laughingly replied.

'That's all very well,' I said, 'but I seem to have heard of someone who built his gate extremely high, out of all proportion to the rest of his house.'

'Good heavens!' exclaimed Narimasa. 'How remarkable! You must be referring to Yü Ting-kuo.[20] I thought it was only veteran scholars who had heard about such things. Even I, Madam, should not have understood you except that I happen to have strayed in these paths myself.'

'Paths!' said I. 'Yours leave something to be desired. When your servants spread out the mats for us, we couldn't see how uneven the ground was and we stumbled all over the place.'

'To be sure, Madam,' said Narimasa. 'It has been raining,

and I am afraid it is a bit uneven. But let's leave it at that. You'll be making some other disagreeable remark in a moment. So I shall be off before you have time.' And with this he went away.

'What happened?' asked the Empress when I rejoined her. 'Narimasa seemed terribly put out.'

'Oh no,' I answered. 'I was only telling him how our carriage could not get in.' Then I withdrew to my own room.

I shared this room with several of the younger ladies-in-waiting. We were all sleepy and, without paying much attention to anything, dozed off immediately. Our room was in the east wing of the house. Though we were unaware of the fact, the clasp of the sliding-door in the back of the western ante-room [21] was missing. Of course the owner of the house knew about this, and presently he came and pushed open the door.

'May I presume to come in?' he said several times in a strangely husky and excited voice. I looked up in amazement, and by the light of the lamp that had been placed behind the curtain of state [22] I could see that Narimasa was standing outside the door, which he had now opened about half a foot. The situation amused me. As a rule he would not have dreamt of indulging in such lecherous behaviour; as the Empress was staying in his house, he evidently felt he could do as he pleased. Waking up the young women next to me, I exclaimed, 'Look who is there! What an unlikely sight!' They all sat up and, seeing Narimasa by the door, burst into laughter. 'Who are you?' I said. 'Don't try to hide!' 'Oh no,' he replied. 'It's simply that the master of the house has something to discuss with the lady-in-waiting in charge.'

'It was your gate I was speaking about,' I said. 'I don't remember asking you to open the sliding-door.'

'Yes indeed,' he answered. 'It is precisely the matter of the gate that I wanted to discuss with you. May I not presume to come in for a moment?'

'Really!' said one of the young women. 'How unpleasant! No, he certainly cannot come in.'

'Oh, I see,' said Narimasa. 'There are other young ladies in the room.' Closing the door behind him, he left, followed by our loud laughter.

How absurd! Once he had opened the door, he should obviously have walked straight in, without bothering to ask for permission. After all, what woman would be likely to say, 'It's all right. Please come in'?

On the following day I told the Empress about the incident. 'It does not sound like Narimasa at all,' she said, laughing. 'It must have been your conversation last night that roused his interest in you. Really, I can't help feeling sorry for the poor man. You have been awfully hard on him.'

One day when the Empress was giving orders about the costumes for the little girls who were to wait upon the Princess Imperial,[23] Narimasa asked, 'Has Your Majesty decided on the colour of the garments[24] that will cover the girls' vests?' This made us all laugh; and surely no one could blame us for being amused. Next Narimasa discussed the Princess's meals. 'I believe it would look rather clumsy, Your Majesty, if they were served in ordinary utensils. If I may say so, she ought to have a *smahl* platter and a *smahl* tray.'[25]

'And be waited upon,' I added, 'by little girls with those garments that cover their vests.'

'You should not make fun of him as the others do,' the Empress told me afterwards. 'He is a very sincere man, and I feel sorry for him.' I found even her reprimand delightful.

Once when I was busy attending the Empress a messenger came and said that Narimasa had arrived and wished to tell me something. Overhearing this, the Empress said, 'I wonder what he will do this time to make himself a laughing-stock. Find out what he has to say.' Delighted by her remark, I decided to go out myself, rather than send a maid. 'Madam,' announced Narimasa, 'I told my brother, the Middle Counsellor,[26] what you said the other night about the gate. He was most impressed and asked me to arrange a meeting for him at some convenient time when he could hear what you had to say.'

I wondered whether Narimasa would make some reference to

his own visit the other night and I felt my heart pounding; but he said nothing further, merely adding as he left, 'I should like to come and see you quietly one of these days.'

'Well,' said the Empress when I returned, 'what happened?' I told her exactly what Narimasa had said, adding with a smile, 'I should hardly have thought it was so important that he had to send a special message for me when I was in attendance. Surely he could have waited until I had settled down quietly in my own room.'

'He probably thought you would be pleased to hear of his brother's high opinion and wanted to let you know at once. He has the greatest respect for his brother, you know.' Very charming the Empress looked as she said this.

8. *The Cat Who Lived in the Palace*

The cat who lived in the Palace had been awarded the headdress of nobility and was called Lady Myōbu. She was a very pretty cat, and His Majesty saw to it that she was treated with the greatest care.[27]

One day she wandered on to the veranda, and Lady Uma, the nurse in charge of her, called out, 'Oh, you naughty thing! Please come inside at once.' But the cat paid no attention and went on basking sleepily in the sun. Intending to give her a scare, the nurse called for the dog, Okinamaro.

'Okinamaro, where are you?' she cried. 'Come here and bite Lady Myōbu!' The foolish Okinamaro, believing that the nurse was in earnest, rushed at the cat, who, startled and terrified, ran behind the blind in the Imperial Dining Room,[28] where the Emperor happened to be sitting. Greatly surprised, His Majesty picked up the cat and held her in his arms. He summoned his gentlemen-in-waiting. When Tadataka, the Chamberlain,[29] appeared, His Majesty ordered that Okinamaro be chastised and banished to Dog Island. The attendants all started to chase the dog amid great confusion. His Majesty also reproached Lady

Uma. 'We shall have to find a new nurse for our cat,' he told her. 'I no longer feel I can count on you to look after her.' Lady Uma bowed; thereafter she no longer appeared in the Emperor's presence.

The Imperial Guards quickly succeeded in catching Okinamaro and drove him out of the Palace grounds. Poor dog! He used to swagger about so happily. Recently, on the third day of the Third Month,[30] when the Controller First Secretary paraded him through the Palace grounds, Okinamaro was adorned with garlands of willow leaves, peach blossoms on his head, and cherry blossoms round his body. How could the dog have imagined that this would be his fate? We all felt sorry for him. 'When Her Majesty was having her meals,' recalled one of the ladies-in-waiting, 'Okinamaro always used to be in attendance and sit opposite us. How I miss him!'

It was about noon, a few days after Okinamaro's banishment, that we heard a dog howling fearfully. How could any dog possibly cry so long? All the other dogs rushed out in excitement to see what was happening. Meanwhile a woman who served as a cleaner in the Palace latrines ran up to us. 'It's terrible,' she said. 'Two of the Chamberlains are flogging a dog. They'll surely kill him. He's being punished for having come back after he was banished. It's Tadataka and Sanefusa who are beating him.' Obviously the victim was Okinamaro. I was absolutely wretched and sent a servant to ask the men to stop; but just then the howling finally ceased. 'He's dead,' one of the servants informed me. 'They've thrown his body outside the gate.'

That evening, while we were sitting in the Palace bemoaning Okinamaro's fate, a wretched-looking dog walked in; he was trembling all over, and his body was fearfully swollen.

'Oh dear,' said one of the ladies-in-waiting. 'Can this be Okinamaro? We haven't seen any other dog like him recently, have we?'

We called to him by name, but the dog did not respond. Some of us insisted that it was Okinamaro, others that it was not. 'Please send for Lady Ukon,'[31] said the Empress, hearing our discussion. 'She will certainly be able to tell.' We immediately went to Ukon's room and told her she was wanted on an urgent matter.

'Is this Okinamaro?' the Empress asked her, pointing to the dog.

'Well,' said Ukon, 'it certainly looks like him, but I cannot believe that this loathsome creature is really our Okinamaro. When I called Okinamaro, he always used to come to me, wagging his tail. But this dog does not react at all. No, it cannot be the same one. And besides, wasn't Okinamaro beaten to death and his body thrown away? How could any dog be alive after being flogged by two strong men?' Hearing this, Her Majesty was very unhappy.

When it got dark, we gave the dog something to eat; but he refused it, and we finally decided that this could not be Okinamaro.

On the following morning I went to attend the Empress while her hair was being dressed and she was performing her ablutions. I was holding up the mirror for her when the dog we had seen on the previous evening slunk into the room and crouched next to one of the pillars. 'Poor Okinamaro!' I said. 'He had such a dreadful beating yesterday. How sad to think he is dead! I wonder what body he has been born into this time. Oh, how he must have suffered!'

At that moment the dog lying by the pillar started to shake and tremble, and shed a flood of tears. It was astounding. So this really was Okinamaro! On the previous night it was to avoid betraying himself that he had refused to answer to his name. We were immensely moved and pleased. 'Well, well, Okinamaro!' I said, putting down the mirror. The dog stretched himself flat on the floor and yelped loudly, so that the Empress beamed with delight. All the ladies gathered round, and Her Majesty summoned Lady Ukon. When the Empress explained what had happened, everyone talked and laughed with great excitement.

The news reached His Majesty, and he too came to the Empress's room. 'It's amazing,' he said with a smile. 'To think that even a dog has such deep feelings!' When the Emperor's ladies-in-waiting heard the story, they too came along in a great crowd. 'Okinamaro!' we called, and this time the dog rose and limped about the room with his swollen face. 'He must have a meal prepared for him,' I said. 'Yes,' said the Empress, laughing happily, 'now that Okinamaro has finally told us who he is.'

The Chamberlain, Tadataka, was informed, and he hurried along from the Table Room.[32] 'Is it really true?' he asked. 'Please let me see for myself.' I sent a maid to him with the following reply: 'Alas, I am afraid that this is not the same dog after all.' 'Well,' answered Tadataka, 'whatever you say, I shall sooner or later have occasion to see the animal. You won't be able to hide him from me indefinitely.'

Before long, Okinamaro was granted an Imperial pardon and returned to his former happy state. Yet even now, when I remember how he whimpered and trembled in response to our sympathy, it strikes me as a strange and moving scene; when people talk to me about it, I start crying myself.

9. On the First Day of the First Month[33]

On the first day of the First Month and on the third of the Third I like the sky to be perfectly clear.

On the fifth of the Fifth Month I prefer a cloudy sky.

On the seventh day of the Seventh Month it should also be cloudy; but in the evening it should clear, so that the moon shines brightly in the sky and one can see the outline of the stars.[34]

On the ninth of the Ninth Month there should be a drizzle from early dawn. Then there will be heavy dew on the chrysanthemums, while the floss silk that covers them will be wet through and drenched also with the precious scent of blossoms.[35] Sometimes the rain stops early in the morning, but the sky is still overcast, and it looks as if it may start raining again at any moment. This too I find very pleasant.

10. *I Enjoy Watching the Officials*

I enjoy watching the officials when they come to thank the Emperor for their new appointments. As they stand facing His Majesty with their batons[36] in their hands, the trains of their robes trail along the floor. Then they make obeisance and begin their ceremonial movements[37] with great animation.

11. *The Sliding Screen in the Back of the Hall*

The sliding screen in the back of the hall in the north-east corner of Seiryō Palace is decorated with paintings of the stormy sea and of the terrifying creatures with long arms and long legs that live there.[38] When the doors of the Empress's room were open, we could always see this screen. One day we were sitting in the room, laughing at the paintings and remarking how unpleasant they were. By the balustrade of the veranda stood a large celadon vase, full of magnificent cherry branches; some of them were as much as five foot long, and their blossoms overflowed to the very foot of the railing. Towards noon the Major Counsellor,[39] Fujiwara no Korechika, arrived. He was dressed in a cherry-coloured Court cloak, sufficiently worn to have lost its stiffness, a white under-robe, and loose trousers of dark purple; from beneath the cloak shone the pattern of another robe of dark red damask. Since His Majesty was present, Korechika knelt on the narrow wooden platform before the door and reported to him on official matters.

A group of ladies-in-waiting was seated behind the bamboo blinds. Their cherry-coloured Chinese jackets hung loosely over their shoulders with the collars pulled back; they wore robes of wistaria, golden yellow, and other colours, many of which showed beneath the blind covering the half-shutter. Presently the noise of the attendants' feet told us that dinner was about to be served in the Daytime Chamber,[40] and we heard cries of 'Make way. Make way.'

The bright, serene day delighted me. When the Chamberlains had brought all the dishes into the Chamber, they came to announce that dinner was ready, and His Majesty left by the middle door. After accompanying the Emperor, Korechika returned to his previous place on the veranda beside the cherry blossoms. The Empress pushed aside her curtain of state and came forward as far as the threshold.⁴¹ We were overwhelmed by the whole delightful scene. It was then that Korechika slowly intoned the words of the old poem,

> The days and the months flow by,
> But Mount Mimoro lasts forever.⁴²

Deeply impressed, I wished that all this might indeed continue for a thousand years.

As soon as the ladies serving in the Daytime Chamber had called for the gentlemen-in-waiting to remove the trays, His Majesty returned to the Empress's room. Then he told me to rub some ink on the inkstone. Dazzled, I felt that I should never be able to take my eyes off his radiant countenance. Next he folded a piece of white paper. 'I should like each of you,' he said, 'to copy down on this paper the first ancient poem that comes into your head.'

'How am I going to manage this?' I asked Korechika, who was still out on the veranda.

'Write your poem quickly,' he said, 'and show it to His Majesty. We men must not interfere in this.' Ordering an attendant to take the Emperor's inkstone to each of the women in the room, he told us to make haste. 'Write down any poem you happen to remember,' he said. 'The Naniwazu⁴³ or whatever else you can think of.'

For some reason I was overcome with timidity; I flushed and had no idea what to do. Some of the other women managed to put down poems about the spring, the blossoms, and such suitable subjects; then they handed me the paper and said, 'Now it's your turn.' Picking up the brush, I wrote the poem that goes,

35

The years have passed
And age has come my way.
Yet I need only look at this fair flower
For all my cares to melt away.

I altered the third line, however, to read, 'Yet I need only look upon my lord.'[44]

When he had finished reading, the Emperor said, 'I asked you to write these poems because I wanted to find out how quick you really were.

'A few years ago,' he continued, 'Emperor Enyū ordered all his courtiers to write poems in a notebook. Some excused themselves on the grounds that their handwriting was poor; but the Emperor insisted, saying that he did not care in the slightest about their handwriting or even whether their poems were suitable for the season. So they all had to swallow their embarrassment and produce something for the occasion. Among them was His Excellency, our present Chancellor, who was then Middle Captain of the Third Rank.[45] He wrote down the old poem,

Like the sea that beats
Upon the shores of Izumo
As the tide sweeps in,
Deeper it grows and deeper –
The love I bear for you.

But he changed the last line to read, "The love I bear my lord!", and the Emperor was full of praise.'

When I heard His Majesty tell this story, I was so overcome that I felt myself perspiring. It occurred to me that no younger woman[46] would have been able to use my poem and I felt very lucky. This sort of test can be a terrible ordeal: it often happens that people who usually write fluently are so overawed that they actually make mistakes in their characters.

Next the Empress placed a notebook of *Kokin Shū* poems before her and started reading out the first three lines of each one, asking us to supply the remainder. Among them were several famous poems that we had in our minds day and night; yet for some strange reason we were often unable to fill in the missing lines. Lady Saishō, for example, could manage only ten, which hardly qualified her as knowing her *Kokin Shū*. Some of the other women, even less successful, could remember only about half a dozen poems. They would have done better to tell the Empress quite simply that they had forgotten the lines; instead they came out with great lamentations like 'Oh dear, how could we have done so badly in answering the questions that Your Majesty was pleased to put to us?' – all of which I found rather absurd.

When no one could complete a particular poem, the Empress continued reading to the end. This produced further wails from the women: 'Oh, we all knew that one! How could we be so stupid?'

'Those of you,' said the Empress, 'who had taken the trouble to copy out the *Kokin Shū* several times would have been able to complete every single poem I have read. In the reign of Emperor Murakami there was a woman at Court known as the Imperial Lady[47] of Senyō Palace. She was the daughter of the Minister of the Left who lived in the Smaller Palace of the First Ward, and of course you have all heard of her. When she was still a young girl, her father gave her this advice: "First you must study penmanship. Next you must learn to play the seven-string zither better than anyone else. And also you must memorize all the poems in the twenty volumes of the *Kokin Shū*."

'Emperor Murakami,' continued Her Majesty, 'had heard this story and remembered it years later when the girl had grown up and become an Imperial Concubine. Once, on a day of abstinence,[48] he came into her room, hiding a notebook of *Kokin Shū* poems in the folds of his robe. He surprised her by seating himself behind a curtain of state; then, opening the book, he asked, "Tell me the verse written by such-and-such a poet, in such-and-such a year and on such-and-such an occasion." The lady understood what was afoot and that it was all in fun, yet the possibility of making a mistake or forgetting one of the poems must have worried her greatly. Before beginning the test, the

Emperor had summoned a couple of ladies-in-waiting who were particularly adept in poetry and told them to mark each incorrect reply by a *go* stone.[49] What a splendid scene it must have been! You know, I really envy anyone who attended that Emperor even as a lady-in-waiting.

'Well,' Her Majesty went on, 'he then began questioning her. She answered without any hesitation, just giving a few words or phrases to show that she knew each poem. And never once did she make a mistake. After a time the Emperor began to resent the lady's flawless memory and decided to stop as soon as he detected any error or vagueness in her replies. Yet, after he had gone through ten books of the *Kokin Shū*, he had still not caught her out. At this stage he declared that it would be useless to continue. Marking where he had left off, he went to bed. What a triumph for the lady!

'He slept for some time. On waking, he decided that he must have a final verdict and that if he waited until the following day to examine her on the other ten volumes, she might use the time to refresh her memory. So he would have to settle the matter that very night. Ordering his attendants to bring up the bedroom lamp, he resumed his questions. By the time he had finished all twenty volumes, the night was well advanced; and still the lady had not made a mistake.

'During all this time His Excellency, the lady's father, was in a state of great agitation. As soon as he was informed that the Emperor was testing his daughter, he sent his attendants to various temples to arrange for special recitations of the Scriptures. Then he turned in the direction of the Imperial Palace and spent a long time in prayer. Such enthusiasm for poetry is really rather moving.'

The Emperor, who had been listening to the whole story, was much impressed. 'How can he possibly have read so many poems?' he remarked when Her Majesty had finished. 'I doubt whether I could get through three or four volumes. But of course things have changed. In the old days even people of humble station had a taste for the arts and were interested in elegant

38

pastimes. Such a story would hardly be possible nowadays, would it?'

The ladies in attendance on Her Majesty and the Emperor's own ladies-in-waiting who had been admitted into Her Majesty's presence began chatting eagerly, and as I listened I felt that my cares had really 'melted away'.

12. *When I Make Myself Imagine*

When I make myself imagine what it is like to be one of those women who live at home, faithfully serving their husbands – women who have not a single exciting prospect in life yet who believe that they are perfectly happy – I am filled with scorn. Often they are of quite good birth, yet have had no opportunity to find out what the world is like. I wish they could live for a while in our society, even if it should mean taking service as Attendants,[50] so that they might come to know the delights it has to offer.

I cannot bear men who believe that women serving in the Palace are bound to be frivolous and wicked. Yet I suppose their prejudice is understandable. After all, women at Court do not spend their time hiding modestly behind fans and screens, but walk about, looking openly at people they chance to meet. Yes, they see everyone face to face, not only ladies-in-waiting like themselves, but even Their Imperial Majesties (whose august names I hardly dare mention), High Court Nobles,[51] senior courtiers, and other gentlemen of high rank. In the presence of such exalted personages the women in the Palace are all equally brazen, whether they be the maids of ladies-in-waiting, or the relations of Court ladies who have come to visit them, or housekeepers, or latrine-cleaners, or women who are of no more value than a roof-tile or a pebble. Small wonder that the young men regard them as immodest! Yet are the gentlemen themselves any less so? They are not exactly bashful when it comes to looking at the great people in the Palace. No, everyone at Court is much the same in this respect.

Women who have served in the Palace, but who later get married and live at home, are called Madam and receive the most respectful treatment. To be sure, people often consider that these women, who have displayed their faces to all and sundry during their years at Court, are lacking in feminine grace. How proud they must be, nevertheless, when they are styled Assistant Attendants, or summoned to the Palace for occasional duty, or ordered to serve as Imperial envoys during the Kamo Festival! Even those who stay at home lose nothing by having served at Court. In fact they make very good wives. For example, if they are married to a provincial governor and their daughter is chosen to take part in the Gosechi dances,[52] they do not have to disgrace themselves by acting like provincials and asking other people about procedure. They themselves are well versed in the formalities, which is just as it should be.

13. *Depressing Things*

A dog howling in the daytime. A wickerwork fish-net in spring.[53] A red plum-blossom dress[54] in the Third or Fourth Months. A lying-in room when the baby has died. A cold, empty brazier. An ox-driver who hates his oxen. A scholar whose wife has one girl child after another.[55]

One has gone to a friend's house to avoid an unlucky direction,[56] but nothing is done to entertain one; if this should happen at the time of a Seasonal Change, it is still more depressing.

A letter arrives from the provinces, but no gift accompanies it. It would be bad enough if such a letter reached one in the provinces from someone in the capital; but then at least it would have interesting news about goings-on in society, and that would be a consolation.

One has written a letter, taking pains to make it as attractive as possible, and now one impatiently awaits the reply. 'Surely the messenger should be back by now,' one thinks. Just then he returns; but in his hand he carries, not a reply, but one's own letter, still twisted or knotted[57] as it was sent, but now so dirty and crumpled that even the ink-mark on the outside has disappeared. 'Not at home,' announces the messenger, or else, 'They said they were observing a day of abstinence and would not accept it.' Oh, how depressing!

Again, one has sent one's carriage to fetch someone who had said he would definitely pay one a visit on that day. Finally it returns with a great clatter, and the servants hurry out with cries of 'Here they come!' But next one hears the carriage being pulled into the coach-house, and the unfastened shafts clatter to the ground. 'What does this mean?' one asks. 'The person was not at home,' replies the driver, 'and will not be coming.' So saying, he leads the ox back to its stall, leaving the carriage in the coach-house.

With much bustle and excitement a young man has moved into the house of a certain family as the daughter's husband. One day he fails to come home, and it turns out that some high-ranking Court lady has taken him as her lover. How depressing! 'Will he eventually tire of the woman and come back to us?' his wife's family wonder ruefully.

The nurse who is looking after a baby leaves the house, saying that she will be back presently. Soon the child starts crying for her. One tries to comfort it by games and other diversions, and even sends a message to the nurse telling her to return immediately. Then comes her reply: 'I am afraid that I cannot be back this evening.' This is not only depressing; it is no less than hateful. Yet how much more distressed must be the young man who has sent a messenger to fetch a lady friend and who awaits her arrival in vain!

It is quite late at night and a woman has been expecting a visitor. Hearing finally a stealthy tapping, she sends her maid to open the gate and lies waiting excitedly. But the name announced by the maid is that of someone with whom she has absolutely no connexion. Of all the depressing things this is by far the worst.

With a look of complete self-confidence on his face an exorcist prepares to expel an evil spirit from his patient. Handing his mace, rosary, and other paraphernalia to the medium who is assisting him, he begins to recite his spells in the special shrill tone that he forces from his throat on such occasions. For all the exorcist's efforts, the spirit gives no sign of leaving, and the Guardian Demon fails to take possession of the medium.[58] The relations and friends of the patient, who are gathered in the room praying, find this rather unfortunate. After he has recited his incantations for the length of an entire watch,[59] the exorcist is worn out. 'The Guardian Demon is completely inactive,' he tells his medium. 'You may leave.' Then, as he takes back his rosary, he adds, 'Well, well, it hasn't worked!' He passes his hand over his forehead, then yawns deeply (he of all people!) and leans back against a pillar for a nap.

Most depressing is the household of some hopeful candidate who fails to receive a post during the period of official appointments.[60] Hearing that the gentleman was bound to be successful, several people have gathered in his house for the occasion; among them are a number of retainers who served him in the past but who since then have either been engaged elsewhere or moved to some remote province. Now they are all eager to accompany their former master on his visit to the shrines and temples, and their carriages pass to and fro in the courtyard. Indoors there is a great commotion as the hangers-on help themselves to food and drink. Yet the dawn of the last day of the appointments arrives and still no one has knocked at the gate. The people in the house are nervous and prick up their ears.

Presently they hear the shouts of fore-runners and realize that the high dignitaries are leaving the Palace. Some of the servants were sent to the Palace on the previous evening to hear the news and have been waiting all night, trembling with cold; now they come trudging back listlessly. The attendants who have remained faithfully in the gentleman's service year after year cannot bring themselves to ask what has happened. His former retainers, however, are not so diffident. 'Tell us,' they say, 'what appointment did His Excellency receive?' 'Indeed,' murmur the servants, 'His Excellency was Governor of such-and-such a province.' Everyone was counting on his receiving a new appointment,[61] and is desolated by this failure. On the following day the people who had crowded into the house begin to slink away in twos and threes. The old attendants, however, cannot leave so easily. They walk restlessly about the house, counting on their fingers the provincial appointments that will become available in the following year. Pathetic and depressing in the extreme!

One has sent a friend a verse that turned out fairly well. How depressing when there is no reply-poem![62] Even in the case of love poems, people should at least answer that they were moved at receiving the message, or something of the sort; otherwise they will cause the keenest disappointment.

Someone who lives in a bustling, fashionable household receives a message from an elderly person who is behind the times and has very little to do; the poem, of course, is old-fashioned and dull. How depressing!

One needs a particularly beautiful fan for some special occasion and instructs an artist, in whose talents one has full confidence, to decorate one with an appropriate painting. When the day comes and the fan is delivered, one is shocked to see how badly it has been painted. Oh, the dreariness of it!

A messenger arrives with a present at a house where a child has been born or where someone is about to leave on a journey. How depressing for him if he gets no reward![63] People should always reward a messenger, though he may bring only herbal balls or hare-sticks.[64] If he expects nothing, he will be particularly pleased to be rewarded. On the other hand, what a terrible let-down if he arrives with a self-important look on his face, his heart pounding in anticipation of a generous reward, only to have his hopes dashed!

A man has moved in as a son-in-law; yet even now, after some five years of marriage, the lying-in room has remained as quiet as on the day of his arrival.[65]

An elderly couple who have several grown-up children, and

who may even have some grandchildren crawling about the house, are taking a nap in the daytime. The children who see them in this state are overcome by a forlorn feeling, and for other people it is all very depressing.[66]

To take a hot bath when one has just woken is not only depressing; it actually puts one in a bad humour.

Persistent rain on the last day of the year.[67]

One has been observing a period of fast, but neglects it for just one day – most depressing.[68]

A white under-robe in the Eighth Month.[69]

A wet-nurse who has run out of milk.

14. *Hateful Things*

One is in a hurry to leave, but one's visitor keeps chattering away. If it is someone of no importance, one can get rid of him by saying, 'You must tell me all about it next time'; but, should it be the sort of visitor whose presence commands one's best behaviour, the situation is hateful indeed.

One finds that a hair has got caught in the stone on which one is rubbing one's inkstick, or again that gravel is lodged in the inkstick, making a nasty, grating sound.

Someone has suddenly fallen ill and one summons the exorcist. Since he is not at home, one has to send messengers to look for him. After one has had a long fretful wait, the exorcist finally arrives, and with a sigh of relief one asks him to start his incantations. But perhaps he has been exorcizing too many evil spirits recently; for hardly has he installed himself and begun praying when his voice becomes drowsy. Oh, how hateful!

A man who has nothing in particular to recommend him discusses all sorts of subjects at random as though he knew everything.

An elderly person warms the palms of his hands over a brazier and stretches out the wrinkles. No young man would dream of behaving in such a fashion; old people can really be quite shameless. I have seen some dreary old creatures actually resting their feet on the brazier and rubbing them against the edge while they speak. These are the kind of people who in visiting someone's house first use their fans to wipe away the dust from the mat and, when they finally sit on it, cannot stay still but are forever spreading out the front of their hunting costume[70] or even tucking it up under their knees. One might suppose that such behaviour was restricted to people of humble station; but I have observed it in quite well-bred people, including a Senior Secretary of the Fifth Rank in the Ministry of Ceremonial and a former Governor of Suruga.

I hate the sight of men in their cups who shout, poke their fingers in their mouths, stroke their beards, and pass on the wine to their neighbours with great cries of 'Have some more! Drink up!' They tremble, shake their heads, twist their faces, and gesticulate like children who are singing, 'We're off to see the Governor.' I have seen really well-bred people behave like this and I find it most distasteful.

To envy others and to complain about one's own lot; to speak badly about people; to be inquisitive about the most trivial matters and to resent and abuse people for not telling one, or, if one does manage to worm out some facts, to inform everyone in the most detailed fashion as if one had known all from the beginning – oh, how hateful!

One is just about to be told some interesting piece of news when a baby starts crying.

A flight of crows circle about with loud caws.

An admirer has come on a clandestine visit, but a dog catches sight of him and starts barking. One feels like killing the beast.

One has been foolish enough to invite a man to spend the night in an unsuitable place – and then he starts snoring.

A gentleman has visited one secretly. Though he is wearing a tall, lacquered hat,[71] he nevertheless wants no one to see him. He is so flurried, in fact, that upon leaving he bangs into something with his hat. Most hateful! It is annoying too when he lifts up the Iyo blind[72] that hangs at the entrance of the room,

45

then lets it fall with a great rattle. If it is a head-blind, things are still worse, for being more solid it makes a terrible noise when it is dropped. There is no excuse for such carelessness. Even a head-blind does not make any noise if one lifts it up gently on entering and leaving the room; the same applies to sliding-doors. If one's movements are rough, even a paper door will bend and resonate when opened; but, if one lifts the door a little while pushing it, there need be no sound.

One has gone to bed and is about to doze off when a mosquito appears, announcing himself in a reedy voice. One can actually feel the wind made by his wings and, slight though it is, one finds it hateful in the extreme.

A carriage passes with a nasty, creaking noise. Annoying to think that the passengers may not even be aware of this! If I am travelling in someone's carriage and I hear it creaking, I dislike not only the noise but also the owner of the carriage.

One is in the middle of a story when someone butts in and tries to show that he is the only clever person in the room. Such a person is hateful, and so, indeed, is anyone, child or adult, who tries to push himself forward.

One is telling a story about old times when someone breaks in with a little detail that he happens to know, implying that one's own version is inaccurate – disgusting behaviour!

Very hateful is a mouse that scurries all over the place.

Some children have called at one's house. One makes a great fuss of them and gives them toys to play with. The children become accustomed to this treatment and start to come regularly, forcing their way into one's inner rooms and scattering one's furnishings and possessions. Hateful!

A certain gentleman whom one does not want to see visits one at home or in the Palace, and one pretends to be asleep. But a maid comes to tell one and shakes one awake, with a look on her face that says, 'What a sleepyhead!' Very hateful.

A newcomer pushes ahead of the other members in a group; with a knowing look, this person starts laying down the law and forcing advice upon everyone – most hateful.

46

A man with whom one is having an affair keeps singing the praises of some woman he used to know. Even if it is a thing of the past, this can be very annoying. How much more so if he is still seeing the woman! (Yet sometimes I find that it is not as unpleasant as all that.)

A person who recites a spell himself after sneezing.[73] In fact I detest anyone who sneezes, except the master of the house.

Fleas, too, are very hateful. When they dance about under someone's clothes, they really seem to be lifting them up.

The sound of dogs when they bark for a long time in chorus is ominous and hateful.

I cannot stand people who leave without closing the panel behind them.

How I detest the husbands of nurse-maids! It is not so bad if the child in the maid's charge is a girl, because then the man will keep his distance. But, if it is a boy, he will behave as though he were the father. Never letting the boy out of his sight, he insists on managing everything. He regards the other attendants in the house as less than human, and, if anyone tries to scold the child, he slanders him to the master. Despite this disgraceful behaviour, no one dare accuse the husband; so he strides about the house with a proud, self-important look, giving all the orders.

I hate people whose letters show that they lack respect for worldly civilities, whether by discourtesy in the phrasing or by extreme politeness to someone who does not deserve it. This sort of thing is, of course, most odious if the letter is for oneself, but it is bad enough even if it is addressed to someone else.

As a matter of fact, most people are too casual, not only in their letters but in their direct conversation. Sometimes I am quite disgusted at noting how little decorum people observe when talking to each other. It is particularly unpleasant to hear some foolish man or woman omit the proper marks of respect when addressing a person of quality; and, when servants fail to use honorific forms of speech in referring to their masters, it is very bad indeed. No less odious, however, are those masters who, in addressing their servants, use such phrases as 'When you were good enough to do such-and-such' or 'As you so kindly re-marked'. No doubt there are some masters who, in describing their own actions to a servant, say, 'I presumed to do so-and-so'![74]

Sometimes a person who is utterly devoid of charm will try to create a good impression by using very elegant language; yet he only succeeds in being ridiculous. No doubt he believes this refined language to be just what the occasion demands, but, when it goes so far that everyone bursts out laughing, surely something must be wrong.

It is most improper to address high-ranking courtiers, Imperial Advisers, and the like simply by using their names without any titles or marks of respect; but such mistakes are fortunately rare.

If one refers to the maid who is in attendance on some lady-in-waiting as 'Madam' or 'that lady', she will be surprised, delighted, and lavish in her praise.

When speaking to young noblemen and courtiers of high rank, one should always (unless Their Majesties are present) refer to them by their official posts. Incidentally, I have been very shocked to hear important people use the word 'I' while conversing in Their Majesties' presence.[75] Such a breach of etiquette is really distressing, and I fail to see why people cannot avoid it.

A man who has nothing in particular to recommend him but who speaks in an affected tone and poses as being elegant.

An inkstone with such a hard, smooth surface that the stick glides over it without leaving any deposit of ink.

Ladies-in-waiting who want to know everything that is going on.

Sometimes one greatly dislikes a person for no particular reason – and then that person goes and does something hateful.

A gentleman who travels alone in his carriage to see a procession or some other spectacle. What sort of a man is he? Even though he may not be a person of the greatest quality, surely he should have taken along a few of the many young men who are anxious to see the sights. But no, there he sits by himself (one can see his silhouette through the blinds), with a proud look on his face, keeping all his impressions to himself.

A lover who is leaving at dawn announces that he has to find his fan and his paper.[76] 'I know I put them somewhere last night,' he says. Since it is pitch dark, he gropes about the room, bumping into the furniture and muttering, 'Strange! Where on earth can they be?' Finally he discovers the objects. He thrusts the paper into the breast of his robe with a great rustling sound; then he snaps open his fan and busily fans away with it. Only now is he ready to take his leave. What charmless behaviour! 'Hateful' is an understatement.

Equally disagreeable is the man who, when leaving in the middle of the night, takes care to fasten the cord of his head-dress. This is quite unnecessary; he could perfectly well put it gently on his head without tying the cord. And why must he spend time adjusting his cloak or hunting costume? Does he really think someone may see him at this time of night and criticize him for not being impeccably dressed?

A good lover will behave as elegantly at dawn as at any other time. He drags himself out of bed with a look of dismay on his face. The lady urges him on: 'Come, my friend, it's getting light. You don't want anyone to find you here.' He gives a deep sigh, as if to say that the night has not been nearly long enough and that it is agony to leave. Once up, he does not instantly pull on his trousers. Instead he comes close to the lady and whispers whatever was left unsaid during the night. Even when he is dressed, he still lingers, vaguely pretending to be fastening his sash.

Presently he raises the lattice, and the two lovers stand together by the side door while he tells her how he dreads the coming day, which will keep them apart; then he slips away. The lady watches him go, and this moment of parting will remain among her most charming memories.

Indeed, one's attachment to a man depends largely on the elegance of his leave-taking. When he jumps out of bed, scurries about the room, tightly fastens his trouser-sash, rolls up the

49

sleeves of his Court cloak, over-robe, or hunting costume, stuffs
his belongings into the breast of his robe and then briskly secures
the outer sash – one really begins to hate him.

15. *The Palace of the First Ward*

The Palace of the First Ward is also known as the Palace of
Today; and, when His Majesty is staying there, it is called Seiryō
Palace. The Empress's residence is to the north and connected to
it by galleries on the left and right. Sometimes His Majesty proceeds along these galleries to visit the Empress, but usually it is
the Empress who visits him. In front of the Empress's building
is a charming little garden, planted with shrubs and flowers, and
surrounded by a bamboo fence.

On the tenth day of the Second Month, with the sun shining
down from a clear, peaceful sky, His Majesty was playing the
flute under the eaves near the western part of the gallery. He was
attended by that excellent flautist, Takatō, the Senior Assistant
Governor-General. They played the Takasago[77] tune in unison
several times, and Takatō explained various points about the
flute to His Majesty. To describe the scene as 'most splendid'
would be hopelessly inadequate. I was sitting behind the bamboo
blinds with some other women, and, as I observed everything,
I felt that I had never in my life been unhappy.

Next the Emperor started to play the song of Suketada. Now,
this Suketada[78] was a Secretary in the Bureau of Carpentry who
had been appointed Chamberlain; but, since he was extremely
uncouth, the high-ranking ladies and gentlemen at Court had
nicknamed him 'rough crocodile' and written a song about him:

> Who can stand next to this fine fellow?
> Truly is he of Owari stock![79]

(His mother was, in fact, the daughter of a certain Kanetoki
from Owari Province.) Hearing the Emperor play this tune,
Takatō sat down next to him and said, 'Would Your Majesty be

50

pleased to blow a little more loudly? Suketada cannot possibly hear, and even if he did he wouldn't understand.'

'How so?' replied the Emperor. 'I am sure he would recognize the tune.' For a while he continued to play softly, then walked down the gallery in the direction of the Empress's building. 'He certainly cannot hear me from here,' explained His Majesty. 'Now I can really let myself go!' So saying, he blew out the tune heartily, and it was most delightful.

16. *Things That Make One's Heart Beat Faster*

Sparrows feeding their young. To pass a place where babies are playing. To sleep in a room where some fine incense has been burnt. To notice that one's elegant Chinese mirror has become a little cloudy. To see a gentleman stop his carriage before one's gate and instruct his attendants to announce his arrival. To wash one's hair, make one's toilet, and put on scented robes; even if not a soul sees one, these preparations still produce an inner pleasure.

It is night and one is expecting a visitor. Suddenly one is startled by the sound of rain-drops, which the wind blows against the shutters.

17. *Things That Arouse a Fond Memory of the Past*

Dried hollyhock.[80] The objects used during the Display of Dolls.[81] To find a piece of deep violet[82] or grape-coloured material that has been pressed between the pages of a notebook.

It is a rainy day and one is feeling bored. To pass the time, one starts looking through some old papers. And then one comes across the letters of a man one used to love.

Last year's paper fan.[83] A night with a clear moon.[84]

18. *A Palm-Leaf Carriage Should Move Slowly*

A palm-leaf carriage should move slowly, or else it loses its dignity. A wickerwork carriage,[85] on the other hand, should go fast. Hardly has one seen it pass the gate when it is out of sight, and all that remains is the attendants who run after it. At such moments I enjoy wondering who the passengers may be. But, if a wickerwork carriage moves slowly, one has plenty of time to observe it, and that becomes very dull.

19. *Oxen Should Have Very Small Foreheads*

Oxen should have very small foreheads with white hair; their underbellies, the ends of their legs, and the tips of their tails should also be white.

I like horses to be chestnut, piebald, dapple-grey, or black roan, with white patches near their shoulders and feet; I also like horses with light chestnut coats and extremely white manes and tails – so white, indeed, that their hair looks like mulberry threads.

I like a cat whose back is black and all the rest white.

20. *The Driver of an Ox-Carriage*

The driver of an ox-carriage should be a big man; his greying hair should have a slightly reddish tint, and his face should be ruddy. He should also look intelligent.

Attendants and escorts should be slim. I prefer gentlemen also to be on the slender side, at least when young. Stout men always strike me as sleepy-looking.

I like page-boys to be small. They should have beautiful hair that hangs loosely, lightly touching their necks. Their voices must be attractive and their speech respectful; for these are the marks of an adept page.

21. *A Preacher Ought To Be Good-Looking*

A preacher ought to be good-looking. For, if we are properly to understand his worthy sentiments, we must keep our eyes on him while he speaks; should we look away, we may forget to listen. Accordingly an ugly preacher may well be the source of sin. . .

But I really must stop writing this kind of thing. If I were still young enough, I might risk the consequence of putting down such impieties, but at my present stage of life I should be less flippant.

Some people, on hearing that a priest is particularly venerable and pious, rush off to the temple where he is preaching, determined to arrive before anyone else. They, too, are liable to bring a load of sin on themselves and would do better to stay away.

In earlier times men who had retired from the post of Chamberlain [86] did not ride at the head of Imperial processions; in fact, during the year of their retirement they hardly ever appeared outside their houses, and did not dream of showing themselves in the precincts of the Palace. Things seem to have changed. Nowadays they are known as 'Fifth Rank Chamberlains' and given all sorts of official jobs.

Even so, time often hangs heavily on their hands, especially when they recall their busy days in active service. Though these Fifth Rank Chamberlains keep the fact to themselves, they know they have a good deal of leisure. Men like this frequently repair to temples and listen to the popular priests, such visits eventually becoming a habit. One will find them there even on hot summer days, decked out in bright linen robes, with loose trousers of light violet or bluish grey spread about them. Sometimes they will have taboo tags [87] attached to their black lacquered head-dresses. Far from preferring to stay at home on such inauspicious days, they apparently believe that no harm can come to anyone bent on so worthy an errand. They arrive hastily, converse with

53

the priest, look inside the carriages [88] that are being lined up outside the temple, and take an interest in everything.

Now a couple of gentlemen who have not met for some time run into each other in the temple, and are greatly surprised. They sit down together and chat away, nodding their heads, exchanging funny stories, and opening their fans wide to hold before their faces so as to laugh more freely. Toying with their elegantly decorated rosaries, they glance about, criticizing some defect they have noticed in one of the carriages or praising the elegance of another. They discuss various services that they have recently attended and compare the skill of different priests in performing the Eight Lessons or the Dedication of Sutras. [89] Meanwhile, of course, they pay not the slightest attention to the service actually in progress. To be sure, it would not interest them very much; for they have heard it all so often that the priest's words could no longer make any impression.

After the priest has been on his dais for some time, a carriage stops outside the temple. The outriders clear the way in a somewhat perfunctory fashion, and the passengers get out. They are slender young gentlemen, clad either in hunting costumes or in Court cloaks that look lighter than a cicada's wings, loose trousers, and unlined robes of raw silk. As they enter the temple, accompanied by an equal number of attendants, the worshippers, including those who have been there since the beginning of the service, move back to make room for them; the young men install themselves at the foot of a pillar near the dais. As one would expect from such people, they now make a great show of rubbing their rosaries and prostrating themselves in prayer. The priest, convinced by the sight of the newcomers that this is a grand occasion, launches out on an impressive sermon that he presumes will make his name in society. But no sooner have the young men settled down and finished touching their heads on the floor than they begin to think about leaving at the first opportunity. Two of them steal glances at the women's carriages outside, and it is easy to imagine what they are saying to each other. They recognize one of the women and admire her elegance;

then, catching sight of a stranger, they discuss who she can be. I find it fascinating to see such goings-on in a temple.

Often one hears exchanges like this: 'There was a service at such-and-such a temple where they did the Eight Lessons.' 'Was Lady So-and-So present?' 'Of course. How could she possibly have missed it?' It is really too bad that they should always answer like this.

One would imagine that it would be all right for ladies of quality to visit temples and take a discreet look at the preacher's dais. After all, even women of humble station may listen devoutly to religious sermons. Yet in the old days ladies almost never walked to temples to attend sermons; on the rare visits that they did undertake they had to wear elegant travelling costume,[90] as when making proper pilgrimages to shrines and temples. If people of those times had lived long enough to see the recent conduct in the temples, how they would have criticized the women of our day!

22. *When I Visited Bodai Temple*

When I visited Bodai Temple to hear the Eight Lessons for Confirmation,[91] I received this message from a friend: 'Please come back soon. Things are very dreary here without you.' I wrote my reply on a lotus petal:

> Though you bid me come,
> How can I leave these dew-wet lotus leaves
> And return to a world so full of grief?[92]

I had been truly moved by the ceremony and felt that I could remain forever in the temple. So must Hsiang Chung have felt when he forgot about the people who were impatiently awaiting him at home.[93]

23. Smaller Shirakawa

Smaller Shirakawa is the residence of His Excellency, the Major Captain of the Smaller Palace of the First Ward. When the Eight Lessons for Confirmation were performed there under the auspices of the High Court Nobles, it was a very magnificent thing, and everyone went to hear the readings. We had been warned that late-comers would be unable to bring their carriages near the hall, so we all hurried to get up with the dew.[94] And what a crowd there was! The carriages in front of the building were so crowded together that each was supported on the shafts of the one behind, and even people in the third row were close enough to hear the service. It was about the middle of the Sixth Month; the heat was overpowering. The only way to feel a little cooler was to gaze at the lotuses growing in the pond.

With the exception of the Ministers of the Left and the Right,[95] all the High Court Nobles were present. They wore laced trousers and Court cloaks lined with violet, through which one could make out the light yellow of their linen robes. Those gentlemen who had lately reached adult age were attired in white trouser-skirts and laced trousers of bluish grey, which gave an impression of coolness. Sukemasa, the Imperial Adviser, was dressed in a rather youthful fashion that seemed informal for so solemn an occasion. In every way it was a fascinating spectacle.

The bamboo blinds in the main room had been rolled up high. At the threshold of the veranda the High Court Nobles were seated in long rows facing inside, while on the veranda itself several senior courtiers and young noblemen, beautifully attired in hunting costumes and Court cloaks, wandered up and down, chatting agreeably. Sanekata, the Captain of the Guards, and Nagaakira, the Gentleman-in-Waiting, having both been brought up in this house, knew their way about better than the others and walked about freely. There were also two young noblemen, still only children, whom I greatly enjoyed watching.

Towards noon the Middle Captain of the Third Rank (as the

56

Chancellor, Michitaka, was then styled) arrived at Smaller Shirakawa. Over a thin silk robe of dark orange he wore a dazzling white one of glossy silk; his Court cloak was lined with violet, and his laced trousers were the same colour, while his trouser-skirt was of deep red material. One might imagine that his costume would have settled too warm next to the light, cool attire of the other gentlemen; in fact he seemed perfectly clad. His fan, with its slender, lacquered frame, was slightly different from the others, but it was covered with red paper of the same tint. As I looked at all the men gathered there with their fans, I had the impression that I was seeing a field of pinks in full bloom.

Since the priest had not yet mounted his dais, the attendants placed before the guests small tables on which to serve refreshments.

Yoshichika, the Middle Counsellor, looked better than ever; his appearance was infinitely charming. . . . (It occurs to me that perhaps I should not refer to such distinguished gentlemen by name; yet otherwise how shall I be sure of their identity in later years?) The summer robes of most of the men were dyed in magnificent shades, and together they shone with such dazzling lustre that it was hard to single out any particular colour as being the most distinctive. Yoshichika's linen robe was so discreet that one might have thought it was an ordinary Court cloak. He was constantly glancing towards the carriages and sending messages to the ladies. Everyone found this delightful.

Before long there was no room left for further carriages; the new arrivals had to be pulled up beside the pond. Catching sight of one of these, Yoshichika sent word to Sanekata: 'Please find me someone suitable for delivering a message.' Having chosen one of the household attendants, Sanekata brought him to Yoshichika, who gave his instructions. People standing near by were speculating about the contents of this message, but I was too far away to hear.

Presently the messenger, looking so self-important that people could not help laughing, swaggered over to the carriage that Yoshichika had indicated and spoke to the lady inside. 'No doubt she's busy with a poem,' someone joked, as the messenger stood there waiting. 'Come, Captain Sanekata, why don't *you* frame a reply?' It was amusing to see how everyone, from the most dignified High Court Noble down to the ordinary people standing out in the open, was watching the carriage with mounting impatience. At last the man began walking off – had she finally given him a message? – only to be summoned back by a wave of the lady's fan. It occurred to me that she may have made a mistake in the wording of her poem. But after taking such a long time? This was certainly not the proper way to do things.

'Well, well, what was her answer? What did she say?' people asked when the messenger finally returned; but he would divulge nothing. On being summoned by Yoshichika, the messenger started to report in a pompous, measured style. 'Be quick about it!' Michitaka interposed. 'Say what you have to say without straining for effect! And mind you don't make any mistakes!' 'Well, Sir,' I heard the messenger say, 'it really does not matter how I report such a reply.'

The Major Counsellor, Fujiwara no Tamemitsu, craned his neck forward. He seemed the most curious of all.

After the messenger had reported, Michitaka remarked, 'It seems to be the case of bending a very straight tree and breaking it in the process.'[96] Tamemitsu burst out laughing, and everyone joined in without quite knowing why. I wondered whether the lady could hear them.

'But look here,' said Yoshichika to the messenger. 'What did she say before she called you back? Tell us her exact words without trying to improve on them!'

'Well, Sir,' said the messenger, 'she was a long time without replying at all. When I said that I had better be going, she called me back.'

'And whose carriage is it – who is she?' Yoshichika asked, just as the priest mounted his dais and everyone fell silent. While the entire congregation was attending to the service, the lady's carriage disappeared as if it had vanished from the face of the earth. I remember that its inner blinds and other fittings looked brand new. The lady had worn a set of dark purple robes [97] over a violet garb of figured material; above it all was a thin cloak of dark red; her formal skirt with its printed pattern had been allowed to spread so that its train hung over the back of the carriage. Who could she be, I wondered, and was her reaction to Yoshichika's message as improper as it seemed? I have heard people suggest that no reply at all is better than a bad one, with which I quite agree.

Seihan, the priest who officiated at the morning service, looked resplendent on his dais; nothing could have been more impressive. But we did not want to stay. For one thing, the heat was overpowering. Besides, we had set out in the morning with the intention of hearing only part of the service, and had various things to finish at home that could not be put off. However, since our carriage was in the forefront, with row after row of other carriages piled up behind us like waves, it was impossible to retreat. We sent messages to the occupants of the other carriages saying that we should like to leave as soon as the morning service was over. No doubt delighted at the possibility of coming a little closer to the dais, they immediately began to make an opening for us.

Seeing us leave so early, many of the onlookers, including some elderly High Court Nobles, made quite audible jokes at our expense; but we paid no attention and refused to reply. As we were squeezing our way out, Yoshichika laughingly called to me, 'Ah, you do well to depart!' [98] Overcome by the heat, I paid no attention to this quip, but later I sent a man with the message, 'Your Excellency, too, will surely be among the five thousand.' And so we left the crowd and returned home.

I remember a certain carriage that remained outside Smaller Shirakawa from the very beginning of the services until the last day. Not once did anyone go up to speak to the person who occupied it. I was much impressed by this mysterious vehicle that stood there as immobile as a carriage in a picture. 'Who can it be in that splendid carriage?' I said. 'How can one find out?' Overhearing me, Tamemitsu remarked, 'It does not look very splendid to me. Quite the contrary – I am sure the occupant is an odious creature.' I was amused by his comment.

After the twentieth of the month the Middle Counsellor became a priest, which caused me much regret. That the cherry blossoms should scatter in the wind is the way of this world; but the Counsellor had certainly not reached the age of 'waiting for the dew to fall'.

24. *It Is So Stiflingly Hot*

It is so stiflingly hot in the Seventh Month that even at night one keeps all the doors and lattices open. At such times it is delightful to wake up when the moon is shining and to look outside. I enjoy it even when there is no moon. But to wake up at dawn and see a pale sliver of a moon in the sky – well, I need hardly say how perfect that is.

I like to see a bright new straw mat that has just been spread out on a well-polished floor.[99] The best place for one's three-foot curtain of state is in the front of the room near the veranda. It is pointless to put it in the rear of the room, as it is most unlikely that anyone will peer in from that direction.[100]

It is dawn and a woman is lying in bed after her lover has taken his leave. She is covered up to her head with a light mauve robe that has a lining of dark violet; the colour of both the outside and the lining is fresh and glossy.[101] The woman, who appears to be asleep, wears an unlined orange robe and a dark crimson skirt of stiff silk whose cords hang loosely by her side, as if they have been left untied. Her thick tresses tumble over each other in cascades, and one can imagine how long her hair must be when it falls freely down her back.[102]

Near by another woman's lover is making his way home in the misty dawn. He is wearing loose violet trousers, an orange hunting costume, so lightly coloured that one can hardly tell whether it has been dyed or not, a white robe of stiff silk, and a scarlet robe of glossy, beaten silk. His clothes, which are damp from the mist, hang loosely about him. From the dishevelment of his side locks one can tell how negligently he must have tucked his hair into his black lacquered head-dress when he got up. He wants to return and write his next-morning letter[103] before the dew on the morning glories has had time to vanish; but the path seems endless, and to divert himself he hums 'The sprouts in the flax fields'.[104]

As he walks along, he passes a house with an open lattice. He is on his way to report for official duty, but cannot help stopping to lift up the blind and peep into the room.[105] It amuses him to think that a man has probably been spending the night here and has only recently got up to leave, just as happened to himself. Perhaps that man too had felt the charm of the dew.[106]

Looking round the room, he notices near the woman's pillow an open fan with a magnolia frame and purple paper; and at the foot of her curtain of state he sees some narrow strips of Michinoku paper and also some other paper of a faded colour, either orange-red or maple.

The woman senses that someone is watching her and, looking up from under her bedclothes, sees a gentleman leaning against the wall by the threshold, a smile on his face. She can tell at once that he is the sort of man with whom she need feel no reserve. All the same, she does not want to enter into any familiar relations with him, and she is annoyed that he should have seen her asleep.[107]

'Well, well, Madam,' says the man, leaning forward so that the upper part of his body comes behind her curtains, 'what a long nap you're having after your morning adieu! You really are a lie-abed!'

'You call me that, Sir,' she replied, 'only because you're annoyed at having had to get up before the dew had time to settle.'

Their conversation may be commonplace, yet I find there is something delightful about the scene.

Now the gentleman leans further forward and, using his own fan, tries to get hold of the fan by the woman's pillow. Fearing his closeness, she moves further back into her curtain enclosure, her heart pounding. The gentleman picks up the magnolia fan and, while examining it, says in a slightly bitter tone, 'How standoffish you are!'

But now it is growing light; there is a sound of people's voices, and it looks as if the sun will soon be up. Only a short while ago this same man was hurrying home to write his next-morning letter before the mists had time to clear. Alas, how easily his intentions have been forgotten!

While all this is afoot, the woman's original lover has been busy with his own next-morning letter, and now, quite unexpectedly, the messenger arrives at her house. The letter is attached to a spray of bush-clover, still damp with dew, and the paper gives off a delicious aroma of incense. Because of the new visitor, however, the woman's servants cannot deliver it to her.

Finally it becomes unseemly for the gentleman to stay any longer. As he goes, he is amused to think that a similar scene may be taking place in the house he left earlier that morning.

25. *Flowering Trees*

Plum blossoms, whether light or dark, and in particular red plum blossoms, fill me with happiness. I also like a slender branch of cherry blossoms, with large petals and dark red leaves. How graceful is the wistaria as its branches bend down covered with whorls of delicately coloured petals!

The *u no hana*[108] is a more modest plant and deserves no special praise; yet it flowers at a pleasant time of the year, and I enjoy thinking that a *hototogisu* may be hiding in its shade. When passing through the plain of Murasaki[109] on one's way back from the Festival, it is lovely to see the white of the *u no hana* blossoms in the shaggy hedges near the cottages. They look like thin, white robes worn over a costume of yellowish green.

At the end of the Fourth Month and the beginning of the Fifth the orange trees have dark green leaves and are covered with brilliant white flowers. In the early morning, when they have been sprinkled with rain, one feels that nothing in the world can match their charm; and, if one is fortunate enough to see the fruit itself, standing out like golden spheres among the flowers, it looks as beautiful as that most magnificent of sights, the cherry blossoms damp with morning dew. But I need say no more; so much has been written about the beauty of the orange trees in the many poems that link them with the *hototogisu*.[110]

The blossom of the pear tree is the most prosaic, vulgar thing in the world. The less one sees this particular blossom the better, and it should not be attached to even the most trivial message.[111] The pear blossom can be compared to the face of a plain woman; for its colouring lacks all charm. Or so, at least, I used to think. Knowing that the Chinese admire the pear blossom greatly and praise it in their poems, I wondered what they could see in it and made a point of examining the flower. Then I was surprised to find that its petals were prettily edged with a pink tinge, so faint that I could not be sure whether it was there or not. It was to the pear blossoms, I recalled, that the poet likened the face of Yang Kuei-fei when she came forth in tears to meet the Emperor's messenger – 'a spray of pear blossom in spring, covered with drops of rain'[112] – and I realized that this was no idle figure of speech and that it really is a magnificent flower.

The purple blossoms of the paulownia are also delightful. I confess that I do not like the appearance of its wide leaves when they open up. . . . But I cannot speak of the paulownia as I do of the other trees; for this is where that grandiose and famous bird of China makes its nest, and the idea fills me with awe.[113] Besides, it is this tree that provides the wood for the zithers from which come so many beautiful sounds. How can I have used such a commonplace word as 'delightful'? The paulownia is not delightful; it is magnificent.

The melia tree is ugly, but I find its flowers very pretty indeed. One always sees them on the fifth day of the Fifth Month, and there is something charming about these dried-up, oddly shaped little flowers.[114]

26. *Festivals*

There is nothing to equal the Festival of the Fifth Month,[115] when the scents of the iris and the sage-brush mingle so charmingly. From the Ninefold Enclosure of the Imperial Palace down to the cottages of the common folk, there is not a place where people are not busy covering their roofs with leaves of iris and branches of sage-brush. Everyone wants his own house to be decorated most luxuriantly. All this is a splendid thing which never occurs on any other occasion.

On the actual day of the festival the sky is usually cloudy. Herbal balls, decorated with braided strings of many colours, have been brought to the Empress's palace by the Bureau of the Wardrobe, and they are now attached to the pillars on both sides of the main hall in which stands Her Majesty's curtain-dais.[116] They replace the chrysanthemums that have been hanging there ever since the ninth day of the Ninth Month, wrapped in their plain cases of raw silk. The herbal balls are supposed to remain on the pillars until the next Chrysanthemum Festival; but whenever people need a string, they tear a piece off the herbal balls, so that before long nothing is left.

During the course of this festive day gifts are exchanged, and young people decorate their hair with iris; they attach taboo tags to their clothes, and adorn their coats and Chinese jackets with long iris roots or sprigs of azalea, orange, and other attractive plants, which they secure to their sleeves with plaited cords dyed in uneven shadings. Though there is nothing new about any of this, it is very charming. After all, do people tire of the cherry trees because they blossom every spring?

The little girls who trip along the streets are also decorated with iris, but the flowers they wear are smaller than those worn by the grown-ups. The children are proud of themselves and keep looking at the flowers on their sleeves, comparing them with those of their companions. This is all delightful, as are the little pages who play with the girls and snatch away their iris, making them burst into tears.

I also like to see melia flowers wrapped in purple paper; thinly rolled iris leaves done up in green paper and attached to people's clothing; and iris roots tied to white paper. Some very elegant men enclose long iris roots in their letters, and it is a pleasure to watch the women who have received the contents discussing them with their companions and showing each other their replies. People who have chosen this day to send letters to a well-born girl or to a high-ranking gentleman at Court exude a particular grace. Indeed the Iris Festival is nothing but a delight until the *hototogisu* brings the day to an end by announcing its name.

27. *Trees*

The maple and the five-needled pine, the willow and the orange tree. The Chinese hawthorn* has a rather vulgar name; but, when all the other trees have lost their blossoms, its dark red leaves shine out impressively from the green surroundings.[117]

I shall say absolutely nothing about the spindle tree.

I realize that it is not a specific tree, but I must mention the name 'parasite tree' since I find it so moving.[118]

I particularly enjoy the *sakaki* on occasions like the Imperial sacred dances at the special festivals.[119] Among all the trees in the world this is the one that people have always regarded as the tree of the Divine Presence – a very pleasant thought.

The camphor tends to grow by itself, avoiding clusters of other trees. There is something rather frightening about its tangled branches, and this estranges one from it; yet it is because the tree is divided into a thousand branches that it has been evoked to describe people in love.[120] (By the way, I wonder who was the first person to know how many branches it had.)

One does not see the *hinoki* cypress very often; but the palace of 'three ridges, four ridges' was built with the wood of this tree.[121] In the Fifth Month it gives a pleasant imitation of the sound of rain.

* 'Side tree'.

The maple is an insignificant tree in itself; but its red-tinged leaves, all spread in the same direction, look very pretty on the branches, and there is something charming about its flowers, which seem as fragile as dried-up insects.

It is rare to come across the large-leaved cypress,[122] and not much is said about it; but I understand that pilgrims returning from Mitake often bring back branches of the tree as souvenirs. These branches are said to be rough and disagreeable to touch. Yet the tree has been given a name meaning 'tomorrow he will become a cypress'. What can be the point of such a prediction, and for whom was it made? I should really like to know.

The privet is also an uncommon tree. Its best feature is its tiny, delicate leaves.

The melia and the wild pear tree.

The pasania oak. It is strange that just this tree among all the evergreens should be mentioned as the one whose leaves do not change.

Of the trees that grow far away in the hills the so-called white oak is the least familiar; in fact about the only time one sees even its leaves is when they are being used to dye the robes worn by gentlemen of the second or third ranks. Though there is nothing very splendid or unusual about the tree, one always has the illusion that it is covered with snow, and it moves me greatly to recall the poem that Hitomaro wrote about the journey of the Storm God to Izumo.[123]

Whether it be a plant or a tree, a bird or an insect, I can never be indifferent to anything that is connected with some special occasion or that has once moved or delighted me.

The *yuzuriha* has an abundance of pretty leaves, all green and glossy; but its stem is quite different from what one would expect, for it is red and glittering. There is something a little vulgar about its colour, yet I really like the tree. No one pays the slightest attention to it during most of the year, but on the last day of the Twelfth Month it comes into its own. I understand that the food offered to the dead on that day is spread out on *yuzuriha*[124] leaves, and this I find very touching. It appears that the same leaves are used to serve tooth-hardening food, which is meant to prolong life. How can this be? It is of this tree also that the poet has written, 'When the leaves turn red'. Indeed the *yuzuriha* is full of promises.

The common oak is a magnificent tree. To think that the God of Leaves lives there![125] It is also fascinating that Captains and Lieutenants of the Middle Palace Guards should be named after this tree.

The hemp palm is an ill-shaped tree; but it is in the Chinese style[126] and does not grow outside the houses of common people.

28. *Birds*

The parrot does not belong to our country, but I like it very much. I am told that it imitates whatever people say.[127]

The *hototogisu*, the water-rail, and the snipe; the starling, the siskin, and the fly-catcher. They say when the copper pheasant cries for its mate it can be consoled if one puts a mirror before it – a very moving thought.[128] What misery these birds must suffer if they are separated from each other by a gorge or a ravine!

If I were to write down all my thoughts about the crane, I should become tiresome. How magnificent when this bird lets out its cry, which reaches up to the very heavens!

The red-headed sparrow, the male grosbeak, the kinglet.

The heron is an unpleasant-looking bird with a most disagreeable expression in its eyes. Yet, though it has nothing to recommend it, I am pleased to think that it does not nest alone in Yurugi Wood.[129]

The box bird.[130]

Among water fowl it is the mandarin duck that affects me most. How charming to think that the drake and his mate take turns in brushing the frost 'from each other's wings'![131]

The gull. The river plover – alas, that he should have lost his mate![132]

The distant cry of wild geese is a most moving sound.

It is charming to think of the wild duck sweeping the frost from its wings.[133]

The poets have extolled the *uguisu*[134] as a splendid bird, and so indeed it is; for both its voice and its appearance are most elegant and beautiful. Alas that it does not sing in the Ninefold Enclosure of the Palace! When I first heard people say this, I thought they must be mistaken; but now I have served for ten years in the Palace, and, though I have often listened for it, I have never yet heard its song. The bamboos in the Palace gardens and the plum trees with red blossoms should certainly attract these birds.[135] Yet not one of them comes here, whereas outside the Palace, in the paltry plum tree of some commoner's house, one hears the *uguisu* warbling joyfully.

At night the *uguisu* is silent. Obviously this bird likes its sleep, and there is nothing we can do about that.

In the summer and autumn the *uguisu*'s voice grows hoarse. Now the common people change its name to 'insect eater' or something of the kind, which strikes me as both unpleasant and unseemly. I should not mind if it were an ordinary bird like the sparrow; but this is the magnificent *uguisu*, whose song in the spring has moved writers to praise that season in both poetry and prose. How splendid it would be if the *uguisu* would sing only in the spring.[136] Yet it is wrong to despise this bird just because its voice deteriorates in the later seasons. After all, should we look down on men or women because they have been ravaged by age and are scorned by the world? There are certain birds, like the kite and the crow, that people disregard entirely and would never bother to criticize; it is precisely because the *uguisu* is usually held in such high regard that people find fault with it when they can.

I remember that on a certain occasion, when we had decided to watch the return of the High Priestess's procession from the Kamo Festival and had ordered the attendants to stop our carriages in front of Urin and Chisoku Temples, a *hototogisu* began to sing, not wanting to be hidden on this festive day. An *uguisu* sang in unison, perfectly imitating his voice. I was surprised by what lovely music these birds can make when they sing together high in the trees.

Having written so many good things about the *uguisu*, how can I properly praise the *hototogisu*? What a joy it is in the Fifth Month to hear its voice ring out triumphantly as if to say, 'My season has come!' The poets describe the *hototogisu* as lurking in the *u no hana* and the orange tree; and there is something so alluring about the picture of this bird half hidden by the blossoms that one is almost overcome with envy. During the short summer nights in the rainy season one sometimes wakes up and lies in bed hoping to be the first person to hear the *hototogisu*. Suddenly towards dawn its song breaks the silence; one is charmed, indeed one is quite intoxicated. But alas, when the Sixth Month comes, the *hototogisu* is silent. I really need say no more about my feelings for this bird. And I do not love the *hototogisu* alone; anything that cries out at night delights me – except babies.

29. *Elegant Things*

A white coat worn over a violet waistcoat.

Duck eggs.

Shaved ice mixed with liana syrup and put in a new silver bowl.[137]

A rosary of rock crystal.

Wistaria blossoms. Plum blossoms covered with snow.

A pretty child eating strawberries.

30. *Insects*

The bell insect and the pine cricket; the grasshopper and the common cricket; the butterfly and the shrimp insect; the mayfly and the firefly.

I feel very sorry for the basket worm. He was begotten by a demon, and his mother, fearing that he would grow up with his father's frightening nature, abandoned the unsuspecting child, having first wrapped him in a dirty piece of clothing. 'Wait for me,' she said as she left. 'I shall return to you as soon as the autumn winds blow.' So, when autumn comes and the wind starts blowing, the wretched child hears it and desperately cries, 'Milk! Milk!'[138]

The clear-toned cicada.

The snap-beetle also impresses me. They say that the reason it bows while crawling along the ground is that the faith of Buddha has sprung up in its insect heart. Sometimes one suddenly hears the snap-beetle tapping away in a dark place, and this is rather pleasant.

The fly should have been included in my list of hateful things;[139] for such an odious creature does not belong with ordinary insects. It settles on everything, and even alights on one's face with its clammy feet. I am sorry that anyone should have been named after it.[140]

The tiger moth is very pretty and delightful. When one sits close to a lamp reading a story, a tiger moth will often flutter prettily in front of one's book.

The ant is an ugly insect; but it is light on its feet and I enjoy watching as it skims quickly over the surface of the water.

31. *In the Seventh Month*

In the Seventh Month, when there are fierce winds and heavy showers, it is quite cool and one does not bother to carry a fan. On such days I find it is pleasant to take a nap, having covered myself with some clothing that gives off a faint smell of perspiration.[141]

32. *Unsuitable Things*

A woman with ugly hair wearing a robe of white damask.
Hollyhock worn in frizzled hair.
Ugly handwriting on red paper.
Snow on the houses of common people. This is especially regrettable when the moonlight shines down on it.[142]
A plain wagon[143] on a moonlit night; or a light auburn ox harnessed to such a wagon.
A woman who, though well past her youth, is pregnant and walks along panting. It is unpleasant to see a woman of a certain age with a young husband; and it is most unsuitable when she becomes jealous of him because he has gone to visit someone else.
An elderly man who has overslept and who wakes up with a start; or a greybeard munching some acorns that he has plucked. An old woman who eats a plum and, finding it sour, puckers her toothless mouth.
A woman of the lower classes dressed in a scarlet trouser-skirt. The sight is all too common these days.
A handsome man with an ugly wife.
An elderly man with a black beard and a disagreeable expression playing with a little child who has just learnt to talk.
It is most unseemly for an Assistant Captain of the Quiver Bearers[144] to make his night patrol in a hunting costume. And, if he wanders outside the woman's quarters, ostentatiously clad in his terrifying red cloak, people will be sure to look down on him. They disapprove of his behaviour and taunt him with remarks like 'Are you searching for someone suspicious?'
A Lieutenant in the Imperial Police who serves as a Chamberlain of the Sixth Rank, and therefore has access to the Senior Courtiers' Chamber, is regarded as being splendid beyond words.[145] Country folk and people of the lower orders believe that he cannot be a creature of this world: in his presence they tremble with fear and dare not meet his eyes. It is very unsuitable that

such a man should slink along the narrow corridors of some Palace building in order to steal into a woman's room.[146]

A man's trouser-skirt hanging over a curtain of state that has been discreetly perfumed with incense.[147] The material of the trouser-skirt is disagreeably heavy; and, even though it may be shining whitely in the lamp-light, there is something unsuitable about it.

An officer who thinks he is very fashionable in his open over-robe and who folds it thinly as a rat's tail before hanging it over the curtain of state – well, such a man is simply unfit for night patrol. Officers on duty should abstain from visiting the women's quarters; the same applies to Chamberlains of the Fifth Rank.

33. *I Was Standing in a Corridor*

I was standing in a corridor of the Palace with several other women when we noticed some servants passing. We summoned them to us (in what I admit was a rather unladylike fashion) and they turned out to be a group of handsome male attendants and pages carrying attractively wrapped bundles and bags. Trouser-cords protruded from some, and I noticed that others contained bows, arrows, shields, halberds, and swords.[148] 'Whom do these things belong to?' we asked each of the servants in turn. Some of them knelt down respectfully and replied, 'They belong to Lord So-and-so.' Then they stood up and continued on their way, which was all very nice. But others gave themselves airs, or else were embarrassed and said, 'I don't know', or even went off without replying at all, which I found hateful indeed.

34. *Gentlemen Should Always Have Escorts*

Gentlemen should always have escorts. Even young noblemen, however handsome and charming, strike me as dull creatures if they are unescorted.

I have always regarded the position of Controller[149] as a fine and honourable one; but it is a shame that the train of his under-robe should be so short and that he is not provided with an escort.

35. *Once I Saw Yukinari*

Once I saw Yukinari, the Controller First Secretary, engaged in a long conversation with a lady near the garden fence by the western side of the Empress's Office.[150] When at last they had finished, I came out and asked, 'Who was she?' 'Ben no Naishi,'[151] he replied. 'And what on earth did you find to discuss with her for such a long time? If the Major Controller had seen you, she would have left you quickly enough.' 'And who can have told you about that business?' asked Yukinari, laughing.[152] 'As a matter of fact, that is precisely what I was discussing with her. I was trying to persuade her not to leave me even if the Major Controller did see us.'

Yukinari is a most delightful man. To be sure, he does not make any particular effort to display his good points and simply lets people take him as he appears, so that in general he is less appreciated than he might be. But I, who have seen the deeper side of his nature, know what an unusual person he really is. I said this one day to the Empress, who was well aware of it herself. In the course of our conversations he often says, 'A woman yields to one who has taken pleasure in her; a knight dies for one who has shown him friendship.'[153] We used to say that our feelings for each other were like the willows on Tōtōmi Beach.[154]

Yet the young women at Court heartily detest Yukinari and openly repeat the most disagreeable things about him. 'What an ugly man he is!' they say. 'Why can't he recite sutras and poems like other people? He really is most unpleasant.' Yukinari, for his part, never speaks to any of them.

'I could love a woman,' he said one day, 'even if her eyes were

73

turned up,[155] her eyebrows spread all over her forehead, and her nose crooked. But she must have a prettily shaped mouth and a good chin and neck, and I couldn't stand an unattractive voice. Of course I would prefer her not to have any bad feature. There's really something sad about a woman with an ugly face.' As a result, all the Court ladies with pointed chins or other unattractive features have become Yukinari's bitter enemies, and some of them have even spoken badly of him to the Empress.

I was the first person he employed to take messages to the Empress, and he always called on me when he wanted to communicate with her. If I was in my room, he would send for me to the main part of the Palace, or else he would come directly into the women's quarters to give me his message. Even if I was at home, he would write to me or come himself, saying, 'In case you are not returning to Court at once, would you please send someone to Her Majesty informing her that I have such-and-such a message.' 'Surely you could tell a messenger yourself directly,' I said; but he would have none of it.

On one such occasion I suggested to Yukinari that one should 'take things as they are'[156] and not always stick to the same habits. 'But such is my nature,' he replied, 'and that is something one cannot change.'

'Well then,' I said in a surprised tone, 'what is the meaning of "Do not be afraid"?'[157]

Yukinari laughed and said, 'There has no doubt been a lot of talk lately about our being so friendly. But what of it? Even if we were as intimate as people think, that would be nothing to be ashamed of. Really you could let me see your face.'[158]

'Oh no,' I replied, 'I cannot possibly do that. I am extremely ugly, and you said you could never love an ugly woman.'

'Are you really?' he said. 'In that case you had better not let me see you.'

Often thereafter, when it would have been easy for Yukinari to look at me in the normal course of things, he covered his face with a fan or turned aside. In fact he never once saw me. To think that he took what I said about my ugliness quite seriously!

Towards the end of the Third Month it becomes too warm for winter cloaks, and often Chamberlains who are on night watch in the Senior Courtiers' Chamber wear only the over-robes of their Court costumes, leaving off their trouser-skirts and trains. Early one morning in that month, when Lady Shikibu and I had been sleeping in the outer part of a room in the Empress's Office, the sliding-door was pushed open and the Emperor and Empress entered. We were thrown into utter confusion and did not know what to do with ourselves, which greatly amused Their Majesties. Hastily we threw on our Chinese jackets, tucking our hair inside, and then we heaped the bed-clothes and everything else in a great pile. Their Majesties walked across the room and, standing behind this pile, watched the men going between the Palace and the guard-house. Several courtiers approached our room and spoke to us, without suspecting who was inside the room. 'Do not let them see we are here,' His Majesty said with a chuckle.

Before long Their Majesties left. 'Come along, both of you,' said the Empress. I replied that we would come as soon as we had made up our faces, and we stayed where we were.

Lady Shikibu and I were still discussing how splendid Their Majesties had looked when, through a small opening in the blinds (where the frame of our curtain of state was pressed against the sliding-door in the back of the room), we noticed the dark silhouette [159] of a man. At first we thought that it must be Noritaka [160] and continued to talk without paying any particular attention. Presently a beaming face appeared through the opening in the blinds. We still took it to be Noritaka, but after a quick look we were amused to find that we were mistaken. Laughing heartily, we rearranged our curtain of state so that we were properly hidden. Too late, though. The man turned out to be none other than Yukinari; and he had seen me full-face. After all my past efforts this was extremely vexing. Lady Shikibu, on the other hand, had been looking safely in the other direction.

'Well,' said Yukinari, stepping forward, 'now I have really managed to see you completely.'

'We thought it was Noritaka,' I explained, 'and so we didn't bother to hide properly. But why, may I ask, did you examine me so carefully when in the past you said that you would never look at me?'

'I have been told,' said he, 'that a woman's face is particularly attractive when she rises in the morning. So I came here hoping for a chance to peep into one of the ladies' rooms and see something interesting. I was already watching you when Their Majesties were here, but you suspected nothing.'

Then, as I recall, he walked straight into the room.

36. *The Roll-Call of the Senior Courtiers*

The roll-call [161] of the senior courtiers is a delightful event, and I also enjoy it when the gentlemen in attendance on the Emperor have their names called. They tumble out of the buildings with a noisy clatter of footsteps. From the eastern part of Her Majesty's wing of Seiryō Palace I and the Empress's other ladies-in-waiting can follow everything if we listen carefully. How exciting when one hears some close friend answering with his name! It is exciting, too, to hear the voice of a man who is unfamiliar even though one knows he is on duty in the Palace. The women freely discuss the different styles in which the men have responded, and this is very amusing.

As soon as the roll-call is finished, one hears the loud footsteps of the Imperial Guards of the Emperor's Private Office, who come out while twanging their bow-strings. Then the Chamberlain on duty proceeds to the balustrade at the north-east corner of the building, his shoes reverberating noisily on the wooden boards, and adopts the posture that I believe is called 'high kneeling'. Facing the Emperor's Palace, he asks the officer who stands behind him, 'Is so-and-so present? And so-and-so?' – all most impressive. Sometimes the answers are given in a soft voice, sometimes loudly; and sometimes the muster is cancelled, if there are insufficient men present. The Officer of the Guards announces this to the Chamberlain, who asks why the men are absent; when the necessary information has been given, he returns to the Palace to make his report to the Emperor.

Things do not go so smoothly when the Chamberlain on duty is Masahiro.[162] Ever since some young noblemen advised him that he was being too lax about the report of the Officer of the Guards, he gets quite incensed on hearing of any absences among the men; he rebukes them severely, telling them that they must improve their behaviour. As a result Masahiro has become the laughing-stock, not only of the gentlemen at Court, but even of the common guardsmen.

On one occasion Masahiro actually left his shoes on the serving-board in the Emperor's Dining Room. This caused great indignation, and it was said that whoever was responsible should be forced to do purgation. Some women in the Office of Grounds and a few others knew the name of the culprit and could not help feeling sorry for him. 'Whose shoes can these be?' they said. 'There's really no telling.' In the midst of all this excitement Masahiro himself came to fetch the shoes. 'Oh dear,' he said, 'those dirty things[163] belong to me.'

37. *It Is Hateful When a Well-Bred Young Man*

It is hateful when a well-bred young man who is visiting a woman of lower rank calls out her name in such a way as to make everyone realize that he is on familiar terms with her. However well he may know her name, he should slur it slightly as though he had forgotten it. On the other hand, this would be wrong when a gentleman comes at night to visit a lady-in-waiting. In such a situation he should bring along a man who can call out the lady's name for him – a servant from the Office of Grounds if she is in the Imperial Palace, or else someone from the Attendants' Hall; for his voice will be recognized if he calls her name himself. But, when he is visiting a mere under-servant or girl attendant, such a precaution is unnecessary.

38. *Small Children and Babies*

Small children and babies ought to be plump. So ought provincial governors and others who have gone ahead in the world; for, if they· are lean and desiccated, one suspects them of being ill-tempered.

39. *Nothing Can Be Worse*

Nothing can be worse than allowing the driver of one's ox-carriage to be poorly dressed. It does not matter too much if the other attendants are shabby, since they can remain at the rear of the carriage; but the drivers are bound to be noticed and, if they are badly turned out, it makes a painful impression.

The servants who follow one's carriage must have at least a few good points. Some people choose slender young men who look as if they were really made to be after-runners, but then let them wear threadbare hunting costumes and trouser-skirts that are dark at the hems and actually seem to be of shaded material.[164] This is a great mistake; for, as they amble along beside the carriage, these badly dressed young men do not seem to be part of their master's equipage at all.

The fact is that the people in one's employ should always be decently dressed. To be sure, servants often tear their clothes; but, so long as they have been wearing them for some time, this is no great loss and one can let the matter pass.

Gentlemen who have had official servants allotted to their households[165] must certainly not allow them to go about looking slovenly.

When a messenger or a visitor arrives, it is very pleasant, both for the master and for the members of his household, to have a collection of good-looking pages in attendance.

40. *Travelling in My Carriage One Day*

Travelling in my carriage one day, I passed a gentleman's house where I saw someone (probably a servant) spreading straw mats on the ground. I also noticed a young boy of about ten, with long, attractive hair hanging loosely down his back, and a child of about five whose hair was piled up under his jacket and whose cheeks were plump and rosy. The child held a funny little bow and a stick of some sort. It was quite adorable. How I should have liked to stop my carriage, pick them both up, and take them along!

As I continued on my way, I presently came to another house. They were burning incense, and the air was redolent with its scent.

41. *Once When I Was Passing*

Once when I was passing the house of a certain great man, the central gate was open and I could see a palm-leaf carriage, which was beautiful and new, and had inside blinds of a delightful orange tint. It made a splendid sight as it stood there with its shafts resting on the trestles. Several officials of the Fifth and Sixth Ranks were scurrying about in all directions; they had tucked the ends of their long robes under their sashes, and their shining white batons were thrust into the shoulders of their robes. Many escorts were coming and going in full dress, with long, narrow quivers on their backs – most suitable for such a grand household. Then I was charmed to see an extremely pretty kitchen-maid who emerged from the house and asked, 'Have Lord So-and-so's attendants arrived yet?'

42. Herbs and Shrubs

Sweet rush and water oats.

Hollyhock is a most delightful flower. To think that ever since the age of the Gods people have been decorating their hair with it at Festival time![166] The plant itself is also charming.

I like the water-plantain* and, when I hear its name, I am amused to think that it must have a swollen head.

The water-bur and the beach-parsley, the moss and the bear-ivy. I also enjoy the grass when its blades peep bright and green through the snow. Wood-sorrel makes an uncommonly pretty design on figured silk and other material.

Shrubs that grow in precarious places like the mountain's edge make me uneasy, and I find them moving. Stonecrop[167] is especially pitiful; for it grows on crumbling walls and other places that are even more unstable than the mountain's edge. Annoying to think that on a securely plastered wall it probably would not grow at all!

The *kotonashi*† shrub. Either it has no worries, or whatever worries it did have are now gone – both explanations of its name are pleasant.[168]

The *shinobugusa*‡ sounds most pathetic, but it is amazing how vigorously this plant grows on the very edge of roofs and walls.[169]

I am also interested in sage-brush and reed-mace, and I particularly like the leaves of the nut-grass. Bulrush, duckweed, green vine, and the scattered *chigaya* reeds. The so-called horse-tail – I love imagining the sound that the wind makes when it blows through these rushes. Shepherd's purse. A lawn of grass.

Floating lotus leaves are very pretty when they are spread out, large and small, drifting along the calm, limpid water of a pond! If one picks up a leaf and presses it against some object it is the most delightful thing in the world.

* 'High face'.
† 'Nothing wrong'.
‡ 'Grass that endures'.

Goose-grass, snake's beard, and mountain sedge; club moss, crinum, and the common reed.

When the wind blows the arrowroot leaves, one can see that their backs are extremely white and pretty.

43. *Poetic Subjects*

The capital city. Arrowroot. Water-bur. Colts. Hail. Bamboo grass. The round-leaved violet. Club moss. Water oats. Flat river-boats. The mandarin duck. The scattered *chigaya* reed. Lawns. The green vine. The pear tree. The jujube tree. The althea.

44. *Things That Cannot Be Compared*

Summer and winter. Night and day. Rain and sunshine. Youth and age. A person's laughter and his anger. Black and white. Love and hatred. The little indigo plant and the great philodendron. Rain and mist.

When one has stopped loving somebody, one feels that he has become someone else, even though he is still the same person.

In a garden full of evergreens the crows are all asleep. Then, towards the middle of the night, the crows in one of the trees suddenly wake up in a great flurry and start flapping about. Their unrest spreads to the other trees, and soon all the birds have been startled from their sleep and are cawing in alarm. How different from the same crows in daytime!

45. *To Meet One's Lover*

To meet one's lover summer is indeed the right season. True, the nights are very short, and dawn creeps up before one has had a wink of sleep. Since all the lattices have been left open, one can lie and look out at the garden in the cool morning air.

There are still a few endearments to exchange before the man takes his leave, and the lovers are murmuring to each other when suddenly there is a loud noise. For a moment they are certain that they have been discovered; but it is only the caw of a crow flying past in the garden.

In the winter, when it is very cold and one lies buried under the bedclothes listening to one's lover's endearments, it is delightful to hear the booming of a temple gong, which seems to come from the bottom of a deep well. The first cry of the birds, whose beaks are still tucked under their wings, is also strange and muffled. Then one bird after another takes up the call. How pleasant it is to lie there listening as the sound becomes clearer and clearer!

46. *A Lover's Visit*

A lover's visit is the most delightful thing in the world. But when the man is a mere acquaintance, or has come for a casual chat, what a nuisance it can be! He enters the lady's room, where numerous other women are ensconced behind the blinds chatting to each other, and he gives no sign that his visit will be brief. The attendants who have accompanied him sit outside impatiently, convinced that 'the handle of his axe will rot away'.[170] They yawn loudly and complain of their lot. 'Oh, the bondage!' they mutter to themselves. 'Oh, the suffering!'[171] It must already be past midnight.' Probably they do not realize that anyone is listening, and in any case their words mean little.[172] Yet it is disagreeable to hear such remarks, and one's visitor finds that the things he would normally be enjoying on such a visit have lost their charm.

Sometimes the attendants do not dare put their sentiments into words but clearly show them by the look on their faces and by the great groans that they let forth. At such times I find it amusing to recall the poem about the 'waters seething far below'.[173] But, if they go and stand by a fence in the garden and say, 'It looks like rain,'[174] or words to that effect, I find it hateful.

The attendants who accompany young noblemen and other people of quality never behave in this rude way; but such things often happen with men of lower rank. When paying a visit, a man should take along only those attendants whose character is known to him.

47. *Rare Things*

A son-in-law who is praised by his adoptive father; a young bride who is loved by her mother-in-law.

A silver tweezer that is good at plucking out the hair.

A servant who does not speak badly about his master.

A person who is in no way eccentric or imperfect, who is superior in both mind and body, and who remains flawless all his life.

People who live together and still manage to behave with reserve towards each other. However much these people may try to hide their weaknesses, they usually fail.

To avoid getting ink stains on the notebook into which one is copying stories, poems, or the like. If it is a very fine notebook, one takes the greatest care not to make a blot; yet somehow one never seems to succeed.

When people, whether they be men or women or priests, have promised each other eternal friendship, it is rare for them to stay on good terms until the end.

A servant who is pleasant to his master.

One has given some silk to the fuller and, when he sends it back, it is so beautiful that one cries out in admiration.

48. *The Women's Apartments along the Gallery*

The women's apartments along the gallery of the Imperial Palace are particularly pleasant. When one raises the upper part of the small half-shutters, the wind blows in extremely hard;

it is cool even in summer, and in winter snow and hail come along with the wind, which I find agreeable. As the rooms are small, and as the page-boys (even though employed in such august precincts) often behave badly, we women generally stay hidden behind our screens or curtains. It is delightfully quiet there; for one cannot hear any of the loud talk and laughter that disturb one in other parts of the Palace.

Of course we must always be on the alert when we are staying in these apartments. Even during the day we cannot be off our guard, and at night we have to be especially careful. But I rather enjoy all this. Throughout the night one hears the sound of footsteps in the corridor outside. Every now and then the sound will stop, and someone will tap on a door with just a single finger. It is pleasant to think that the woman inside can instantly recognize her visitor. Sometimes the tapping will continue for quite a while without the woman's responding in any way. The man finally gives up, thinking that she must be asleep; but this does not please the woman, who makes a few cautious movements, with a rustle of silk clothes, so that her visitor will know she is really there. Then she hears him fanning himself as he remains standing outside the door.

In the winter one sometimes catches the sound of a woman gently stirring the embers in her brazier. Though she does her best to be quiet, the man who is waiting outside hears her; he knocks louder and louder, asking her to let him in. Then the woman slips furtively towards the door where she can listen to him.

On other occasions one may hear several voices reciting Chinese or Japanese poems. One of the women opens her door, though in fact no one has knocked. Seeing this, several of the men, who had no particular intention of visiting this woman, stop on their way through the gallery. Since there is no room for them all to come in, many of them spend the rest of the night out in the garden – most charming.

Bright green bamboo blinds are a delight, especially when beneath them one can make out the many layers of a woman's clothes emerging from under brilliantly coloured curtains of state.[175] The men who glimpse this sight from the veranda, whether they be young noblemen with their over-robes informally left unsewn in the back, or Chamberlains of the Sixth Rank in their costumes of green, do not as a rule dare enter the room where the woman is seated. It is interesting to observe them as they stand there with their backs pressed to the wall and with the sleeves of their robes neatly arranged. Charming also, when one is watching from the outside, is the sight of a young man clad in laced trousers of dark purple and in a dazzling Court robe over an array of varicoloured garments, as he leans forward into the woman's room, pushing aside the green blind. At this point he may take out an elegant inkstone and start writing a letter, or again, he may ask the woman for a mirror and comb his sidelocks; either is delightful.

When a three-foot curtain of state has been set up, there is hardly any gap between the top of the frame and the bottom of the head-blind; fortunately the little space that remains always seems to come precisely at the face-level of the man who is standing outside the curtains and of the woman who is conversing with him from inside. What on earth would happen if the man was extremely tall and the woman very short? I really cannot imagine. But, so long as people are of normal height, it is satisfactory.

I particularly enjoy the rehearsal before the Special Festival[176] when I am staying in the women's apartments at the Palace. As the men from the Office of Grounds walk along, they hold their long pine torches high above them; because of the cold their heads are drawn into their robes, and consequently the ends of the torches are always threatening to bump into things. Soon there is the pleasant sound of music as the players pass outside the women's apartments playing their flutes. Some of the young noblemen in the Palace, fascinated by the scene, appear in their Court costumes and stand outside our rooms chatting with us, while their attendants quietly order people to make way for their masters. All the voices mingle with the music in an unfamiliar and delightful way.

Since the night is already well advanced, one does not bother to go to bed but waits for the dawn when the musicians and dancers return from their rehearsal. Soon they arrive, and then comes the best part of all when they sing 'The rice flowers from the freshly-planted fields'.[177]

Almost everyone enjoys these things; but occasionally some sober-sides will hurry by, without stopping to watch the scene. Then one of the women calls out laughingly to him, 'Wait a moment, Sir! How can you abandon the charms of such a night? Stay for a while and enjoy yourself!' But evidently the man is in a bad mood, for he scurries along the corridor, almost tumbling over himself in his haste, as though in terror of being pursued and captured.

49. *It Was during One of Her Majesty's Periods of Residence*

It was during one of Her Majesty's periods of residence in the building of the Empress's Office. Although we were somewhat cut off from things, we enjoyed being in such a tall building and the ancient trees that stretched far into the distance behind the Office delighted us. One day it was reported that there was a demon in the main room. Everything had to be taken out, and we arranged the screens and other furniture so as to keep the demon out of the rest of the house. We told the maids to put Her Majesty's curtains of state in the front part of the building, south of the main room, and we women moved into an adjoining chamber.

All the time we could hear the cries of 'Make way!' that preceded the approach of High Court Nobles and senior courtiers as they went from the gate of the Inner Palace Guards past the guard-house of the Left Guards. The cries for the senior courtiers were shorter than those for the High Court Nobles, and we had heated discussions about which were the 'big cries' and which the 'small cries'.[178] Since we had often heard these voices, we were usually able to recognize them. 'That's Lord So-and-so they're announcing,' one of us would say. 'No it isn't,' another woman would insist, and then we would have to send a servant to find out who was right. It was amusing to hear the first woman say, 'Well, you see I knew.'

Early one morning, when a pale moon still hung in the sky, we went out into the garden, which was thick with mist. Hearing us, Her Majesty got up herself, and all the ladies in attendance joined us in the garden. As we strolled about happily, dawn gradually appeared on the horizon. When eventually I left to go and have a look at the guard-house of the Left Guards, all the other women ran after me, crying that they wanted to come along. On our way we heard a group of senior courtiers, who were evidently bound for the Empress's palace, reciting 'So on and so forth – and the voice of autumn speaks'.[179] We therefore hurried back to the palace to converse with the gentlemen on their arrival there. 'So you have been out moon-viewing,' said one of them admiringly and composed a poem in praise of the moon.

Both during the day and at night the senior courtiers were always paying us such visits. High Court Nobles too, unless they were in an uncommon hurry, used to call on us whenever they were going to or from the Imperial Palace.

50. *On the Day after the Naming of the Buddhas*

On the day after the Naming of the Buddhas the screens with the paintings of Hell were carried into the Empress's apartments for her to see. They were terrifying beyond words.[180]

'Look!' said Her Majesty. But I replied that I had no desire to see them; I was so frightened that I went and lay down in my room next door where I could hide myself from the screens.

It was raining very hard. Since the Emperor declared that he was bored, some of the senior courtiers were summoned to the Empress's apartments for a concert. Michikata, the Minor Counsellor, played splendidly on the lute, Lord Narimasa played the thirteen-string zither, Yukinari the ordinary flute, and Captain Tsunefusa the thirteen-pipe flute.[181] They gave a delightful performance of one piece; then, after the sound of the flute had stopped, His Excellency the Major Counsellor, Korechika, chanted the line,

The music stops, but the player will not speak her name.[182]

While all this was going on, I lay out of sight in my room; but now I got up and went into the Empress's apartments. 'Whatever guilt this may bring upon me,'[183] I said as I entered, 'I cannot resist such a charming recitation.' Hearing this, the gentlemen all burst out laughing.

I recall that there was nothing very remarkable about the Major Counsellor's voice; yet it seemed to have been made especially for the occasion.

51. *The Captain First Secretary, Tadanobu*

The Captain First Secretary, Tadanobu,[184] having heard certain false rumours, began to speak about me in the most unpleasant terms. 'How could I have thought of her as a human being?' was the sort of thing he used to say.

One day I learnt that he had gone so far as to speak badly about me in the Senior Courtiers' Chamber. I felt terribly ashamed, but I laughed and said, 'How distressing if what he said were correct! As it is, he's sure to find out the truth soon enough, and then he'll change his mind about me.' Shortly afterwards Tadanobu heard my voice when passing near the Black Door,[185] and, without even glancing at me, he covered his face with his sleeve. Despite his dislike of me, I never tried to explain matters, and let time pass without so much as looking at him.

Towards the end of the Second Month it rained a great deal and time hung on my hands. One day someone told me that Tadanobu was secluded in Seiryō Palace on the occasion of an Imperial Abstinence[186] and that he had been overheard to remark, 'After all, things do seem a bit dreary since I stopped seeing

Shōnagon. I wonder if I shan't send her a message.' 'I don't believe a word of it,' I replied. Yet I spent the entire day in my room, thinking that a messenger might arrive, and by the time I went to the Empress's apartments I found that she had already retired for the night. The ladies-in-waiting on duty were seated in a group near the veranda; they had drawn up a lamp and were playing a game of parts.[187]

'Oh, good!' they cried when they saw me. 'Come and join us!' Yet I felt depressed and wondered why I had come. Instead of joining the women, I sat down by a brazier; but presently they had all gathered round me and we started chatting to each other. Just then there was a loud cry outside the room: 'A messenger is here!'[188]

'That's strange,' I said. 'I've only just arrived. What can have happened since I left my room?' I sent a maid to find out; when she returned, she told me that the man was from the Office of Grounds and that he had a message which he must at all costs deliver to me personally. I went out and asked the man what had happened. 'Here is a letter for you from the Captain First Secretary,' he said. 'Please answer it without delay.'

In view of Tadanobu's attitude, I wondered what sort of a letter he could have written; but, since I did not want to hurry through it then and there, I told the messenger that he could leave and that I would send my reply presently. Tucking the letter in the breast of my robe, I returned to my companions.

We were once more chatting away when the messenger returned and said, 'His Excellency, the Captain, ordered me to bring his letter back to him if there was no immediate reply. Please be quick.' It was all as strange as a tale from Ise.[189] I examined the letter. It was elegantly written on heavy blue paper, and there was nothing about it to worry me. I opened it and read:

> With you it is flower time
> As you sit in the Council Hall
> 'Neath a curtain of brocade.[190]

And below this he had added, 'How does the stanza end?'

I was at a complete loss. If Her Majesty had been there, I should have asked her to look at the letter and give her opinion; but unfortunately she was asleep. I had to prove that I knew the next line of the poem, but were I to write it in my somewhat faltering Chinese characters it would make a bad impression. I had no time to ponder since the messenger was pressing for a reply. Taking a piece of burnt-out charcoal from the brazier, I simply added the following words at the end of Tadanobu's letter:

> Who would come to visit
> This grass-thatched hut of mine?

Then I told the messenger to take it back to Tadanobu. I waited for a reply, but none came.

I spent the night in the Empress's apartments with the other ladies-in-waiting. Very early on the following morning, when I had returned to my own room, I heard Captain Tsunefusa call in a booming voice, 'Is Grass Hut here? Is Grass Hut here?'

'How could anyone with such a vulgar name be staying here?' I asked. 'Now, if you were to ask for Jade Tower, you might get a reply.'[191]

'Ah, good!' said Tsunefusa. 'So you are in your room. I was prepared to go all the way to the Palace to find you.' He then told me what had happened on the previous evening. He and several officials of the Sixth Rank and above (all of them gentlemen of some talent) had been with Tadanobu in the Captain's night-duty room. In the course of their conversation, while they were discussing various people and events, Tadanobu said, 'I have completely broken with Shōnagon. But even now that it is all over between us I find it hard to leave things as they are. I have been waiting for her to make some move to bring us together again, but she does not seem to give it the slightest thought. Really, I find this indifference of hers most galling. . . . Well, tonight I am going to make up my mind about her once and for all and settle things properly.'

'We all discussed the matter,' continued Tsunefusa, 'and it

was decided that he should put you to the test by means of a letter. But, when the messenger returned, he told us that you had gone back to your room and could not read the letter at once. Hearing this, Tadanobu sent the man back again with the instructions, "This time seize her by the sleeve and get a reply from her willy-nilly! But in any case bring back my letter!"

'Despite the heavy rain the messenger was soon back in the night-duty room. "Here it is," he said, producing a letter from the folds of his robe. It was the same blue piece of paper that Tadanobu had sent. We wondered whether you had returned it without perusal. But, when Tadanobu unfolded it, he gave an exclamation of surprise, and we all gathered round him curiously. "What a rogue she is!" he said. "How can one break with a woman like that?" We examined the letter excitedly. "We'll have to send it back to her with the first three lines added,"[192] said someone. "Come, Captain Tsunefusa, you provide the missing lines!" We stayed up until late at night cudgelling our brains for the right words, but in the end we had to give up. We then decided that this was an incident that people must hear about.'

I was quite embarrassed by Tsunefusa's praise. 'So now,' he added, as he hurriedly took his leave, 'you have acquired the name of Grass Hut.' 'That's all very well,' thought I, 'but it's hardly a name I should like to keep indefinitely.'

Just then Norimitsu, the Assistant Master of the Office of Palace Repairs,[193] arrived in my room, 'I thought you would be in the Palace,' he said, 'and I have just been there to tell you how delighted I was by the news.' 'Why so delighted?' I said. 'I haven't heard about any official appointments. What post did you get?' 'No, no,' replied Norimitsu. 'It's about your answer to Tadanobu yesterday evening. I've been waiting all night to tell you how pleased I was. There's never been anything like it.'

He then related the whole story that I had heard from Captain Tsunefusa. 'Tadanobu told us that he would finally make up his mind about you depending on your reply to his letter. If it turned out to be unsatisfactory, he was going to break with you once and for all. When the messenger came back the first time empty-handed, I decided that this was in fact a good sign. The next time, when he returned with your answer, I was so curious to know what you had said that my heart was pounding. To tell the truth, it occurred to me that, if your answer was inadequate, this would reflect on me too as your elder brother. As it turned out, it was not merely adequate; it was outstanding. Everyone in the room praised it warmly, and one of the old men told me, "This is something for you to hear since you're her elder brother."

'Of course I was delighted, but I kept it to myself and simply said, "I am totally incompetent in matters of this kind." "We aren't asking for your criticism," was the reply, "and we don't even expect you to understand what she wrote. But we do want you to tell people about it." This was rather mortifying for your elder brother, but I found some satisfaction in the difficulties they themselves had in framing a reply. "We simply can't find the right opening lines," they said. "But, after all, is there any special reason that we have to send a return poem?"[194] Still they did not give up. Since they realized that to produce a feeble reply would be worse than nothing at all, they stayed there till the middle of the night racking their brains for the proper words.

'Well now, surely we both have good cause to rejoice. Even if I had been given a promotion during the period of official appointments, it would have been as nothing compared to this.' Listening to Norimitsu, I was most vexed at the idea that all these men had been sitting in judgement on me without my knowledge.

(As for the matter of 'younger sister' and 'elder brother', everyone from the Emperor and Empress down knew about it, and even in the Palace people called Norimitsu 'elder brother' instead of designating him by his office.)

Norimitsu and I were still talking when a servant came to my room and told me to report at once to Her Majesty. As soon as I was in her presence I realized that she had called me to discuss what I had written to Tadanobu. 'The Emperor has been here,' she said, 'and he told me that all his gentlemen have your reply written on their fans.' I was amazed and wondered who could have spread the news.

Thereafter Tadanobu no longer hid his face behind his sleeve when we met and he seemed to have altered his opinion of me.

52. *On the Twenty-Fifth of the Second Month*

On the twenty-fifth of the Second Month in the following year Her Majesty moved to the Empress's Office. I did not accompany her but stayed behind in Umetsubo Palace.[195] On the next day a message came from Tadanobu: 'Last night I visited the temple at Kurama. Since the direction to the capital is closed this evening, I am taking a detour and expect to be back before dawn.[196] There is something I must tell you. Please wait for me and be ready to open the door as soon as I knock.'

It happened, however, that Her Highness, the Mistress of the Robes,[197] sent me a message. 'Why stay alone in your room?' she wrote. 'Come and spend the night here.' Accordingly I went to her.

It was late on the following morning when I got up and returned to my room. My maid was waiting for me. 'Last night,' she said, 'someone was knocking very loudly at the door. In the end I had to get up. The visitor ordered me to announce to my mistress that the man who had promised to come had now arrived. I replied that you would pay no attention to such a message and went back to bed.'

I was feeling very annoyed about all this when a messenger came from the Office of Grounds and said, 'His Excellency, the First Secretary, wishes to inform you that he has to leave at once but that first he has something he must tell you.'

If Tadanobu were to visit me in my own room, he would probably open the blinds and do other such bothersome things. The idea made me nervous, so I told the messenger that I was going to the Palace on business; if His Excellency wanted to see me, he should come there. I then went to Umetsubo Palace and had just opened the half-shutters at the east end of the main room when Tadanobu arrived. I asked him to approach the blinds behind which I was sitting. He looked magnificent as he came towards me. His resplendent, cherry-coloured Court cloak was lined with material of the most delightful hue and lustre; he wore dark, grape-coloured trousers, boldly splashed with designs of wistaria branches; his crimson under-robe was so glossy that it seemed to sparkle, while underneath one could make out layer upon layer of white and light violet robes. As the veranda on which he sat was very narrow, he leaned forward so that the top part of his body came almost up to the blind and I could see him clearly. He looked like one of the gentlemen who are depicted by painters or celebrated by the writers of romances.

The plum blossoms in front of the Palace (red ones on the left and white ones on the right) were just beginning to scatter; yet they were still very beautiful. The sun brilliantly lit up the whole scene – a scene that I should have liked everyone to view. To make it still more charming, the woman nestling close to the blinds should have been a young lady-in-waiting with beautiful, long hair cascading over her shoulders. Instead it was I, an old woman who had long since seen her best years, and whose hair had become so frizzled and dishevelled that it no longer looked as if it belonged to her head.[198] To make matters worse, we were still in mourning[199] and most of the ladies at Court wore special clothes, mine all being of such a light grey hue that they hardly seemed to have any colour at all and one could not tell one garment from another. Since Her Majesty was away, I was wearing an ordinary long robe without a formal skirt and train. Alas, there was not one good thing about me, and I quite spoiled the beauty of the scene!

'I am on my way to the Empress's Office,' said Tadanobu. 'Do you want me to take a message? And when will you be going yourself?

'Well,' he continued, 'it was not yet dawn when I left the place where I stayed last night. Since I had already told you my plans, I expected that you would be waiting for me. It was a clear, moonlit night. As soon as I arrived from the West City,[200] I came and knocked on your door. It took me a long time to arouse your maid. When she finally got out of bed, what a vulgar creature she turned out to be and how rudely she answered me!' Tadanobu laughed, and went on: 'It was a terrible disappointment. How can you have left someone like that in your room?'

Tadanobu had good reason to be annoyed, and as I heard his story I was both sorry for him and amused. He left soon after. It occurred to me that the people who had noticed him from the outside must have wondered what sort of delightful woman could be hidden by the screens, while those who were in the back of the room and could see me from behind would never have imagined that there was such a splendid gentleman on the veranda.

At sunset I went up to the Empress's Office. Her Majesty was surrounded by a group of ladies-in-waiting, who were arguing about various romances and citing passages that impressed them as good or clumsy or disagreeable. The Empress herself discussed the qualities and defects of Suzushi and Nakatada.[201] 'Well, Shōnagon,' said one of the ladies-in-waiting, 'let's hear your opinion of these characters. You must tell us at once. Her Majesty is always talking about Nakatada's mean upbringing. What do you think?'

'For my part,' I replied, 'I don't see anything so wonderful about Suzushi. I admit that he may have succeeded in bringing a heavenly maiden down from the sky by his music, but when did he ever do anything important enough to win the hand of an Emperor's daughter?'

'Good!' exclaimed the lady-in-waiting, realizing that I was on Nakatada's side in the debate.

'If you'd seen Tadanobu when he came here today,' the Empress said, 'you would have found him far more splendid than all these romantic heroes.' 'Yes indeed,' put in another of the ladies-in-waiting, 'today he was even more magnificent than usual.'

'It was just so that I could let Your Majesty know at once

about Tadanobu's visit that I came here this evening,' I said, 'but I became involved in your discussion about romances.' Thereupon I told them everything that had happened.

'We've all seen him,' they said, laughing, 'but how could we possibly have pieced the whole story together?' Then they described Tadanobu's visit. 'Oh, the desolation of the West City!' he had said to them. 'If someone had been there to share it with me. . . . The fences are all broken and everything is overgrown with moss.' 'And was there any fern on the tiles?' Lady Saishō[202] had asked. Extremely impressed by her question, Tadanobu had hummed the line, 'It is not far from the city's western gate. . .'

The women were all loud in praising this exchange, and I found their enthusiasm delightful.

53. *When I Stayed Away from the Palace*

When I stayed away from the Palace,[203] I frequently received visits from senior courtiers and other gentlemen. The people of the household where I was staying used to complain about this and criticize me. If my visitors had included anyone to whom I was particularly attached, I should have resented their complaints, but such was not the case. As it happened, I had no desire to meet them. Yet, if a gentleman comes all the way to see one both during the daytime and at night, is it possible to reply that one is not at home and to send him away embarrassed?

Some of the men who visited my house were almost total strangers, and in the end it became too much for me. On the next time when I left Court I therefore decided not to announce where I was going – in fact I told hardly anyone except Tsunefusa and Narimasa.

On one occasion during my absence the Lieutenant of the Guards, Norimitsu, came to see me. In the course of our conversation he mentioned that on the previous day His Excellency the Imperial Adviser, Tadanobu, had insistently questioned him about my whereabouts. 'After all,' Tadanobu had said, 'it hardly seems likely that you would not know where your own sister is staying.' Norimitsu had continued to protest his ignorance, but Tadanobu had become cross and only pressed him the harder. 'I really had a difficult time hiding the truth from him,' said Norimitsu. 'It was all I could do not to burst into laughter. To make matters worse, Tsunefusa was sitting directly next to us with an unconcerned, innocent look. I knew that if I so much as glanced at him I should start giggling. To save myself, I snatched from the table a common piece of seaweed[204] and popped it into my mouth. It must have looked odd, but my ruse saved me from giving away your secret. As it was, Tadanobu decided that I really did not know where you were. I found it all most amusing.'

'Well,' I said, still more emphatically, 'whatever you do, don't tell him!'

Several days passed. Then late one night I heard a loud knocking at the gate. I wondered why anyone should make such a terrible disturbance, especially since the gate was quite near the house and an ordinary knock would have sufficed. I sent one of the servants to find out who was there. It turned out to be a messenger, a soldier in the Imperial Guards, with a letter from Norimitsu.[205] Since everyone was asleep, I drew up a lamp for myself and opened the letter. 'Tomorrow,' I read, 'is the Day of Conclusion of the Sacred Readings.[206] Tadanobu is bound to spend all day in the Palace to attend the Emperor and Empress during their abstinence. If he urges me again to tell him where my younger sister is, there will be no help for it. I shall certainly not be able to hide it this time. Is it all right to let him know where you are? What shall I do? I shall act according to your instructions.'

By way of reply I merely wrapped a little seaweed in a piece of paper and sent it to him.[207] When Norimitsu came to see me later, he told me that all night long Tadanobu had been after him for information. 'Without even waiting to find a suitable place,' said Norimitsu, 'His Excellency took me aside and began interrogating me. I can assure you that it was most disagreeable to be put to the question like that. Besides, you never told me what I should answer, but simply sent that silly bit of seaweed wrapped in paper. I suppose you did it by mistake.'

'What a strange mistake that would be!' I thought. 'Who would ever wrap up such an object and send it to someone?' I was really disgusted with Norimitsu for having so completely missed the point, and without a word I took a piece of paper that was lying under the inkstone and wrote the following poem:

> Tell no man where she lives –
> The diver in the water's depths –
> Such must have been the meaning of her glance.[208]

I gave it to Norimitsu, but he pushed it back with his fan, saying, 'Ah, you have been good enough to write one of your poems for me. But I have no intention of reading it.' And he hurried out of the room.

Norimitsu and I had always been on close terms and tried to help each other, but now, without anything particular having happened, a coolness came between us. Shortly afterwards I received this note from him: 'I know that I may have put you out in some way, but please do not forget our pact. Even though we are apart, remember that I have been your elder brother.'

I have heard Norimitsu say, 'People who are fond of me should spare me their poems or I shall have to regard them as enemies. When you feel that the time has come to break with me, just send one of those things.' So it is possible that Norimitsu never actually read the following poem that I sent in reply to his note:

> Smoothly runs the river of Yoshino
> Between Mount Imo and Mount Se.*
> Yet, should those mountains crumble,
> The river too would vanish from our sight.[209]

In any case he never answered it. At about the same time he was awarded the head-dress of nobility and appointed Assistant Governor of Tōtōmi; and so we parted while still on bad terms.

* 'Younger Sister' and 'Older Brother'.

54. *Things That Give a Pathetic Impression*

The voice of someone who blows his nose while he is speaking. The expression of a woman plucking her eyebrows.[210]

55. *Then a Few Months after Our Visit*

Then a few months after our visit to the guard-house of the Left Guards I was staying at home when I received this message from the Empress: 'Come back quickly. I keep remembering that early morning when you went to the guard-house. How can you be so indifferent to it all? Surely such an experience must have made a deep impression on you.'

In my reply I assured Her Majesty of my profound respect; then, as a personal touch, I added the following: 'How could it fail to make an impression on me when even Your Majesty was so moved by the scene that she referred to us, her mere attendants, as "heavenly maidens hovering in the air"?'[211] The messenger returned presently with these words from the Empress: 'I wonder why you should have said something to bring discredit on Nakatada, who was such a favourite of yours. In any case, leave everything and come back here this very evening. I shall resent it greatly if you don't.'

I sent the messenger back with this reply: 'If Your Majesty had simply said "slightly annoyed", I should consider it a terrible thing. Since you used the word "greatly", I shall return even at the risk of my life.' So saying, I went back to the Palace.

56. *Once When Her Majesty Was Residing*

Once when Her Majesty was residing in the Empress's Office, Perpetual Readings[212] were held in the western part of the main hall. The usual paintings of the Buddha had been hung for the

99

occasion, and several priests were in attendance. On the second day of the readings the voice of a common-sounding woman reached us from the veranda. 'I expect there'll be some scraps from the altar offerings,' she said. 'How could there be any left-overs this early in the service?' replied one of the priests. I wondered who the woman might be and went on to the veranda to have a look. It turned out to be an old nun dressed in a filthy cotton trouser-skirt which was so short and narrow that it seemed more like a sort of tube than an article of clothing. Over this she wore something equally dirty which was presumably meant to be a robe but which came only about five inches below her sash. She really looked like a monkey.

'What do you want, woman?' I asked.

'Madam,' she replied in an affected tone, 'I am a disciple of the Buddha and I was hoping to receive the left-overs from his altar. But these priests are so stingy that they grudge the smallest gift.' She now spoke in a bright, elegant fashion and I was rather touched to see her so crushed by misfortune. Yet there was a gaudiness about her manner that annoyed me and I said, 'So you eat nothing but the Buddha's holy left-overs! How worthy of you!' Seeing my expression she said, 'Why do you suppose that's all I eat? It's only when I can't get anything else that I take left-overs.'

I put some fruit, flat rice cakes, and other things in a basket and gave it to her. She then became extremely familiar and began chatting away. Some of the younger ladies-in-waiting joined us on the veranda and plied her with all sorts of questions, such as 'Do you have a lover?' and 'Where do you live?', to which she replied with jokes and suggestive quips. When one of them asked her whether she could sing and dance, she burst out with

> Who shall share my bed tonight?
> Hitachi no Suke[213] – he's my man!
> His skin is soft to touch.

This was followed by several other songs in a similar vein. Then she started rolling her head round and round, and sang,

The maple leaves of scarlet
That tint Otoko's manly peak
Proclaim that mountain far and wide.[214]

Her behaviour was most unbecoming. The ladies-in-waiting laughed with disgust and said, 'Be off with you!', which I found very amusing. 'Let's give the woman something before we send her packing,' said one of them.

The Empress had heard all this and reprimanded us. 'Why have you made her behave in such an embarrassing way?' she asked. 'I couldn't bear to hear it and I had to stop up my ears. Here, give her this robe and send her away at once!'

The ladies took the robe and threw it at the woman, saying, 'Her Majesty has generously given you this present. Take off your filthy robe and put on this nice clean one.' The nun received it with a deep bow; then, draping it over her shoulders, she began to perform a dance of thanks.[215] She was really too repulsive, and we all went indoors.

Evidently this gift made her feel that she was now fully accepted in Her Majesty's household; thereafter she was always coming and going, and soon she had acquired the nickname of Hitachi no Suke. She still wore her same dirty robe. We wondered what she had done with the one the Empress gave her and we felt quite disgusted with the creature.

One day when Lady Ukon paid a call, Her Majesty told her about the nun. 'My ladies have taken it into their heads to befriend her,' she said. 'She's always coming to see us these days.' Then she asked Lady Kohyōe to give an imitation of the nun. Lady Ukon burst out laughing. 'How can I arrange to see her for myself?' she asked. 'You really must show her to me. Don't think I'll try to take her away. I realize she is Your Majesty's favourite.'

Later there came another nun – a cripple this time, but with a naturally elegant manner. She called to us from the veranda; when we went out, she begged for alms, in such an embarrassed way that we were truly sorry for her. Her Majesty ordered that she be given a robe and the nun prostrated herself on the ground.

Her movements were much the same as the other nun's, but there was nothing unpleasant about her. Just as she was leaving the veranda, weeping for joy, Hitachi no Suke happened to arrive and caught a glimpse of her. Thereafter Hitachi did not visit us again for a long time, and we soon forgot about her.

က

From the tenth day of the Twelfth Month it snowed very heavily. I and the other ladies-in-waiting gathered large quantities of snow and heaped it in lids; then we decided to build a real snow mountain [216] in the garden. Having summoned the servants, we told them it was on Her Majesty's orders, and so they all got to work. Men from the Office of Grounds, who had come to do some sweeping, also joined in, and soon the mountain was rising high above the ground. Next came some officials from the Office of the Empress's Household, who made suggestions and helped build an especially beautiful mountain. There were also a few Assistant Officials from the Emperor's Private Office and some more men from the Office of Grounds, so that soon we had about twenty people working away. In addition messages were sent to the servants off duty, saying that a special stipend would be given to anyone who helped on that day, but that those who did not appear for work could expect nothing. This brought the men rushing out, except for those who lived far away and could not be informed.

When the mountain was finished, officials from the Office of the Empress's Household were summoned and given rolls of silk tied up in sets of two. They threw the rolls on to the veranda, and each of the workmen came and took a set. Having bowed low, they thrust the silk into their robes before withdrawing. Some of the Court gentlemen changed from their formal over-robes into hunting costume and remained in attendance at the Empress's Office.

'Well,' said Her Majesty, 'how long is that mountain likely to last?'

Everyone guessed that it would be ten days or a little more.

'And what do you think?' the Empress asked me.

'It will last till the fifteenth of the First Month,' I declared.

Even Her Majesty found this hard to believe, and the other women insisted that it would melt before the end of the year. I realized I had chosen too distant a date; the mountain would last until the first of the year at the outside, which was the latest day I should have given. Yet there was no taking back what I had said: though I knew the mountain was unlikely to survive till the fifteenth, I stuck to my original prediction.

Towards the twentieth it began raining. There was no sign that the snow was about to melt, but the mountain did shrink a little. 'Oh, Goddess of Mercy of Shirayama,'[217] I prayed frenziedly, 'do not let our mountain melt away!'

On the day we built the mountain Tadataka, the Secretary in the Ministry of Ceremonial, arrived with a message from the Emperor. We gave him a cushion and joined him for a talk. 'Today they're making snow mountains everywhere,' he told us. 'The Emperor has ordered his men to build one in the garden in front of his Palace, and they're also building them in the Eastern Palace and in the Koki and Kyōgoku Palaces.'[218] Hearing this, I wrote a poem and asked the woman standing beside me to recite it:

> That mountain in our garden,
> Which we had thought so rare!
> Everywhere its snowy likeness . . .
> And we can boast of nothing new.

Tadataka was impressed. 'I would not want to spoil the brilliant effect of your poem by making a poor reply,' he said, bowing repeatedly. 'The next time I find myself outside the blinds of some fashionable Court lady I shall repeat your lines.' And with that he took his leave.

I had heard that Tadataka was very fond of poetry, and his behaviour surprised me. When I told the Empress about it, she said, 'He obviously preferred not to reply at all unless he could produce something really good.'

Towards the end of the year the snow mountain seemed to have become smaller, yet it was still very high. About noon one day, when I and some of the other women were sitting out on the veranda, Hitachi no Suke arrived. 'Why haven't we seen you for such a long time?' we asked her. 'Oh, nothing special,' she said. 'It's just that something rather sad happened to me.' 'And what may that be?' we asked. 'Well,' she replied, 'I couldn't help feeling that

> Lucky indeed is she,
> That nunnish diver of the briny depths,
> Who is so laden down with gifts
> That she can scarcely drag herself ashore.'[219]

She drawled out her poem, and we all laughed contemptuously. Since no one was paying much attention, she made her way up to the snow mountain and walked round it before leaving. Later we sent Lady Ukon a message about the visit, and she replied, 'Why didn't you bring her here? It was really too bad to abandon her like that and make her go all the way to that great mountain of yours by herself.' This caused us to burst into laughter again.

New Year came without affecting the snow mountain in any way.

On the first day of the year it again started snowing heavily. I was happily thinking how the snow would gather on the mountain when Her Majesty said, 'This has come at the wrong time. Leave what was there before and brush away all the new snow.'

Very early on the following morning, as I was going from the Palace to my room, I saw a man who looked like a head retainer. He was on his way to the Empress's Office and was shivering with cold. On the sleeve of his night-watch costume, which was as green as a citron leaf, I noticed a piece of paper, also green, attached to a pine twig.[220]

'Who sent this?' I asked him.

'The High Priestess of Kamo,'[221] he replied.

Realizing at once that this must be something pleasant, I carried the letter to the Empress's room. Her Majesty was still in bed, and I did my best to open her lattice-door myself,[222] using for this purpose a *go* board on which I stood as I tried to push up the heavy grating. The lattice was very heavy, but finally one side opened with a creaking sound that wakened the Empress. 'Why are you doing that?' she asked. 'I have a letter from the High Priestess,' I replied, 'which I had to deliver to Your Majesty as quickly as possible.' 'Well,' she said, getting up, 'it certainly is early for a letter.'

Looking inside, she discovered a pair of hare-sticks, each about five inches long. They had been placed end to end so that they looked like a single hare-wand; some paper had been wrapped round the head of the sticks, which were prettily decorated with sprigs of wild orange, club moss, and mountain sedge. But there seemed to be no written message. 'Can this really be all?' said the Empress. Searching more carefully, however, we found the following verse written on a bit of paper wrapped round the end of the stick:

> I thought I heard the woodman's axe
> Echoing through the hills.
> But, oh, it was a gladder sound –
> The cutting of the festive wands.[223]

As I watched the Empress writing her reply to this letter (which turned out to be the beginning of a regular correspondence between her and the High Priestess), I was full of admiration. Determined to make her letter as elegant as the one she had received, Her Majesty took the utmost pains to correct the wording until she considered it just right. The messenger was rewarded with an unlined costume of white material and another of dark red that looked like plum blossom.[224] I enjoyed watching the man set off in the falling snow with the clothes over his shoulder. Unfortunately I never found out what Her Majesty had replied.

Meanwhile our snow mountain, dirty and unattractive though it had become, showed no sign of melting; and one would really have thought that it belonged to the northern land of Koshi.

I prayed that somehow it would survive until the fifteenth. I was convinced that I would win, but some people insisted that it would not outlast the seventh. We had all decided to wait and see what happened when suddenly on the third of the month the Empress was obliged to return to the Imperial Palace. This was a great disappointment, and at first I seriously thought that we would never know the outcome. 'Well,' said everyone (including Her Majesty), 'it was all very delightful. What a shame we couldn't see it to the end!'

I determined then that, if my original guess turned out to be correct, I would show Her Majesty the remaining snow whatever happened. I realized that this would require special steps, so I took advantage of the confusion of packing and moving to summon a gardener who lived in a hut near the wall of the Empress's Office. When he came to the veranda where I was sitting, I told him to take extremely good care of the mountain. 'Make sure it lasts until the fifteenth,' I said, 'and don't let any children climb up and scatter the snow. If you look after it really well and it lasts until the middle of the month, Her Majesty will give you a generous reward, and I too shall show you my gratitude.' So saying, I gave him some cakes and other food that I had got from the reserve that was always kept in the kitchen for poor people.

The gardener beamed. 'That will be quite simple, Madam,' he said, 'I shall certainly guard your mountain for you, though it may be difficult to stop the children from climbing. . .' 'If they refuse to obey,' I said, 'tell them whom they are dealing with!'

I then accompanied Her Majesty back to the Palace and stayed there until the seventh. During this time I was so worried about the mountain that I was forever dispatching under-servants, bathroom servants, and housekeepers with instructions for the gardener. On the seventh I sent him some of the left-overs from the Festival of Young Herbs; when the servants returned, I heard them laughing at the reverent way in which the gardener had received the gifts.

After I had gone home on the seventh, I was still greatly con-

cerned with the mountain and early each morning I sent someone to look at it. On the tenth my messenger delighted me by
saying that it would last for another five days or so. On the night
of the thirteenth, however, it rained very hard, and I thought
with distress that now my mountain must surely have melted. I
stayed awake all night, lamenting that it could not possibly
survive another day, let alone the necessary two. The people who
heard me laughed and said I was mad. As soon as there was a
sound of stirring in the house, I got up and tried to arouse one
of the maids. The lazy wench would not budge. Thoroughly
annoyed, I sent another servant, who was already awake, to
inspect the mountain. 'Well, Madam,' she told me on her return,
'it is now about the size of a round straw cushion. The gardener
has been looking after it very efficiently and has not let any
children come near. It should last like this until tomorrow or
even the next day. The gardener says that he is now confident
of receiving his reward.'

I was overjoyed and decided that, with the arrival of the
fifteenth, I should dash off a poem and send it to the Empress
together with some of the snow in a basket.

Anxiously I awaited the following day, and before dawn I gave
my maid a large chip-basket,[225] telling her to fill the cover with
snow from those parts of the mountain where it was still white.
'Use a rake,' I said, 'and throw away all the dirty snow.'

She was back almost at once with the cover of the chip-basket
dangling, still empty, from her hand. 'It's gone,' she announced.
I was dumbfounded. The splendid poem that I had composed
with such effort, thinking that soon it would be on everyone's
lips, now seemed foolish and useless. 'But how,' I asked de-
jectedly, 'can such a large heap of snow have melted overnight?'

'The gardener was wringing his hands,' the maid said
excitedly. 'He told me that the snow was there until late last
night and he was counting on his reward, but that now of course
he would get nothing.'

Just then a messenger arrived with a note from the Empress

asking whether the snow had lasted. Mortifying as it was, I had to reply that none was left. 'Tell Her Majesty,' I said, 'that the snow, which the older women said would melt last month and in any case before New Year's Day, was still there yesterday at sunset. I don't think I did so badly. If it had actually lasted until today, my prediction would have been *too* accurate. I dare say that during the night someone removed the snow out of spite and flung it away.'

When I returned to the Palace on the twentieth, I discussed the matter with the Empress and told her how amazed I had been by the maid's prompt return and by her news. 'The cover was dangling in her hand,' I said, 'and she had put the box itself on her head like a hat. . . . I was planning to build a beautiful little snow mountain in the lid and to present it to Your Majesty with a fine poem written on white paper.'

The Empress burst out laughing and her ladies-in-waiting joined in. 'I am afraid I have earned a heavy load of sin for having spoiled everything when it meant so much to you,' she said. 'To tell the truth, on the night of the fourteenth I sent some servants to the mountain with orders to destroy it and throw away what was left. Strange that in your reply to my note you guessed exactly what happened.'

It appeared that, when the Empress's servants arrived at the mountain, the old gardener had come out, wringing his hands and begging them not to damage the snow. 'We are acting on Her Majesty's orders,' they had answered. 'And don't tell any-one, or we shall tear down your hut for you.' They then took all the snow and threw it over the wall at the south of the guard-office of the Left Division. According to the servants' report, the mountain was still quite high and the snow would certainly have lasted until the twentieth. 'In fact,' said the Empress, 'I am afraid your mountain might very well have stood there until it started snowing again next winter.' When His Majesty heard the story, he commented to his senior courtiers, 'Who would have thought of having such a strange contest?'

'Well,' said the Empress after she had told me all this, 'now you can see that it is just the same as if you had actually won. So please let me hear your poem.'

The ladies-in-waiting joined her in asking for my poem, but I felt very unhappy and replied, 'After what I have just been told, why should I want to recite it?'

At that moment the Emperor walked into the room and addressed me. 'I have always regarded you as being like other people,' he said, 'but now I see what a remarkable woman you really are.'

This only made me unhappier about my mountain, and I felt I was going to burst into tears. 'Oh, how sad!' I exclaimed. 'What a cruel world we live in! I remember how happy I was when it snowed on New Year's Day and the mountain started getting higher, but then Your Majesty said it had come at the wrong time and gave orders that all the snow should be swept away.'

The Emperor laughed. 'The fact is,' he said, 'that she probably didn't want you to win.'

57. *Splendid Things*

Chinese brocade. A sword with a decorated scabbard. The grain of the wood in a Buddhist statue. Long flowering branches of beautifully coloured wistaria entwined about a pine tree.

Despite his low station a Chamberlain of the Sixth Rank is a splendid thing. To think that he is allowed yellowish-green robes of figured material and cloth that even young noblemen of the finest families are forbidden to wear! A mere Assistant or Subordinate Official in the Emperor's Private Office, who is the son of a commoner and who has gone completely unnoticed while serving under gentlemen of rank with official posts, becomes splendid beyond words after being appointed Chamberlain.

A Chamberlain of the Sixth Rank cuts a magnificent figure when he arrives with an Imperial mandate or when he brings the sweet chestnuts for the Great Council banquet.[226] Observing how he is treated and entertained, one could imagine that he has come down from heaven.

A girl of noble birth has been chosen as Imperial consort; but she is still living at home, where they refer to her as 'Princess'. When a Chamberlain visits her with a message from the Emperor, her lady-in-waiting, before even delivering the letter, first pushes out a cushion for him from behind the blinds. As she does so, she displays the sleeves of her dress – a rare sight for a man of such humble rank.

If, in addition to being a Chamberlain, the messenger belongs to the Imperial Guards, things are still more impressive. He sits down on the cushion, spreading out the skirts of his under-robe, and it is the master of the house himself who gives the man a wine cup. What must be his delight on receiving such treatment!

A Chamberlain can keep company with young noblemen as if he were their equal – yes, with those same young noblemen whose very sight used to overawe him and who in the past would not have deigned to sit in the same room with someone of such low rank. Now it is he who inspires jealousy, especially when people see how closely he attends the Emperor, fanning His Majesty and rubbing the inkstick for him when he wishes to write a letter.

The Chamberlain's term of office is three or four years. During this time he is poorly dressed and there is nothing very elegant about his personal effects; yet he can mix freely with senior courtiers and other superiors. But what does he have to show for it all when his term has expired? I am sure that, as the time approaches for him to receive the head-dress of nobility and forgo the privilege of being admitted into the Presence, he feels sorrier than if he were to lose his own life. It is sad to see how he bustles about the Palace in a frantic effort to secure some last favours from the Emperor. In the past, Chamberlains began lamenting the loss of their privileges from the very beginning of the year when they were to relinquish their posts. Nowadays they compete for new appointments.

I need hardly say how splendid I find a learned Doctor of Literature.[227] He may be of lowly appearance, and of course he is of low rank; but the world at large regards him as an impressive figure. As an Imperial Tutor, he is consulted about all sorts of special matters, and he is free to approach the most eminent members of the Emperor's family. When he has composed one of his prayers for the Emperor or the introduction to some poem, he becomes the object of universal praise.

A learned priest is also splendid. It is impressive enough when he reads his breviary by himself, but how much more so when he is among several Lectors officiating in the Sacred Readings[228] at one of the fixed periods! It is getting dark. 'Why haven't they brought the oil?' says one of the Lectors. 'How late they are in lighting the lamps!' All the Lectors stop reading, but the learned priest continues quietly reciting the scriptures from memory.

An Imperial Procession by the Empress in daytime.

The Empress's birth chamber.[229]

The ceremony of installing a new Empress.[230] On this occasion tables are arranged in front of her dais together with the lion and the Korean dog. Then the people from the Table Office bring in the Imperial Cauldron. As one watches all this, it is difficult to believe that this same Empress was recently an ordinary person known simply as 'Princess'.

The procession of the First Man. His pilgrimage to Kasuga Shrine.

Grape-coloured material.

Anything purple is splendid, be it flowers, thread, or paper. Among purple flowers, however, I do not like the iris despite its gorgeous colour. What makes the costume of Sixth Rank Chamberlains so attractive when they are on night duty is the purple trousers.

A large garden all covered with snow.

The eldest son of our present Emperor is still a child, but how splendid he looks when he is in the arms of Their Excellencies, his handsome young uncles, when he is being served by senior courtiers, or when his horse is led out for inspection! Seeing the

young Prince at such times, one would say that nothing unpleasant could ever happen to him.[231]

58. *One Day When the Emperor Visited Her Majesty's Rooms*

One day when the Emperor visited Her Majesty's rooms, we
heard that he had taken along the lute called Mumyō*[232] and
that some of the ladies-in-waiting were strumming it. We went
to have a look, but no one was playing. One of our group toyed
with the strings and asked what the instrument was called. 'It's
far too insignificant to have a name,'[233] said the Empress. Hearing her reply, I was once more reminded what an admirable
mistress I served.

The Lady of the Shigei Sha,[234] who had come to call on the
Empress, mentioned in the course of conversation that at home
she had a very fine thirteen-pipe flute which she had received
from her late father. Hearing this, His Lordship the Bishop[235]
said, 'Please give it to me. I have a splendid seven-string zither
at home which I hope you will take in exchange.' But the
Shigei Sha paid no attention to him and continued chatting to the
Empress. His Lordship repeated the request several times,
thinking that in the end his sister was bound to reply; but still
she said nothing. Thereupon Her Majesty said, 'No, she
certainly has no intention of exchanging it – any more than one
would exchange the Inakaeji†[236] flute.' It was a delightful remark; but His Lordship, priest though he was, seemed unfamiliar with the name of this particular flute, and he only felt
resentful. (This was at a time when Her Majesty was residing
in the Empress's Office and there was a flute known as Inakaeji
in the Imperial collection.)

The zithers, flutes, and other instruments belonging to the
Emperor have certainly been given some strange names. Among

* 'Nameless'.

† 'No, I will not exchange'.

the lutes are Genshō, Mokuma, Ide, Ikyō, and Mumyō; the six-string zithers have names like Kuchime, Shiogama, and Futanuki. I have also heard about Suirō, Kosuirō, Uda no Hōshi, Kugiuchi, and Hafutatsu;[237] and there are many others whose names I have forgotten. 'Such objects,' I remember Tadanobu saying, 'deserve to be placed on the shelf of honour in Giyō Palace.'[238]

59. A Group of Senior Courtiers

A group of senior courtiers had spent all day playing the zither and flute outside the bamboo blinds of the Empress's apartments in Seiryō Palace. In the evening they retired and went their own ways. When the lamp was brought out, the lattices had not yet been lowered and it was possible to see clearly through the blinds into the Imperial apartments. There sat the Empress, holding her lute lengthwise. She wore a magnificent scarlet robe, and beneath it several layers of beaten and stretched silk. Her sleeve was elegantly draped over the glossy, black lute; and nothing could have been more splendid than the contrast between her dazzlingly white forehead and the dark wood of the instrument. Having glanced at this scene, I went up to one of the women who was standing near by and said, 'The girl whose face was half hidden can certainly not have been as beautiful as this. And she, of course, was a mere commoner.'[239] When she heard this, the woman forced her way into the Empress's room and reported what I had said. Presently she came back and told me that Her Majesty had laughingly asked, 'And do you know what Shōnagon meant by that?', which amused me greatly.

60. Once in the Fifth Month

Once in the Fifth Month during the long spell of rainy weather Captain Tadanobu came and stood next to the bamboo screen by the door leading to the Empress's apartments. He u ;ed a most delightful scent, which it was impossible to identify. The air was very damp.[240] Even though nothing noteworthy took place, there was something peculiarly elegant about the entire scene, which makes me feel bound to mention it. The Captain's scent permeated the screen and lingered there till the following day. Small wonder that the younger ladies-in-waiting should have felt this was something unique!

61. *One of Her Majesty's Wet-Nurses*

One of Her Majesty's wet-nurses who held the Fifth Rank left today for the province of Hyūga. Among the fans given her by the Empress as a parting gift was one with a painting of a travellers' lodging, not unlike the Captain of Ide's residence. On the other side was a picture of the capital in a heavy rainstorm with someone gazing at the scene. In her own hand the Empress had written the following sentence as if it were an ordinary piece of prose[241]: 'When you have gone away and face the sun that shines so crimson in the East, be mindful of the friends you left behind, who in this city gaze upon the endless rains.' It was a very moving message, and I realized that I myself could not possibly leave such a mistress and go away to some distant place.

62. *Annoying Things*

One has sent someone a poem (or a reply to a poem) and, after the messenger has left, thinks of a couple of words that ought to be changed.

One has sewn something in a hurry. The task seems finished, but on pulling out the needle one discovers that one forgot to knot the end of the thread. It is also very annoying to find that one has sewn something back to front.

One day when the Empress was staying in the Southern

Palace,[242] she went to visit His Excellency, her father, in the western wing. I and the other ladies-in-waiting were gathered in the main building with nothing particular to do. We wandered along the corridors, trying to distract ourselves in one way or another. Then a messenger came from Her Majesty. 'A robe is wanted in a hurry,' we were told. 'All of you are to get together and make sure that it is delivered to the Empress, fully sewn, before the next watch.' We were then given some plain silk material.

My companions and I assembled at the front of the main hall, each of us taking a piece of silk and each determined to be the first to finish her work. We sat side by side, not facing each other, and started sewing at great speed. Nurse Myōbu, who did the wide sleeves, finished her work before anyone else. In her haste, however, she did not notice that she had sewn one piece of material inside out. Without even tying the final knot, she laid down the sleeves and stood up.

When it came to putting the different parts of the dress together at the back, we soon realized that there had been a mistake. The ladies laughed and scolded the nurse, saying, 'You'd better do it over again properly.' 'And who do you suppose would admit she had made a mistake in sewing?' said the nurse. 'With patterned silk, of course, one would have to start again if one had mistaken the front for the back, but with plain material like this what does it matter? If anyone has to do her work again, I don't see why it should be me. Ask the girls who still haven't finished their sewing.'

Since she could not be persuaded, the rest of us had to start our work over again. It was really amusing to watch the expressions of Gen Shōnagon, Shin Chūnagon, and the others as they sat there plying their needles and muttering, 'How does she think she can get away with it?' All this because Her Majesty intended to visit the Emperor that evening and had said, 'I shall know that the one who gets her work done first really loves me.'

It is annoying when a messenger delivers a letter to a person not meant to see it. If he simply admitted his mistake, it would not be so bad. But when he begins insisting that he merely carried out orders, it is really infuriating. If I were not afraid that someone might see me I should rush up and strike him.

One has planted some nice clover or *susuki* grass and goes to have a look at it. What a painful and annoying experience to find someone with a long box and a spade who has carefully dug up the plants and is now carrying them away! If a gentleman were present, the fellow would not dare act like this. On being reproached, he answers, 'I've only taken a little,' and hurries off.

A retainer of some grand family comes to the house of a provincial official and speaks to him rudely with an expression implying, 'You may find my manner annoying, but what can you do about it?'

A man snatches a letter that one does not want him to see and takes it into the garden, where he stands reading it. One runs after him in a rage. But one cannot go beyond the curtains; and there one stops, wishing that one could leap out at the man.

A woman is angry with her lover about some trifle and refuses to continue lying next to him. After fidgeting about in bed, she decides to get up. The man gently tries to draw her back, but she is still cross. 'Very well then,' he says, feeling that she has gone too far. 'As you please.' Full of resentment, he buries himself under his bedclothes and settles down for the night. It is a cold night and, since the woman is wearing only an unlined robe, she soon begins to feel uncomfortable. Everyone else in the house is asleep, and besides it would be most unseemly for her to get up alone and walk about. As the night wears on, she lies there on her side of the bed feeling very annoyed that the quarrel did not take place earlier in the evening when it would have been easy to leave. Then she begins to hear strange sounds in the back of the house and outside. Frightened, she gently moves over in bed towards her lover, tugging at the bedclothes, whereupon he annoys her further by pretending to be asleep. 'Why not be stand-offish a little longer?' he asks her finally.

63. *Embarrassing Things*

While entertaining a visitor, one hears some servants chatting without any restraint in one of the back rooms. It is embarrassing to know that one's visitor can overhear. But how to stop them?

A man whom one loves gets drunk and keeps repeating himself.

To have spoken about someone not knowing that he could overhear. This is embarrassing even if it be a servant or some other completely insignificant person.

To hear one's servants making merry. This is equally annoying if one is on a journey and staying in cramped quarters or at home and hears the servants in a neighbouring room.

Parents, convinced that their ugly child is adorable, pet him and repeat the things he has said, imitating his voice.

An ignoramus who in the presence of some learned person puts on a knowing air and converses about men of old.

A man recites his own poems (not especially good ones) and tells one about the praise they have received – most embarrassing.

Lying awake at night, one says something to one's companion, who simply goes on sleeping.

In the presence of a skilled musician, someone plays a zither just for his own pleasure and without tuning it.

A son-in-law who has long since stopped visiting his wife runs into his father-in-law in a public place.

64. *Surprising and Distressing Things*

While one is cleaning a decorative comb, something catches in the teeth and the comb breaks.

A carriage overturns. One would have imagined that such a solid, bulky object would remain forever on its wheels. It all seems like a dream – astonishing and senseless.

A child or grown-up blurts out something that is bound to make people uncomfortable.

All night long one has been waiting for a man who one thought was sure to arrive. At dawn, just when one has forgotten about him for a moment and dozed off, a crow caws loudly. One wakes up with a start and sees that it is daytime – most astonishing.

One of the bowmen in an archery contest stands trembling for a long time before shooting; when finally he does release his arrow, it goes in the wrong direction.[243]

65. *It Was during the Abstinence of the Fifth Month*

It was during the Abstinence of the Fifth Month[244] when Her Majesty was residing in the Empress's Office. The two-span apartment[245] in front of the store-room had been especially decorated for the occasion, and I enjoyed seeing how different it looked.

From the beginning of the month it had been dark and rainy. 'This is becoming a bore,' I said one day. 'I should like to go somewhere to hear a *hototogisu* singing.' The other women enjoyed the idea and said that they wanted to accompany me. One of them suggested a bridge behind Kamo Shrine; it had an unpleasant name, something like Weaver Bridge.[246] 'The *hototogisu* sings there every day,' she said. 'Those aren't *hototogisu*,' said someone else. 'They're cicadas.'

Nevertheless we planned to go there, and on the morning of the fifth day we ordered the men from the Office of the Empress's Household to get our carriage ready. Since it was the rainy season, we decided that no one would object if we left by the gate next to the guard-house at the north of the Palace.[247] The carriage was pulled up to our veranda and four[248] of us climbed inside. 'Can't we get another carriage of our own and go along with them?' asked some of the other women, but the Empress refused. Though they were very disappointed, we set off without listening to their complaints or showing any sympathy.

As we passed the riding-ground, we noticed a throng of noisy people and asked what was happening. It turned out that they were doing archery practice with the great bow. We were invited to stay and watch for a while. 'All the Middle and Minor Captains of the Left Guards Division are here,' we were told. But we saw no one of the kind; there were only a few officials of the Sixth Rank wandering about the place. 'Not very interesting, is it?' said one of the women. 'Let's go on at once.'

So we continued on our way to Kamo, the road reminding us pleasantly of the Festival.[249] Since Lord Akinobu's[250] house lay on our way, someone suggested that we should stop and have a look at it. We told our men to draw the carriage up to the veranda and we all got out. It was a plain, rustic place. The sliding paper-door with pictures of horses, the wickerwork screens, the water-bur blinds – everything seemed deliberately arranged to look old-fashioned. The house itself was designed in the simplest style; but, poor and cramped as everything was, it still had a certain charm. As for the *hototogisu*, they were singing to each other so loudly that we were almost deafened. It really was a shame that Her Majesty was not there to hear them; and we also felt sorry for the women who had wanted so badly to come with us.

'When one visits a new place,' said our host, 'it's always interesting to see the local activities.' He sent for a large quantity of what I took to be rice plants,[251] and also summoned a number of quite pleasant-looking young girls from his own household and some common women from the neighbouring farms. Half a dozen threshed the rice, while a couple of others used a revolving machine of a type that I had never seen before. As they worked, they sang such a strange song that we all burst out laughing and completely forgot about writing our *hototogisu* poems.

Next Lord Akinobu ordered his servants to bring out some small tables of the kind one sees in Chinese pictures, and we were served a meal. Noticing that none of us paid much attention to the food, he said, 'I am afraid this is only rough, country fare.[252] But if you come to this sort of place and don't like the food, you must tell your host quite frankly and he will serve you something more to your taste. You ladies really are the shyest guests I've ever had.' He encouraged us to help ourselves. 'Do have some of these fern sprouts,' he said. 'I picked them with my own hands.'

'But really,' I said, 'how can you expect us to sit here eating in a row like a lot of common maid-servants?'[253]

'Of course,' said Akinobu and ordered his attendants to remove the dishes. 'I should have realized that ladies-in-waiting like you are accustomed to the formality of life in the Palace.' While the servants were bustling about, taking the dishes off the tables and putting everything in order, one of our men came and announced that it was going to rain. So we hurried back to our carriage.

'I should have liked to write my *hototogisu* poem before we left,' I remarked. 'Never mind,' said the others. 'You can do it just as well on our way back.'

Before starting, we picked some long branches of *u no hana*, covered with white blossoms, and decorated our carriage with them, so that they hung out of the blinds and sides. It really looked as though a great white cloak had been spread across the roof. Our attendants were delighted and, laughing loudly, began to stick branches into every possible place, even through the bamboo framework of the carriage. 'There's still room for some here,' they shouted, adding bough after bough. 'And here's another place.'

I was hoping that we would be seen by someone on our way back. Alas, all we met was an occasional indigent priest and a few other people too common to be worth mentioning. As we approached the Palace, we decided that we really could not let the outing come to an end without making sure that someone would see us and spread the news about our carriage. So we stopped next to the Palace of the First Ward and sent a servant to ask for His Excellency, Fujiwara no Kiminobu, the Gentleman-in-Waiting,[254] informing him that we were on our way back from hearing the *hototogisu*. 'I shall be with you at once, my dear ladies,' came the reply. The messenger added that His Excellency had gone to the Attendants' Hall and was hurriedly changing into Court trousers. We replied that we could not possibly wait and told our driver to set off at full speed for Tsuchi Gate.[255] Presently Kiminobu appeared, running after our carriage, and accompanied by a number of attendants and lackeys who had not even had time to put on their shoes. He had managed to get dressed with amazing speed, but was still tying his sash as he dashed along the road. 'Wait a minute!' he shouted. 'Wait a minute!' We told our driver to go still faster and had already reached Tsuchi Gate when Kiminobu caught up with us, gasping for breath and extremely flustered. It was only then that he saw how our carriage was decorated. 'I cannot believe there are real people in there,' he said with a laugh. 'Do get out and let me see you!' The men with him were greatly amused. 'And what about your poems?' he added. 'You must let me hear them.'

'No,' I replied, 'we have to show them to Her Majesty first.'

At that moment it started to rain in earnest. 'I wonder why just this gate had to be built without a roof,' said Kiminobu. 'What a dreadful nuisance on a day like this! How am I ever going to get home? When I started running after your carriage, the only thought in my mind was not to miss you. It did not occur to me that I might be seen. Oh dear, I really must be getting back. How depressing!'

'Come, come!' I said. 'Why don't you go into the Palace with us?'

'In my lacquered cap?' he said. 'How can I do that?'

'Send for something more formal.'

But now it was really raining heavily, and our men, who had no head-covering, pulled in the carriage as quickly as they could.[256] An attendant brought Kiminobu an umbrella from his palace, and someone held it over him while he started to make his way home; he walked slowly this time, and there was a melancholy expression on his face as he looked back at us over his shoulder. I was pleased to see that in his hand he carried nothing but a spray of *u no hana*.

When we came into the Empress's presence, she asked us how things had turned out. The ladies who had been left behind were at first resentful and sullen; but, when we described how Kiminobu had run after us along the First Avenue, they all joined in laughing.

'Well now,' said Her Majesty, 'where are they – your poems?' We explained that we had not written any.

'Really?' she said. 'That is most unfortunate. The gentlemen at Court are sure to hear of your expedition. How are you going to explain that you haven't got a single interesting poem to show for it? You should have dashed off something on the spur of the moment while you were listening to the *hototogisu*. Because you wanted to make too much of it all, you let your inspiration vanish. I'm surprised at you! But you can still make up for it. Write something now. Surely that is not asking too much.'

Everything that Her Majesty said was true, and we were really distressed by our failure. I was discussing possible poems with the other women when a message arrived from Kiminobu. His poem was attached to some of the white blossom, and the paper itself was as white as the flower:

> If only I had known
> That you were off to hear the cuckoo's[257] song,
> I should have sent my heart to join you on your way.

Since the messenger was awaiting a reply, I asked someone to fetch an inkstone from our apartments, but the Empress ordered me to use hers. 'Quickly,' she said. 'Write something on this.' A piece of paper had been placed in the lid.

'Why don't you write the reply?' I said to Lady Saishō.

'No, I'd rather you did it,' she answered.

Meanwhile it had been getting dark, and now the rain started coming down again, accompanied by great claps of thunder, which so terrified us that we could think of nothing except closing the lattices. In our confusion we quite forgot about the messenger.

The thunder continued rumbling until nightfall. When it

eventually stopped, we set about writing our poem in earnest. But just at that moment a group of High Court Nobles and senior courtiers arrived to ask how the Empress had fared in the thunderstorm, and we had to go to the west entrance and talk with them.

Then at last we could concentrate on our poem. But now the other women withdrew, saying that only the person to whom the poem was addressed should be responsible. It was really a nuisance: poetry seemed to be having a bad *karma*[258] that day.

'We shall simply have to keep as quiet as we can about our outing,' I said with a laugh.

'I still see no reason,' said Her Majesty, 'why some of you who went to hear the *hototogisu* can't write a proper poem about it. I suppose it's because you have set your minds against it.' She looked rather cross; yet even this I found charming. 'Yes, Your Majesty,' I said, 'but by now the whole thing's become a bit pointless.'

'Is it all that pointless?' she said.

The matter of the poem was allowed to drop.

〜

A couple of days later when we were discussing our excursion, Lady Saishō mentioned the fern sprouts that Akinobu said he had picked with his own hands. Her Majesty overheard us. 'So that is the sort of thing you remember!' she said, laughing. She picked up a stray piece of paper and wrote, 'A longing for those fern sprouts lingers in her head.'

'Now then,' she said to me, 'you must provide the opening lines.'[259] I was delighted and wrote, 'More than the cuckoo's song she went to hear.'

'Well, Shōnagon,' said the Empress merrily, 'I wonder how you dare mention that bird at all.'

'How so, Your Majesty?' I replied, rather embarrassed. 'In any case,' I continued, 'I have decided to give up writing poetry for good and all. If each time there is a poem to be composed you call on me to do it, I don't see how I can remain in Your

Majesty's service. After all, I don't even know how to count the syllables correctly. How can I be expected to write winter poems in the spring and spring poems in the autumn and poems about chrysanthemums when the plum blossoms are in bloom? I realize that there have been many poets in my family,[260] and of course it's a great satisfaction if one of my verses turns out well and people say, "Of everything written on that day Shōnagon's was the best. But that's what one would expect considering who her father was." The trouble is that I have no particular talent and, if I push myself forward and turn out some doggerel as though I thought it were a masterpiece, I feel I am disgracing the memory of my ancestors.'

I was speaking quite seriously, but the Empress laughed and said, 'In that case you must do exactly as you wish. I shan't ask you to write any more poems.'

Late one evening, not long after this incident, His Excellency the Minister of the Centre, Korechika, who was making elaborate preparations for the Night of the Monkey,[261] gave out subjects on which the Empress's ladies-in-waiting were to write poems. They were all very excited and eagerly set themselves to the task. Meanwhile I stayed with the Empress and talked to her about various things. Presently Korechika caught sight of me. 'Why don't you join the others and write a poem?' he asked. 'Pick your subject.'

'Her Majesty has excused me from poetry,' I said, 'and I don't have to worry about such things any more.'

'How odd!' said Korechika. 'I can hardly believe she would allow that. Very well, you may do as you like at other times, but please write something tonight.'

But I did not pay the slightest attention. When the poems of the other women were being judged, the Empress handed me the following little note:

> Surely it is not you –
> You whom we know as Motosuke's heir –
> That will be missing from this evening's round of verse.

I laughed delightedly and, when Korechika asked me what had happened, I replied with this verse:

Were I not known to be the daughter of that man,
I should have been the very first
To pen a poem for this night of verse.

And I added to Her Majesty that, if my father were anyone else, I should have written a thousand poems for her without even waiting to be asked.

66. *It Was a Clear, Moonlit Night*

It was a clear, moonlit night a little after the tenth of the Eighth Month. Her Majesty, who was residing in the Empress's Office, sat by the edge of the veranda while Ukon no Naishi played the flute for her. The other ladies in attendance sat together, talking and laughing; but I stayed by myself, leaning against one of the pillars between the main hall and the veranda.

'Why so silent?' said Her Majesty. 'Say something. It is sad when you do not speak.'

'I am gazing into the autumn moon,' I replied.

'Ah yes,' she remarked. 'That is just what you should have said.'

67. *One Day When There Were Several People in the Empress's Presence*

One day when there were several people in the Empress's presence, including many senior courtiers and young noblemen, I was leaning against a pillar, chatting with some of the other women. Suddenly Her Majesty threw a note at me. 'Should I love you or should I not?' it said. 'What will you do if I cannot give you first place in my heart?'

No doubt she was thinking of a recent conversation when I

had remarked in her hearing, 'If I do not come first in people's affections, I had just as soon not be loved at all; in fact I would rather be hated or even maltreated. It is better to be dead than to be loved in the second or third place. Yes, I must be first.' Hearing this, someone had said, 'There we have the Single Vehicle of the Law!',[262] and everyone had burst out laughing.

Now the Empress gave me a brush and some paper. I wrote the following note and handed it to her: 'Among the Nine Ranks of lotus seats even the lowliest would satisfy me.'[263]

'Well, well,' said the Empress, 'you seem to have lost heart completely. That's bad. I prefer you to go on thinking as you did before.'

'My attitude depends on the person in question,' I replied.

'That's really bad,' she said, much to my delight. 'You should try to come first in the affections of even the most important people.'

68. His Excellency the Middle Counsellor, Takaie

His Excellency the Middle Counsellor, Takaie,[264] visited the Empress one day and presented her with a fan. 'I have found a most magnificent fan-frame,' he told her. 'I want to have it covered, but it can't be done with ordinary paper. I am looking for something very special.'

'What sort of a frame is it?' asked Her Majesty.

'It's absolutely splendid,' declared Takaie. 'People say they've never seen anything like it before, and they're quite right.'

'Well then,' I said, 'it's not a fan-frame at all. It must be the frame of a jelly-fish.'[265]

'Very amusing!' said Takaie. 'Let's take it that I meant to say that myself.'

This incident deserves to be included in my section on 'embarrassing things',[266] and perhaps I should not have recorded it at all. But I have been told to leave nothing out, and so I really had no choice.

69. Once during a Long Spell of Rainy Weather

Once during a long spell of rainy weather the Secretary of the Ministry of Ceremonial, Nobutsune,[267] arrived at the Empress's palace with a message from His Majesty. A cushion was brought out for him, but he pushed it away even farther than he normally did on these occasions and sat down on the floor.[268]

'Whom do you think that cushion is for?' I asked him.

'If I sat on the cushion after being out in this rain,' he replied with a laugh, 'it would get all nasty and stained with my footmarks.'

'How so?' I said. 'Are you under the impression that the cushion is to *couch* your feet *on*?'[269]

'There's nothing very clever about that remark,' said Nobutsune. 'If I hadn't mentioned my footmarks, you'd never have thought of your little joke.'

He then kept on pointing out that it was he, not I, who was responsible for the joke. At first I found this rather amusing, but after a while I could no longer bear to hear him praising himself so lavishly and, turning to the Empress, I told the following story: 'Many years ago there lived in the palace of the Great Empress[270] an attendant called Enutagi* who, despite her low rank, had made quite a reputation for herself. Fujiwara no Tokikara† (who died while serving as Governor of Mino) was at that time a Chamberlain. One day he called at the room where many of the lower attendants were gathered and said, "So this is the famous Enutagi! Why don't you look like your name?" "I do," she replied, "but it depends on the weather." Everyone, including the High Court Nobles and senior courtiers, found Enutagi amusing, because even when a trap was set for her in advance she always managed to acquit herself cleverly. And the stories about her must be true. They've been handed down for a long time without any change.'

'Yes,' said Nobutsune, 'but it was Tokikara who put the idea

* 'Dog's Vomit'.

† 'Depending on the Weather'.

into her head.[271] As for myself,' he continued, 'I can compose a good poem in either Chinese or Japanese on any subject you give me.'

'Really?' I replied. 'Very well, I'll give you a subject and you will kindly write me a poem in Japanese.'

'Splendid,' said Nobutsune. 'But why only one subject? I can just as well handle a whole lot.'

Hearing his boast, the Empress herself proposed a subject, at which Nobutsune promptly took his leave, saying, 'Dear me, how frightening! I'd better be off.'

'He has an appalling hand,' someone explained after he had left the room. 'Whether in Chinese characters or Japanese script, the results are equally poor. People are always laughing at him about it. That's why he had to escape.'

One day when Nobutsune was serving as Intendant in the Office of Palace Works[272] he sent a sketch to one of the craftsmen explaining how a certain piece of work should be done. 'Kindly execute it in this fashion,' he added in Chinese characters. I happened to notice the piece of paper and it was the most preposterous writing I had ever seen. Next to his message I wrote, 'If you do the work in this style, it will certainly turn out strangely.' The document found its way to the Imperial apartments, and everyone who saw it was greatly amused – except, of course, Nobutsune, who was furious and after this held a grudge against me.

70. *When the Lady of the Shigei Sha Entered the Crown Prince's Palace*

When the Lady of the Shigei Sha entered the Crown Prince's palace on the tenth of the First Month,[273] the ceremonies were carried out with great splendour. She wrote frequently to her sister, the Empress, but they did not actually meet.[274] Then on the tenth of the following month the Shigei Sha sent Her Majesty a message that she would come to see her.

In honour of this visit the Empress's apartments were decorated even more beautifully than usual, and everything was especially cleaned and polished. We ladies-in-waiting also prepared ourselves carefully.

The Shigei Sha arrived very late at night and was taken to the two-span apartment that had been prepared for her in the eastern wing of the Tōka Palace. As soon as it was dawn the lattices were raised, and presently her father, the Chancellor,[275] arrived in a carriage with his wife.

In the morning I attended the Empress while her hair was being dressed. A four-foot curtain of state had been placed across the main hall, facing the back of the room. Her Majesty was seated in the front part of the room, while a group of ladies-in-waiting was gathered behind the curtain of state. Hardly any furniture had been put out – only a straw mat with a cushion for Her Majesty and a round brazier.

While her hair was being done, the Empress asked me whether I knew the Shigei Sha. 'How could I possibly know her, Your Majesty?' I replied. 'The only time I came near her was during the memorial service at Shakuzen Temple,[276] and then I just glimpsed her from the back.'

'Very well then,' said the Empress, 'sit behind me and, if you look through the space between the curtain and that pillar, you'll be able to see her. Isn't she beautiful?' I was overjoyed to see the Shigei Sha and longed for the time when I would get a really good view of her.

Now the Empress's hair had been dressed, and she was ready to be robed. Over a three-layered scarlet dress of beaten silk she wore two plum-red robes, one of heavily embroidered material and the other more lightly worked. 'Tell me,' she said. 'Do you think the plum red really goes with dark scarlet? I know this isn't the season for plum red, but I can't stand colours like light green.'[277]

Unusual though the combination was, Her Majesty looked beautiful. The colour of her clothes went perfectly with her complexion and, as I gazed at her, I was impatient to have a proper look at the Shigei Sha to see whether she was equally pretty.

Presently Her Majesty crept out[278] from where she had been sitting. Some of the women noticed how I had installed myself by the curtains and was peering at the people in the other part of the room. 'What a way to behave!' they said, much to my amusement. 'Very suspicious.'

Since the hall was wide open, with no other curtains or screens, I had an extremely good view. Her Highness, the Chancellor's wife, wore a white robe over two dresses of scarlet silk, and a formal skirt with a long train. Lifting the folds of her skirt, she moved towards the back of the room. Since she was turned sideways, I could not see her properly.

The Shigei Sha, who had moved back a little, was now facing in my direction. She had on several plum-red under-robes of different shades, an unlined costume of deep red damask, a long, flowing robe of darkish red, and an over-robe of richly embroidered light green silk which made her look very young. She held her fan steadily in front of her face. Altogether she was magnificent.

His Excellency, the Chancellor, wore a light violet Court cloak, laced trousers of light green material, and a scarlet under-robe. He faced towards us, leaning against one of the pillars between the main part of the hall and the veranda and fastening the cord round the neckband of his cloak in a loose knot. At the sight of his beautiful daughters he smiled with delight and chatted away in his usual bantering fashion.

I glanced again at the Shigei Sha, who was looking extraordinarily pretty. But, when I turned back to Her Majesty and saw her tranquil expression, her charming features which had recently taken on a more adult cast,[279] and her complexion which went so beautifully with her scarlet clothes, I realized that no one in the world could equal her. . .

Now the attendants brought water for the Shigei Sha's ablutions. As I recall, there were altogether six attendants – two young maids and four servants of lower rank – and they came along the galleries through Senyō and Jōgan Palaces.[280] I noticed that only half a dozen ladies-in-waiting were seated under the Chinese roof at our end of the gallery. There was not enough room for all the Shigei Sha's ladies, and the others had gone back after escorting their mistress to Tōka Palace.

The young attendants were very pretty in their loose, cherry-coloured coats, under-skirts of light green and plum red, and long trains; I enjoyed watching them take the basin of water from the servants and place it next to the Shigei Sha. Also in attendance were Lady Shōshō, the daughter of Sukemasa (Director of the Bureau of Imperial Stables), and Lady Saishō, the daughter of the Gentleman of Kitano of the Third Rank; they were seated next to the Empress, and the embroidered silk of their Chinese jackets emerged charmingly from beneath the curtain of state. The Palace Girls who were helping the Shigei Sha with her ablutions wore divided skirts of green and shaded material, Chinese jackets, waistband ribbons, and shoulder sashes; their faces were heavily powdered. The servants passed them what was needed for the ablutions, and I was pleased to see how everything was done with proper ceremony in the Chinese style.

When the time came for the Empress's morning meal, the Palace hairdresser arrived to do the hair of the Lady Chamberlains and of the attendants who were to serve Her Majesty. The screen behind which I had been peeping was now pushed aside and I felt exactly like a demon who has been robbed of his straw coat.[281] I had not seen nearly enough and, rather annoyed by the interruption, I moved next to one of the pillars where I could go on watching the scene from between a bamboo blind and a curtain of state. However, my train and the skirts of my robe stuck out under the blind. His Excellency, the Chancellor, happened to notice this and said in a reproachful tone, 'Who can it be – she whom I dimly glimpse through a clearing in the mist?'[282]

'It must be Shōnagon,' replied the Empress. 'She is very curious to see what is going on.'

'Oh, how embarrassing!' said the Chancellor, with a smug look. 'I've known her for a long time and I hate her to see what ugly daughters I have.'

Then the attendants brought in the Shigei Sha's meal. 'Really,' said the Chancellor, 'I'm becoming jealous. Now Their Ladyships have been served. I do hope they'll finish their meals quickly so that I and my old woman can start on the scraps.'[283] He continued joking like this all day long.

Presently the Major Counsellor and the Middle Captain of the Third Rank[284] arrived with Matsugimi. The Chancellor, who had been waiting for them impatiently, picked up the little boy and put him on his knees in a most charming way. The veranda was too narrow for the men's formal Court costumes, and their under-robes trailed all over the floor.

The Major Counsellor looked extremely handsome, and the Middle Captain was impressive for his age. As I observed the two young men, it occurred to me that, while the Chancellor could be expected to have such splendid sons, their mother's good fortune must be the result of some special *karma*.[285] The Chancellor told them to sit down on the straw cushions that were spread on the veranda; but they hastily took their leave, explaining that they had to report for duty.

Shortly afterwards a secretary (I do not know his name) came from the Ministry of Ceremonial with a message from the Emperor for his wife. The attendants placed a cushion for him in the room at the north of the buttery and he sat down, while the Empress hastened to write her reply.

Before there was even time to remove the cushion, Chikayori, the Minor Captain of the Inner Palace Guards, arrived bearing a letter from the Crown Prince to the Shigei Sha. Since there was no room for Chikayori on the veranda of the gallery, his cushion was placed at the east of the main veranda. He handed over the letter, which, after the Shigei Sha had examined it, was read in turn by the Chancellor and his wife and also by the Empress. 'You had better make haste with your reply,' the Chancellor told the Shigei Sha; but she did not seem to be in any hurry. 'Why aren't you writing?' said the Chancellor. 'I suppose it's because I am watching you. Otherwise you'd have answered at once without any prompting from me.' I was delighted to see the girl blushing slightly as she smiled at her father's words. Now her mother also told her to hurry up and produce an answer. She accordingly sat down, facing the back of the room, and started to write with the help of her mother, who came and sat next to her. I noticed that the Shigei Sha was looking more and more embarrassed.

As a gift for the messenger the Empress produced a formal, wide-sleeved robe of light green material together with a trouser-skirt. These were pushed out from beneath her blind, and the Middle Captain of the Third Rank gave them to the man. It was clear from his attitude as he took the clothes and left that he was not too pleased with his reward.

Meanwhile Matsugimi babbled away; everyone was delighted and made a great fuss over him. 'I don't suppose there would be any harm in passing him off as the Empress's child,' said the Chancellor. Of course he was joking, but his words made me worry about why Her Majesty had not yet done what His Excellency had in mind.[286]

At about the Hour of the Sheep the Emperor appeared with a great rustling of silk robes. So sudden was his arrival that there was not even time to announce that the mats leading to the entrance had been laid out for him. The Empress joined her husband and they both promptly retired to the curtain-dais, while the ladies-in-waiting went and sat in the front of the anteroom. I noticed that the gallery was full of senior courtiers. The Chancellor summoned servants from the office of the Empress's Household and made them bring fruit and other dishes to be eaten with wine. 'Now let everyone get drunk,' he said. And everyone did get drunk.[287] The gentlemen began to exchange remarks with the ladies-in-waiting and they all found each other extremely amusing.

At sunset His Majesty got up and called for the Major Counsellor, Yamanoi. Then, having ordered his gentlemen to help him on with his Court robes, he left for his Palace.[288] He was resplendent in his cherry-blossom Court cloak and his crimson robe which reflected the light of the evening glow – but His Majesty is such an awe-inspiring figure that I cannot continue writing about him like this.

Yamanoi was not on very close terms with his brothers. He looked magnificent, handsomer even than Korechika; but unfortunately people were always running him down.

As he set out for his Palace, the Emperor was escorted by His Excellency the Chancellor, the Major Counsellor Yamanoi, the Middle Captain of the Third Rank, and the Director of the Imperial Storehouse.[289] Later, Lady Uma no Naishi arrived with a message from His Majesty asking the Empress to come to him. She did not want to go, however, and replied that it was impossible for her that evening. 'That will never do,' said the Chancellor when he heard this. 'You must go to him at once.'

There was also a constant stream of messengers from the Crown Prince. Ladies-in-waiting who had come from the Emperor's Palace and from the Crown Prince's residence were bustling about, urging Her Majesty and the Shigei Sha to make haste and join their husbands.

'Very well,' said the Empress, 'but first you must escort my sister.'

'How can I possibly go ahead of you?' asked the Shigei Sha.

'Whatever you may say,' insisted the Empress, 'it is *I* who will see *you* off.' I found their conversation both amusing and delightful. Eventually the two sisters agreed that the one who had farther to go should leave first, and so the Shigei Sha went before the Empress. After she had gone, the Chancellor and the other gentlemen departed; then finally Her Majesty set off for the Emperor's Palace. The people who accompanied the Chancellor were laughing so heartily at his jokes that they almost fell off the bridge.[290]

71. *On the Last Day of the Second Month*

On the last day of the Second Month, when there was a strong wind, a dark grey sky, and a little snow, a man from the Office of Grounds came to the Black Door and asked to speak to me. He then approached and gave me a note which he said was from Kintō, the Imperial Adviser.[291] It consisted of a sheet of pocket-paper on which was written,

> And for a moment in my heart
> I feel that spring has come.

The words were most appropriate for the weather; but what concerned me was that I was bound to produce the opening lines. I asked the messenger which gentlemen were present, and he gave me their names. They were all the type of men to put me on my mettle; but it was Kintō's presence among them that made me most reluctant to give a commonplace answer. I felt very alone and wished that I could show the note to Her Majesty and discuss my predicament; but I knew that she was lying down with the Emperor.

The man from the Office of Grounds urged me to hurry; and I realized that if, in addition to bungling my reply, I was slow about it, I should really disgrace myself. 'It can't be helped,' I thought and, trembling with emotion, wrote the following lines:

> As though pretending to be blooms
> The snow flakes scatter in the wintry sky.[292]

I handed my poem to the messenger and anxiously wondered how Kintō and the others would receive it. If their verdict was unfavourable I would rather not hear it, I thought as I eagerly awaited the news.

It turned out that the Captain of the Middle Palace Guards (who at that time held the rank of Middle Captain in the Inner Palace Guards) was present when my answer arrived, and he told

135

me that Toshikata, the Imperial Adviser,[293] gave the following judgement: 'After this she deserves to be appointed to the Palace Attendants' Office.'

72. *Masahiro Really Is a Laughing-Stock*

Masahiro really is a laughing-stock. I wonder what it is like for his parents and friends. If people see him with a decent-looking servant, they always call for the fellow and laughingly ask how he can wait upon such a master and what he thinks of him. There are skilled dyers and weavers in Masahiro's household, and when it comes to dress, whether it be the colour of his under-robe or the style of his cloak, he is more elegant than most men; yet the only effect of his elegance is to make people say, 'What a shame someone else isn't wearing these things!'

And how strangely he expresses himself! Once, when he was due to report for night duty at the Palace, he ordered that the clothes and other things he would need should be brought from his house. 'Send *two* servants,' he said. One man came and said that he could easily carry everything. 'You're an odd fellow,' said Masahiro. 'How can one man bring the things of two people? After all, can you put two measures in a one-measure jar?'[294] No one had the slightest idea what he meant; but there was loud laughter.

On another occasion a messenger brought Masahiro a letter from someone, asking for an immediate reply. 'You hateful fellow!' said Masahiro. 'Has someone been putting peas on the stove?[295] And who's stolen the ink and brush I had in this residence? Very odd! I could understand people taking rice or wine. . .' And again everyone laughed.

When the Empress Dowager was ill, Masahiro was sent from the Palace to inquire after her. When he came back, people asked which of her gentlemen-in-waiting had been present. He named a few people, four or five in all. 'Was no one else there?' 'Well, there were some others,' replied Masahiro, 'but they had all left.'

It is amazing that we could still laugh at him – so accustomed were we to hearing his foolishness.

One day when I was alone he came up to me and said, 'My dear lady, I have something I must tell you at once – something that I've just heard.' 'And what may that be?' I asked. He approached my curtain. 'I heard someone who instead of saying, "Bring your body closer," used the phrase, "Bring up your five parts."'[296] And again I burst into laughter.

On the middle night during the period of official appointments Masahiro was responsible for filling the lamps with oil. He rested his foot on the cloth under the pedestal of one of the lamps and, since the cloth happened to have been freshly oiled, his foot stuck to it. As soon as he started to walk off, the lamp fell over and, as he hurried along with the cloth stuck to his foot, the lamp dragged after him, making a terrible clatter.

One day when he thought he was alone in the Table Room, neither of the First Secretaries having reported for duty, Masahiro took a dish of beans that was lying there and went behind the Little Screen.[297] Suddenly someone pulled aside the screen – and there was Masahiro, stealthily munching away at the beans. Everyone who saw him was convulsed with laughter.

73. *On the Last Day of the Fourth Month*

On the last day of the Fourth Month we made a pilgrimage to Hase Temple by way of Yodo Ferry.[298] Our carriage was put on the ferry, and as we crossed the river I observed the iris, water-oats, and other plants that grew out of the water. They looked quite short; but, when we told our attendants to pluck some of them, I discovered that they had extremely long stems. I enjoyed watching the passing boats laden with water-oats,[299] and it occurred to me that this was the sort of scene described in the song of Takase Pool.[300]

When we returned on the third of the following month, it was raining heavily. We saw men and children setting out to pick irises;[301] they wore tiny sedge hats and their clothes were tucked up high on their legs. It was just like a screen painting.

74. *Things That Lose by Being Painted*

Pinks, cherry blossoms, yellow roses. Men or women who are praised in romances as being beautiful.

75. *Things That Gain by Being Painted*

Pines. Autumn fields. Mountain villages and paths. Cranes and deer. A very cold winter scene; an unspeakably hot summer scene.

76. *During the Long Rains in the Fifth Month*

During the long rains in the Fifth Month, there is something very moving about a place with a pond. Between the dense irises, water-oats, and other plants one can see the green of the water; and the entire garden seems to be the same green colour. One stays there all day long, gazing in contemplation at the clouded sky – oh, how moving it is!

I am always moved and delighted by places that have ponds – not only in the winter (when I love waking up to find that the water has frozen over) but at every time of the year. The ponds I like best are not those in which everything is carefully laid out; I much prefer one that has been left to itself so that it is wild and covered with weeds. At night in the green spaces of water one can see nothing but the pale glow of the moonlight. At any time and in any place I find moonlight very moving.

77. *In the First Month When I Go to a Temple*

In the First Month when I go to a temple for a retreat I like the weather to be extremely cold; there should be snow on the ground, and everything should be frozen. If it looks like rain, however, I feel most dissatisfied.

Once I went on a pilgrimage to Hase Temple. While our rooms were being prepared, our carriage was pulled up to the foot of the log steps that lead to the temple. Young priests, wearing only their sashes and under-robes, and with those things called high clogs on their feet,[302] were hurrying up and down the steps without the slightest precaution, reciting verses from the Sacred Storehouse[303] or such scraps from the sutras as came into their heads. It was very appropriate to the place, and I found it charming. Later, when we started to climb the steps, we were terrified and kept close to the side, clinging to the banisters. I was amused to see that the priests walked as freely as on an ordinary wooden floor.

Presently a priest told us that our rooms were ready and asked us to go to them directly; he brought us some overshoes and helped us out of our carriage. Among the pilgrims who had already arrived I saw some who were wearing their clothes inside out,[304] while others were dressed in formal style with trains on their skirts and Chinese jackets. The sight of so many people shuffling along the corridors in lacquered leather shoes and short clogs was delightful and reminded me of the Palace.

Several acolytes and some young men who had the run of the temple grounds and buildings followed us, saying, 'There's a drop now,' 'Here the corridor goes up,' and so on. Close behind us came another group (I have no idea who they were), and they tried to push their way ahead of us. 'Wait a moment,' our guides said. 'These are ladies of quality. You people must keep your distance.' Some bowed and fell back; but others paid no attention at all and hurried ahead, each determined to be the first before the Buddha.

On the way to our rooms we had to pass in front of rows of strangers. I found this very unpleasant; but, when I reached the chapel and got a view past the dog-barrier[305] and right up to the sanctuary, I was overcome with awe and wondered how I could have stayed away for so many months. My old feelings were aroused and they overwhelmed all else.

The lamps that lit the sacred image in the sanctuary were not permanent ones, but had been brought by pilgrims as offerings. They burnt with terrifying brightness, and in their light the Buddha glittered brilliantly. Priest after priest reverently entered the sanctuary, and, kneeling on the platform of worship,[306] held up his petition in both hands and read it aloud. So many people were bustling about that it was hard to make out what any particular priest was saying; but occasionally I could distinguish a strained voice pronouncing some phrase like 'One thousand platforms[307] on behalf of Lord So-and-so'.

I was kneeling down to pray, with the sash of my skirt hanging loosely over my shoulders,[308] when a priest came up to me and said, 'I have brought you this.' He was carrying a bough of anise, and I was delighted by the gesture.

Presently another priest came from the dog-barrier. He told us that he had satisfactorily recited all our petitions and asked how long we expected to remain in retreat; he also gave us the names of some other people who were staying in the temple. When he had gone, the attendants brought us a brazier and some fruit. Our washing-water was poured into a bucket, and I noticed that we had been given a basin without handles. A priest called for our servants and explained where they would be lodged; then, one at a time, the servants went off to their cells.

Now the bell rang for the recitation of the sutras. It was very comforting to think that it rang for me. In the cell next to ours a solitary gentleman was prostrating himself in prayer. At first I thought that he might be doing it because he knew we were listening; but soon I realized that he was absorbed in his devotions, which he continued hour after hour. I was greatly moved. When he rested from his prayers, he started reading the sutras in a voice that was no less impressive for being somewhat inaudible. I was wishing that he would read more loudly so that I might hear every word; but instead he stopped and blew his nose – not in a noisy, unpleasant way but gently and discreetly. I wondered what he could be praying for so fervently and hoped that his wish might be granted.[309]

Usually when we stayed in temples the days passed rather quietly. The male attendants and boys who accompanied us would spend a good deal of time visiting the priests in their cells, and we were left with very little to do. Then the stillness of the day would be broken by the loud noise of the conch-shell.[310] Or a messenger would arrive with an elegantly folded letter and offerings to pay for a recitation of the sutras; laying everything down, he would call for the acolytes in a voice so powerful that it echoed among the hills. Sometimes the booming of the temple bell became louder and louder until I was overcome with curiosity about who had asked for the readings. Then someone would mention the name of a great family, adding, 'It is a service of instruction and guidance[311] for Her Ladyship's safe delivery.' An anxious period indeed, I thought, and would begin praying for the lady's well-being.

All this happened at an ordinary time, when life in the temple was fairly peaceful. In the First Month things are in an uproar. People are constantly arriving with their requests, and as I watch them I sometimes forget all about my own devotions.

One day at sunset a large party came to the temple, evidently intending to stay for a retreat. The acolytes bustled about efficiently, installing tall screens (which looked so heavy that I should not have thought they could possibly carry them) and flopping straw mats noisily on the floor. The visitors were taken directly to their quarters, and soon I heard a loud rustling sound as a blind was hung over the dog-barrier to separate their rooms from the sanctuary. All the arrangements were carried out in a most effortless fashion: the acolytes were used to their job.

Presently I heard another rustling sound – this time of silk. It came from a large group of elderly ladies, discreet in manner and distinguished in appearance, who were apparently leaving their quarters and returning home. 'Be careful about fire,' I heard one of them say. 'These rooms are very dangerous.' Among their party was a boy of about seven who called for the attendants and spoke to them in a proud, charming voice[312] that I found very attractive. There was also an adorable child, about two years old, who was coughing drowsily. I wished that the mother or someone else would address its nurse by name so that I might find out who these people were.

The service continued all night, and it was so noisy that I could not get to sleep. After the matins[313] I finally dozed off, only to be woken by a reading of the sutra consecrated to the temple Buddha. The priests were reciting loudly and raucously, without making any effort to sound solemn. From their tone I gathered that they were travelling monks and, as I listened to their voices, which had awakened me so abruptly, I found myself being strangely moved.

I also remember a pleasant-looking young gentleman, evidently from a good family, who did not stay in his cell at night and performed all his devotions during the daytime. He was attractively dressed in wide, bluish-grey trousers and many layers of white robes. Several pages had accompanied him on his pilgrimage, and I enjoyed watching how respectfully they attended him. They had provided their master with a special screen, behind which he occasionally prostrated himself in prayer.

When staying at temples, I enjoy wondering who the strangers are; and it is also pleasant to recognize people one knows.

The young men who visited the temple were apt to wander near the women's quarters and spend more time looking in that direction than at the Buddha. Sometimes they would call for one of the sextons and, after a whispered consultation, set off for some other part of the temple. I saw nothing wrong in their behaviour.

At the end of the Second and beginning of the Third Months, when the cherry blossoms were in bloom, I made another pleasant retreat to the temple. Two or three good-looking gentlemen, apparently travelling incognito, arrived while I was there. They were elegantly dressed in cherry-blossom and willow robes, and they looked very distinguished with the ends of their laced trousers neatly tucked up and fastened. They were accompanied by a very proper-looking attendant, who held an attractively decorated bag of provisions. Their page-boys, who carried flowering branches of cherry blossom, wore hunting costumes of plum red and bright green, with varicoloured under-robes and skirts printed with scattered patches of colour. Also in their party was a slender retainer, who looked extremely attractive as he beat the gong at the entrance to the temple. I recognized one of the gentlemen. Of course he had no way of knowing that I was at the temple, and he did not notice me as he passed near where I stood. Though I had no particular desire to meet him, this rather saddened me. 'If only I could let him know!' I thought, and found my feelings somewhat strange.

Whenever I go to stay in a temple, or indeed in any new place, it seems pointless to be accompanied only by servants. One needs a few companions of one's own class with whom one can chat congenially. There may be some suitable women even among one's maids; the trouble is that one knows all too well what they are going to say. Gentlemen appear to have the same idea; for I notice that whenever they go on a pilgrimage they take along a few agreeable companions.

78. *Things That Give a Hot Feeling*

The hunting costume of the head of a Guards escort.
A patchwork surplice.
The Captain in attendance at the Imperial Games.[314]
An extremely fat person with a lot of hair.
A zither bag.
A Holy Teacher performing a rite of incantation at noon in the Sixth or Seventh Month. Or at the same time of the year a copper-smith working in his foundry.

79. Shameful Things

A thief has crept into a house and is now hiding in some well-chosen nook where he can secretly observe what is going on. Someone else comes into the dark room and, taking an object that lies there, slips it into his sleeve. It must be amusing for the thief to see a person who shares his own nature.[315]

Priests on night duty are often confronted with shameful things, especially if they are light sleepers.[316] For they are liable to overhear groups of young women joking about other people, abusing them, and venting their spite on them; all this is bound to arouse a sense of shame in the priest who lies next door, hearing everything they say. Some of the Emperor's elderly ladies-in-waiting angrily tell the girls not to be so noisy; but they pay no attention and continue gossiping until finally they doze off without the slightest regard for decorum. Even after they are asleep, the priest still feels it is shameful.

A man's heart is a shameful thing. When he is with a woman whom he finds tiresome and distasteful, he does not show that he dislikes her, but makes her believe she can count on him. Still worse, a man who has the reputation of being kind and loving treats a woman in such a way that she cannot imagine his feelings are anything but sincere. Yet he is untrue to her not only in his thoughts but in his words; for he speaks badly about her to other women just as he speaks badly about those women to her. The woman, of course, has no idea that she is being maligned; and, hearing his criticisms of the others, she fondly believes he loves her best. The man for his part is well aware that this is what she thinks. How shameful!

When a woman runs into a lover with whom (alas!) she has broken for good, there is no reason for her to be ashamed if he regards her as heartless. But if the lover shows that he has not been even slightly upset by their parting, which to her was so sad and painful and difficult, she is bound to be amazed by the man and to wonder what sort of a heart he can have. Oblivious of his own callous attitude, her abandoned lover carried on a glib conversation in which he criticizes the behaviour of other men.

How shameful when a man seduces some helpless Court lady and, having made her pregnant, abandons her without caring in the slightest about her future!

80. *Things That Have Lost Their Power*

A large boat which is high and dry in a creek at ebb-tide.

A woman who has taken off her false locks to comb the short hair that remains.

A large tree that has been blown down in a gale and lies on its side with its roots in the air.

The retreating figure of a *sumō* wrestler who has been defeated in a match.[317]

A man of no importance reprimanding an attendant.

An old man who removes his hat, uncovering his scanty top-knot.

A woman, who is angry with her husband about some trifling matter, leaves home and goes somewhere to hide. She is certain that he will rush about looking for her; but he does nothing of the kind and shows the most infuriating indifference. Since she cannot stay away for ever, she swallows her pride and returns.

81. *Awkward Things*

One has gone to a house and asked to see someone; but the wrong person appears, thinking that it is he who is wanted; this is especially awkward if one has brought a present.

One has allowed oneself to speak badly about someone without really intending to do so; a young child who has overheard it all goes and repeats what one has said in front of the person in question.

Someone sobs out a pathetic story. One is deeply moved; but it so happens that not a single tear comes to one's eyes – most awkward. Though one makes one's face look as if one is going to cry, it is no use: not a single tear will come. Yet there are times when, having heard something happy, one feels the tears streaming out.

82. When the Emperor Returned from His Visit to Yawata

When the Emperor returned from his visit to Yawata, he halted his palanquin before reaching the Empress Dowager's gallery and sent a messenger to pay his respects.[318] What could be more magnificent than to see so august a personage as His Majesty seated there in all his glory and honouring his mother in this way? At the sight tears came to my eyes and streamed down my face, ruining my make-up. How ugly I must have looked.

It was also very impressive to see the Imperial Adviser, Captain Tadanobu, who had been chosen as Imperial messenger. He proceeded to the gallery on horseback, accompanied by four escorts on foot, all magnificently attired, and by some mounted escorts who were elegantly slender. Spurring his horse, he trotted along the wide, clear expanse of the Second Avenue.[319] Then, dismounting at a short distance from the gallery, he waited by the bamboo blinds at the side, where the Master of the Empress Dowager's Household came for the message. Having received the reply, Tadanobu remounted and, once more spurring his horse, returned to the Emperor. What a magnificent sight when he stood by the Imperial palanquin making his report! I imagined the Empress Dowager's feelings as she watched her son, passing with his retinue. My heart leapt with joy, and tears came to my eyes – much to the amusement of the people who were watching me. Even common people are delighted if things go well for their children; when one imagines what the Empress Dowager must have felt, it is really awe-inspiring.

83. *One Day We Heard That His Excellency*

One day we heard that His Excellency, the Chancellor, was
going to appear at the Black Door and we all gathered in the
corridor to watch him. Presently he emerged and, making his
way through our group, remarked, 'Oh, what an impressive
collection of ladies! It must make you laugh to see the foolish
old man.'[320]

The women next to the door raised the bamboo blinds, and
one could see the varied colours of their many-layered robes at
the openings of their sleeves. Korechika, the Provisional Major
Counsellor, helped his father on with his shoes. The Major
Counsellor was a handsome, impressive figure as he stood in
the narrow corridor, beautifully dressed with his long train pro-
truding from beneath his under-robe. 'Imagine having one's
shoes[321] picked up by a Major Counsellor!' I thought. 'The
Chancellor is indeed the grandest of them all.'

Seated in a row were Yamanoi, the Major Counsellor, his
younger brothers, and some other gentlemen; their robes made
a sea of black all the way from the wall of Fujitsubo Palace to the
front of Tōka Palace. The Chancellor, looking extremely slender
and elegant, stopped for a moment to adjust his sword. Meanwhile His Excellency the Senior Steward, Fujiwara no Michinaga, was standing in front of Seiryō Palace. It occurred to me
that he would probably not make obeisance to his own brother;
but I was mistaken, for when the Chancellor advanced a few steps
Michinaga knelt down in a most respectful attitude. It was a
splendid moment, and I wondered what merit the Chancellor
could have accumulated to deserve such glory in this life.

Lady Chūnagon, having announced that it was a day of
abstinence, recited her prayers in an exemplary fashion. 'Let us
have your rosary for a moment,' said one of the ladies, adding,
'Do you suppose those prayers of yours are going to put you in
the same class as His Excellency?' She and the others then
gathered round Lady Chūnagon, laughing loudly; but their

jokes did nothing to detract from the Chancellor's splendour. When we mentioned this to the Empress, she smiled and said, 'To become a Buddha is better still.'[322] Once again I was overcome with admiration for my mistress.

I frequently told Her Majesty about the way in which Michinaga had made obeisance. 'So he's still your favourite!' she said with a smile. If the Empress had lived to see how brilliantly Michinaga advanced in later years,[323] she would have understood still better why I was so impressed by the scene.

84. *I Remember a Clear Morning*

I remember a clear morning in the Ninth Month when it had been raining all night. Despite the bright sun, dew was still dripping from the chrysanthemums in the garden. On the bamboo fences and criss-cross hedges I saw tatters of spider webs; and where the threads were broken the raindrops hung on them like strings of white pearls. I was greatly moved and delighted.

As it became sunnier, the dew gradually vanished from the clover and the other plants where it had lain so heavily; the branches began to stir, then suddenly sprang up of their own accord. Later I described to people how beautiful it all was. What most impressed me was that they were not at all impressed.

85. *On the Sixth of the Month*

On the sixth of the month people come in throngs carrying young herbs for the festival on the following day.[324] One year, when some children were spreading out the herbs, I asked them to tell me the name of a particular plant that I had never seen before. It took them a long time to answer. 'Come on,' I said. 'What is it called?' The children looked at each other and one of them replied, 'It's called *miminagusa*.'*[325] 'That stands to reason,' I said with a laugh. 'It certainly doesn't look as if it could hear anything.' The children had also brought some pretty chrysanthemums, and the following poem occurred to me:

> Pluck them or pinch them as you may,
> Indifferent they remain,
> These earless plants who hear not what I say.
> Yet, since there are so many blossoms here,
> Surely some chrysanthemums must hear.[326]

I should have liked to recite the lines to them, but, being children, they would not have understood.

86. *One Day a Man from the Office of Grounds*

One day a man from the Office of Grounds brought me a packet wrapped in white paper and decorated with a magnificent branch of plum blossom. He said that it was from Yukinari, the Controller First Secretary. I eagerly examined the parcel; it looked as if it contained a painting, but instead I found a couple of the objects known as square cakes[327] packed next to each other. I also found a twisted letter written in the style of a Submission[328]:

A Presentation:
One packet of Square Cakes,
The aforesaid packet being herewith respectfully presented
    in accordance with established precedent
To Madam Shōnagon.

Below this came the date and the signature, Mimana no Nariyuki,[329] and at the end: 'Your humble servant would have liked to present this in person but, fearing lest he be too ill-favoured to show himself by daylight, he has forborne from coming.'[330]

* 'Earless plant'.

It was most elegantly written, and I showed it to Her Majesty. 'What a beautiful hand!'[331] she said, taking the letter. 'And what an amusing idea!'

'But how shall I reply?' I asked. 'Should I reward the messenger? If only someone could tell me!'

'I hear Korenaka's voice,' said Her Majesty. 'Call him and ask what to do.' I went out to the veranda and ordered a servant to tell the Major Controller of the Left that I had something to say to him. Presently he appeared, having arranged his clothing very carefully. 'I have not called you on behalf of Her Majesty,' I said, 'but for a personal matter. If a servant brings this sort of parcel to someone like Lady Ben[332] or me, should he be given a reward?'

'No,' replied Korenaka, 'one should simply eat the cakes. But why do you ask, Madam? Has some member of the Great Council sent you this?'

'How could you suppose such a thing?' I said.

Then, by way of reply to Yukinari, I took a piece of thin, bright red paper and simply wrote, 'The servant who would not present the cold cakes in person strikes me as being very cold himself.'[333] I attached my note to a magnificent branch of red plum blossom and dispatched it.

Almost immediately Yukinari arrived and sent in the message, 'Your servant humbly presents himself.' When I went out to meet him, he said, 'I was sure that when you received my parcel you would send me a poem. What a splendid answer you produced instead! Women who are pleased with themselves never miss an opportunity to scatter their poems in all directions. I am delighted to be on friendly terms with someone who is different. I should get little pleasure from a woman who was always turning out poems. In fact I should consider that she was being inconsiderate.'

Later I heard that Yukinari had told the story to the Chancellor in the presence of a large group of courtiers. 'People like Norimitsu and Nariyasu[334] are delighted with her note,' Yukinari had said. Hearing this, the Chancellor had strongly commended my reply. . . . But it is most unattractive to blow my own trumpet like this.

87. *One Night the Empress's Ladies-in-Waiting*

One night the Empress's ladies-in-waiting were engaged in a heated discussion. 'When they are making batons for the new Chamberlains of the Sixth Rank,' said one of them, 'why do they use wood from the planks at the south-east corner of the Empress's Office?[335] Surely they could just as well take it from the east or west sides of the building. Or, for that matter, why not use wood from the south-east corner to make batons for Chamberlains of the Fifth Rank?'

'I see nothing very interesting in that,' said another of the ladies. 'It is the names given to different types of clothing that I find strange. They often seem to have been chosen at random. I can see why the name "thin and long" should have been given to long robes.[336] But why "sweat garment" for women's loose coats? Surely they should be called "long train" like the robes worn by boys. And why "Chinese robe"? The proper name would be "short robe". I suppose they call it that because it's worn by the Chinese. "Over-robe", "over-trousers", and "under-robe" all make sense. And so does "big mouth" since the opening of the trousers is greater than the length. But the name *hakama* for trouser-skirt is pointless. And why "insertions" for laced trousers? They should be known as "leg clothes", "leg bags", or something of the sort.'[337]

'Well, well,' I said, 'what a noise you're making! I myself have nothing to add on the subject and I wish you'd all go to sleep.' As if in reply to my words came the peevish voice of the priest on night duty: 'That would be a great shame,' he said, much to our surprise and amusement. 'Do please continue talking all night.'

88. *On the Tenth Day of Each Month*[338]

On the tenth day of each month the Empress ordered that Dedications of Sutras and of Images be made on behalf of the late Chancellor. In the Ninth Month the service was held in the Empress's Office with many Court Nobles and senior courtiers in attendance. Seihan was the preacher, and his sermon was so sad that everyone wept, including the young people, who as a rule are not very sensitive to the pathos of things.[339]

When it was finished, the gentlemen drank wine and recited Chinese poems. Captain Tadanobu quoted the lines,

Where is he now
When moon and autumn have returned at the appointed time?[340]

It was splendid, and I wondered how he could have thought of such an appropriate passage. I made my way through the crowd of ladies to where the Empress was standing, and found that she was on the point of leaving. 'Wasn't he magnificent?' she said. 'Those lines were just right for the occasion.' 'Yes, Your Majesty,' I said. 'I wanted to tell you about it, so I had a quick glance at the ceremony and then came to look for you. The more I think about his quotation, the more impressed I am.'

'Indeed,' said Her Majesty, 'I can see why you would be more impressed than anyone.'[341]

One day Tadanobu sent someone especially to ask for me, but I did not go. Later when we met by accident he said, 'Why do you refuse to be on close terms with me? It is very strange, for I know you do not dislike me. Surely a friendship that has lasted all this time cannot end so coldly. At present I can visit you here whenever I want, but the time may come when that will be impossible and then what will there be to show for our relationship?'

'Indeed,' I replied, 'it would not be difficult for us to come together. But, if we did, I could no longer go on praising you, and that would be a great shame. As things are, when I am in

Her Majesty's presence with all the other ladies gathered about, I am forever singing your praises as though it were my function in life. But, if we did as you want, how could that continue? Then it would go against my conscience to say anything nice about you. So please just think of me fondly and don't take things any further.'

'How so?' he said, laughing. 'There are many people on intimate terms who praise each other far more than mere acquaintances ever do.'

'If I did not find that sort of thing so distasteful,' I replied, 'I should certainly accept your proposal. But I can't stand men or women who praise their lovers and who get angry if someone says the slightest thing against them.'

'That doesn't make you sound very dependable,' said Tadanobu, which amused me greatly.[342]

89. *One Evening Yukinari, the Controller First Secretary*

One evening Yukinari, the Controller First Secretary, came to the Empress's Office and stayed there talking until late at night.

'Tomorrow is a day of Imperial Abstinence,' he said as he left, 'and I have to remain in the Palace. I must certainly go home before the Hour of the Ox.'[343]

On the following morning a messenger brought me several sheets of Kōya paper of the type the Chamberlains use in the Emperor's Private Office. 'Today,' I read, 'my heart is full of memories of our meeting. I had hoped that I might stay until the morning telling you of bygone tales, but the cock's crow forced me to take my leave. . . '[344] It was a long letter, very elegantly written and contrived to give an impression that was quite contrary to the truth.[345] I was much impressed and replied, 'Can the cock's crow that we heard so late at night be that which saved the Lord of Meng-ch'ang?'[346] Yukinari answered, 'It is said that the cock's crow opened the barrier of Han Ku and allowed the

Lord of Meng-ch'ang to escape in the nick of time with his three thousand followers.[347] But we are concerned with a far less distant barrier – the Barrier of Ōsaka.'* I then sent him this poem:

> There may be some who are deceived
> By the cock's crow that falsely breaks
> The stillness of the night.
> But such a fraud will not beguile
> The Barrier of Ōsaka,
> Where lovers have their trysts.

And as a postscript: 'I am told that the gate-keeper is a very shrewd man.'

Yukinari promptly replied:

> I have heard it said
> That Ōsaka's Barrier can be freely crossed.
> No need here for the cock to crow:
> This gate is ever opened wide,
> And waits each wanderer who comes.[348]

Bishop Ryūen was much impressed by this exchange. Bowing deeply, he took the first of the letters and brought it to the Empress; later he showed her all the others also.

When I met Yukinari a little later, he laughed and said, 'I am sorry that my poem was too much for you and that in the end you never answered. By the way, all the senior courtiers have seen your letters.'

'Well then,' I replied, 'you must have a very high opinion of me. If one has been impressed by a letter one finds it a shame not to let other people see it. Since *your* letters, on the other hand, were rather poor, I hid them carefully and didn't let anyone get a glimpse. So our intentions were equally good.'

Yukinari laughed. 'You really have an unusual way of thinking things out before you speak,' he said. 'Most women would have answered with something like, "I did not like your letters. They are too shallow."'

* 'Slope of Meetings'.

'Far from resenting that comment,' I said, 'I am most grateful for it.'

'Well,' said Yukinari, 'it's a good thing you've hidden my letters. It would have been very sad and painful for me if you had shown them to anyone. Please go on hiding them in future.'

Not long afterwards I met Captain Tsunafusa. 'Did you know that Yukinari has been singing your praises?' he said. 'He told me about the conversation after your exchange of letters the other day. It is a great pleasure to hear people praising a woman one loves.'

I was delighted by his sincere manner and said, 'So now I have two things to make me happy: first being praised by Yukinari and secondly being included among those you love.'

'That's strange,' Tsunafusa said. 'You speak as though it were something new.'

90. On a Dark, Moonless Night in the Fifth Month

On a dark, moonless night in the Fifth Month we heard several voices saying, 'Are any of the ladies-in-waiting here?'

'What an odd way to speak!' said the Empress. 'Go and see who it is.'

I went on to the veranda and asked, 'Who is there with that loud, ringing voice?'

By way of reply, someone raised the blind and gently thrust in an object, which turned out to be a branch of narrow-leaved bamboo.

'Oh,' I said, 'so it's this gentleman!' [349]

'Come,' said one of the people who had brought the branch, 'let's go and report this to the Palace.' And off they went – the Middle Captain, the new Middle Captain, [350] the Sixth Rank Chamberlain, and the others in the group. Yukinari, the Controller First Secretary, stayed behind. 'How oddly they behave!' he said, looking at them as they left. 'We were picking bamboo branches in front of Seiryō Palace and were intending to write a few poems when someone suggested that we might go to the Empress's Office and invite the ladies-in-waiting to join in. You didn't take long to show them you knew what they meant by the bamboo, and they left in a hurry. Most amusing! I wonder where you heard that story. It isn't something most people would recognize.'

'I had no idea that "gentleman" was a name for bamboo,' I said. 'I must have made rather a poor impression.'[351]

'To be sure,' said Yukinari. 'It's not something one could be expected to know.'

While we were deep in our conversation, the men returned, reciting the verse, 'He called it "this gentleman".'[352]

'And what about the poems you intended to write?' Yukinari asked the men. 'I find it very strange that you should come back without them.'

'But how could we possibly find an adequate reply? It's better to make no answer at all than an unsatisfactory one. In any case the story is already being noised about the Palace. His Majesty has heard it and he is delighted.'

They recited the passage over and over again, with Yukinari joining in. It was a delightful scene and many of the ladies-in-waiting came out to have a look. After a few minutes of conversation the gentlemen said they had to return to the Palace. As they left they continued reciting in chorus the line about the bamboo, and one could hear their voices until they reached the guard-house of the Left Division.

Very early on the following morning Lady Shōnagon no Myōbu arrived with a letter from the Emperor reporting the story to Her Majesty. The Empress sent for me in her room and asked if the report was correct. 'I do not know,' I replied. 'I said it without thinking. Perhaps Lord Yukinari arranged it all to my advantage.'

'Well, even if he did,' said Her Majesty, smiling, 'you still came out of it pretty well.'

The Empress is always delighted when she hears that one of us has been praised by the courtiers, and she congratulates the fortunate woman in a most charming way.

91. *A Year after Emperor Enyū's Death*

A year after Emperor Enyū's death[353] people ceased to wear mourning. It was a most moving time. Everyone from His Majesty himself down to the late Emperor's attendants remembered how things had been when the poet wrote about the 'flowery clothes'.[354]

One day when it was raining heavily a child, whose straw coat made him look like a basket worm, came to Tōzammi's[355] room and presented a formal letter attached to a large branch that had been peeled white.

'Where does this come from?' said the maid. 'Madam is observing abstinence both today and tomorrow. Her shutters are closed.' Then, opening the upper part of the shutters, she took in the letter and brought it to her mistress.

'It is a day of abstinence,' said Tōzammi, leaving the letter on top of the lattice. 'I cannot possibly read it.'

On the following morning Tōzammi washed her hands and asked her maid for the 'account of scrolls'.[356] Kneeling down, she took the strange-looking document and slowly opened it. The handwriting, which was traced on heavy, nut-brown paper, was very weak, as though done by some old priest:

> Here we keep our sombre, oak-dyed clothes
> In memory of him who died.
> But in the capital no doubt
> The clothes are changed to brighter hues.[357]

Tōzammi was extremely shocked and wondered who could have sent it. The Archbishop of Niwa[358] occurred to her as a possibility, yet surely he could not have written such a letter. So who was responsible? It must be the Fujiwara Major Counsellor, since he was Director of the late Emperor's household. She

157

would have liked to let Their Majesties know about it at once; but the Masters of Divination had told her that she must be extremely prudent during the period of abstinence and she restrained her impatience until the two days had passed. On the following morning she wrote her answer to the poem and sent it to the residence of the Fujiwara Major Counsellor, whence a further poem came in reply.

Tōzammi now hurried off to the Empress, taking along the two letters she had received. On arrival she explained what had happened, and the Emperor, who was in the room at the time, heard everything. Her Majesty glanced indifferently at the letters. 'This doesn't look like the writing of the Fujiwara Major Counsellor,' she said. 'It must be from some priest.' 'But who?' said Tōzammi. 'Who among the high nobility or clergy would do such a thing? Can it be Lord So-and-so? Or perhaps it's Bishop So-and-so.'

Seeing Tōzammi so perplexed and curious, the Emperor smiled and said, 'Your letter reminds me of something I've seen here.' Opening a small cupboard,[359] he took out still another letter.

'Oh dear. Do tell me what this is all about,' said Tōzammi insistently. 'My head is aching. I really must know.' She gave a bitter laugh.

Finally the Emperor spoke. 'The demon-child who brought you the letter happens to work as an assistant for one of the servants in our kitchen. But I think it may have been Lady Kohyōe who plotted the whole thing.'[360]

Now Her Majesty burst out laughing. 'Oh!' exclaimed Tōzammi, tugging at the sleeve of the Empress's robe and shaking it. 'How could Your Majesty have played such a trick on me? I never suspected anything like that. Before even opening the letter, I specially washed my hands and knelt down.' Tōzammi laughed and I was delighted by the proud, angry look on her face. There was also loud laughter in the kitchen when the servants heard what had happened.

Returning to her own apartments, Tōzammi sent for the child

from the Imperial kitchen and showed him to her maid who had originally taken the letter. 'Yes, that's the boy,' said the maid. 'Who wrote the letter, child, and who handed it to you?' The boy gave a foolish laugh and ran away without a word.

Later the Fujiwara Major Counsellor was told the story and chuckled with delight.

92. Things Without Merit

An ugly person with a bad character.

Rice starch that has become mixed with water. . . . I know that this is a very vulgar item and everyone will dislike my mentioning it. But that should not stop me. In fact I must feel free to include anything, even tongs used for the parting-fires.[361] After all, these objects do exist in our world and people all know about them. I admit they do not belong to a list that others will see. But I never thought that these notes would be read by anyone else, and so I included everything that came into my head, however strange or unpleasant.[362]

93. Outstandingly Splendid Things

What can possibly equal the ceremonies performed in His Majesty's presence on the occasion of the Special Festivals? The rehearsal is also delightful. . . . A bright sun shone in the peaceful spring sky, and in the garden in front of Seiryō Palace mats had been spread out by men of the Housekeeping Office.[363] The Imperial messengers sat facing north, while the dancers faced the Emperor. (But perhaps my memory is mistaken on this point.[364]) Assistant Officials of the Emperor's Private Office placed little tables in front of each of the noblemen in attendance. One after another the guests took the bowl and, after holding it for a while poured some of the wine into a thing called a Yaku shell and drank.

This was followed by the 'gathering of remains'.[365] I find it bad enough to see men doing this; but now to my surprise a lot of women emerged from the fire-huts,[366] which I had thought were empty, and began helping themselves to the left-overs in a most unsightly way. The women who roughly pushed themselves forward, determined to take as much as possible, actually got less than the ones who darted out nimbly and snatched the first things they could find. I was much amused to see how cleverly they used the little huts as store-rooms for their spoils.

As soon as the men from the Housekeeping Office had removed the mats, some workers arrived from the Office of Grounds, each carrying a broom, and levelled off the sand in the garden.

On the day of the rehearsal even the musicians [367] are allowed to come and go freely in His Majesty's presence. As they reached the front of Shōkyō Palace, one could hear the sound of their flutes and of the wooden clappers beating time. I impatiently waited for them to arrive at Seiryō Palace. Presently they emerged by the side of the fence that surrounds the bamboo garden; they were singing Udo Beach [368] to the strumming of their zithers, and, seeing them, I could hardly control my joy. Now two of the dancers ran forward to start the first dance. They stood facing the Emperor, with the sleeves of their robes joined in exactly the right way. The other dancers came out one by one, tapping their feet in time with the music. Having adjusted their costumes – the cords of their short-sleeved jackets, the collar of their over-robes, their head-dress, and the rest – they began dancing to the accompaniment of The Little Pines [369] and other such songs. It was really splendid, and I could gladly have watched them all day as they danced, moving their wide sleeves like great wheels. I felt very sorry when they had finished but consoled myself with the thought that there was another dance to come. I was disappointed, however; for now the musicians walked off, carrying their zithers on their shoulders, and the performers immediately danced behind the bamboos. They made a most elegant picture as they glided gracefully away, their cloaks removed from one shoulder to let the sleeve hang down and the long trains of their glossy silk under-robes stretching out in all directions and becoming entwined with each other. . . . But I am afraid it all seems rather commonplace when put into words.

Now they had gone, and I was left with the sad thought that there would be no more dancing that day. The High Court Nobles and others who had been watching also left, making me feel very forlorn and regretful.

Things are different when the Special Festival is held at Kamo; for then one can look forward to the Sacred Dance of the Return.[370] I remember one such evening. As the smoke rose in slender wisps from the bonfires in the garden, I listened to the clear, delicate, charmingly tremulous sound of the flute that accompanied the sacred dances. The singing also moved me greatly. Delighted by the scene, I hardly noticed that the air was piercingly cold, that my robes of beaten silk were icy, and that the hand in which I held my fan was almost frozen. Afterwards the director summoned the dancers, and I enjoyed seeing how pleased he looked when they came running towards him.[371]

When I am staying at home, I am not satisfied with simply watching the procession as it passes on its way back from the Shrine in the evening. Often I will go all the way to Kamo to see the dances. On arrival I tell my men to place the carriage under the great trees. The smoke of the pine torches trails along the ground; and by their light the cords of the dancers' jackets and the lustre of their silken robes look even more beautiful than in the daytime.

It is delightful too when the dancers move in rhythm with the sacred songs, stamping their feet on the boards of the wooden bridge. The sound of running water blends with the music of the flute, and surely even the Gods must enjoy such a scene.[372]

Among the dancers was a certain Captain in the Inner Palace Guards who performed every year on this occasion and who had always impressed me greatly. He had recently died, and I had heard that his spirit was haunting the first bridge at the upper shrine. I found the idea very frightening and did not think that

I should be able to enjoy the dances fully. Yet, when the time came, I was totally absorbed by their beauty.

'It is always so sad when the Special Festival at Iwashimizu comes to an end,' remarked one of the ladies-in-waiting. 'Why don't the dancers give a repeat performance after they return to the Palace? What a delight that would be! I find it such a shame to see the dancers leaving one after another as soon as they've received their rewards.'

Hearing this, the Emperor said that he would summon the dancers after they returned on the following day and order them to perform. 'Will you really do that, Your Majesty?' said the lady. 'Oh, how splendid!' The ladies-in-waiting were all delighted with this decision, and they crowded round Her Majesty, begging her to make sure that the Emperor would not change his mind.

As a result we had the great pleasure of seeing the dancers give a special performance on their return from the Shrine.[373] The ladies, however, had not really expected that the extra dance would really take place, and when they heard that the dancers had been summoned into the Presence they were not prepared. In their eagerness to reach the hall, they bumped into things and behaved in the most insane way; those who had been in their rooms when the news came rushed helter-skelter to the Palace and, not caring in the slightest that they could be seen by courtiers, attendants, and others whom they passed, lifted their skirts over their heads as they ran.[374] No wonder that people laughed at them!

94. *When His Excellency, the Chancellor, Had Departed*

When His Excellency, the Chancellor, had departed from among us, there was much stir and movement in the world.[375] Her Majesty, who no longer came to the Imperial Palace, lived in the Smaller Palace of the Second Ward.[376] Though I had done nothing to deserve it, things became very difficult for me and I spent a long time at home. One day, when I was particularly concerned about Her Majesty and felt I could not allow our separation to continue, the Captain of the Left Guards Division came to see me. 'I called on Her Majesty today,' he said, 'and found it very moving. Her ladies were dressed as elegantly as ever, with their robes, skirts, and Chinese jackets perfectly matching the season. The blind was open at the side and, when I looked in, I saw a group of about eight ladies, elegantly seated next to each other. They wore Chinese jackets of tawny yellow, light violet skirts, and robes of purple and dark red. Noticing that the grass in the garden outside the palace had been allowed to grow very high and thick, I told them they should have it cut. "We've left it like this on purpose so that we might admire the dew when it settles on the blades." The voice was Lady Saishō's and I found her reply delightful.

'Several of the ladies spoke about you and said it was a shame you were staying at home. "Now that Her Majesty is living in a place like this," they told me, "she feels that Shōnagon should come back into waiting regardless of what business she may have at home. Why won't she return when Her Majesty wants her so much?" I definitely had the impression that they wanted me to pass this on to you. So please go. There's a charm about the place that will stir you deeply. The peonies in front of the terrace have a delightful Chinese air.'

'No,' I replied. 'Since they dislike me so much, I've come to dislike them.'

'You must try to be generous,' he said with a smile.

Shortly afterwards I visited the Empress. I had no way of telling what she thought about it all; but I did hear some of her ladies-in-waiting whisper, 'She is on close terms with people who are attached to the Minister of the Left.'[377] I was coming from my room when I saw them all standing there muttering to each other. Noticing me, they became silent and each of them went about her own business. I was not used to being treated like this and found it most galling. Thereafter Her Majesty summoned me on several occasions, but I paid no attention, and a long time passed without my visiting her. No doubt the ladies-in-waiting made out that I belonged to the enemy camp and told all sorts of lies about me.

One day, when there had been an unaccustomed silence from the Empress and I was sitting at home sunk in gloomy thoughts, a housekeeper brought me a letter. 'Her Majesty ordered that this should be sent to you secretly by Lady Sakyō,' she told me. Yet there could be no reason for such secrecy when I was living at home. Examining the letter, I gathered that it was a personal message from Her Majesty and my heart was pounding as I opened it. There was nothing written on the paper. It had been used to wrap up a single petal of mountain rose, on which I read the words, 'He who does not speak his love.'[378] I was overjoyed; what a relief after the long, anxious days of silence! My eyes filled with 'the things that one knows first of all'.[379] 'The ladies-in-waiting are all wondering why you have stayed away so long,' said the housekeeper, who had been watching me. 'They consider it very strange, especially since you know how much Her Majesty is always thinking of you. Why don't you go?' Then she added, 'I have a short errand near by. I'll be back for your answer presently.'

But as I prepared to write my answer, I realized that I had completely forgotten the next line of the poem. 'Amazing!' I muttered. 'How can one possibly forget an old poem like that? I know it perfectly well and yet it just won't come.' Hearing this, a small page-boy who happened to be in the room said, '"Yet feels its waters seething underneath" – those are the words Madam.' Of course! How on earth could they have slipped my mind? To think that I should have to be taught by a mere child!

Shortly after sending my reply, I visited the Empress. Not knowing how she would receive me, I felt unusually nervous and remained half hidden behind a curtain of state. 'Are you a new-comer here?' asked Her Majesty with a laugh. 'I am afraid it was not much of a poem,' she went on, 'but I felt it was the sort of

164

thing I should write. When I do not see you, Shōnagon, I am wretched all the time.'

Her Majesty had not changed. When I told her about the page-boy who had reminded me of the missing words, she was most amused. 'That's just the sort of thing that can happen,' she said, laughing, 'especially with old poems that one considers too familiar to take seriously.'

Then she told me the following story: 'Some people were organizing a game of riddles[380] when one of them, a clever man and a good player, said that he would like to set the first riddle presented by the team of the left, to which he belonged. His team-mates cheerfully agreed, feeling confident that he would produce something good.

'When all the people in the team of the left had made up their riddles, they began to select the ones that would actually be used. "Please tell us what yours is going to be?" they said to the man. "No," he replied. "You must simply trust me. After speaking as I did, I am hardly likely to come out with something that will disappoint you." His team-mates assumed that he must be right; but, when the day of the game drew near, they again asked him to let them know his riddle. "What if you should have produced something very strange?" they said. "Well," he said angrily, "I don't know. If you are so uncertain about my riddle, you had better not depend on me at all." When the day arrived, his partners were very worried about what he would do.

'The participants, men and women of quality including several senior courtiers, were divided into two teams and seated in rows. The time came to present the first set of riddles, and our man was chosen to lead off for the team of the left. He looked as if he had prepared his entry with great care, and all the players gazed at him anxiously, wondering what they would hear. "Your riddle! Your riddle!" they said impatiently.

'Finally he came out with "A bow drawn in the sky", which delighted the members of the opposing team. His partners were dumbfounded and disgusted with him. Surely, they thought, he must be working for the other side and trying to make his own team lose.

'Meanwhile his opponent on the team of the right was laughing at him. "Dear me!" he said, beginning to pout. "I haven't the slightest idea." And, instead of answering the riddle, he began making jokes.

'"I've won!" cried the man who had posed the riddle. "A point for our side!" A token was duly given to the team of the left.[381]

'"Disgraceful!" said the members of the other team. "Everyone knows the answer to that riddle. They certainly shouldn't get a point."

'"But he said he did not know," replied the man. "How can you claim he hasn't lost?" In this and in each of the subsequent contests he argued so effectively that his side won.

'Later the player who had failed to answer the first riddle was being taken to task by his team-mates. "We admit," they said, "that people can forget the answers to the most obvious questions and have to concede defeat. But what possible reason could you have to say you didn't know?"[382] And they made him pay a forfeit.'

When the Empress had finished her story, all the ladies burst out laughing. 'The people on the team of the right had good reason to be annoyed with their man,' said one of them. 'I can see why they were disappointed. And how furious the other team must have been to hear their candidate lead off with such a silly riddle!'

'Indeed,' I thought, 'how could anyone possibly forget something so simple and commonplace?'

95. On the Tenth Day of the First Month

On the tenth day of the First Month there were thick clouds in the sky but the sun shone through brightly. In a rough, uncultivated field behind a poor dwelling-house grew a young peach tree. Little branches sprouted thickly all over it; I noticed that the leaves were green on one side while on the other they were dark and glossy as if coloured with a deep red dye.

A slender youth, with beautiful hair and wearing a torn hunting costume, had climbed the tree. At the foot stood a little boy; he had on short clogs, and over a plum-red under-robe he wore a white hunting costume tucked up so that it bulged at the waist. 'Come on!' he called to the youth in the tree. 'Cut me a nice branch.'

Just then a small group of girls arrived. They too had pretty hair and their jackets were torn; though their skirts were faded, the colours still looked quite attractive. 'Please cut us some branches,' they shouted to the lad. 'Choose some that we can make into nice hare-sticks. Master sent us for them.'

When the youth in the tree started to throw down branches, the children ran for them helter-skelter, each taking her share and crying, 'Lots for me! Lots for me!' It was a delightful scene.

Then a man in a dirty trouser-skirt came running along and said that he too wanted some branches. The boy asked him to wait for a moment, whereupon the man began shaking the tree. The boy was terrified and clung on like a monkey, which I found most amusing. One is likely to come across similar scenes when the plum trees start bearing fruit.

96. *Two Handsome Men*

Two handsome men are absorbed in a game of backgammon. Though they have been playing all day, they still do not seem tired and order a servant to light the lamp on a short stand. One of the players holds the dice in his hand and, before finally placing them in the box, prays earnestly for a good throw. The other player puts his dice-box on the board. As he sits there waiting, he tucks in the collar of his hunting costume, which has begun to creep up over his face,[383] and shakes his sagging lacquered cap. 'How could anyone possibly lose after reciting all those charms?' he seems to be saying as he stares impatiently at his opponent. What a proud look he has!

A high-ranking gentleman is about to start a game of *go*. He loosens the sash of his cloak and with a negligent air picks up the stones from his box and starts placing them on the board. Meanwhile his opponent, who is of lower rank, sits respectfully at some distance from the board, bending forward, and each time that he reaches out to place a stone he has to push aside his sleeve with the other hand. It is a delightful scene.

97. *Things That Give a Clean Feeling*

An earthen cup. A new metal bowl.
A rush mat.
The play of the light on water as one pours it into a vessel.
A new wooden chest.

98. *Things That Give an Unclean Feeling*

A rat's nest.
Someone who is late in washing his hands in the morning.
White snivel, and children who sniffle as they walk.
The containers used for oil.
Little sparrows.[384]
A person who does not bathe for a long time even though the weather is hot.[385]
All faded clothes give me an unclean feeling, especially those that have glossy colours.

99. *Adorable Things*

The face of a child drawn on a melon.[386]
A baby sparrow that comes hopping up when one imitates the

squeak of a mouse;[387] or again, when one has tied it with a thread round its leg and its parents bring insects or worms and pop them in its mouth – delightful!

A baby of two or so is crawling rapidly along the ground. With his sharp eyes he catches sight of a tiny object and, picking it up with his pretty little fingers, takes it to show to a grown-up person.

A child, whose hair has been cut like a nun's,[388] is examining something; the hair falls over his eyes, but instead of brushing it away he holds his head to the side. The pretty white cords of his trouser-skirt are tied round his shoulders, and this too is most adorable.

A young Palace page, who is still quite small, walks by in ceremonial costume.

One picks up a pretty baby and holds him for a while in one's arms; while one is fondling him, he clings to one's neck and then falls asleep.

The objects used during the Display of Dolls.

One picks up a tiny lotus leaf that is floating on a pond and examines it. Not only lotus leaves, but little hollyhock flowers, and indeed all small things, are most adorable.

An extremely plump baby, who is about a year old and has a lovely white skin, comes crawling towards one, dressed in a long gauze robe of violet with the sleeves tucked up.

A little boy of about eight who reads aloud from a book in his childish voice.

Pretty, white chicks who are still not fully fledged and look as if their clothes are too short for them; cheeping loudly, they follow one on their long legs, or walk close to the mother hen.

Duck eggs.

An urn containing the relics of some holy person.

Wild pinks.

100. *Presumptuous Things*

A child who has nothing particular to recommend him yet is used to being spoilt by people.

Coughing.

One is about to say something to a person who is obviously embarrassed, but then he speaks first – very strange.

A child of about four, whose parents live near by, comes to one's house and behaves mischievously. He picks up one's things, scatters them about the place, and damages them. As a rule he is held in check and cannot do as he wishes, but, when his mother is with him, he feels that he can assert himself. 'Let me see that, Mama,' he says, tugging at her skirts and pointing to some coveted object. The mother tells him that she is talking to grown-up people and pays no more attention to him, whereupon the child manages to take hold of the object by himself, picks it up, and examines it – oh, how hateful! Instead of snatching the thing from him and hiding it, the mother simply says, 'You naughty child!' Then she adds with a smile, 'You mustn't do that. You'll damage it, you know.' The mother is hateful too. Since it would be unseemly to say anything, one has to sit there in silence, anxiously watching the child.

101. *Squalid Things*

The back of a piece of embroidery.

The inside of a cat's ear.

A swarm of mice, who still have no fur, when they come wriggling out of their nest.

The seams of a fur robe that has not yet been lined.

Darkness in a place that does not give the impression of being very clean.

A rather unattractive woman who looks after a large brood of children.

A woman who falls ill and remains unwell for a long time. In the mind of her lover, who is not particularly devoted to her, she must appear rather squalid.

102. *People Who Seem to Suffer*

The nurse looking after a baby who cries at night.

A man with two mistresses who is obliged to see them being bitter and jealous towards each other.

An exorcist who has to deal with an obstinate spirit. He hopes that his incantations will take effect quickly; but often he is disappointed and has to persevere, praying that after all his efforts he will not end up as a laughing-stock.

A woman passionately loved by a man who is absurdly jealous.

The powerful men who serve in the First Place never seem to be at ease though one would imagine that they had a pleasant enough life.

Nervous people.

103. *Enviable People*

One has been learning a sacred text by heart; but, though one has gone over the same passage again and again, one still recites it haltingly and keeps on forgetting words. Meanwhile one hears other people, not only clerics (for whom it is natural) but ordinary men and women, reciting such passages without the slightest effort, and one wonders when one will ever be able to come up to their standard.

When one is ill in bed and hears people walking about, laughing loudly and chatting away as if they did not have a care in the world, how enviable they seem!

Once on the day of the Horse in the Second Month I decided to visit Inari. By the time I had reached the Middle Shrine I was already worn out; yet I kept going and was on my way to the Upper Shrine when a group of people passed me. Though they had evidently started after I did, they strode briskly up the hill without the slightest look of discomfort – very enviable.

I had made haste to leave at dawn, but by the Hour of the Snake[389] I was still only half way to the top. To make matters worse, it was gradually becoming hot, and I felt really wretched. When I stopped to rest, I began crying from exhaustion and wondered why I had come on this pilgrimage when there were so many people who had never even thought of making the effort. Just then I saw a woman in her thirties walking down the hill. She was not wearing a travelling costume, but had simply tucked up the bottom of her skirts. 'I am making the pilgrimage seven times today,' she declared to the people she met on her way. 'I've been up three times already and there won't be any trouble about the other four times. I have to be back by the Hour of the Sheep.'[390] She was a woman I could hardly have noticed if I had met her anywhere else; but at that moment I wished I could change places with her.

∽

I greatly envy people who have nice children, whether they grow up to be priests or become ordinary men and women.

Women who have beautiful hair with tresses that fall splendidly over their shoulders.

People of high rank who are always surrounded by respectful attendants are most enviable.

People who have a good hand, who are skilful at composing poems, and who are always chosen first when there is a letter to be written. . . . Several women are attending a lady of quality who wishes a letter to be written on her behalf to an important person. Obviously many of them are suited for the task (it is not likely that *all* her women will have writing as feeble as the tracks of a bird's feet); yet the lady especially summons a woman who is not in the room and, producing her own inkstone, tells her to write the letter. This is bound to make the others envious. The fortunate woman may be one of the older members of the household, whose writing is of the most elementary kind; yet she will set herself to the task with enthusiasm. On the other hand she may be an experienced calligrapher. Perhaps the letter is going to some High Court Noble; or possibly it is intended to introduce a young woman who is hoping to take service in the Palace. The writer is instructed to do her very best, and she begins by carefully selecting the paper. Meanwhile her fellow attendants gather round and make envious jokes.

On first learning the zither or the flute, one is extremely envious of experienced players and wonders when one will ever reach that stage.

The nurse of the Emperor or of the Crown Prince.

The women in the Palace who are privileged to see His Majesty's consorts.

People who can afford to build their own Chapel of Meditation and pray there in the evening and at dawn.

When one's opponent has a lucky throw of dice in backgammon, he is most enviable.

A saint who has really given up all thoughts of the world.

104. *Things That One Is in a Hurry to See or to Hear*

Rolled dyeing, uneven shading, and all other forms of dappled dyeing.

When a woman has just had a child, one is in a hurry to find out whether it is a boy or a girl. If she is a lady of quality, one is obviously most curious; but, even if she is a servant or someone else of humble station, one still wants to know.

Early in the morning on the first day of the period of official appointments one is eager to hear whether a certain acquaintance will receive his governorship.

A letter from the man one loves.

105. *While We Were in Mourning for the Chancellor*

While we were in mourning for the Chancellor, Her Majesty had to leave the Palace on the occasion of the Great Purification at the end of the Sixth Month. Since the Empress's Office lay in an unlucky direction, she proceeded to the Dining Hall of the High Court Nobles.[391] It was terribly hot that first evening and so dark that one could not see anything. We spent a rather anxious night in our cramped quarters. On the following morning, when we got up and looked about, we found that the building was a low, flat structure with a tiled roof that gave it a peculiar, Chinese air. There were none of the usual lattices, only bamboo blinds hanging down all round the room. Yet the place was strangely charming.

While we were staying there, I and the other ladies-in-waiting used to go into the garden for a walk every morning. Conspicuous among the plants were the masses of flowers known as yellow day-lilies which grew along the bamboo fence and looked just right in front of this particular building.

The Time Office[392] was directly next door, and the gong sounded different from usual. Some of the younger ladies in our group were curious to hear it, and one day about twenty of them ran over to the building and climbed the high bell-tower. I stayed at the bottom and looked up at them. As they stood there in their light grey skirts, Chinese jackets, matching dresses of unlined silk, and scarlet petticoats, they really looked as if they might have descended from heaven (though one could hardly have called them angels). I also enjoyed watching the faces of some of the other ladies who, though quite as young as the ones in the tower, could not join them because of their own superior rank, and were looking up at them enviously.

When the sun had set, the older women joined the younger ones under the cover of darkness, and they all set off for the guard-house. It appears that, when they arrived there, they played about and laughed so noisily that the guard-house attendants became angry. 'What a way to behave!' they exclaimed and accused the ladies of having climbed into the chairs normally occupied by the High Court Nobles and of having upset and damaged the benches used by the members of the Great Council of State. But the women paid no attention.

Perhaps because the building was very old and covered with tiles, it became unspeakably hot at night, and we slept outside the blinds. All day long, centipedes kept falling from the ceiling (this also because the building was so old), and great droves of hornets flew into our room; this we found very frightening.

Every day senior courtiers came to call, and often they stayed talking until late at night. When one of them heard a lady-in-waiting say something about the Dining Hall, he delighted us by reciting, 'Who would have believed it? That the grounds of the Great Council would so soon become a pleasure garden.'

Autumn came, but in our cramped quarters no 'cooling wind'[393] was wafted from any side. We could, however, hear the sound of the autumn insects.

On the eve of the Empress's return to the Palace on the eighth, the two stars[394] seemed closer than usual. This too was no doubt because the building and its garden were so cramped.

106. *One Day Captain Tadanobu, the Imperial Adviser, Came to Call*

One day Captain Tadanobu, the Imperial Adviser, came to call in the company of Captain Nobukata. I went out on the veranda with some of the other ladies-in-waiting, and we chatted with the two gentlemen. In the course of our conversation, I suddenly asked Tadanobu, 'Which poem will you be reciting tomorrow?'

'Why, of course,' he answered after a moment's thought, 'it will be the one about the Fourth Month in this world of men.'[395]

I was delighted that he should have remembered an old poem like this and that he should have replied so adroitly. Unlike women, men are liable to forget old poems,[396] even the ones they have written themselves, and so I was especially impressed by Tadanobu's feat. The allusion, of course, was lost on the other women behind the screen and on Captain Nobukata, who was standing in front.

107. *It Was Late at Night*

It was late at night on the same day, the last of the Third Month. There had been a large number of senior courtiers next to the first door of the long corridor in the Palace, but one by one they had slipped away, and now no one remained but the Captain First Secretary, Tadanobu, Captain Nobukata of the Minamotos, and a certain Chamberlain of the Sixth Rank. They spoke about all sorts of things, chanted passages from the sutras, and recited Japanese poems.

'Now the night is over,' declared Tadanobu. 'Let us go home.' And he added the line, '"The tears they shed on parting will turn to dew when morning comes".'[397] Nobukata joined him in reciting the poem, and it was delightful to hear them.

'She really is in a hurry – that Weaver of yours!' I remarked.

'I thought of that quotation on the spur of the moment,' replied Tadanobu, looking very cross. 'The situation happened to remind me of a parting at dawn. What a shame that you should have to tease us like that! In this palace one is always sorry when one has made some inadvertent remark.' Since it was becoming very light, Tadanobu added, 'It is impossible for the God of Kazuraki to remain here any longer.'[398] And the gentlemen made their way home through the thick grass in the garden.

When the time actually came for the Tanabata Festival, I hoped to be able to say something about this conversation. In the meantime, however, Tadanobu had become an Imperial Adviser, and it seemed unlikely that I would see him. I planned to write a letter that might be delivered by someone from the Office of Grounds; but I was pleasantly surprised to receive a personal visit from him on the seventh of the month. Would Tadanobu remember our conversation? If I brought it up casually, he would no doubt put his head to the side with a questioning look, and I should have to remind him of what had been said. As it turned out, he replied without the slightest hesitation, and this really delighted me. For months I had been wondering when our conversation would be mentioned again (here, I am afraid, my fanciful nature was at work), and now I was most impressed to find that he had remembered everything and prepared his answer. Nobukata, who like Tadanobu had been annoyed on the previous occasion, again accompanied him on this visit, but obviously remembered nothing. 'Really!' Tadanobu exclaimed. 'Do you mean to say you've forgotten how she criticized me at dawn that day?' 'Ah, to be sure, to be sure,' replied Nobukata, laughing – most pathetic.

In our discussion of men and women Tadanobu and I often used the terminology of *go*. Thus, when we wanted to imply that two people were on intimate terms, we would say that they had 'yielded their hands' or 'filled up the spaces'. Or again we would use expressions like 'he's going to keep his hand' or 'the time has come to part the pieces' (meaning 'so-and-so has become far too familiar').[399] In this way we could understand each other without letting anyone else know what we had in mind.

Nobukata heard about our language and one day he came up to me and inquired what it was all about. Since I refused to tell him, he went to Tadanobu and reproachfully asked him for an explanation. Out of regard for their friendship Tadanobu let him into the secret.

Nobukata now anxiously awaited a chance to display his new knowledge. One day he came to our building and asked to speak to me. 'Is there a *go* board here?' he began. 'What would you say if I too wanted to play? Would you yield your hand to me? I am just as good as Tadanobu, you know. You mustn't discriminate against me.'

'If I played like that,' I replied, people could well speak of a roving eye.'[400]

When Nobukata told Tadanobu about this, he was delighted that I had given a happy answer. Yes, I really like people who remember things.

One day, after Tadanobu's promotion to the rank of Imperial Adviser had been decided, I was in His Majesty's presence. 'Tadanobu is wonderful at reciting Chinese poetry,' I said. 'Now that he has been promoted, who is going to be left to give us lines like "Hsiao of K'uai-chi, having visited the ancient tomb"? Your Majesty had better make sure that he continues coming here, even if it means that he has to wait a little longer for his new post. It would be too sad to lose him.' The Emperor burst out laughing. 'I shall tell him what you have said,' he replied, 'and I shall withhold the appointment.'

Tadanobu received his promotion all the same. I was feeling very sorry about this when one day Nobukata came to see me. By now he was convinced that he was in no way Tadanobu's inferior and gave himself great airs. I spoke to him about Tadanobu and said, 'He can recite the Chinese poem, "Had not yet reached the term of thirty"[401] in a delightfully original way.'

'But why shouldn't I be just as good? In fact I shall try to do it even better.' So saying, Nobukata recited the poem in question.

'That's not bad at all,' I said when he had finished.

'Oh dear!' said Nobukata. 'Why can't I recite it as well as he does?'

'There's a particular charm,' I explained, 'in the way Tadanobu recites the passage about "the term of thirty".' At this Nobukata left with a bitter chuckle.

Some time later, when Tadanobu was visiting the headquarters of the Inner Palace Guards, Nobukata made a point of seeing him and reported what I had said, requesting that he teach him the passage. Tadanobu laughingly agreed.

I was unaware of all this when one day I heard someone reciting verse outside my room. The style was remarkably like Tadanobu's. 'Who's that?' I called out in surprise. It was

Nobukata who replied. 'You'll be amazed,' he said. 'Yesterday Tadanobu visited our guard-house and I asked him to let me hear how he recited poetry. As soon as he had done so, I was able to say the verses in a way that everyone found extremely similar to his. Just now when you asked who was there, you certainly did not sound as if you found my style unattractive.'

I was delighted to think that he had made this special effort and, since he had now begun to recite the precise poem that I had mentioned earlier, I went out and spoke to him.

'I owe this new talent of mine to Tadanobu,' he said when he saw me. 'I should turn in his direction and make obeisance.'

Thereafter, though I often avoided people who came to visit me in my room (my usual excuse being that I was on duty in the Palace), I was always at home to Nobukata when he arrived reciting his poem. I told the Empress the story and she was much amused.

෨

One day, during an Imperial Abstinence at the Palace, Nobu-kata ordered a certain Clerk[402] in the Right Division of the Inner Palace Guards (his name was Mitsu-something-or-other) to bring me a letter. It was written on a double sheet of Michinoku paper and said, 'I had intended to come and see you today but was prevented by the Imperial Abstinence. What do.you think of "had not yet reached the term of thirty"?'

'I believe you must already have got beyond that term,' I replied. 'Indeed you must by now be as old as Chu Mai-ch'en when he admonished his wife.'[403]

Once again Nobukata was annoyed and he reported my answer to the Emperor, who in turn discussed it with the Empress when he visited her. 'How could Shōnagon possibly know such a thing?' he said, laughing. 'Chu Mai-ch'en was over forty[404] when he reprimanded his wife, and it makes Nobukata sad that someone should have written to him like that.'

When I heard about this, I was convinced that Nobukata had taken leave of his senses.[405]

108. The Name 'Kokiden'

The name 'Kokiden' was given to the Imperial Lady who was the daughter of the Major Captain of the Left Division residing in Kanin Palace. In her service was a lady called Sakyō (the daughter of a woman by the name of Uchifushi*), who was loved by Nobukata and courted by him. People used to laugh at him about this liaison. One day Nobukata came to the Empress's Office, where Her Majesty was then residing. 'I should have stood night watch here from time to time,' he told her, 'but Your Majesty's ladies have not treated me properly and so I have been avoiding this place. If only I had been assigned to the night duty room in the Palace, I should faithfully have carried out my responsibilities.'

The other ladies agreed with him, but I interrupted and said, 'Yes, indeed. Some people like to have a place where they can lie down and rest.[406] When they have found such a place they go there all the time, but as for coming here. . .'

'I shall never tell you anything again,' said Nobukata in a voice that was both solemn and bitter. 'I confided in you as a friend, but you have treated the matter as if it were common gossip.'

'Very odd!' I replied. 'What on earth have I said? There was nothing in my remark that you could possibly object to.'

When I nudged the lady next to me, she turned to Nobukata with a laugh and said, 'Yes, why should you be so annoyed by a harmless remark?'

'No doubt Shōnagon put you up to saying that,' exclaimed Nobukata furiously.

'I dislike hearing other people gossip,' I said, 'and I certainly don't go in for that sort of thing myself.' With this the other ladies and I all left.

A few days later Nobukata again addressed me bitterly. 'You have been spreading shameful things about me,' he said, 'when

* 'Lying Down'.

180

all along it was a story concocted by some of the senior courtiers to make people laugh at me.'

'In that case,' I replied, 'it would appear that I am not the only one to blame. Really, I find your attitude very strange.'

Thereafter Nobukata broke entirely with Sakyō.

109. *Things That are Distant Though Near*

Festivals celebrated near the Palace.[407]

Relations between brothers, sisters, and other members of a family who do not love each other.

The zigzag path leading up to the temple at Kurama.[408]

The last day of the Twelfth Month and the first of the First.

110. *Things That are Near Though Distant*

Paradise.[409]

The course of a boat.[410]

Relations between a man and a woman.

111. *Gentlemen of the Fifth Rank*

Officials in the Ministry of Ceremonial, the Left Division of the Outer Palace Guards, and the Office of Scribes are delighted to belong to the Fifth Rank;[411] but it is hardly a position that Chamberlains of the Sixth Rank would covet.

A man who has been awarded the head-dress of nobility, and who serves as a Provisional Governor or in some other Fifth Rank post, usually lives in a small, shingled house. Sometimes he will surround it with a new fence made of strips of cypress, next to which he will build a shelter for carriages, and he will tether his oxen to the trees that cluster directly in front of the house and let them graze there – all very hateful. He is also likely to have an attractive garden, and inside the house, Iyo blinds suspended by cords of purple leather and sliding-doors that have been covered with material; at night he gives instructions that the main gate should be securely closed. Considering that he is a man without the slightest prospects in life, all this show is most distasteful.[412] An official of this rank should not have his own house at all. So long as no uncle or elder brother is already living there, he had better stay with his parents or, of course, with his parents-in-law. Alternatively it is quite proper for him to live in a house whose owner is absent or in the house of a close friend who is serving in the provinces and has no use for it. If none of this is possible, he can always arrange to stay for a while in one of the many houses that belong to Imperial Princesses or to the children of the Empress Dowager; then, when he has obtained a good post for himself, he can move into a more permanent place.

112. *When a Woman Lives Alone*

When a woman lives alone, her house should be extremely dilapidated, the mud wall should be falling to pieces, and if there is a pond, it should be overgrown with water-plants. It is not essential that the garden be covered with sage-brush;[413] but weeds should be growing through the sand in patches, for this gives the place a poignantly desolate look.

I greatly dislike a woman's house when it is clear that she has scurried about with a knowing look on her face, arranging everything just as it should be, and when the gate is kept tightly shut.

113. *When a Court Lady Is on Leave*

When a Court lady is on leave from the Palace, it is pleasant if she can stay with her parents. While she is there, people are always coming and going, there is a lot of noisy conversation in the back rooms, and the clatter of horses' hoofs resounds outside. Yet she is in no danger of being criticized.[414]

Things are very different if she is staying in someone else's house. Let us suppose that a man comes to visit the lady, either openly or in secret. He stands by the front gate and says to her, 'I did not know you were at home, else I should certainly have called on you before. When will you return to Court?' If it is a man she has set her heart on, the lady cannot possibly leave him standing outside and she opens the front door for him.

Then, to her great annoyance, she hears the owner of the house, who has evidently decided that there is too much noise and that it is dangerous to leave the door unbolted so late at night. 'Has the outer gate been closed?' he asks the porter. 'No, Sir,' says the latter in a disgruntled tone. 'There's still a visitor in the house.' 'Well, be sure to close it as soon as he's left. There have been a lot of burglaries recently.' This is especially irking for the lady since the man who is with her can hear everything. Meanwhile the servants are constantly peeping in to see whether the guest is getting ready to leave – much to the amusement of the attendants who have accompanied him on his visit. Then the attendants start imitating the owner's voice. Oh, what a scolding there would be if he heard them!

Sometimes the lady will receive visits from a man who does not show any tender feelings for her in either his looks or his words. Presumably he must care for her; else why would he continue his visits night after night? Nevertheless the man may turn out to be quite harmless and will leave her saying, 'It's really getting late. And I suppose it *is* rather dangerous to keep the gate open at this hour.'

One can tell if a man really loves one, because he will insist on staying all night however much one may urge him to leave. Time after time the night watchman has made his rounds, and now he exclaims in a very audible voice, 'Good heavens! The dawn has come' (as if it were so surprising) 'and someone's gone and left the gate wide open all night. Such carelessness!' Then he securely bolts the gate, though it is now light and there is no need for such precautions. How unpleasant it all is!

183

Yes, things are a great deal better when one is staying with one's own parents. Parents-in-law, however, are the most awkward of all, since one is always worrying about what they are going to think. I imagine that it must also be difficult to stay with an elder brother.

What I really like is a house where no one cares about the gate either in the middle of the night or at dawn, and where one is free to meet one's visitor, whether he be an Imperial Prince or a gentleman from the Palace. In the winter one can stay awake together all night with the lattices wide open. When the time comes for him to leave, one has the pleasure of watching him playing upon his flute as he goes; if a bright moon is still hanging in the sky, it is a particular delight. After he has disappeared, one does not go to bed at once, but stays up, discussing the visitor with one's companions, and exchanging poems; then gradually one falls asleep.

114. *It Is Delightful When There Has Been a Thin Fall of Snow*

It is delightful when there has been a thin fall of snow; or again when it has piled up very high and in the evening we sit round a brazier at the edge of the veranda with a few congenial friends, chatting till darkness falls. There is no need for the lamp, since the snow itself reflects a clear light. Raking the ashes in the brazier with a pair of fire-tongs, we discuss all sorts of moving and amusing things.

It already seems to be quite late at night when we hear the sound of footsteps. We all look up, wondering who it may be. A man is approaching – the type of man that often visits us unannounced on such occasions. 'I was wondering how you ladies were enjoying today's snow,' he says. 'I had intended to come and see you earlier, but I was held up all day in some other place.'

'Ah!' says one of us and quotes the poem about 'the man who

came today'.[415] Then, with a great deal of laughter, we begin talking about what has happened since the morning and about all sorts of other things. The visitor has been offered a round cushion, but he prefers to sit on the wooden veranda with one leg hanging over the edge.

The conversation goes on until the bell announces that dawn has come. The ladies sitting behind the blinds and the man in front[416] feel that they still have many things to tell each other; but he has to be off before daylight. As he gets ready to leave, he charmingly recites, 'Snow lay upon such-and-such hills'.[417] Then he is gone. If he had not been there, we should certainly not have stayed up all night like this; it was he who made the occasion so delightful, and now we start discussing what an elegant man he is.

115. *One Evening during the Reign of Emperor Murakami*

One evening during the reign of Emperor Murakami, when it had been snowing very heavily, and the moon was shining brightly, His Majesty ordered that some snow be heaped on to a platter. Then a branch of plum blossom was stuck into it, and the Emperor told someone to hand the platter to Hyōe, the Lady Chamberlain. 'Let us have a poem about this,' he said to her. 'What will you give us?'

'The moon, the snow, the flowers,'[418] she replied, much to His Majesty's delight. 'To have composed a special poem for the occasion,' he said, 'would have been the ordinary thing to do. But to find a line that fits the moment so beautifully – that is really hard.'

On another day, when Lady Hyōe was accompanying Emperor Murakami, His Majesty stopped for a moment in the Senior Courtiers' Chamber, which was empty at the time, and, noticing that some smoke was coming out of the square brazier, said, 'What can that be? Go and have a look.' Lady Hyōe went and examined the brazier, then returned with this delightful poem, which she recited to the Emperor:

> What do I see in the open sea,
> Or aflame in the open fire?
> It must be a frying frog I see,
> Or a woman diver rowing home.[419]

In fact a frog had jumped into the fire and was burning away.

116. *When I First Went into Waiting*

When I first went into waiting at Her Majesty's Court, so many different things embarrassed me that I could not even reckon them up and I was always on the verge of tears. As a result I tried to avoid appearing before the Empress except at night, and even then I stayed hidden behind a three-foot curtain of state.

On one occasion Her Majesty brought out some pictures and showed them to me, but I was so ill at ease that I could hardly stretch out my hand to take them. She pointed to one picture after another, explaining what each represented. Since the lamp had been put on a low tray-stand, one could view the pictures even better than in the daytime, and every hair of my head was clearly visible. I managed to control my embarrassment and had a proper look. It was a very cold time of the year and when Her Majesty gave me the paintings I could hardly see her hands;[420] but, from what I made out, they were of a light pink hue that I found extraordinarily attractive. I gazed at the Empress with amazement. Simple as I was and unaccustomed to such wonderful sights, I did not understand how a being like this could possibly exist in our world.

At dawn I was about to hurry back to my room when Her Majesty said, 'Even the God of Kazuraki would stay a little longer.' So I sat down again, but I leant forward sideways in such a way that Her Majesty could not see me directly, and kept the lattice shut. One of the ladies who came into the room noticed this and said that it should be opened. A servant heard her and started towards it, but Her Majesty said, 'Wait. Leave the lattice as it is.' The two women went out, laughing to each other.

Her Majesty then asked me various questions and finally said, 'I am sure you want to return to your room. So off you go! But be sure to come again this evening – and early too.'

As soon as I had crept out of Her Majesty's presence and was back in my room, I threw open all the lattices and looked out at the magnificent snow.

During the day I received several notes from Her Majesty telling me to come while it was still light. 'The sky is clouded with snow,' she wrote, 'and no one will be able to see you clearly.'

Noticing my hesitation, the lady in charge of my room[421] urged me, saying, 'I don't know how you can stay shut up like this all day long. Her Majesty has granted you the extraordinary good fortune of being admitted into her presence, and she must certainly have her reasons. To be unresponsive to another person's kindness is a most hateful way to behave.' This was enough to make me hurry back to the Empress; but I was overcome with embarrassment, and it was not easy for me.

On my way I was delighted to see the snow beautifully piled on top of the fire huts. When I entered Her Majesty's room, I noticed that the usual square brazier was full to the brim with burning charcoal and that no one was sitting next to it. The Empress herself was seated in front of a round brazier made of Shen[422] wood and decorated with pear-skin lacquer. She was surrounded by a group of high-ranking ladies who were in constant attendance upon her. In the next part of the room a tightly packed row of ladies-in-waiting sat in front of a long, rectangular brazier, with their Chinese jackets worn in such a way that they trailed on the floor. Observing how experienced they were in their duties and how easily they carried them out, I could not help feeling envious. There was not a trace of awkwardness in any of their movements as they got up to deliver notes to Her Majesty from the outside and sat down again by the brazier, talking and laughing to each other. When would I ever be able to manage like that, I wondered nervously. Still further in the back of the room sat a small group of ladies who were looking at pictures together.

After a while I heard the voices of outrunners loudly ordering people to make way. 'His Excellency, the Chancellor, is coming,' said one of the ladies, and they all cleared away their scattered belongings. I retired to the back of the room; but despite my modesty, I was curious to see the great man in person and I peeped through a crack at the bottom of the curtain of state where I was sitting. It turned out that it was not Michitaka, but his son, Korechika, the Major Counsellor. The purple of his Court cloak and trousers looked magnificent against the white snow. 'I should not have come,' he said, standing next to one of the pillars, 'because both yesterday and today are days of abstinence. But it has been snowing so hard that I felt bound to call and find out whether all was well with you.'

'How did you manage?' said Her Majesty. 'I thought that all the paths were buried.'

'Well,' replied Korechika, 'it occurred to me that I might move your heart.'[423]

Could anything surpass this conversation between the Empress and her brother? This was the sort of exchange that is so eloquently described in romances; and the Empress herself, arrayed in a white dress, a robe of white Chinese damask, and two more layers of scarlet damask over which her hair hung down loosely at the back, had a beauty that I had seen in paintings but never in real life: it was all like a dream.

Korechika joked with the ladies-in-waiting, and they replied without the slightest embarrassment, freely arguing with him and contradicting his remarks when they disagreed. I was absolutely dazzled by it all and found myself blushing without any particular reason. Korechika ate a few fruits and told one of the servants to offer some to the Empress. He must have asked who was behind the curtain of state and one of the ladies must have told him that it was I; for he stood up and walked to the back of the room. At first I thought he was leaving, but instead he came and sat very close to me; he began to talk about various things he had heard about me before I came into waiting and asked whether they were true. I had been embarrassed enough when I had been looking at him from a distance with the curtain of state between us; now that we were actually facing each other I felt extremely stupid and could hardly believe that this was really happening to me.

In the past, when I had gone to watch Imperial Processions and the like, Korechika had sometimes glanced in the direction of my carriage; but I had always pulled the inner blinds close together, and hidden my face behind a fan for fear that he might see my silhouette through the blinds. I wondered how I could ever have chosen to embark on a career for which I was so ill-suited by nature. What on earth should I say to him? I was bathed in sweat and altogether in a terrible state. To make matters worse, Korechika now seized the fan behind which I had prudently hidden myself, and I realized that my hair must be scattered all over my forehead in a terrible mess; no doubt everything about my appearance bespoke the embarrassment I felt at that moment.

I had hoped Korechika would leave quickly, but he showed no sign of doing so; instead he sat there, toying with my fan and asking who had done the paintings on it. I kept my head lowered and pressed the sleeve of my Chinese jacket to my face – so tightly indeed, that bits of powder must have stuck to it, making my complexion all mottled.

The Empress, who no doubt realized how desperately I wanted Korechika to leave, turned to him and said, 'Look at this notebook. Whose writing do you suppose it is?' I was relieved to think that now he would finally go; but instead he asked her to have the book brought to him so that he could examine it. 'Really,' she said. 'You can perfectly well come here yourself and have a look.' 'No I can't,' he replied. 'Shōnagon has got hold of me and won't let go.' It was a very fashionable sort of joke but hardly suited to my rank or age, and I felt terribly ill at ease. Her Majesty held up the book, in which something had been written in a cursive script, and looked at it. 'Well indeed,' said Korechika, 'whose can it be? Let's show it to Shōnagon. I am sure she can recognize the handwriting of anyone in the world.' The aim of all these absurd remarks, of course, was to draw me out.

As if a single gentleman were not enough to embarrass me, another one now arrived, preceded by outrunners who cleared the way for him. This gentleman too was wearing a Court cloak, and he looked even more splendid than Korechika. He sat down and started telling some amusing stories, which delighted the ladies-in-waiting. 'Oh yes,' they said, laughing, 'we saw Lord So-and-so when he was –.' As I heard them mention the names of one senior courtier after another, I felt they must be talking about spirits or heavenly beings who had descended to earth. Yet, after some time had passed and I had grown accustomed to Court service, I realized that there had been nothing very impressive about their conversation. No doubt these same ladies, who talked so casually to Lord Korechika, had been just as embarrassed as I when they first came into waiting, but had little by little become used to Court society until their shyness had naturally disappeared.

The Empress spoke to me for a while and then asked, 'Are you really fond of me?' 'But Your Majesty,' I replied, 'how could I possibly not be fond of you?' Just then someone sneezed loudly in the Table Room. 'Oh dear!' said the Empress. 'So you're telling a lie.[424] Well, so be it.' And she retired into the back of the room.

To think that Her Majesty believed I was lying! If I had said that I was *fairly* fond of her, that would have been untrue. The real liar, I thought, was the sneezer's nose. Who could have done such a terrible thing? I dislike sneezes at the best of times, and whenever I feel like sneezing myself I deliberately smother it. All the more hateful was it that someone should have sneezed at this moment. But I was still far too inexperienced to say anything that might have repaired the damage: and, since the day was dawning, I retired to my room. As soon as I arrived, a servant brought me an elegant-looking letter, written on fine, smooth paper of light green. 'This is what Her Majesty feels,' I read.

How, if there were no God Tadasu in the sky,
And none to judge what is the truth and what a lie,
How should I know which words were falsely said?

My emotions were a jumble of delight and dismay, and once again I wished I could find out who had sneezed on the previous night. 'Please give Her Majesty the following reply,' I said, 'and help me to make up for the harm that has been done.

"A simple sneeze might give the lie
To one whose love is small,
But sad indeed that she who truly loves,
Should suffer from so slight a thing![425]

The curse of God Shiki[426] is of course very terrible."'
Even after I had sent my reply I still felt most unhappy and wondered why someone should have had to sneeze at such an inopportune moment.

117. *People Who Look Pleased with Themselves*

A man who sneezes before anyone else on the morning of New Year's Day.[427]

A man who has obtained an appointment as Chamberlain for his dear son at a time when the competition is very keen.

A man who has received the governorship of one of the first-class provinces that is being offered in the current period of official appointments. 'What a splendid appointment!' people say and congratulate him warmly, to which he smugly replies, 'How so? I've been ruined.'

A young man who has been chosen out of several candidates to be adopted as son-in-law.

191

An exorcist who has succeeded in bringing a very stubborn spirit under control.

A player in a game of hidden rhymes who quickly discovers the concealed character.[428]

During a small-bow contest one of the archers coughs. The man who is about to shoot is distracted by the sound and becomes nervous; but he manages to control himself and his arrow shoots off with a loud twang, hitting the target. How pleased he looks with himself!

In a game of *go* a greedy player switches his attention to a different part of the board, not quite realizing what a large number of stones he is likely to capture there.[429] His opponent is unable to keep his 'eyes' in the new sector, and the greedy player manages to win several stones. Oh, how pleased he looks! He laughs proudly, feeling happier about this windfall than he would about an ordinary gain.

At long last a man has received the governorship for which he has been waiting. He looks radiantly happy. In the past everyone treated him with rudeness and disdain; but, painful as it was, he bore it all patiently, realizing that he had no choice. Now even his superiors respect the man and play up to him with remarks like, 'I am entirely at Your Excellency's service.' He is attended by women and surrounded by elegant furnishings and clothing that he has never known before.[430] Seeing all this, one wonders whether he can really be the same man whom even simple servants used to scorn. Then this fortunate governor is appointed Middle Captain in the Inner Palace Guards. Oh, what a triumphant look he has on his face! To be a captain of the Guards seems far grander to him than it would to a young nobleman who received the same appointment.[431]

High office is, after all, a most splendid thing. A man who holds the Fifth Rank or who serves as Gentleman-in-Waiting is liable to be despised; but when this same man becomes a Major Counsellor, Great Minister, or the like, one is overawed by him and feels that nothing in the world could be as impressive. Of course even a provincial governor has a position that should impress one; for after serving in several provinces, he may be appointed Senior Assistant Governor-General and promoted to the Fourth Rank, and when this happens the High Court Nobles themselves appear to regard him with respect.

After all, women really have the worse time of it. There are, to be sure, cases where the nurse of an Emperor is appointed Assistant Attendant or given the Third Rank and thus acquires great dignity. Yet it does her little good since she is already an old woman. Besides, how many women ever attain such honours? Those who are reasonably well born consider themselves lucky if they can marry a governor and go down to the provinces. Of course it does sometimes happen that the daughter of a commoner becomes the principal consort of a High Court Noble and that the daughter of a High Court Noble becomes an Empress.[432] Yet even this is not as splendid as when a man rises by means of promotions. How pleased such a man looks with himself!

Who pays any attention to a Palace Chaplain when he walks by?[433] Though he may recite the scriptures in a most impressive manner and may even be quite good-looking, women despise a low-ranking priest, which is very sad for him. Yet, when this same man becomes a Bishop or Archbishop, people are overwhelmed with awe and respect, and everyone is convinced that the Buddha himself has appeared among them.

118. *Winds*

A stormy wind. At dawn, when one is lying in bed with the lattices and panelled doors wide open, the wind suddenly blows into the room and stings one's face – most delightful.

A cold, wintry wind.

In the Third Month the moist, gentle wind that blows in the evenings moves me greatly.

Also moving is the cool, rainy wind in the Eighth and Ninth Months. Streaks of rain are blown violently from the side, and I enjoy watching people cover their stiff robes of unlined silk with the padded coats that they put away after the summer rains.[434] In this season they would like to dispense even with their unlined robes, which have become quite sweltering; instead they are caught off guard by the sudden change in weather and have to dress still more warmly than before.

Towards the end of the Ninth Month and the beginning of the Tenth the sky is clouded over, there is a strong wind, and the yellow leaves fall gently to the ground, especially from the cherry trees and the elms. All this produces a most pleasant sense of melancholy. In the Tenth Month I love gardens that are full of trees.

119. *On the Day after a Fierce Autumn Wind*

On the day after a fierce autumn wind everything moves one deeply. The garden is in a pitiful state with all the bamboo and lattice fence knocked over and lying next to each other on the ground. It is bad enough if the branches of one of the great trees have been broken by the wind; but it is a really painful surprise to find that the tree itself has fallen down and is now lying flat over the bush-clover and the valerians. As one sits in one's room looking out, the wind, as though on purpose, gently blows the leaves one by one through the chinks of the lattice-window, and one finds it hard to believe that this is the same wind which yesterday raged so violently.

On one such morning I caught sight of a woman creeping out from the main hall and emerging a few feet on to the veranda. I could see that she was a natural beauty. Over a dress of dull purple she wore an unlined robe of tawny cloth and a formal robe of some light material. The noise of the wind must have kept her awake during the night and she had just got up after sleeping late. Now she knelt on the veranda and looked into her mirror. With her long hair being blown about and gently puffed up by the wind, she was a truly splendid sight. As she gazed at the scene of desolation in the garden, a girl of about seventeen – not a small girl, but still not big enough to be called grown-up – joined her on the veranda. She wore a night-dress of light violet and over that a faded blue robe of stiff silk, which was badly coming apart at the seams and wet from the rain. Her hair, which was cut evenly at the ends like miscanthus in a field, reached all the way down to her feet, falling on to the veranda beyond the bottom of her robe. Looking at her from the side, I could make out the scarlet of her trouser-skirt, the only bright touch in her costume.

In the garden a group of maids and young girls were collecting the flowers and plants that the wind had torn up by the roots and were propping up some that were less damaged. Several women were gathered in front of me by the blind, and I enjoyed seeing how envious they looked as they watched the young people outside and wished that they might join them.

120. *Wind Instruments*

I love the sound of the flute: it is beautiful when one hears it gradually approaching from the distance, and also when it is played near by and then moves far away until it becomes very faint.

There is nothing so charming as a man who always carries a flute when he goes out on horseback or on foot. Though he keeps the flute tucked in his robe and one cannot actually see it, one enjoys knowing it is there.

I particularly like hearing familiar tunes played on a flute. It is also very pleasant at dawn to find that a flute had been left next to one's pillow by a gentleman who has been visiting one; presently he sends a messenger to fetch the instrument and, when one gives it to him carefully wrapped up, it looks like an elegant next-morning letter.

A thirteen-pipe flute is delightful when one hears it in a carriage on a bright, moonlit night. True, it is bulky and rather awkward to play – and what a face people make when they blow it![435] But they can look ungraceful with ordinary flutes also.

The flageolet is a very shrill instrument, the autumn insect it most resembles being the long cricket. It makes a terrible noise, especially when it is played badly, and it is not something one wants to hear near by. I remember one of the Special Festivals at Kamo, when the musicians had not yet come into His Majesty's presence. One could hear the sound of their flutes from behind the trees, and I was just thinking how delightful it was when suddenly the flageolets joined in. They became shriller and shriller, until all the ladies, even those who were most beautifully groomed, felt their hair standing on end.[436] Then the procession came before the Emperor with all the string and wind instruments playing in splendid unison.

121. *Things Worth Seeing*

The Chancellor's pilgrimage to Kamo.

The Special Festival at Kamo. On one cold, overcast day the snow began to come down in scattered flakes, falling on the blue and white robes of the people in the procession and on the flowers that they wore in their head-dress.[437] I found the sight immensely delightful. The sheaths of the dancers' swords shone magnificently, and the cords of their jackets, which hung over the sheaths, were so bright that they might have been polished. Beneath the printed material of their trouser-skirts I could see the brilliant, glossy silk of their under-robes, and for a moment I wondered whether they were made of ice. I was relishing the beauty of the procession when the envoys appeared.[438] They were certainly a most undistinguished lot, having been chosen from among provincial governors and the like, common-looking men not worth one's attention. Yet so long as their faces were hidden by the sprays of wistaria in their head-dress, it was not too unpleasant to see them go by. While we were still watching the dancers, the musicians appeared, wearing willow-

coloured robes and yellow roses in their head-dress. They were
insignificant men of low rank, but it was delightful to hear them
chanting,

> The princess pines that grow outside
> All-powerful Kamo Shrine –[439]

and beating the measure very loudly with their fans.

◌

What can compare with an Imperial Progress? When the
Emperor passes in his palanquin, he is as impressive as a God
and I forget that my work in the Palace constantly brings me into
his presence. Not only His Majesty himself, but even people like
Ladies of the Escort, who usually are of no importance, overawe
me when I see them in an Imperial Progress. I particularly enjoy
watching the Assistant Directors of the Bureau of Imperial
Attendants[440] as they walk past holding the cords of the Imperial palanquin, and also the Captains of the Inner Palace
Guards, who serve as its escorts.

The Return Procession of the High Priestess from Kamo is a
magnificent sight. I recall one year when everything was especially beautiful. On the day of the Festival itself we had stopped our
carriage on that splendidly wide road, the First Avenue, and had
sat there for a long time, hiding our faces behind our fans and
waiting for the procession to arrive. A hot sun shone through the
carriage blinds, dazzling us and making us perspire in a most unsightly fashion. On the following day we set out very early to see
the High Priestess's procession. Though the sun had risen,
the sky was overcast. As we reached the gates of Urin and
Chisoku Temples, we noticed a number of carriages decorated
with branches of faded hollyhock and maple. We could hear a
loud chorus of *hototogisu*. This was the bird whose song so
fascinated me that I would lie awake at night waiting for it.[441]
I was just thinking how delightful it was that I could now hear
great numbers of these birds without making the slightest effort
when an *uguisu* joined in with his rather croaky voice. He

197

sounded as if he were trying to imitate the beautiful song of the *hototogisu*, and I found this unpleasant though at the same time rather amusing.

While we sat in our carriage waiting impatiently for the procession, we saw a group of men in red coming from the Upper Shrine. 'What's happening? Is the procession on its way?' we asked them; but they replied that they had no idea and continued down the road, carrying the High Priestess's empty palanquins.[442] It impressed me deeply that the High Priestess herself had travelled in one of these palanquins; but I was rather disturbed at the thought that low fellows like these could have come close to her sacred presence.

Though we had been told that there might be a long wait, the High Priestess and her retinue soon arrived from the Upper Shrine. First we could see the fans come into sight, then the yellow-green robes of the gentlemen from the Emperor's Private Office. It was a splendid sight. The men wore their under-robes in such a way that the white material stood out against the yellowish-green of their outer robes, and I was reminded so much of white *u no hana* blossoms in a green hedge that I almost expected to find a *hototogisu* lurking there.

On the previous day I had noticed several of these young noblemen crowded together in a carriage. They had taken down the blinds, and I could see that they were messily dressed in hunting costumes and violet cloaks; altogether they had made a very bizarre impression. Today these same young men were beautifully attired in full Court costume and ready to take part in the High Priestess's banquet, to which they had been invited as extra guests.[443] They looked extremely demure as one by one they passed, each in his own carriage; and the young Palace pages who followed were also very attractive.

After the Procession had gone, things got out of hand. Everyone wanted to be the first to leave and there was a great crush of carriages, which I found rather frightening. I stuck my fan out of the window to summon my attendants. 'Don't be in such a hurry,' I scolded them. 'Go slowly.' Since they paid not the

198

slightest attention and continued to push ahead, I became very flustered and ordered them to pull up the carriage in a place where the road was a little wider. The men were very impatient and it annoyed them to have to stop.

I enjoyed watching the carriages as they hurried along the road, each one trying to forge ahead of another. I allowed them all to get a good start before letting my men continue. It was a delightful road, rather like the paths that lead up to mountain villages. The thick hedges on both sides looked rough and shaggy; they were covered with *u no hana*, but the flowers had not yet come into bloom. I told my men to break off some of the branches and stuck them here and there in the carriage; they looked very pretty, all the more so since the decorations of maple and holly-hock had unfortunately begun to fade.

When I had glanced down the road from the distance, it had seemed impossible that all the carriages would get through, but now as we gradually advanced I was pleased to see it was not as crowded as I had thought. I noticed that the carriage of one man – I have no idea who he can have been – was following close behind mine, and I decided that this was much more pleasant than being alone on the road. When we came to a fork where our paths separated, he leaned out and recited the line, 'That scatter on the peak',[444] which I found delightful.

122. *In the Fifth Month*

In the Fifth Month I love going up to a mountain village. When one passes a marsh on the way, a thick covering of weeds hides the water and it seems like a stretch of green grass; but as the escort walk across these patches, the water spurts up under their feet though it is quite shallow. The water is incredibly clear and looks very pretty as it gushes forth.

Where the road runs between hedges, a branch will sometimes thrust its way into the carriage. One snatches at it quickly, hoping to break it off; alas, it always slips out of one's hand.

199

Sometimes one's carriage will pass over a branch of sage-brush, which then gets caught in the wheel and is lifted up at each turn, letting the passengers breathe its delicious scent.

123. *During the Hot Months*

During the hot months it is a great delight to sit on the veranda, enjoying the cool of the evening and observing how the outlines of objects gradually become blurred. At such a moment I particularly enjoy the sight of a gentleman's carriage, preceded by outriders clearing the way. Sometimes a couple of commoners will pass in a carriage with the rear blinds slightly raised. As the oxen trot along, one has a pleasant sense of freshness. It is still more delightful when the sound of a lute or flute comes from inside the carriage, and one feels sorry when it disappears in the distance. Occasionally one catches a whiff of the oxen's leather cruppers; it is a strange, unfamiliar smell, but, absurd as it may seem, I find something rather pleasant about it.

On a very dark night it is delightful when the aroma of smoke from the pine-torches at the head of a procession is wafted through the air and pervades the carriage in which one is travelling.

124. *One Has Carefully Scented a Robe*

One has carefully scented a robe and then forgotten about it for several days.[445] When finally one comes to wear it, the aroma is even more delicious than on freshly scented clothes.

125. *When Crossing a River*

When crossing a river in bright moonlight, I love to see the water scatter in showers of crystal under the oxen's feet.

126. *Things That Should Be Large*

Priests. Fruit. Houses. Provision bags. Inksticks for inkstones.
Men's eyes: when they are too narrow, they look feminine.[446]
On the other hand, if they were as large as metal bowls, I should
find them rather frightening.
Round braziers. Winter cherries.[447] Pine trees. The petals of
yellow roses.
Horses as well as oxen should be large.

127. *Things That Should Be Short*

A piece of thread when one wants to sew something in a
hurry.
A lamp stand.
The hair of a woman of the lower classes should be neat and
short.
The speech of a young girl.

128. *Nothing Annoys Me So Much*

Nothing annoys me so much as someone who arrives at a
ceremony in a shabby, poorly decorated carriage. It is not so bad
if the person has come to hear a sermon with the aim of clearing
himself of sin; but even then a very inelegant carriage is bound
to make a bad effect.
At the Kamo Festival, of course, such negligence is quite in-
excusable. Yet there are people who actually attend the ceremony
in carriages where plain white robes have been hung up instead
of the proper blinds. Even when one has carefully equipped one's
carriage in honour of the great day, making sure that the blinds
and other fittings are exactly right, and has set out for the ceremony confident that one presents a fairly elegant appearance

to the world, it is most unpleasant to see a near-by carriage that is superior to one's own, and one wonders why it had to appear at just that place. How much more galling must it be for someone who is travelling in a really shabby carriage!

At the time of the Festival, when the carriages of the young noblemen go up and down the avenue, it really makes one's heart pound with excitement if one of them pushes its way between the others and stops close to one's own. I remember one year when, wishing to be sure of a good view, I hurried my servants and set out early in the morning. As a result I had to wait a long time for the procession to arrive. The suffocating heat added to my impatience, and I moved about restlessly in my carriage. I was just standing up to stretch myself when I saw a group of about eight carriages moving quickly along the avenue, one directly behind the other. They came from the direction of the High Priestess's palace and the passengers were senior courtiers, Assistant Officials of the Emperor's Private Office, Controllers, Minor Counsellors, and other gentlemen who were to attend the High Priestess's banquet as extra guests. It was a delightful surprise to find that things had already started.

The senior courtiers ordered that dishes of watered rice be served to some of the more distinguished outriders at the head of the procession. Servants came down to the galleries, and held the horses by the bridles. Then those of the outriders whose fathers were important men partook of the watered rice. It was a pleasant scene, but I felt rather sorry for the lesser riders.

When the High Priestess's palanquin was carried along the avenue, I enjoyed seeing how all the people pulled down the blinds of their carriages, hastily raising them as soon as the High Priestess had passed.

Now a carriage came and stood directly in front of mine. I complained bitterly, but the attendants paid no attention and simply said, 'Why shouldn't we stay here?' Not knowing how to argue with such men, I sent a message to the owner of the carriage. It was really rather an amusing situation.[448]

Although the carriages were already squeezed together tightly new ones kept arriving. The passengers were people of high rank, accompanied by numerous attendants who travelled in carriages behind them. I was wondering how they could possibly find room when I saw the outriders leap off their horses and briskly force the other carriages to move back. I was most impressed by the way in which they managed to get their masters' carriages, and then those of the attendants, into the spaces that had been cleared; but it was rather pathetic to observe the owners of the simple carriages as they harnessed their oxen and jogged along, looking for some new place. The grander carriages, of course, could not be treated in such a cavalier fashion.

Though there were many splendid carriages in the crowd, I also noticed quite a few that had an ugly, rustic look and whose humble occupants were forever summoning their servants and giving them their babies to hold.

129. *There Was a Man in the Corridor*

'There was a man in the corridor early this morning who had no business to be here,' I heard one of the ladies-in-waiting say. 'His servant was holding an umbrella over him when he left.' I was listening to her story with interest when suddenly I realized that she was talking about a visitor of mine. He was admittedly a gentleman of rather low rank, but he was perfectly acceptable and there was no reason why I should not receive him. I was still feeling rather put out when a letter came from Her Majesty, with a message that I was to reply at once. Opening it in great excitement, I found a drawing of a large umbrella. One could see nothing of the person underneath except the fingers round the handle. Below were written the words, 'Since dawn first shed its light over Mount Mikasa's peak.'[449]

Knowing that the Empress attached the greatest importance to our behaviour even in very trivial affairs, I had been hoping that no one would tell her about this somewhat embarrassing and disagreeable incident. Now I realized that she had in fact heard the rumour. I was dismayed, yet at the same time amused, and, taking another piece of paper, I drew a picture of rain falling heavily and wrote underneath,

> My name, though innocent of rain,
> Has long been spattered by unfounded tales.

'So it must all be a matter of wet clothes,' I added and sent the message to the Empress, who laughingly told the story to Lady Ukon and some of the other gentlewomen.

130. When the Empress Was Staying in the Third Ward

When the Empress was staying in the Third Ward, a palanquin arrived full of irises for the Festival of the Fifth Day and Her Majesty was presented with herbal balls from the Palace. The Mistress of the Robes and a few of the younger ladies prepared special balls, which they attached to the clothing of the Princess Imperial and of the little Prince.[450] Then other very pretty herbal balls arrived from other palaces. Someone also brought a green-wheat cake;[451] I presented it to Her Majesty on the elegant lid of an inkstone on which I had first spread a sheet of thin green paper carrying the words, 'This has come from across the fence.'[452] The Empress tore off a piece of the paper and wrote the following splendid poem:

> Even on this festive day,
> When all are seeking butterflies and flowers,
> You and you alone can see
> What feelings hide within my heart.

131. Captain Narinobu Has an Amazing Memory

Captain Narinobu has an amazing memory for voices. When several people are conversing, it is usually impossible to tell who

204

is who unless one is very familiar with their manner of speaking. Men in particular have difficulty in recognizing people from their voices or their looks, and it is amazing how Narinobu can identify people even when they are speaking in hushed tones.

132. *I Have Never Come across Anyone with Such Keen Ears*

I have never come across anyone with such keen ears as Masamitsu, the Minister of the Treasury.[453] I believe he could hear the sound of a mosquito's eyelash falling on the floor.

Once during my stay in the west wing of the Empress's Office, Masamitsu was in the room when I was having a talk with the new Captain of the Inner Palace Guards (the Great Minister's adopted son). 'What do you think about paintings on fans?' murmured someone who was standing near the Captain. 'Don't answer,' I whispered. 'That man over there will soon be leaving. Wait until he has gone.' My voice was so soft that the Captain himself could not hear me. 'What's that? What's that?' he said, straining his ears. Masamitsu, however, clapped his hands and cried, 'Shocking! If you speak about me like that, Madam, I shall stay here all day long.' Both the Captain and I were astounded to realize that Masamitsu had heard what I said.

133. *I Hate Seeing a Dusty, Dirty-Looking Inkstone*

I hate seeing a dusty, dirty-looking inkstone with an inkstick that has been used in a slovenly way so that it is rubbed down on only one side. It also makes an unpleasant impression if someone puts a cap on a writing-brush whose head has become large and shaggy.

One can judge a woman's nature by looking at her mirror, her inkstone, or any other belongings of this kind. Nothing gives

such a neglected impression as an inlaid inkstone-case when dust
has collected in cracks at the corners.

It is even more important for a man to keep his writing-table
in perfect order. If his inkstone-case is not made in several tiers,
it should have two fitted boxes, and its gold lacquer design should
be attractive without looking contrived; his inkstick, brush, and
other equipment should all be chosen to attract attention.

Some people seem to think that the actual appearance of their
writing utensils is unimportant. They have a box of plain black
lacquer with a cracked lid;[454] into this they put a tiled inkstone,
which is broken on one side and whose every crack is so embedded with dust that one feels that a lifetime would not be long
enough to clean it properly. They rub a little ink on the stone,
barely blackening the surface, and pour water over it all out of a
celadon jug, whose tortoise-shaped spout is broken so that there
is only a gaping neck. Yet they are quite content to let people see
this unsightly collection of objects.

When one takes another person's inkstone to practise some
calligraphy or write a letter, it is very unpleasant if the owner
says, 'Would you mind not using that brush?' One feels awkward if one puts it down at once; yet to continue writing is sheer
impudence. Since people know my views on this matter, they
often come to borrow my brush, and I never raise any objection.
Sometimes it will be a woman who has a poor hand yet who
always wants to be writing something. She picks up a brush
which one has used until it has acquired just the right hardness,
and very awkwardly she soaks it in ink. 'Is there anything inside
this chest?' she asks as she starts scribbling something on the lid.
Then she flings one's brush down on its side so that the head is
immersed in the ink. Her behaviour is hateful, yet how can one
bring oneself to tell her so?

When one is sitting in front of someone who is writing, it is
very unpleasant to be told, 'Oh, how dark it is! Please get out
of my light.' I also find it painful to be scolded by someone when
I have been peeping at his calligraphy. This sort of thing does
not happen with a man one loves.

134. *Letters are Commonplace*

Letters are commonplace enough, yet what splendid things they are! When someone is in a distant province and one is worried about him, and then a letter suddenly arrives, one feels as though one were seeing him face to face. Again, it is a great comfort to have expressed one's feelings in a letter even though one knows it cannot yet have arrived. If letters did not exist, what dark depressions would come over one! When one has been worrying about something and wants to tell a certain person about it, what a relief it is to put it all down in a letter! Still greater is one's joy when a reply arrives. At that moment a letter really seems like an elixir of life.

135. *Shrines*

Furu, Ikuta, Tatsuta, Hanafuchi, and Mikuri. The sacred shrine of the cryptomeria.[455] It is interesting that this tree should be a sign of virtue.

The deity of Koto no Mama deserves the trust that people put in him. I enjoy knowing that this is the shrine 'where every prayer's been glibly answered by the God'.[456]

The deity of Aridōshi. It was past his shrine that Tsurayuki was riding when his horse was taken ill and he was told that this was due to the anger of the God; he then dedicated a poem to the God whereupon his horse was cured – a delightful incident.[457]

I wonder whether the usual explanation for the name *Aridōshi* is correct.[458] Long ago there was an Emperor who liked only young people and who ordered that everyone over forty should be put to death. The older people therefore went and hid in remote provinces, leaving the capital to their juniors. Now there was a Captain of the Guards whose parents were both almost seventy. They were absolutely terrified, realizing that, if even people of forty were proscribed, their own position was precarious indeed. The Captain, however, a most devoted son, who could not live without seeing his parents at least once a day, refused to let them go off to some distant hiding-place. Instead he spent night after night secretly digging a hole under his house and, when it was finished, he made it into a room where he installed his parents and went to visit them frequently, informing the Imperial authorities and everyone else that they had disappeared.

(Why should His Majesty have decided on this policy? After all, he had no need to concern himself with people who lived quietly at home and minded their own business.)

Since his son was a Captain, I imagine that the father was a High Court Noble or something of the sort. In any case he was a very clever, knowing old gentleman, and the Captain, despite his youth, was also able and intelligent, so that His Majesty regarded him as the outstanding young man of the day.

At this time the Emperor of China was planning to capture our country by tricking His Majesty, and for this purpose he was constantly sending puzzles to test His Majesty's ability. On one occasion he sent a round, glossy, beautifully planed log about two feet long and asked, 'Which is the base and which is the top?'[459] Since there was absolutely no way of telling, His Majesty was in great distress – so much so that the young Captain felt sorry for him and told his father what had happened. 'All you need do,' said the old man, 'is to go to a rapid river, hold the log straight up, and throw it sideways into the water. It will then turn round by itself and the end that faces downstream will be the top. Mark the wood accordingly and return it to the Chinese Emperor.' The Captain went to the Palace and, pretending to have thought of a plan by himself, told His Majesty that he would try to solve the puzzle. Accompanied by a group of people he proceeded to a river, threw in the log, and made a mark on the end that faced downstream. The log was then sent back and turned out to be correctly marked.

On another occasion the Chinese Emperor sent a pair of

208

identical snakes, each about two feet in length, and the test was to tell which was male and which female. Since no one had the faintest idea, the Captain again consulted his father, who told him to place the snakes next to each other and to hold a long straight twig near their tails. 'The one that moves its tail,' he said, 'will be the female.' The son followed this advice and, as predicted, one of the snakes remained still while the other one moved; the Captain marked them accordingly and sent them back to China.

A long time afterwards the Chinese Emperor dispatched to His Majesty a small jewel with seven curves and a passage that ran right through all the curves and was open at both ends. 'Please pass a thread through the jewel,' he wrote. 'This is something that everyone in our country knows how to do.' Outstanding craftsmen were summoned, but their skill was of no avail; everyone, from the High Court Nobles down, admitted defeat. Once more the Captain went to his father. 'You must capture two large ants,' said the old man. 'Tie narrow threads round their middles and attach slightly thicker threads to the ends. Then smear some honey opposite one of the openings and place the ants at the opposite end.' The Captain told this to His Majesty and two ants were duly put next to the opening. As soon as they smelt the honey, they started crawling through the passage and rapidly emerged at the other end. The threaded jewel was then returned to China, where it was decided that, after all, the inhabitants of Japan were clever people and there was no point in sending them any more puzzles.

Greatly impressed by the Captain's achievement, His Majesty asked what he could do for him and what rank he desired. 'I want no rank or office at all,' declared the young man. 'Grant only that all the old people who have gone and hidden themselves be searched out and told that they may safely return to the capital.' 'That is a simple matter,' said the Emperor. The old people were delighted when they heard the news and the Captain was appointed Great Minister. Evidently the Captain's father became a God; for it is said that the deity of Aridōshi appeared in a dream one night to someone who had come on a pilgrimage and that he recited the following poem:

Who is there who does not know
That the God of Aridōshi was so named
From the passage of the ants through a seven-curved jewel?[460]

136. Things That Fall from the Sky

Snow. Hail. I do not like sleet, but when it is mixed with pure white snow it is very pretty.

Snow looks wonderful when it has fallen on a roof of cypress bark.

When snow begins to melt a little, or when only a small amount has fallen, it enters into all the cracks between the bricks, so that the roof is black in some places, pure white in others – most attractive.

I like drizzle and hail when they come down on a shingle roof. I also like frost on a shingle roof or in a garden.

137. Clouds

I love white, purple, and black clouds, and rain clouds when they are driven by the wind. It is charming at dawn to see the dark clouds gradually turn white. I believe this has been described in a Chinese poem that says something about 'the tints that leave at dawn'.[461]

It is moving to see a thin wisp of cloud across a very bright moon.

138. People Who Have Changed as much as if They had been Reborn

Someone who has been serving as a mere maid-of-honour is appointed to be the nurse of an Imperial Prince. She no longer bothers with a Chinese jacket or a formal skirt, and, weaving a simple white dress, she lies down next to the young prince and stays with him inside his curtain-dais. Summoning her former colleagues, she sends them to her room with messages or gives them letters to deliver. Words do not suffice to describe her behaviour.

What a splendid thing it is for a Subordinate Official[462] in the Emperor's Private Office when he is promoted to the rank of Chamberlain! One cannot believe that he is the same man who last year in the Eleventh Month had to carry a zither during the Special Festival. When one sees him walking along in the company of young noblemen, one really wonders where he can have sprung from. This applies also to men who have been given the rank of Chamberlain after serving in other offices, but in their case the change is not quite so impressive.

139. One Day, When the Snow Lay Thick on the Ground

One day, when the snow lay thick on the ground and was still coming down heavily, I saw some gentlemen of the Fourth and Fifth Ranks who had a fresh complexion and a pleasant, youthful look. Their beautifully coloured Court robes, which they wore over their night-watch costumes, were tucked up at the bottom and showed the marks of their leather belts.[463] Their dark purple trousers stood out beautifully against the white snow. I could also see their under-jackets, some of scarlet, others dyed a beautiful rose-yellow. The men had opened their umbrellas, but since it was very windy the snow came at them from the side

and they bent forward slightly as they walked. The sparkling
white snow covered them all the way to the tips of their lacquered
leather shoes or short clogs – a magnificent sight.

140. *Towards the End of the Eighth Month*

Towards the end of the Eighth Month I was on my way to the
temple at Uzemasa[464] when I saw a crowd of peasants working
in the fields. The ears of rice had started to grow out and the men
were busily reaping the plants. True indeed were the poet's
words when he wrote,

> They were pulling out the sprouts.
> Now already autumn's stolen up.[465]

Yes, it was only the other day that I had seen them planting the
fields as I set out on a pilgrimage for Kamo, and it was already
time for the harvest.

On this occasion all the workers were men. Bending down, they
pulled out the plants, seized them by their green roots with one
hand, and cut off the ears with a knife or something of the sort[466]
held in their other hand. They seemed to work with such ease
that I really felt like including their skill among 'impressive
things'. How on earth did they manage it? I was fascinated to
observe how they put all the plants together in bundles with the
bright red ears on top.

The huts inhabited by these peasants looked most peculiar.

141. *Shortly after the Twentieth of the Ninth Month*

Shortly after the twentieth of the Ninth Month I went on a
pilgrimage to Hase Temple and spent the night in a very simple
lodging. Being exhausted, I fell at once into a sound sleep.

When I woke up late at night, the moonlight was pouring in
through the window and shining on the bed-clothes of all the

other people in the room. Its clear white brilliance moved me greatly. It is on such occasions that people write poems.

142. *A Family Has Finally Arranged the Marriage*

A family has finally arranged the marriage of their daughter; but the new son-in-law stops visiting his wife. Then one day he runs into his father-in-law in a public place. Surely the young man cannot help feeling rather sorry for his wife and her family.[467]

A certain young man, who had been adopted as son-in-law by a very powerful family, ended by neglecting his wife for months at a time. The wife's nurse and others called ill luck down on his head, and all the household spoke strongly against him. In the First Month of the following year, however, he was appointed Chamberlain. 'This is really going to surprise everyone,' people said. 'How on earth could he get the promotion when he is on such bad terms with his wife's family?' Reports of this gossip must certainly have reached his ears.

In the Sixth Month the young Chamberlain, elegantly attired in over-trousers of silk damask, a glossy white under-robe lined with dark red, and a short-sleeved black jacket, was among the crowd of people who attended a recitation of the Eight Lessons. It so happened that his carriage was standing close to that of the girl whom he had forsaken – so close, in fact, that he could have hung the cord of his jacket over the kite's tail[468] of her carriage. 'I wonder how she will take it,' said one of the ladies in the girl's suite, and they all felt very sorry for her. Yet the young man evidently did not care in the slightest about his wife's pathetic situation or about what people were thinking; for afterwards it was reported that he had sat in his carriage with an expression of complete indifference.

143. *To Feel That One is Disliked by Others*

To feel that one is disliked by others is surely one of the saddest things in the world, and no one, however foolish, could wish such a thing on himself. Yet everywhere, whether it be in the Palace or at home in the bosom of the family, there are some people who are naturally liked and others who are not.

Not only among people of good birth, where it goes without saying, but even among commoners, children who are adored by their parents naturally attract the attention of outsiders, and everyone makes a great fuss over them. If they are attractive children, it is only natural that their parents should dote on them. How could it be otherwise? But, if the children have nothing particular to recommend them, one can only assume that such devotion comes merely from the fact of being parents.

I imagine that there can be nothing so delightful as to be loved by everyone – one's parents, one's master, and all the people with whom one is on close terms.

144. *Men Really Have Strange Emotions*

Men really have strange emotions and behave in the most bizarre ways. Sometimes a man will leave a very pretty woman to marry an ugly one. Surely a gentleman who frequents the Palace should choose as his love the prettiest girl of good family he can find. Though she may be of such high standing that he cannot hope to make her his wife, he should, if he is really impressed by the girl, languish for her unto death.

Sometimes, too, a man will become so fascinated by a girl of whom he has heard favourable reports that he will do everything in his power to marry her even though they have never even met.

I do not understand how a man can possibly love a girl whom other people, even those of her own sex, find ugly.[469]

I remember a certain woman who was both attractive and good-natured and who furthermore had excellent hand-writing. Yet when she sent a beautifully written poem to the man of her choice, he replied with some pretentious jottings and did not even bother to visit her. She wept endearingly, but he was indifferent and went to see another woman instead. Everyone, even people who were not directly concerned, felt indignant about this callous behaviour, and the woman's family was much grieved. The man himself, however, showed not the slightest pity.

145. *Sympathy is the Most Splendid of All Qualities*

Sympathy is the most splendid of all qualities. This is especially true when it is found in men, but it also applies to women. Compassionate remarks, of the type 'How sad for you!' to someone who has suffered a misfortune or 'I can imagine what he must be feeling' about a man who has had some sorrow, are bound to give pleasure, however casual and perfunctory they may be. If one's remark is addressed to someone else and repeated to the sufferer, it is even more effective than if one makes it directly. The unhappy person will never forget one's kindness and will be anxious to let one know how it has moved him.

If it is someone who is close to one and who expects sympathetic inquiries, he will not be especially pleased, since he is merely receiving his due; but a friendly remark passed on to less intimate people is certain to give pleasure. This all sounds simple enough, yet hardly anyone seems to bother. Altogether it seems as if men and women with good heads rarely have good hearts. Yet I suppose there must be some who are both clever and kind.

146. *It is Absurd of People to Get Angry*

It is absurd of people to get angry because one has gossiped about them. How can anyone be so simple as to believe that he is free to find fault with others while his own foibles are passed over in silence? Yet when someone hears that he has been discussed unfavourably he is always outraged, and this I find most unattractive.

If I am really close to someone, I realize that it would be hurting to speak badly about him and when the opportunity for gossip arises I hold my peace. In all other cases, however, I freely speak my mind and make everyone laugh.

147. *Features That I Particularly Like*

Features that I particularly like in someone's face continue to give a thrill of delight however often I see the person. With pictures it is different. If I look at them too often, they cease to attract me; indeed, I never so much as glance at the beautiful paintings on the screen that stands near my usual seat.

There is something really fascinating about beautiful faces. Though an object such as a vase or a fan may be ugly in general, there is always one particular part that one can gaze at with pleasure. One would expect this to apply to faces also; but, alas, there is nothing to recommend an ugly face.

148. *Pleasing Things*

Finding a large number of tales that one has not read before. Or acquiring the second volume of a tale whose first volume one has enjoyed. But often it is a disappointment.

Someone has torn up a letter and thrown it away. Picking up the pieces, one finds that many of them can be fitted together.

One has had an upsetting dream and wonders what it can mean. In great anxiety one consults a dream-interpreter, who informs one that it has no special significance.

A person of quality is holding forth about something in the past or about a recent event that is being widely discussed.

Several people are gathered round him, but it is oneself that he keeps looking at as he talks.

A person who is very dear to one has fallen ill. One is miserably worried about him even if he lives in the capital and far more so if he is in some remote part of the country. What a pleasure to be told that he has recovered!

I am most pleased when I hear someone I love being praised or being mentioned approvingly by an important person.

A poem that someone has composed for a special occasion or written to another person in reply is widely praised and copied by people in their notebooks. Though this is something that has never yet happened to me, I can imagine how pleasing it must be.

A person with whom one is not especially intimate refers to an old poem or story that is unfamiliar. Then one hears it being mentioned by someone else and one has the pleasure of recognizing it. Still later, when one comes across it in a book, one thinks, 'Ah, this is it!' and feels delighted with the person who first brought it up.

I feel very pleased when I have acquired some Michinoku paper, or some white, decorated paper, or even plain paper if it is nice and white.

A person in whose company one feels awkward asks one to supply the opening or closing line of a poem. If one happens to recall it, one is very pleased. Yet often on such occasions one completely forgets something that one would normally know.

I look for an object that I need at once, and I find it. Or again, there is a book that I must see immediately; I turn everything upside down, and there it is. What a joy!

When one is competing in an object match[470] (it does not matter what kind), how can one help being pleased at winning?

I greatly enjoy taking in someone who is pleased with himself and who has a self-confident look, especially if he is a man. It is amusing to observe him as he alertly waits for my next repartee; but it is also interesting if he tries to put me off my guard by adopting an air of calm indifference as if there were not a thought in his head.

I realize that it is very sinful of me, but I cannot help being pleased when someone I dislike has a bad experience.

It is a great pleasure when the ornamental comb that one has ordered turns out to be pretty.

I am more pleased when something nice happens to a person I love than when it happens to myself.

Entering the Empress's room and finding that ladies-in-waiting are crowded round her in a tight group, I go next to a pillar which is some distance from where she is sitting. What a delight it is when Her Majesty summons me to her side so that all the others have to make way!

149. *One Day, When Her Majesty Was Surrounded by Several Ladies*

One day, when Her Majesty was surrounded by several ladies, I remarked in connexion with something that she had said, 'There are times when the world so exasperates me that I feel I cannot go on living in it for another moment and I want to disappear for good. But then, if I happen to obtain some nice white paper, Michinoku paper, or white decorated paper, I decide that I can put up with things as they are a little longer. Or, if I can spread out a finely woven, green straw mat and examine the white bordering with its vivid black patterns, I somehow feel that I cannot turn my back on this world, and life actually seems precious to me.'

'It really doesn't take much to console you,' said the Empress, laughing. 'I wonder what sort of a person it was who gazed at the moon on Mount Obasute.'[471]

The ladies who were in attendance also teased me. 'You've certainly found a cheap prayer for warding off evil,' they said.

Some time later, when I was staying at home and absorbed in various petty worries, a messenger brought me twenty rolls of

218

magnificent paper from Her Majesty. 'Come back quickly,' she wrote, adding, 'I am sending you this because of what you told me the other day. It seems to be of poor quality, however, and I am afraid you will not be able to use it for copying the Sutra of Longevity.'[472] It delighted me that Her Majesty should have remembered something that I myself had completely forgotten. Even if an ordinary person had sent me the present, I should have been overjoyed. How much more pleasing when it came from the Empress herself! I was so excited that I could not frame a proper reply, but simply sent Her Majesty this poem:

> Thanks to the paper that the Goddess gave,
> My years will now be plenteous as the crane's.[473]

'Make sure that the Empress is asked the following,' I told the messenger. 'Am I expecting too many years?' My reward for the messenger, a general maid from the Table Room, was an unlined green costume.

Then I immediately used the paper I had received to write my collection of notes.[474] I felt a glow of delight and all my worries began to disappear.

A couple of days later a messenger dressed in red arrived with a straw mat. 'Here you are,' he said. 'And who may you be?' said my maid severely. 'Such impudence!' However, the man simply put down the mat and left. I told the maid to ask him where he came from, but he had already disappeared. She brought me the mat, which was an unusually beautiful one with a splendid white border, of the type used by high dignitaries. I felt it must be the Empress who had sent it, but as I was not quite sure I told someone to look for the messenger. Everyone was greatly puzzled, but I did not think the matter was worth discussing since the messenger was nowhere to be found.[475] It occurred to me that, if he had delivered the mat to the wrong place, he would be sure to come back and say so. I should have liked to send someone to Her Majesty's palace to discover the truth of the affair. Then I decided that the mystery must be deliberate and that the mat could only have come from the

Empress. This thought filled me with joy. Having heard nothing further after two days, I knew there could be no doubt about the matter, and I sent a message to Lady Sakyō telling her what had happened. 'Has any of this come to your ears?' I asked. 'Please inform me secretly of what you have heard. In any case do not let anyone know that I have asked you.'

'Her Majesty did it all in great secret,' was Lady Sakyō's reply. 'On no account tell anyone now or later that I informed you.'

Delighted that everything I had suspected was now clear, I wrote a letter, telling the messenger to lay it on the balustrade in Her Majesty's palace when no one was looking. In his nervousness, however, he placed it in such a way that it fell off the side and landed under the stairs.

150. *On about the Twentieth of the Second Month*

On about the twentieth of the Second Month His Excellency the Chancellor ordered that a Dedication of the Full Canon of the Sutras take place in the temple known as Shakuzen in Hōkō Palace.[476] It was arranged that Her Majesty should attend the service as well as the Empress Dowager and, on the first of the month, she proceeded to the Palace of the Second Ward.[477] It was late at night when we arrived and, since I was tired, I went directly to bed.

When I got up the next morning, the sun was shining brightly and I noticed that everything in the Palace was spick and span, beginning with the bamboo blinds, which looked as if they had only been hung on the previous day. I was delighted by all I saw, and wondered when they had managed to decorate the rooms so elegantly and to install the lion and the Korean dog.

At the foot of the stairs leading into the garden there was a cherry tree covered with what appeared to be magnificent blossoms. I was surprised that it should have bloomed so early, and it occurred to me that, if the cherry was already out, the plum trees must be at their height. Then I realized that the flowers were artificial.[478] Their tint, however, was in no way inferior to that of real blossoms. What skill must have been needed to make them look so life-like! It saddened me to think that they would all be ruined if it started to rain. The palace had been constructed on a site previously occupied by several small houses, and the trees in the garden did not show to full advantage; the building itself, however, had an immediate appeal.

In the morning His Excellency, the Chancellor, arrived to call on the Empress. He was wearing bluish-grey trousers of heavily figured silk and a cherry-blossom cloak, over three scarlet robes. The Empress and the other ladies were dressed in the most splendid costumes made of glossy, plum-blossom material, some with heavily figured designs, others decorated with embroidery. On top they wore Chinese jackets of light green, willow green, or red plum-blossom.

Watching the Chancellor as he sat down in front of the Empress and started talking to her, I wished that I could somehow arrange to let outsiders have a glimpse of the scene, so that they might observe how perfectly she made her replies.

'What more could Your Majesty desire?' said the Chancellor, looking towards the Empress's ladies-in-waiting. 'Really, I can't help feeling envious when I see all these splendid women seated round you side by side. There's not a single one of them who is not well-born. Oh, how magnificent to be attended by such ladies! I hope you are kind to them. If they knew what you were really like, I doubt whether they would crowd into your service as they do. Despite your shamefully mean nature I have served you loyally since you were born. And never once have you given me so much as a piece of cast-off clothing. . . . Yes, I might as well tell you openly what I think.'

We were all greatly amused and burst out laughing. 'I'm being quite serious,' said the Chancellor. 'How dare you laugh at me?' . . .

Several of the women gathered to talk about the costumes and fans they would use on the day of the ceremony, each being determined to outdo the others in elegance. In the midst of the discussion, however, one of them exclaimed, 'Why should I take so much trouble? I shall simply appear as I am.' 'Oh dear, there she goes again!' said the others in a rather spiteful tone.

In the evenings many of the ladies-in-waiting went home to make their preparations for the great event; under the circumstances Her Majesty could not very well stop them from leaving the palace. The Chancellor's wife called on the Empress every day and even at night. His Excellency's young daughters also paid regular visits, and a messenger came daily from the Imperial Palace. In fact the Empress was surrounded by people, and it was all very pleasant.

As the days went by, the condition of the cherry-blossoms in front of the palace did not improve, and the sun gave them an unpleasant, withered look. One morning, after it had rained all night, I got up early and went into the garden. By this time the blossoms were really not worth looking at, and I remarked that they could hardly be compared to the faces of tearful lovers forced to say farewell.[479] Her Majesty overheard me. 'What's happened to them?' she said in surprise. 'I know it was raining last night.' Just then a crowd of attendants and servants arrived from the Chancellor's residence. They rushed up to the tree and tore down all the blossoms. 'His Excellency said we should remove them while it was still dark so that no one would see us,' I heard one of the attendants say. 'The sun's already out and it's going to be awkward. Come on. We'd better do it quickly.' I was most amused and, if they had been people of quality, I should have liked to ask them whether they had thought of Kanezumi's poem, 'Let him tell me what he will'.[480] Instead I simply inquired who they were and said they had no right to steal the blossoms. The men ran away with much laughter, gathering speed as they went and dragging the branches behind them. After they had gone, I realized that the Chancellor's idea[481] had been a very happy one indeed. After all, what pleasure would there have been in seeing a mass of wet blossoms coiled round

222

the tree and sticking to the branches? Then I went back inside the palace.

Presently a man arrived from the Housekeeping Office to open the lattices, and some women from the Office of Grounds came to clean the rooms. When they had finished, Her Majesty got up. She noticed at once that the blossoms had disappeared. 'Oh dear!' she said. 'Where have they all gone? I heard you say something about thieves earlier this morning, but I thought they had taken only a few of the branches. Did you see who they were?'

'No, Your Majesty,' I replied. 'It was still too dark to see anything properly. I could only make out some white forms moving about in the garden. I thought they might be stealing the blossoms, so I called out to them.'

'All the same,' said the Empress with a laugh, 'why should anyone want to steal cherry-blossoms? I am sure it must have been His Excellency who ordered some of his men to remove the branches secretly.'

'Oh no,' said I, 'that doesn't seem at all likely. It must have been the spring breeze.'

'If you go on speaking like that,' said the Empress, 'it means you have something to hide. No one has stolen those blossoms. It was the spring rain.'[482] One could hardly be surprised that Her Majesty should have guessed the truth, yet I was greatly impressed.

Since the Chancellor was about to arrive, I withdrew into the back of the room, knowing that he would find my dishevelled 'morning face' extremely unseasonal.[483] As soon as he entered, I heard him explain in a surprised tone, 'Good heavens! The blossoms have disappeared? How could you let them be stolen? What sleepyheads you all are not to have noticed it.'

'And yet,' I murmured, 'you must certainly have known about the theft before I did.'

He caught my words instantly. 'Ah,' he said, laughing loudly, 'so *you* knew about it. I expected as much. Most people who went into the garden wouldn't have seen that anything was missing. I was sure that, if anyone noticed, it would be you or Saishō.'

'Yes,' said the Empress with a charming smile, 'Shōnagon knew who was responsible. But she pretended to believe that it was the spring breeze. And you, Sir, have been telling us a lie.'[484] Then in the most elegant way imaginable she recited the lines,

> The time must now have come
> To till the rice fields in the hills.[485]

'How extremely annoying of my men to let themselves be seen!' said the Chancellor. 'I particularly told them to be careful. It really is a misery to have such fools in one's service. . . . But it was a very pleasant idea of Shōnagon's to have invented the spring breeze.' And he recited a few words from the poem about the rice fields.

'Yes indeed,' said the Empress, 'it was quite ingenious of Shōnagon, considering that it was only a simple remark.'[486] Then she added with a smile, 'I can't help wondering what it must have been like to see those men stealing the flowers this morning.'

'Shōnagon understood everything from the beginning,' said the Counsellor's little boy. 'It was she who pointed out how sad it would be if the blossoms were drenched by the rain.' I was amused to see how annoyed the Chancellor looked when he heard this.

∽

Towards the ninth of the month I announced that I was returning home. 'Don't go yet,' said the Empress. 'Wait until the ceremony is a little nearer.' But I left the Palace all the same. Then at about noon on an unusually calm, sunny day I received the following message from Her Majesty: 'Have the flowers laid bare their hearts?[487] You must not fail to let me know.'

'It would be premature to speak of autumn,' I replied, 'yet I feel myself ascending nine times towards you in the night.'

∽

On the evening when the Empress set out for the Smaller Palace of the Second Ward,[488] no arrangements had been made about

224

the seating in the carriages, and each of the women rushed to secure a place for herself. I and three of the more important ladies-in-waiting stood watching this unpleasant scene. 'What a chaotic way of getting into carriages!' I said, laughing. 'It's as bad as the Return Procession.[489] They're all in such a state that they look as if they might collapse at any moment. Well, it can't be helped. If there's no room for us in these carriages, Her Majesty is bound to hear why we haven't reached the Second Ward and she'll send another for us.'

When all the other women had pushed themselves into the carriages, a gentleman from the Office of the Empress's Household asked whether anyone was left. 'Yes,' I replied, 'we're still here.' He came up and asked our names. 'Very strange!' he exclaimed when we had told him. 'I thought that everyone had found a place by now. Why are you ladies so late? We were on the point of putting the serving-women into this last carriage. Really, I find your behaviour most peculiar.' He ordered that a carriage be pulled up.

'If that's how it is,' I said, 'put the servants in first as you planned, and we can go later.'

'Outrageous!' said the gentleman. 'What an unpleasant nature you have!'[490]

The other ladies and I then stepped into the carriage that had been intended for the serving-women. We laughed to see how dark it was inside.[491]

When we reached the palace in the Second Ward, we found that the Empress's palanquin had arrived early and that everything had been arranged for her. Since Her Majesty had ordered that I be brought into her presence as soon as I arrived, Ukyō, Kosakon, and some of the other young ladies had been examining each of the carriages; but there had been no sign of me. The passengers went to the Empress's room in groups of four[492] and gathered round her. 'How odd!' she exclaimed after some time. 'Why is Shōnagon not among you?' No one could answer.

When the last carriage was drawn up outside the palace, the

young ladies finally saw me. 'Why are you so late?' they said. 'Her Majesty hasn't stopped asking about you.' As they led me into her presence, I looked about the palace and was greatly impressed. It was amazing that in such a short time things could have been arranged to look as if the Empress had lived there for years.

'Why didn't you come sooner?' said Her Majesty, when she saw me. 'I've been asking everyone about you.' As I did not answer, the ladies who had travelled with me laughed loudly and said, 'It really couldn't be helped, Your Majesty. People who travel last can't very well arrive early. As it was, we almost missed that last carriage, but the serving-women took pity on us and let us use it. And what a dark, wretched carriage it was!'

'I am rather surprised at the man who was in charge of the travelling arrangements,' said the Empress. 'Why didn't you say something? I can see that those of you who are unfamiliar with these things might hesitate to speak, but surely one of you, Uemo for instance, could have tried to help.'

'But, Your Majesty,' said Uemo, 'why did they all have to push ahead of each other like that?'

It occurred to me how unpleasant it must be for the ladies who were standing near by to hear this.

'Indeed,' said Her Majesty with a look of annoyance, 'I see no excuse for such undignified behaviour. The seating arrangements should have been carefully planned in advance.'

'I'm sure it was my fault,' I said, trying to smooth things over. 'I took a long time coming from my room, and that made them all very impatient.'

Hearing that on the following day Her Majesty would be attending the recitation of the newly dedicated sutras, I went to visit her in her room in the evening. On my way I looked into the hall at the northern end of the Southern Palace. Several lamps were standing on trays, and by their light I could see that the room was full of women. Some were seated behind screens in small groups of three or four; others had retired alone behind curtains of state; still others had gathered to make their toilet,

226

to attach the cords to their formal skirts or to sew their robes, which they had arranged in piles on the floor. As I observed them elaborately arranging their hair, it occurred to me that I would probably never again see anything as splendid as the next day's ceremony.

'I understand that Her Majesty is to set out tomorrow morning at the Hour of the Tiger,'[493] said one of the ladies-in-waiting when she saw me. 'And why didn't you come until now? Someone sent you a fan with a message to ask what you were doing.'

I had already put on my full ceremonial robes so that I might be ready in case the Empress did leave as early as the Hour of the Tiger; but the sun rose and there was still no sign of her. Then, hearing that the carriages were to be brought up to the western wing of the palace near the part of the hall that was covered by Chinese eaves, we all went out to the corridor. The ladies-in-waiting who had recently come into service and were unaccustomed to ceremonies of this kind looked very nervous. Her Majesty now proceeded to the western wing, where the Chancellor was residing, and together with five other ladies (Lady Shigeisha, the Chancellor's third and fourth daughters, the Chancellor's wife, and his sister-in-law) she seated herself behind some blinds to watch us getting into the carriages.

As each carriage arrived at the entrance, the Major Counsellor and the Middle Captain of the Third Rank,[494] one on either side, rolled up the outer and inner blinds and helped the ladies. If we had all been able to stay closely together, we should not have been so conspicuous, but as it was our names were called out individually from a list and we had to go forward in groups of four. Presently my turn came and I walked towards the carriage that had been assigned to me. To say that I was terribly uncomfortable would be an understatement. The thought of the Empress watching me from behind the blinds and possibly thinking that I was ugly made me so miserable that I started perspiring and felt that my beautifully arranged hair was standing on end. When I had finally managed to get past the blinds and came close to the carriage, I saw to my extreme embarrassment that two handsome young gentlemen (the Counsellor and the Captain) were standing by the entrance, smiling broadly. It was just like a dream. Nevertheless I managed to reach the carriage without collapsing. I am afraid I cannot have cut a very fine figure, but I did my best.

When we had all got into our carriages, they were pulled out into the Second Avenue and left there, with the shafts resting on the trestles. They looked splendid, standing one behind the other as on the occasion of some grand festival, and I felt my heart pounding at the thought that the onlookers must be as impressed as I was. Several men of the Fourth, Fifth, and Sixth Ranks strolled up to the carriages and addressed elegant remarks to the ladies inside.

The Chancellor, in company with all the senior courtiers and many other gentlemen, now came out to greet the Empress Dowager. Since Her Majesty's palanquin was not to leave until the Empress Dowager had passed the palace, I expected that there would be a tiresome wait, but it was not long before the procession arrived. There were fifteen carriages in all, with the Empress Dowager's Chinese-style carriage in front followed by four that were occupied by nuns. Through the back entrances, one could see the nuns' crystal rosaries, grey stoles, and other vestments. The blinds were still lowered, but I could make out the light violet colour of the inner hangings, which were a slightly darker shade towards the edges. In the remaining ten carriages sat ladies-in-waiting, elegantly dressed in Chinese jackets of cherry-blossom material, skirts of scarlet or occasionally light violet, and coats of stiff silk. Though there was a bright sun, the sky was covered with mist, giving a pale green effect. Against this light the colours of the ladies' Court robes made a splendid combination, even surpassing in elegance the varied designs of their Chinese jackets.

The Chancellor, his younger brother, and the other gentlemen of his suite now came out to pay their respects to the Empress Dowager. It was a magnificent sight, and we were all wild with admiration. No doubt the men for their part were impressed by our twenty carriages, which stood in a row along the avenue.

Her Majesty's palanquin had still not left, and I was becoming impatient. Finally eight Palace Girls were led up on horseback, wearing blue formal skirts shaded darker towards the edges, waistband ribbons, and shoulder sashes, which all fluttered attractively in the breeze. One of the girls called Buzen was on intimate terms with Shigemasa, the doctor.[495] Noticing that she had on a pair of grape-coloured trousers, Yamanoi, the Major Counsellor, laughed and said, 'So they have allowed Shigemasa to wear the forbidden colour?'[496]

The row of horses on which the Palace Girls were riding came to a halt, and just then the Empress's palanquin appeared. The Empress Dowager's retinue had seemed splendid enough, but it was as nothing compared to this new sight. By now the sun was high in the sky, making the onion-flower[497] decoration, the glossy curtains, and everything else glitter brilliantly. The attendants pulled the cords and the palanquin moved off. As the ladies watched its curtains swaying gently with the motion, they were so impressed that their hair literally stood on end; later even those who had been most beautifully groomed complained how messy their hair had become. It was indeed a fantastically impressive moment, and I too was overcome with awe, wondering how it was possible that I should be in daily attendance on such a magnificent Empress. After the palanquin had passed, the attendants came forward and yoked the oxen to our carriages. We then started moving along the avenue behind the Empress, our hearts full of the most inexpressible joy and pride.

When Her Majesty reached Shakuzen Temple, a group of musicians by the great outer gate played Korean and Chinese music,[498] and there were performances of the Lion Dance and the Dance of the Korean Dog. So loud was the sound of the thirteen-pipe flute and the tabor that I became quite giddy. I wondered to which of the Buddha's realms I had been wafted and felt that I was floating up into the sky with the music.

Presently the procession entered the temple enclosure, where

I saw numerous pavilions with brocade curtains, closed off by bright green blinds and surrounded by hangings. It was all so splendid that I could not believe we were still in this world of ours. Our carriages were pulled up before the Empress's gallery, where the Major Counsellor and the Captain, who were still on duty, asked us to get out as quickly as possible. I had been embarrassed enough when stepping into the carriage; but here things were still more awkward, since it was brighter and we were more exposed than we had been at the palace. Nevertheless I was able to cast an admiring glance at Korechika, the Major Counsellor, as he stood there looking imposingly handsome in an under-robe whose train seemed far too long for such a narrow place. Raising the carriage blinds, he told us to make haste. I felt that the artificial locks, which I had tucked together with my own hair under my Chinese jacket,[499] were in disorder and must look very strange. It was so light in the temple enclosure that one could easily distinguish the shades of blackness and redness in our hair. All this made me extremely embarrassed, and at first I could not bring myself to step out of the carriage. 'Please get out before me,' I asked the lady who was sitting in the back; but evidently she was just as shy as I, for she turned to the Major Counsellor, who was standing directly outside the carriage, and said, 'Would you be so good as to step back a little? You are too kind to us.'

'How timid you ladies are!' he remarked with a laugh as he stepped back a few paces. Since we still hesitated, he again walked up to us. 'It was Her Majesty who told me to come,' he explained. 'She said I should get you out of the carriages in such a way that people like Munetaka would not see you.[500] That's the only reason I'm here.' He then helped us out of the carriage and led us to the Empress. I felt very grateful to her for having given these instructions on our behalf.

As I approached the Empress, I noticed that about eight ladies who had travelled in the first carriages, were installed at the edge of the veranda, from where they could have a good view of the ceremony. Her Majesty was seated on a platform about two feet high. 'I have brought you Shōnagon and the others,' announced Korechika, 'and I did not let anyone get a look at them.' The Empress said she wanted to see us and emerged from her curtain of state. She had not changed her clothes since I saw her before and was still wearing the same Chinese jacket; but she was dazzlingly beautiful. Where else would one ever see a red Chinese robe like this? Beneath it she wore a willow-green robe of Chinese damask, five layers of unlined robes of grape-coloured silk, a robe of Chinese gauze with blue prints over a plain white background, and a ceremonial skirt of elephant-eye[501] silk. I felt that nothing in the world could compare with the beauty of these colours.

'How do I look today?' Her Majesty asked me.

'Magnificent,' I replied, realizing at once how inadequate a response this was.

'I am afraid you must have become rather impatient waiting for my palanquin,' she said. 'We were delayed by the Master of the Household.[502] He was afraid that if people saw him accompanying me in the same under-robe that he had worn when he was with the Empress Dowager there might be some criticism. So he ordered his women to sew a new under-robe, and that is why we were so late. What a taste he has for elegance!'

It was very bright on the gallery and I could see Her Majesty's hair more closely than usual. I was absolutely fascinated by the beauty of her front parting, which was combed at a slight angle pointing towards the ornament that held up the hair over her forehead.

A pair of three-foot curtains of state had been placed together in such a way that I was separated from the other ladies. A mat had been spread behind the curtains, its borders parallel to the lower beam of the gallery. On it were seated Lady Chūnagon, the daughter of Captain Tadagimi (the Chancellor's uncle), and Lady Saishō, the granddaughter of the Minister of the Right.

'Please go to the gentlemen's hall,' said the Empress to Lady Saishō, 'and see what is happening.'

Saishō, however, realized what Her Majesty had in mind.

231

'Surely there is enough room for all three of us to sit here and have a good view,' she said.[503]

'Very well then,' said the Empress. She summoned me to come closer and sit on the mat. Seeing this, one of the ladies-in-waiting who was seated on a lower level laughingly remarked that I was just like a page-boy who had been given special permission to enter the Senior Courtiers' Chamber. 'I wonder if Her Majesty is trying to be funny,' said a second lady, and still another commented that my position was more like that of a mounted escort. Despite their quips, I was delighted by the honour of sitting beside Her Majesty to watch the ceremony. I suppose this sounds rather conceited, yet how can I remain silent about something that really happened? Of course I was treated far too kindly, and no doubt many knowing people of the type who are always ready to find fault with others maliciously blamed our gracious Empress for her indiscretion in befriending someone like me. And it is true that I was favoured in a way that a woman in my position does not deserve.

From where I was sitting I had a splendid view of the galleries occupied by the Empress Dowager and the other important people. His Excellency, the Chancellor, now started a round of visits, going first to the gallery of the Empress Dowager, where he stayed for a while, and then coming to us. The two Major Counsellors and the Captain of the Third Rank had already arrived. The Captain was still wearing his Guards uniform with a bow and quiver at his waist, which suited the occasion admirably.[504] A large group of senior courtiers and other gentlemen of the Fourth and Fifth Ranks whom he had brought along as an escort sat in a row next to him. As the Chancellor entered Her Majesty's gallery, he looked round at the occupants. The ladies-in-waiting, including Madam, the Mistress of the Robes, were all dressed in Chinese jackets and formal skirts with trains; Her Excellency, the Chancellor's wife, wore a wide-sleeved Court robe over her skirt.

'Ah,' exclaimed the Chancellor, 'you look like something out of a picture. But please don't go about later saying that you were

uncomfortable today in your stiff clothes.[505] And you, my girls,'
he added, turning to his third and fourth daughters, 'be ready to
help Her Majesty off with her formal skirt and train. Remember
that she is the mistress of you all. It is in front of *her* gallery that
the Guards have been ordered to take up their positions. Do you
suppose everyone has such an honour?' Then he burst into tears.
Everyone who saw him thought that he had good reason to
weep, and they themselves felt tears coming to their eyes.[506]

When the Chancellor noticed that my Chinese jacket was made
of red silk with five patterns embroidered in cherry-coloured
thread, he laughed and said, 'We've suddenly found ourselves
short of a red robe for one of the priests. I wish we could borrow
that jacket of yours. It looks exactly like a clerical vestment.[507]
In any case I'm sure you made it by shortening a priest's robe.'

'Yes,' said Korechika, who had moved towards the rear of the
gallery, 'it must be the robe of Bishop Sei.'[508]

Bishop Ryūen wore a robe of thin, red material, a purple stole,
a light mauve jacket, and a pair of loose trousers. The bluish tint
of his shaved head made him look very attractive, and one could
easily have taken him for the Bodhisattva Jizō.[509] It was funny to
see him surrounded by ladies-in-waiting. 'How unpleasant for
him to be among the women!' someone said with a laugh. 'I'm
sure he'd prefer to be walking along solemnly with all those
priestly dignitaries.'

Matsugimi, who had accompanied his father, was brought to
see us. He wore a grape-coloured Court cloak, a dark violet robe
of beaten damask, and a jacket of plum-red material. Escorted
by the usual crowd of gentlemen of the Fourth and Fifth Ranks,
he was led into the midst of the ladies in the Empress's gallery.
Then something went wrong and he started to cry loudly; but
even this was very charming.

The ceremony began. Texts of the Full Canon were placed
on red lotus flowers,[510] one scroll on each petal, and carried
by a procession of clerics, High Court Nobles, senior courtiers,
gentlemen of the Sixth Rank, and many other gentlemen. It was
most awe-inspiring.

Next came the Great Procession round the Holy Image, and then the officiating priest appeared and recited the Prayer for Salvation.[511] Later there was a performance of dances.

After I had watched these ceremonies all day long, my eyes were aching. Towards evening a Chamberlain of the Fifth Rank arrived with a letter for the Empress from the Palace. A stool was brought out for him and placed in front of the gallery; as he sat there waiting for Her Majesty's reply, the Chamberlain made a very splendid sight.

The next gentleman to arrive was Norimasa, the Secretary in the Ministry of Ceremonial. 'Her Majesty is to return to the Palace this evening,' he announced, 'and I have been ordered to escort her. This is an Imperial Command.' Norimasa then remained in the gallery, waiting for the Empress to leave. 'First I must go to the palace in the Second Ward,' she said. Just then the Chamberlain-Controller brought an Imperial message for the Chancellor, who, after reading it, told his daughter that she must do exactly what His Majesty desired. The Empress then made preparations to return directly to the Imperial Palace.

Meanwhile attendants also brought Her Majesty some charming gifts and a note from the Empress Dowager, who referred to the 'salt-kilns of Chika'[512] and the like.

When the ceremony was over, the Empress Dowager left; but now she was escorted by only about one half of the High Court Nobles and household officials who had accompanied her on her arrival.[513]

The servants of the Empress's ladies-in-waiting had not been informed that Her Majesty was returning to the Imperial Palace, and in the evening they all went to the residence in the Second Ward, where they stayed until late at night waiting for their mistresses. Meanwhile in the Palace the ladies were waiting for their maids to bring them their night clothes. They felt extremely cold in their elegant ceremonial robes, to which they were unaccustomed, and they spoke furiously, but of course to no avail, about their servants. 'How could you be so stupid?' they asked when they finally arrived on the following morning; but they had to agree that their maids' explanation was entirely reasonable.

On the day after the ceremony it started raining. 'This shows what a good *karma*[514] I must have,' the Chancellor told the Empress. 'Don't you agree?' One could well understand why he was so relieved.

151. *At Noon When the Sun Is Shining Brightly*

At noon when the sun is shining brightly or at night when one imagines it is the Hour of the Rat,[515] it is always delightful to hear the Emperor summon his gentlemen to the Imperial Bedchamber when he has retired. I love to hear His Majesty playing the flute in the middle of the night.[516]

152. *Captain Narinobu Is a Son of His Reverend Highness*

Captain Narinobu is a son of His Reverend Highness, the Minister of Military Affairs. He is not only extremely handsome but has a delightful nature. I can well imagine how Kanesuke's daughter[517] must have suffered when he abandoned her and she had to accompany her father to his post in Iyo. No doubt the Captain, having heard that she was to leave at dawn, came to visit her on the previous night. How beautiful he must have looked in his Court cloak as he made his way home by the pale moonlight!

In the past he used frequently to come and talk with me, and he would say very disagreeable things about people. There was in those days a certain lady-in-waiting called Hyōbu[518] who was scrupulous about performing abstinence and the like and who used her family name at Court.[519] She had been adopted by some family like the Tairas and wanted to be known by their name, but the young ladies-in-waiting found it amusing always to call her by her original surname.

Lady Hyōbu was not particularly good-looking; in fact it was hard to find anything to recommend her. Yet she was always pushing herself forward in the Palace. The Empress observed this and one day she mentioned how she disliked such behaviour. But out of malice everyone refrained from warning the lady.

At this time I was living with Shikibu no Omoto in quarters that had been arranged for us in the Palace of the First Ward. It was a charming little room under the eaves directly opposite the eastern gate, and we stayed there all the time, inviting only people whom we liked. The Empress herself used to come and visit us.

One rainy evening, when the Empress had said that we must all spend the night in the Palace, Shikibu no Omoto and I went to bed in the southern ante-room. Presently there was a loud knocking at the door. We agreed that it would be a nuisance to have a visitor, and pretended to be asleep. But then someone called my name loudly and I heard the Empress say, 'Go and wake her, I'm sure she's only pretending.' Lady Hyōbu came in and tried to wake me, but I did not stir. Hyōbu reported this to the Empress and then went out to the veranda and began a conversation with my visitor. I did not think this would last very long, but the night wore on and still they were chatting away. It seemed fairly certain that the visitor was Narinobu. What on earth could they be discussing all that time? I lay in bed, chuckling to myself – something that the couple on the veranda could hardly have suspected. When dawn came, my visitor finally went home.

'What a terrible man!' I thought. 'If he ever comes again, I shall refuse to speak to him. What can they have found to say to each other all night?'[520] Just then Hyōbu pushed open the sliding-door and came in.

On the following morning she heard Shikibu and me talking in our ante-room and joined us. 'A man who comes in such a heavy rain-storm to visit a woman deserves some sympathy,' she declared. 'However much he may have made her worry and suffer during the past days, surely she should forgive him when he arrives with his clothes all drenched.'

I wondered what gave her such an idea. If a man has been visiting one night after night and then comes again despite a heavy downpour, it shows that he cannot bear to be separated for even a single evening and one has good reason to be impressed. If, on the other hand, he has made one worry by letting several days go by, one is bound to question his sincerity even if he should choose to appear on a stormy night. But no doubt people have different feelings about these matters.

Narinobu is in fact devoted to a woman who has quick wits and a mind of her own, and who also impresses him as being kindhearted.[521] But he has several other attachments, not to mention his wife, and he cannot come very often. If he chooses such a terrible night to visit the woman, it can only be because he knows people will talk and praise him for his devotion. Of course, if he had no feeling for her at all, he would not bother to invent such stratagems.

When it is raining, I feel absolutely miserable. I entirely forget how beautiful the weather was earlier in the day and everything seems hateful, whether I am in one of the beautiful galleries in the Palace or in a very ordinary house. Nothing gives me the slightest pleasure, and I can think of one thing only: when will the rain stop?

When the moon is shining I love to receive a visitor, even if it is someone who has not come to see me for ten days, twenty days, a month, a year, or perhaps seven or eight years, and who has been inspired by the moonlight to remember our previous meetings. Even if I am in a place where it is hopelessly difficult to receive visitors and where one is constantly in fear of being seen, I will allow the man to speak with me, though we may have to stand up all the time. And then, if it is at all possible, I will keep him with me for the night.

Moonlight[522] makes me think of people who are far away and also reminds me of things in the past – sad things, happy things,

things that delighted me – as though they had just happened. I do not like 'The Tale of Komano' in the slightest, for its language is old-fashioned and it contains hardly anything of interest. Yet I am always moved by the moonlight scene[523] in which one of the characters recalls past events and, producing a moth-eaten fan, recites the line, 'My horse has come this way before.'[524]

My dislike of rain is so profound that even a little shower strikes me as hateful. It only needs to rain and the most splendid ceremonies, occasions that I should otherwise have found delightful and affecting, become a pointless nuisance. Why then should I be so impressed when a man comes to see me dripping with rain and full of complaints?

Captain Ochikubo (he who quarrelled with Captain Katano) is certainly an attractive character; and what makes one like him so much is that he visited the heroine not only on the night when it was raining but also on the two previous nights.[525] (I remember that he had to wash his feet on arrival. How disgusting they must have been!) If he hadn't visited the lady on the previous nights, there would have been nothing so admirable about his coming on the rainy one.

I am delighted when a man visits me on a very windy night. Then I really feel that he cares for me.

I also like having a visitor when it is snowing. A secret visit is especially enjoyable; as one waits for the man, one whispers to oneself, 'Can he forget?'[526] It is very pleasant, too, when one is staying in a place where one can receive a visitor openly and he arrives in clothes that are cold and damp from the snow. He may be wearing a hunting costume, an over-robe, the yellow-green robes of a Chamberlain, or, best of all, a proper Court cloak; but, even if he is dressed in a short green robe, I am quite content so long as it has been moistened by the snow.

In the old days Chamberlains always used to wear their yellow-green robes when visiting women at night, and if they had got wet in the rain they would wring them out. But nowadays they all seem to wear their short green robes,[527] even for daytime visits.

How handsome the Chamberlains looked when they came dressed in yellow-green, especially those who were also serving as Guards officers!

After they have heard my views on this subject, I wonder whether there will be any gentlemen who refrain from visiting their ladies in the rain.

∽

One bright, moonlit night a messenger thrust a note into the ante-room where I was staying. On a sheet of magnificent scarlet paper I read the words, 'There is nothing.'[528] It was the moonlight that made this so delightful; I wonder whether I would have enjoyed it at all on a rainy night.

153. *On One Occasion a Man*

On one occasion a man, who invariably sent me a letter after we had spent the night together, declared that he saw no point in our relationship and that he had nothing more to say to me. There was no word from him on the next day. 'When dawn appeared'[529] without the usual next-morning letter, I could not help feeling rather gloomy. 'Well,' I thought as the day advanced, 'he really meant what he says.'

It rained very hard on the day after that. Noon came and still I had heard nothing from him: obviously he had forgotten all about me. Then in the evening, while I was sitting on the edge of the veranda, a child arrived with an open umbrella in one hand and a letter in the other. I opened the letter and read it with more than usual haste. 'The rain that swells the water'[530] was the message, and I found this more charming than if he had sent me a whole sheaf of poems.

154. One Day the Sky, Which until Then Had Been Quite Clear.

One day the sky, which until then had been quite clear, was suddenly covered with dark clouds and there was a snow-storm. Feeling rather depressed, I went and looked outside: the snow was already lying thickly on the ground. It was still coming down heavily when I noticed a slender, handsome man, who looked like an after-runner and who was sheltered under an umbrella, arriving at the house next door. I watched with delight as he entered through the fence and delivered a letter. It was a knotted letter written on a sheet of pure white paper (either Michinoku or decorated paper); I could see that the ink-seal on the outside was frozen and that the dark lines of the characters became fainter towards the ends.[531] As the lady to whom the letter was addressed opened it, I was able to observe that it had been knotted into a very narrow strip and that there were delicate indentations in the paper where it had been folded. The ink was extremely dark in some places, light in others, and the columns of writing, which covered both sides of the paper, came very close together. Even from where I was standing it was a great pleasure to watch the lady as she read the letter carefully, then read it all over again. I wondered what it actually said and, seeing her smile, became even more curious. I was too far away, however, to make it out; the most I could do was to guess at a few of the characters that were written in particularly dark ink.

∽

An attractive woman, whose hair tumbles loosely over her forehead, has received a letter in the dark. Evidently she is too impatient to wait for a lamp; instead she takes some fire-tongs, and, lifting a piece of burning charcoal from the brazier, laboriously reads by its pale light. It is a charming scene.

155. *The Thunder Guards are Awe-Inspiring*

The Thunder Guards are awe-inspiring when they appear during a violent thunderstorm.[532] The Major and Middle Captains and the other officers of the two Guards divisions make a delightful sight as they post themselves next to the lattices in the Palace. When the thunder has abated, one of the Major Captains orders the soldiers to 'go up' or 'go down'.[533]

156. *One Has Taken a Roundabout Way*

One has taken a roundabout way to avoid an unlucky direction. It is late at night when one approaches home, and the carriage attendants walk with their heads bent to protect themselves against the terrible cold. Finally one arrives and pulls up a brazier. It is delightful enough when live embers cover the entire surface, but it is a particular pleasure to find a glowing ember under a covering of ash. Then one starts talking to one's companions and does not even notice that the fire had gone out. Often a maid will lay some fresh charcoal on top and light it; this annoys me greatly, though it is all right if she lights the fire in the centre. It is also very annoying when a maid rakes all the embers to the sides of the brazier, then piles up some new charcoal in the middle and places the burning embers on top.

157. *One Day, When the Snow Lay Thick on the Ground*

One day, when the snow lay thick on the ground and it was so cold that the lattices had all been closed, I and the other ladies were sitting with Her Majesty, chatting and poking the embers in the brazier.

'Tell me, Shōnagon,' said the Empress, 'how is the snow on Hsiang-lu peak?'[534]

I told the maid to raise one of the lattices and then rolled up the blind all the way. Her Majesty smiled. I was not alone in recognizing the Chinese poem she had quoted; in fact all the ladies knew the lines and had even rewritten them in Japanese. Yet no one but me had managed to think of it instantly.

'Yes indeed,' people said when they heard the story. 'She was born to serve an Empress like ours.'

158. *The Boys Employed by Masters of Divination*

The boys employed by Masters of Divination know their job very well. When their employer has gone to perform a service of purification, the boys recite the invocations in his place, and everyone accepts this as normal. Again, if a patient has lost consciousness, the boys quickly and expertly sprinkle cold water on his face without a word from their master. It makes me envious to see how clever they are, and I only wish I could have such boys in my service.

159. *Once in the Third Month*

Once in the Third Month I spent a period of abstinence in a friend's house. It was a modest place and the trees in the garden were not worth noticing. One of them was called a willow; but it was broad-leaved and had none of the willow's usual charm.

'It doesn't look like a willow at all,' I remarked.

'All the same,' insisted the people of the house, 'it is a kind of willow.'

The following poem then occurred to me:

> Ah, what a house this is,
> Where the eyebrows of the willow's leaves
> Grow so impudently broad
> That they make the spring itself lose face![535]

During this same period of abstinence I went to stay in another rather simple house. On the second day, when I was becoming very bored and wishing that I could return at once to the Palace, I was delighted to receive a letter from the Empress. Her Majesty's poem had been beautifully copied by Lady Saishō on a sheet of light green paper:

> So hard to bear
> These past two days –
> How could I have lived
> Those years gone by?[536]

To this Lady Saishō had added her own message: 'Already I feel as if it were a thousand years.[537] Please hurry back tomorrow morning. Don't even wait for the sun to rise.' Lady Saishō's words were charming enough; but the Empress's letter overwhelmed me and, instead of sending a perfunctory reply, I composed this poem:

> How sadly have I viewed these long spring days
> From my poor dwelling-place,
> When even one who lives above the clouds[538]
> Has found them hard to bear!

And to Lady Saishō I wrote, 'Perhaps I shall not even survive this night but suffer the Captain's sad fate.'[539]

I returned to the Palace at dawn on the following day. 'I did not like your poem about the long spring days,' said the Empress when she saw me. 'My ladies also criticized it severely.'[540]

This made me very unhappy, but no doubt Her Majesty had good reason to reproach me.

160. *Once When I Had Gone to Kiyomizu Temple*

Once when I had gone to Kiyomizu Temple for a retreat and was listening with deep emotion to the loud cry of the cicadas a special messenger brought me a note from Her Majesty written on a sheet of red-tinted Chinese paper:

> Count each echo of the temple bell
> As it tolls the vespers by the mountain's[541] side.
> Then you will know how many times
> My heart is beating out its love for you.

'What a long stay you are making!' she added. 'Surely you realize how much I miss you.' Since I had forgotten to bring along any suitable paper, I wrote my reply on a purple lotus petal.[542]

161. *On the Twenty-Fourth of the Twelfth Month*

On the twenty-fourth of the Twelfth Month the Empress arranged that there should be a Naming of the Buddhas. It must have been well past midnight when the Leader finished the first service and we all left the temple, some to return home, others to set out for a secret tryst. I shared a carriage with some other people and we had a delightful drive.

The snow had been coming down for days, but in the morning it had stopped and now there was a strong wind. Here and there one could see a patch of black earth where the snow had been blown away; but the roof-tops were completely white, and even the wretched huts of the poor people were very pretty under their covering of snow, evenly lit by a pale moon as though they were thatched with silver. The icicles, which seemed to have been deliberately hung in different lengths from all the eaves, were incredibly beautiful and looked like waterfalls of crystal.

The outer blinds of our carriage had been pulled up and, since there were no inner curtains, the moonlight came right inside. I could see a lady who was covered in about eight layers of light violet, red plum, white, and other robes; over this she wore a cloak of dark violet, which shone with a brilliant lustre. Next to her sat a gentleman in laced trousers of grape-coloured material with a heavily figured design; he wore several white robes, and at the opening of his sleeves one could see the yellow rose and scarlet of his under-robes; he had undone the dazzlingly white sash of his Court cloak, which he wore off one shoulder so that one had a clear view of the robes beneath. He sat in such a way that one of his legs reached into the front of the carriage and any passer-by would have found his posture delightful.

The lady had slipped into the back of the carriage to avoid the brilliance of the moonlight, but much to her embarrassment the gentleman now pulled her forward. Again and again he recited the words, 'Piercing cold, it spreads like ice.'[543] It was a delightful scene, and I should have liked to spend the entire night travelling in the carriage; but, alas, we soon reached our destination.

162. *It Is Delightful for the Master of a Household*

When a group of ladies-in-waiting are on leave from Court and have gathered in a room, it is delightful for the master of the household to hear them exchanging flattering remarks about their mistresses and gossiping about the latest news from the Palace.

ↄ

I should like to live in a large, attractive house. My family would of course be staying with me; and in one of the wings I should have a friend, an elegant lady-in-waiting from the Palace, with whom I could converse. Whenever we wished, we should meet to discuss recent poems and other things of interest. When my friend received a letter, we should read it together and write our answer. If someone came to pay my friend[544] a visit, I should receive him in one of our beautifully decorated rooms, and if he was prevented from leaving by a rain-storm or something of the sort, I should warmly invite him to stay. Whenever my friend went to the Palace, I should help her with her preparations and see that she had what was needed during her stay at Court. For everything about well-born people delights me.

But I suppose this dream of mine is rather absurd.

163. *Times When One Should Be on One's Guard*

When one meets people who have a bad reputation. Such people often give a more sincere impression than those of good repute.

When one travels by boat. I remember one such excursion. It was a beautiful clear day and the sea was so calm that its surface looked like a sheet of light green, glossy silk. I was travelling with a group of young women, and none of us had the slightest sense of danger. Dressed in our short jackets, we helped the boatmen at the oars, singing song after song as we rowed. It was a most delightful trip, and I only wished that someone of high rank were there to see us gliding across the water.

Then all of a sudden a violent wind blew up and the sea became terribly rough. We were beside ourselves with fear. As we rowed back to the shore, the waves leapt over the boat, and I could not believe that this was the same sea that a little while ago had been so smooth.

When one thinks of it, sailors are the bravest people in the world. Even in reasonably shallow water their vessels are far too flimsy to be safe. Yet they do not hesitate to embark on a sea of any depth – perhaps even a thousand fathoms – entrusting their lives to a boat so heavily loaded that the water comes up almost to the edge. The common people who man the boat run up and down, never giving a thought to the danger; and, though it looks as if the slightest rocking would capsize it, one sees them banging down into the hold half a dozen great pine logs two or three feet in circumference. Amazing!

People of quality travel in boats with cabins. These, of course, seem far safer, especially if one is in the rear; but if one is near the side one gets very dizzy. The ropes that keep the oars in place – the 'fast cords' as they are called – look extraordinarily weak. What if one of them were to snap? Surely the rower would be plunged into the sea. Yet I have never seen anyone using heavy ropes.

I remember one journey on such a boat. We had a charming cabin, fitted with head-blinds, double doors, and lattices. Though the boat did not seem quite as sturdy as most of its kind, I felt as if I were in a snug little house. But when I looked out and saw the other boats, I was really frightened. Those in the distance looked as frail as bamboo leaves that have been made into toy boats and scattered across the water.[545] When we finally returned to the harbour, lights were shining in all the boats, which was a delightful sight. On the following morning I was very moved to observe people rowing out to sea in those tiny vessels known as sampans; as they moved slowly into the distance, the white waves behind the boats did in fact 'disappear without a trace'.[546]

When all is said and done, only common people should go in boats. There are dangers enough when one travels by land, but then at least one has the firm ground under one's feet and that is a great comfort.

The sea is a frightening thing at the best of times. How much more terrifying must it be for those poor women divers who have to plunge into its depths for their livelihood![547] One wonders what would happen to them if the cord round their waist were to break. I can imagine men doing this sort of work, but for a woman it must take remarkable courage. After the woman has been lowered into the water, the men sit comfortably in their boats, heartily singing songs as they keep an eye on the mulberry-bark cord that floats on the surface. It is an amazing sight, for they do not show the slightest concern about the risks the woman is taking. When finally she wants to come up, she gives a tug on her cord and the men haul her out of the water with a speed that I can well understand. Soon she is clinging to the side of the boat, her breath coming in painful gasps. The sight is enough to make even an outsider feel the brine dripping. I can hardly imagine this is a job that anyone would covet.

164. *A Certain Lieutenant*

A certain lieutenant in the Right Division of the Outer Palace Guards looked down on his parents and was ashamed that people should see them.[548] When they were journeying up to the capital from Iyo Province, he pushed them both into the sea and they drowned. People were dismayed by his action and regarded it as shameful. Yet on the fifteenth day of the Seventh Month the man said that he was going to celebrate the Festival of the Dead in honour of his parents and he began to busy himself with preparations. When the Holy Teacher, Dōmei,[549] was told about this, he wrote the following poem, which I find really delightful:

> A man who drowned his parents in the ocean's depths
> Now celebrates the feast of Bon –
> A sorry sight indeed!

165. *Once I Wrote down a Poem*

Once I wrote down in my notebook a poem that had greatly appealed to me. Unfortunately one of the maids saw it and recited the lines clumsily. It really is awful when someone rattles off a poem without any proper feeling.

166. *If a Servant Girl*

If a servant girl says about someone, 'What a delightful gentleman he is!' one immediately looks down on him, whereas if she insulted the person in question it would have the opposite effect. Praise from a servant can also damage a woman's reputation.

Besides, people of that class always manage to express themselves badly when they are trying to say something nice.

167. *One Evening Korechika*

One evening Korechika, the Major Counsellor, came to the Palace and lectured to the Emperor on literature, his visit lasting as usual until late at night. Gradually the ladies in attendance on Their Majesties retired by ones and twos to lie down behind their screens or curtains of state, until I was the only one left. I was struggling to keep myself awake when I heard the officer of the Guards announce, 'The Ox, fourth quarter.'[550]

'It's already dawn,' I murmured.

'Well then, Your Majesty,' said Korechika, 'it is no longer worth while to go to bed.'

I was shocked by his remark. After all, even if Korechika felt no need for sleep himself, why should he prevent His Majesty from resting? If there had been other ladies in the room, I should have said something since my voice would not have been recognized among theirs, but as it was I found it wiser to stay silent. Meanwhile the Emperor dozed off, leaning against a pillar. 'Look at him!' said Korechika to the Empress. 'How can he possibly sleep now that dawn is here?'

'Yes indeed,' said Her Majesty, and burst out laughing. But the Emperor was deaf to it all.

There was a young girl in the Palace who was employed as a maid by one of the housekeepers. She had caught a cock and was keeping it in her room, intending to take it home on the following day. Somehow or other the bird was found by a dog and fled all the way to the end of the gallery, letting out the most piercing squawks. Everyone woke up, including the Emperor, who came to himself with a start and asked what had happened. Korechika replied by loudly declaiming the words from the Chinese poem, 'The prudent monarch rises from his sleep'.[551] My own eyes were heavy with sleep, but the magnificent way in

249

which Korechika recited the line made me open them wide. Their Majesties were both delighted, and complimented the Counsellor on his apt quotation. Such things are really very splendid.

At about midnight on the following evening, when the Emperor had retired to his bedchamber and I had just called for my servant, Korechika came up to me. 'Are you going to your room?' he said. 'Let me escort you.' Having hung my ceremonial over-skirt and my Chinese jacket on a screen, I allowed him to accompany me.

His Court cloak looked dazzlingly white in the bright moonlight. I noticed that his loose trousers were a bit too long and that he stepped on them as he walked. At one point he held my sleeve and said, 'Be careful not to trip.' Then, as he continued guiding me along the corridors, he recited the line, 'As the traveller journeys by the dying moon's faint light'.[552] I was overjoyed at the quotation – so much so, indeed, that Korechika laughingly remarked, 'You do let yourself get excited by such things, don't you?' Yes, I thought, but how can one help being impressed when someone recites poetry so beautifully?

168. *One Day I Was in the Apartment*

One day I was in the apartment of Her Highness, the Mistress of the Robes,[553] together with Mama, the nurse of the Lord Bishop, when I noticed a man coming along the wooden balcony outside the room. He seemed to be on the verge of tears. 'A terrible thing has happened to me,' he said. 'I don't know where to appeal.' 'Well,' we asked, 'what is it?' 'I was obliged to leave home for a while,' he replied, 'and while I was absent my miserable house was burnt down. For the past several days I have had to live like a hermit-crab, squeezing myself into other people's houses.[554] The fire started in one of the hay-lofts belonging to the Imperial Stables and quickly spread to my home. There is only a fence between the two buildings, and one of the lads in the bed-

250

room just escaped being burnt alive. They didn't save a single object.'

We all burst out laughing at this, including the Mistress of the Robes; I took a sheet of paper and wrote,

> If the vernal sun burns strong enough
> To sprout the young grass roots,
> Even a place like Yodo Plain
> Can ill survive its heat.[555]

'Kindly give him this,' I told Mama, throwing the paper to her. With loud laughter Mama handed the poem to the man. 'Madam has presented you with this,' she explained, 'because she is so sorry for you at having lost your house.'

'What does the record-slip[556] say?' he asked. 'How much is she giving me?'

'Read it first,' said one of the ladies.

'But how can I, Madam?' he asked. 'Neither of my eyes is up to that.'

'Well then, ask someone to read it for you,' said the lady. 'We can't help you. The Empress has sent for us and we must go to the Palace directly. But with such a splendid document in your hands, you have nothing more to worry about.'

Roaring with laughter, we set off for the Palace. 'I wonder if he's shown it to anyone yet,' said one of my companions after a while. 'How furious he will be when he hears what it really is!'

When we saw Her Majesty, Mama told her what had happened, and there was a lot more laughter. The Empress herself joined in, saying, 'How can you all be so mad?'

169. *A Young Man Has Lost His Mother*[557]

A young man has lost his mother; the father loves him dearly but marries again, and the stepmother turns out to be a very dis-agreeable woman. The son is no longer allowed into the main

251

part of the house and lives in one of the wings or in a guest room. This is a pleasant enough room with some outstanding paintings on the screens and panels. An old nurse, or possibly a maid who used to work for his mother, looks after his wardrobe.

He is very popular at Court; even the Emperor enjoys his company and frequently summons him to join in concerts. The young man has an extraordinarily amorous nature. For all this, he is constantly unhappy and nothing in the world seems to please him. The only person to whom he feels close is his elder sister; she is married to a High Court Noble, who dotes upon her and regards her as unique. The young man confides all his feelings to this sister and she is his great consolation in life.

170. *I Cannot Stand a Woman Who Wears Sleeves of Unequal Width*[558]

I cannot stand a woman who wears sleeves of unequal width. If she has several layers of robes, the added weight on one side makes her entire costume lop-sided and most inelegant; if she is dressed in thick wadded clothes, the uneven balance prevents them from closing properly in front, and this too is very unsightly. When a woman wears a robe with sleeves of different width, all her robes must be cut in the same style.

The smartest robes, after all, are those with evenly matched sleeves that people have worn since ancient times. I don't mind if both the sleeves are very wide, but such robes are rather awkward for Court ladies in ceremonial dress.

The fashion of unequal sleeves is just as unattractive for men as for women, since it produces the same lop-sided effect. Yet nowadays everyone seems to have his clothes cut like this, whether he is wearing a fine ceremonial robe or a light summer garment. Fashionable, good-looking people really dress in a most inconvenient way.

171. *Illnesses*

Chest trouble. Illnesses caused by evil spirits. Beriberi. Illnesses that cannot be properly identified yet that make people lose all their appetite.

Once I saw a girl of about eighteen with magnificent hair that hung in thick tresses all the way to her feet; she was nicely plump and had splendid white skin.[559] Apart from her charming features, she was obviously of good breeding. At the moment she was suffering from a very bad toothache. Her hair was in great disorder and where it hung over her forehead it was damp with tears. Quite unconscious of this she kept pressing her hand against her flushed cheek, which made a delightful effect.

On another occasion I saw a girl in an unlined robe of soft white material, an attractive trouser-skirt, and a bright aster cloak. She had a terrible pain in her chest. Her fellow ladies-in-waiting visited her one after another, while outside her room a crowd of young noblemen had come to inquire about her. 'How dreadfully sad!' they exclaimed. 'Has she ever suffered from this before?' In fact none of them seemed particularly concerned, except one who, being the girl's lover, was obviously very distressed about her illness. Since their relations were secret, he was frightened of attracting attention and, though he entered her room, he did not dare come too close. I found it fascinating to watch him standing there, his eyes full of anxiety.

She bound back her beautiful long hair[560] and sat up in bed, saying that she was going to be sick. It was painful to see how ill she looked, yet there was something charming about her appearance.

The Empress, having heard about the girl's condition, sent a priest who was known for his skill in performing the Sacred Readings. He installed himself behind a curtain of state and started to intone his sutras. Since it was a very small room, it was impossible to provide screens and curtains for all the ladies who had come to visit their friend and who now wanted to hear the recitation. They were therefore clearly exposed to view and, while the priest read the scriptures, he kept glancing in their direction, which no doubt earned him a heavy load of guilt.

172. *I Cannot Bear Men to Eat*

I cannot bear men to eat when they come to visit ladies-in-waiting in the Palace. I also object to women who offer food to their male guests. Sometimes these women become quite insistent and say they will do nothing until the man has eaten. In such cases he is bound to give in; after all, he cannot very well put his hand in front of his mouth or turn his head the other way with a look of disgust. For my part, even if a man arrived very late and very drunk, I should never offer him so much as a bowl of watered rice. If he thinks I am heartless and decides not to repeat his visit – well then, let him stay away!

Of course, if I am at home and one of the maids brings my visitor something from the kitchen, there is nothing I can do about it. Yet I find this just as disagreeable.

173. *It Is Very Annoying*

It is very annoying, when one has visited Hase Temple and has retired into one's enclosure, to be disturbed by a herd of common people who come and sit outside in a row, crowded so close together that the tails of their robes fall over each other in utter disarray. I remember that once I was overcome by a great desire to go on a pilgrimage. Having made my way up the log steps, deafened by the fearful roar of the river,[561] I hurried into my enclosure, longing to gaze upon the sacred countenance of Buddha. To my dismay I found that a throng of commoners had settled themselves directly in front of me, where they were incessantly standing up, prostrating themselves, and squatting down again. They looked like so many basket-worms as they crowded together in their hideous clothes, leaving hardly an inch of space between themselves and me. I really felt like pushing them all over sideways.

Important visitors always have attendants to clear such pests from their enclosures; but it is not so easy for ordinary people like me. If one summons one of the priests who is responsible for looking after the pilgrims, he simply says something like 'You there, move back a little, won't you?' and, as soon as he has left, things are as bad as before.

174. *The Way in Which Carpenters Eat*

The way in which carpenters eat is really odd. When they had finished the main building and were working on the eastern wing, some carpenters squatted in a row to have their meal; I sat on the veranda and watched them. The moment the food was brought, they fell on the soup bowls and gulped down the contents. Then they pushed the bowls aside and finished off all the vegetables. I wondered whether they were going to leave their rice; a moment later there wasn't a grain left in the bowls.[562] They all behaved in exactly the same way, so I suppose this must be the custom of carpenters. I should not call it a very charming one.

175. *One Night in the Ninth Month*

One night in the Ninth Month a certain lady was visited by a young man who, though not of the highest nobility, was known for his elegance and keen wits. He left before dawn when the moon still hung in the sky, bathing the whole landscape with its beautiful light. Determined that the lady should think back fondly on their parting,[563] he whispered to her every endearment that he knew. She stood watching for a long time as he disappeared into the distance, believing that this was the last she would see of him that night. The scene was beautiful beyond words.

Her lover, however, had only pretended to be leaving; presently he came back and hid behind a garden fence, intending to let the lady know he was still there. Just then she glanced in his direction and recited the words, 'Like the moon that lingers in the dawning sky.'[564] According to what the man told people later, the moonlight seemed to be shining like a great lamp only a few inches from where the lady was standing, and he was so overcome by the sight that he left without a word.

176. *It Often Happens That a Court Lady*

It often happens that a Court lady is obliged to borrow someone's carriage to travel to or from the Palace. The owner declares that he is only too delighted to be of service, but the carriage attendants do not conceal their annoyance. The drivers shout at the oxen even more roughly than usual and force them to trot along so rapidly that the lady finds it all most disagreeable. The outrunners, looking extremely vexed, keep muttering that they must hurry if they are to be home before dark. Obviously the master himself was none too pleased about lending the carriage, and the lady decides she will never apply to him again even in an emergency.

With Lord Naritō, however, things are totally different. Whether in the middle of the night or at dawn, no lady who borrows his carriage suffers even the slightest embarrassment. He must certainly have trained his attendants carefully. If Naritō is travelling at night and sees some lady's carriage that is stuck in a deep rut and surrounded by a group of furious drivers, he sends his own carriage over to goad the oxen and help the carriage on its way. A man who shows such concern for mere strangers must have given his attendants the most careful instructions about looking after the passengers in his own carriage.

177. *A Young Bachelor*[565]

A young bachelor of an adventurous nature comes home at dawn, having spent the night in some amorous encounter. Though he still looks sleepy, he immediately draws his inkstone to him and, after carefully rubbing it with ink, starts to write his next-morning letter. He does not let his brush run down the paper in a careless scrawl, but puts himself heart and soul into the calligraphy. What a charming figure he makes as he sits there by himself in an easy posture, with his robe falling slightly open! It is a plain unlined robe of pure white, and over it he wears a cloak of rose-yellow or crimson. As he finishes his letter, he notices that the white robe is still damp from the dew, and for a while he gazes at it fondly.

Then he makes arrangements for delivering his letter. Instead of calling one of the ladies in attendance, he takes the trouble to get up and select a page-boy who seems suitable for the task. Summoning the boy to his side, he whispers his instructions and hands over the letter. The page leaves for the lady's house, and for some time the gentleman watches him disappear in the distance. As he sits there, he quietly murmurs some appropriate passage from the sutras.

Now one of his servants comes to announce that his washing-water and morning gruel have been prepared in the neighbouring wing. The gentleman goes there, and soon he is leaning against the reading-desk and looking at some Chinese poems, from which he now and then reads out a passage that he has particularly enjoyed – altogether a charming sight.

Presently he performs his ablutions and changes into a white Court cloak, which he wears without any trousers. Thus attired, he starts reciting the sixth scroll of the Lotus Sutra from memory. A pious gentleman indeed – or so one might think, except that at just this moment the messenger returns (he cannot have had far to go) and nods encouragingly to his master, who thereupon instantly interrupts his recitation and, with what might strike one as sinful haste, transfers his attention to the lady's reply.

178. *It Is Noon on a Summer Day*

It is noon on a summer day and the weather is so hot that one does not know what to do with oneself. One keeps waving one's fan, but there is not a breath of cool air; then, just as one is hurrying to put one's hands in a bowl of iced water, a letter arrives. It is written on a sheet of fine, brilliantly red paper and attached to a Chinese pink in full bloom. Without thinking, one lays aside one's fan (which was not doing much good in any case) and imagines how deeply one's friend must feel to have taken all this trouble on such a suffocating day.

179. *The Floor-Boards in the Ante-Room*[566]

The floor-boards in the ante-room are shining so brightly that they mirror everything near by, and some crisp new straw matting has been placed near the three-post curtain of state. The curtains themselves give a lovely cool impression; when one pushes them, they glide smoothly back, opening far wider than one expected and revealing the lady of the house, who under the faded dark robe she is using as her bedclothing wears a white unlined gown of raw silk and a crimson trouser-skirt.

By the light of the lamp one can see that the blinds further back in the room have been raised all the way; below them several women, including a couple of ladies-in-waiting, girl attendants, and others, sit leaning against the raised beam between the ante-room and the veranda. In another part of the room some more ladies are huddled together under a closed blind. A fire is smouldering deep in the incense-burner, giving out a scent that is vaguely melancholy and full of a calm elegance.[567]

258

Late in the evening there is a stealthy tap outside. A lady-in-waiting (the one who always knows what is happening) hurries to the gate and lets in the gentleman visitor. Then with a smug look on her face she stealthily leads him to the lady who has been awaiting his arrival.

From one side of the hall comes the beautiful sound of lute music. The player plucks the strings so gently that even when the murmur of conversation dies down one can barely make out the notes.

180. *At First Dawn a Carriage Passes*

At first dawn a carriage passes along the near-by avenue. The gentleman who is travelling in it has raised the blinds so that he can enjoy the beautiful pale moon, and one is delighted to hear him recite in a most elegant voice, 'As the traveller goes by the dying moon's faint light.'[568]

It is delightful also when a man on horseback recites poetry at dawn. I remember that once I heard a splendid line of verse accompanied by the flapping of a horse's mud-shields. Who could the rider be? When I put aside what I was doing and looked out, I was dismayed to see that he was a vulgar commoner.

181. *A Handsome Young Gentleman*

A handsome young gentleman is riding along on horseback, beautifully dressed in a Court cloak, over-robe, and hunting costume, with the full array of his varicoloured under-robes emerging at the opening of his sleeves. Still in his saddle, he hands an elegantly knotted letter to the servant who accompanies him on foot. It is delightful to observe how the man looks up at his master as he takes the letter from him.

182. *The House Had a Spacious Courtyard*

The house had a spacious courtyard and was shadowed by tall pine trees. To the south and east the lattice-windows were all wide open. It gave a cool feeling when one looked inside. In the main room was a four-foot curtain of state and in front of it a round hassock on which a priest was kneeling. He was in his early thirties and quite handsome. Over his grey habit he wore a fine silk stole – altogether the effect was magnificent. Cooling himself with a clove-scented fan, he recited the Magic Incantation of the Thousand Hands.[569]

I gathered that someone in the house was seriously ill,[570] for now a heavily built girl with a splendid head of hair edged her way into the room. Clearly this was the medium to whom the evil spirit was going to be transferred. She was wearing an unlined robe of stiff silk and long, light-coloured trousers.

When the girl had sat down next to the priest in front of a small three-foot curtain of state, he turned round and handed her a thin, highly polished wand.[571] Then with his eyes tightly shut he began to read the mystic incantations, his voice coming out in staccato bursts as he uttered the sacred syllables. It was an impressive sight, and many of the ladies of the house came out from behind the screens and curtains and sat watching in a group.

After a short time the medium began to tremble and fell into a trance. It was awesome indeed to see how the priest's incantations were steadily taking effect. The medium's brother, a slender young man in a long robe who had only recently celebrated his coming of age, stood behind the girl, fanning her.

Everyone who witnessed the scene was overcome with respect. It occurred to me how embarrassed the girl herself would feel to be exposed like this if she were in her normal state of mind. She lay there groaning and wailing in the most terrible way, and, though one realized that she was in no actual pain,[572] one could not help sympathizing with her. Indeed, one of the patients'

260

friends, feeling sorry for the girl, went up to her curtain of state and helped to rearrange her disordered clothing.

Meanwhile it was announced that the patient was a little better. Some young attendants were sent to the kitchen to fetch hot water and other requisites. Even while they were carrying their trays they kept darting uneasy glances at the exorcist. They wore pretty unlined robes and formal skirts whose light mauve colour was as fresh as on the day they were dyed – it made a most charming effect.

By the Hour of the Monkey[573] the priest had brought the spirit under control and, having forced it to beg for mercy, he now dismissed it. 'Oh!' exclaimed the medium. 'I thought I was behind the curtains and here I am in front. What on earth has happened?' Overcome with embarrassment, she hid her face in her long hair and was about to glide out of the room when the priest stopped her and, after murmuring a few incantations, said, 'Well, my dear, how do you feel? You should be quite yourself by now.' He smiled at the girl, but this only added to her confusion.

'I should have liked to stay a little longer,' said the priest, as he prepared to leave the house, 'but I am afraid it is almost time for my evening prayers.' The people of the house tried to stop him. 'Please wait a moment,' they said. 'We should like to make an offering.' But the priest was obviously in a great hurry and would not stay. At this point a lady of noble rank, evidently a member of the family, edged her way up to the priest's curtain of state and said, 'We are most grateful for your visit, Your Reverence. Our patient looked as if she might well succumb to the evil spirit, but now she is well on the way to recovery. I cannot tell you how delighted we are. If Your Reverence has any free time tomorrow, would you please call again?'

'I fear we are dealing with a very obstinate spirit,' the priest replied briefly, 'and we must not be off our guard. I am pleased that what I did today has helped the patient.'[574] So saying, he took his leave with an air of such dignity that everyone felt the Buddha himself had appeared on earth.[575]

183. *Things That are Unpleasant to See*

Someone in a robe whose back seam is crooked.

People who wear their clothes with the collars pulled back.

A High Court Noble's carriage that has dirty blinds.

People who insist on bringing out all their children when they receive a visit from someone who rarely comes to see them.

Boys who wear high clogs[576] with their trouser-skirts. I realize that this is the modern fashion, but I still don't like it.

Women in travelling costumes who walk in a great hurry.[577]

A priest who is acting as a Master of Divination and who wears a paper head-dress[578] to perform a service of purification.

A thin, ugly woman who has dark skin and wears a wig.

A lean, hirsute man taking a nap in the daytime.[579] Does it occur to him what a spectacle he is making of himself? Ugly men should sleep only at night, for they cannot be seen in the dark and, besides, most people are in bed themselves. But they should get up at the crack of dawn, so that no one has to see them lying down.[580]

A pretty woman looks even prettier when she gets up after taking a nap on a summer day. But an unattractive woman should avoid such things, for her face will be all puffy and shining and, if she is not lucky, her cheeks will have an ugly, lop-sided look. When two people, having taken a nap together in the daytime, wake up and see each other's sleep-swollen faces, how dreary life must seem to them!

A dark-skinned person looks very ugly in an unlined robe of stiff silk. If the robe is scarlet,[581] however, it looks better, even though it is just as transparent. I suppose one of the reasons I do not like ugly women to wear unlined robes is that one can see their navels.

184. *When the Middle Captain*

When the Middle Captain of the Left Guards Division was still Governor of Ise, he visited me one day at my home. There was a straw mat at the edge of the veranda, and I pulled it out for him. This notebook of mine happened to be lying on the mat, but I did not notice it in time. I snatched at the book and made a desperate effort to get it back; but the Captain instantly took it off with him and did not return it until much later. I suppose it was from this time that my book began to be passed about at Court.

185. *It Is Getting So Dark*

It is getting so dark that I can scarcely go on writing; and my brush is all worn out. Yet I should like to add a few things before I end.

I wrote these notes at home, when I had a good deal of time to myself and thought no one would notice what I was doing. Everything that I have seen and felt is included. Since much of it might appear malicious and even harmful to other people, I was careful to keep my book hidden. But now it has become public, which is the last thing I expected.

One day Lord Korechika, the Minister of the Centre, brought the Empress a bundle of notebooks. 'What shall we do with them?' Her Majesty asked me. 'The Emperor has already made arrangements for copying the "Records of the Historian".'[582]

'Let me make them into a pillow,' I said.[583]

'Very well,' said Her Majesty. 'You may have them.'

I now had a vast quantity of paper at my disposal, and I set about filling the notebooks with odd facts, stories from the past, and all sorts of other things, often including the most trivial material. On the whole I concentrated on things and people that I found charming and splendid; my notes are also full of poems and observations on trees and plants, birds and insects. I was sure that when people saw my book they would say, 'It's even worse than I expected. Now one can really tell what she is like.' After all, it is written entirely for my own amusement and I put things down exactly as they came to me. How could my casual jottings possibly bear comparison with the many impressive books that exist in our time? Readers have declared, however, that I can be proud of my work. This has surprised me greatly; yet I suppose it is not so strange that people should like it, for, as will be gathered from these notes of mine, I am the sort of person who approves of what others abhor and detests the things they like.[584]

Whatever people may think of my book, I still regret that it ever came to light.

LIST OF ABBREVIATIONS

E.J.H.	R. K. Reischauer, *Early Japanese History*, Princeton, 1937.
Hyōshaku	Kaneko Motoomi, *Makura no Sōshi Hyōshaku*, Tokyo, 1927.
Ikeda-Kishigami	Ikeda Kikan and Kishigami Shinji, *Makura no Sōshi*, Nihon Koten Bungaku Taikei ed., Tokyo, 1958.
Sansom, *History*	Sir George Sansom, *A History of Japan*, vol. i, London, 1958.
W.P.B.	Arthur Waley, *The Pillow-Book of Sei Shōnagon*, London, 1928.
W.S.P.	Ivan Morris, *The World of the Shining Prince*, Penguin Books, 1969.

NOTES

1. The famous opening words of *The Pillow Book* constitute an elliptical sentence. Their literal meaning is 'As for spring the dawn', but some predicate like 'is the most beautiful time of the day' must be understood. The same applies to the opening phrases of each of the four paragraphs in this section.

2. See App. 1. New Year's Day was, and still is, an occasion for paying one's respects to the Emperor and to other superiors (*W.S.P.*, p. 167). It also marked an increase in one's own age, thus corresponding in some ways to the Western birthday.

3. The Festival of Young Herbs was one of the seven national festivals listed in the code of 718 (see App. 1). Derived from Han China, it had been observed at the Japanese Court since the reign of Emperor Saga in the early ninth century. The 'seven herbs' (parsley, borage, etc.) were plucked and made into a gruel which was supposed to ward off evil spirits and to protect one's health throughout the year. In the Palace a bowl of this gruel was ceremoniously presented to the Emperor (see *W.S.P.*, p. 169).

4. Normally the grounds near the Palace were kept clear of plants, weeds, etc.; but at this time of the year it was possible to find 'young herbs', since they were hidden by the snow. (In this translation Palace with a capital P invariably refers to the Imperial Palace in Heian Kyō, App. 3c.)

5. The Festival of the Blue Horses was an annual ceremony in which twenty-one horses from the Imperial stables were paraded before the Emperor in the great courtyard in front of the Ceremonial Palace. (See App. 1.) The custom, which had existed in ancient China, was imported to Japan early in the eighth century. Originally the horses were steel grey (hence the name 'blue'); but, since such horses were very rare and

267

since white was the colour of purity in Shintō ritual, they were replaced in the early tenth century by white horses.

6. The Central Gate: refers to the Taiken Mon, the main eastern gate of the Greater Imperial Palace. A huge wooden cross-beam was fixed on the ground and joined the two main pillars of the gate.

7. Senior courtier: a gentleman of the Fourth or Fifth Rank who had the privilege of waiting in attendance on the Emperor in the Senior Courtiers' Chamber; in certain special cases gentlemen of the Sixth Rank were also accorded this privilege (see note 86) and they too were known as senior courtiers.

   For ranks and offices see App. 2 and *W.S.P.*, pp. 78–80.

   'Left Division' is an abbreviation of 'Outer Palace Guards, Left Division', one of the Imperial Guards regiments in charge of the outer gates of the Palace and also responsible for patrolling the Palace grounds. Their guard-house was on the route of the Blue Horse procession.

8. On the eighth day of the First Month presents of silk and brocade were given to the Imperial Princesses, and many of the Court ladies were promoted in rank. All those who had been so favoured went to present their formal thanks to the emperor.

9. Full-moon gruel: a special gruel eaten on the fifteenth day of the First Month (see *W.S.P.*, p. 170 and App. 1). Its name derived from the fact that the full moon in the lunar calendar was invariably on the fifteenth of the month. A stick of peeled elder-wood was used to stir the gruel, and it was believed that, if a woman was struck on the loins with such a stick, she would soon give birth to a male child. (N.B. the fifteenth of the First Month was also dedicated to Shintō deities representing the male element.) It therefore became customary on this day for women to run about the house hitting each other playfully with these sticks. The custom,

which survived in rural districts until fairly modern times, possibly had phallic origins, and it may be related to the country dances in which the participants whacked each other with large wooden phalli.

10. The young man was a *muko* (son-in-law). According to the standard systems of marriage among the Heian upper classes, the husband either moved in with his wife's family, or continued living at home and visited her more or less regularly to spend the night. For details see Ivan Morris, 'Marriage in the World of Genji', *Asia*, spring 1968.

11. According to some of the commentators, the woman was Shōnagon herself; the description certainly fits.

12. 'Empress' in this translation always refers to Fujiwara no Sadako, Michitaka's daughter in whose Court Sei Shōnagon served as lady-in-waiting.

13. Colours of clothes in Heian literature frequently referred, not to single colours, but to certain fashionable combinations produced by lining the costume with material of a different colour from the outside. A 'cherry-coloured' cloak, for instance, was one whose outside was white and whose lining was red or violet.

14. The Festival: refers to the Kamo Festival, the main Shintō celebration of the year, which was observed in the middle of the Fourth Month (see *W.S.P.*, p. 173, and App. 1).

15. *Hototogisu*: usually translated 'cuckoo'; but the *hototogisu* (*cuculus poliocephalus*) is a far more poetic type of bird with none of the cuckoo's cheeky associations, and I prefer to leave it in the original (cf. *uguisu*, note 134). The name, *hototogisu*, is an onomatopoeia derived from the bird's characteristic cry of *ho-to-to*; in Heian times people accordingly described the *hototogisu* as 'announcing its name'.

16. Dyeing was one of the great arts of the Heian period, as well as a pastime for women of quality. It was done with particular

care when the clothes were to be worn during the Kamo Festival. The three forms mentioned here are: border shading, in which the material becomes darker towards the bottom of the garment; uneven shading, in which the material is dyed unevenly all over; and rolled dyeing, in which the material is rolled up before being immersed in the dye.

17. Women's language was traditionally far less influenced by Chinese and contained a much larger proportion of 'pure' Japanese words and constructions. In the *Sangenbon* texts the title of this section is: 'Cases in which people say the same thing, but sound different'.

18. Popular Buddhist beliefs at the time included the following: 'If a man becomes a priest, his father and mother are saved until the seventh generation' and 'When a child takes the Vows, nine of his relations are reborn in Heaven.'

19. The events described in this section occurred towards the very end of the period covered by *The Pillow Book* (see App. 5). It was in the Eighth Month of 999 that Empress Sadako moved from the Palace to Narimasa's house in the Third Ward. The move was necessitated by her pregnancy, which made her ritually unclean (see *W.S.P.*, pp. 107–8) and therefore unable to stay under the same roof as the Emperor. The palace in the Second Ward, where she would normally have gone, had burnt down and she was obliged to move into Narimasa's comparatively modest residence.

   Four-pillared gates could normally be built only by men of the Second Rank or above (*W.S.P.*, p. 80). Because of the Empress's visit, however, Narimasa had been given special permission to add two extra pillars to his gate.

20. Yü Kung (Ukō) of the Former Han dynasty was so proud of his son, Ting Kuo (Teikoku), that he ordered a specially high gate to be built in front of his house; this was to permit the passage of the great retinues that he knew would one day

accompany the young man. Narimasa, even though he has 'strayed along these paths' (i.e. the paths of Chinese scholarship), seems to be mixing up the name of the son and that of the father (who was not nearly so well known); Shōnagon does not take him up on the mistake – an interesting omission in view of her reputation for being learned (cf. the end of note 112).

It should be borne in mind that Shōnagon and Narimasa are speaking to each other through a screen, and that they are kneeling on straw mats in the same room as the Empress but at such a distance from her that she cannot hear their conversation (*W.S.P.*, p. 46).

21. The layout of Heian rooms is difficult to suggest in translation; I have tried to make my equivalents as simple as possible, and in a few cases I have slightly abbreviated the descriptions when the details seemed unimportant.

The term *hisashi*, which is particularly intractable to smooth translation, referred to a part of the room that was covered by deep eaves and that was situated between the main part of the room and the open veranda; the *hisashi* was normally divided into four sections, designated as north, south, east, and west (in the present passage we find western *hisashi*). 'Ante-room' is probably the best equivalent, but it must be remembered that the *hisashi* was not a separate room. Latticed shutters or gratings divided the *hisashi* from the open veranda, the main part of the room was separated from the *hisashi* by blinds or curtains or both (see App. 4b). Great importance was attached to geographical directions both within and outside the house (see *W.S.P.*, p. 137). Since the Heian house faced south, north can conveniently be translated as 'back' (of the house, room, etc.).

22. *Kichō* (curtain of state or curtain-frame): a piece of furniture that played a most important part in Heian domestic architecture. Analogous to the Indian pardah, it was a portable frame, about six feet high and of variable width,

which supported opaque hangings and was mainly aimed at protecting the women of the house from being seen by men and strangers (*W.S.P.*, p. 48, and App. 4b). When reading *The Pillow Book*, we should remember that Shōnagon and her companions spent a good part of their time ensconced behind *kichō*.

23. Princess Imperial refers to Princess Osako, Emperor Ichijō's eldest daughter, who was born to Sadako in 996, and who came with the Empress to Narimasa's house in 999.

24. Narimasa does not know the name of the over-garment in question and is obliged to use an absurd circumlocution; it is much as if a man were to say 'the garment that covers a woman's shoulders' for 'shawl'.

25. Instead of the normal *chiisai* ('small'), Narimasa says *chūsei*. According to Waley, this is an affection; but it sounds more like a provincial dialect, probably from Mimasaka Province near the Inland Sea, where his father had been Assistant Governor. Anything in the way of a provincialism was bound to amuse Shōnagon and her companions. According to another theory, it was a type of student dialect that Narimasa retained from his days at the University, but this seems far-fetched.

26. Middle Counsellor: one of six officials of the Third Rank who served in the Great Council of State, the central bureaucracy of the Heian government (App. 2). Narimasa refers to his elder brother, Taira no Korenaka (*c.* 944–1006), who later became Assistant Governor-General of the Government Headquarters in Kyūshū. Shōnagon appears to have had more respect for Korenaka than for his younger brother, whom she clearly regarded as a figure of fun.

    What impressed Korenaka, of course, was Shōnagon's neat allusion to Ting Kuo (note 20).

27. Cats had been imported from the Continent, and there are several references to them in Heian chronicles and literature.

The diary of Fujiwara no Sanesuke, for instance, contains the momentous entry (on the nineteenth day of the Ninth Month in 999) that one of the Palace cats gave birth to a litter of kittens, that the birth-ceremony was attended by no lesser dignitaries than the Ministers of the Left and of the Right, and that Uma no Myōbu was appointed nurse to the litter. Myōbu no Omoto may well have been one of the kittens born on this occasion. Readers of *The Tale of Genji* will recall the important part played by a cat in the Kashiwagi-Nyosan story. Emperor Ichijō was known to be particularly fond of cats, and there were several in his Palace; few, however, were elevated to the nobility.

Head-dress of nobility: originally this referred to the ceremonial head-dress given by the Emperor to gentlemen of the Fifth Rank and above. It was a small, round, black cap with a protuberance sticking up in the back and a wide, stiff ribbon hanging down.

Lady Myōbu: *Myōbu* originally designated a lady who, either by marriage or in her own right, belonged to the Fifth Rank or above; from the tenth century the term was applied to any woman of medium rank. *Omoto* was a general term for high-ranking ladies-in-waiting, especially those serving in the Imperial Palace.

28. Imperial Dining Room: this was the room in which ceremonial meals were served to the Emperor in the mornings and evenings; his real meals were eaten in another room.

29. Chamberlain: one of the officials in the Emperor's Private Office which was in charge of matters relating to the Emperor and his Palace. This office had been established early in the ninth century as a means of simplifying the cumbrous Chinese administration and of concentrating power. For a time it was the most important organ of government, relegating many of the older departments to political insignificance.

30. i.e., on the occasion of the Jōmi Festival earlier in the same

273

month. On this day the dogs in the Palace were frequently decorated with flowers and leaves.

31. Ukon was one of the ladies in the Palace Attendants' Office, a bureau of female officials who waited on the Emperor.

    Almost certainly Ukon recognizes Okinamaro, but pretends that it is a different dog in order to spare him further punishment (cf. Shōnagon's own reply to Tadataka on p. 33).

32. Table Room: a room with a large table adjoining the Imperial Dining Room (note 28) and used mainly by the the Emperor's ladies-in-waiting.

    Tadataka , of course, does not enter the Empress's room, but stands outside the blinds, where he cannot actually see the dog.

33. In this section Shōnagon lists the Five Festivals, see App. 1.

34. The Weaver Festival is derived from a Chinese legend about the love of the Weaver and the Herdsman represented by the stars Vega and Altair respectively. Because of her love for the Herdsman, the Weaver neglected her work on the clothes for the gods, while the Herdsman neglected his cattle. As a punishment the Heavenly Emperor put the two stars on opposite sides of the Milky Way, decreeing that they should be allowed to meet only once a year, namely on the seventh day of the Seventh Month, when a company of heavenly magpies use their wings to form a bridge that the Weaver can cross to join her lover. The magpies, however, will not make the bridge unless it is a clear night; if it rains, the lovers must wait until the next year. During the Tanabata Festival poems are written in dedication to the two starry lovers, and women pray to the Weaver for skill in weaving, sewing, music, poetry, and other arts. The peculiar name of the month may derive from these customs. Altars with offerings and incense were set up outside the palaces and private houses on the night of the seventh.

35. Floss silk covers were put over the chrysanthemums on the eve of the Chrysanthemum Festival (see note 33 and *W.S.P.*, p. 177), either to protect them from the dew or, according to another theory, so that one might enjoy these scent-impregnated covers, which, incidentally, were believed to protect people from old age if they rubbed their bodies with them.

36. Baton: a flat stick held by officials in the right hand on occasions when they wore Court costume; instructions concerning details of Court ceremony were sometimes written on the batons or on pieces of paper pasted to them. For gentlemen of the Fifth Rank and above the batons were ivory; otherwise they were wood.

37. Ceremonial movements: a complicated series of movements performed when giving thanks to the Emperor or on other formal occasions, and so elegant and stylized as to be equivalent to a dance, in which the various gestures and poses are intended to express the joy and gratitude of the performer.

38. For the importance attached to geographical directions see note 21.

   North-east, lit. ox-tiger, was the unlucky direction according to traditional Chinese beliefs (see *W.S.P.*, p. 137). Directions were frequently named by reference to the Chinese Zodiac.

   Seiryō Palace, lit. Pure and Fresh Palace, was the normal residence of the reigning Emperor. The Empress's room was used by her when she came from her own palace, the Koki Den, to stay with the Emperor; the sliding screen 'protected' this room from the northern veranda of the Palace by scaring away any evil spirits that might be lurking in the vicinity. The terrifying creatures with long arms and legs were, of course, imaginary; they were of Chinese origin.

39. His Excellency the Major Counsellor: Major Counsellors were among the top officials in the Great Council of State (App. 2).

The present incumbent was Fujiwara no Korechika, the elder brother of the Empress, who received the appointment in 992. Two years later he became Minister of the Centre; but in 996 he was exiled from the capital, ostensibly because of a scandal involving a former Emperor, but in fact because of the rivalry of his uncle, Michinaga (see *W.S.P.*, p. 71). Korechika was noted for his good looks, and many commentators have regarded him as a (or even the) model for the Shining Prince, the hero of *The Tale of Genji*.

40. Daytime Chamber: the main room of Seiryō Palace.

41. Threshold: the threshold between the main part of the room and the *hisashi* (note 21).

42. Taken from the *Manyō Shū*, but with a few minor changes. Mimoro, in eastern Yamato, is the site of an ancient Shintō shrine mentioned in the *Kojiki*. The mountain is associated with the idea of the everlasting power promised to the Japanese Imperial line by the Shintō deities. Korechika no doubt has in mind the continued prosperity of the Empress, his sister.

43. Naniwazu: famous poem attributed to the Korean scholar, Wani (who is said to have introduced Chinese writing into Japan), and later to Emperor Nintoku (*c.* 400). The second attribution was made by Ki no Tsurayuki in his preface to the *Kokin Shū*: 'The Naniwazu is the first poem to have been composed by an Emperor.'
    The poem is as follows:

> Ah, this flower that bloomed
> In the port of Naniwa
> And was hidden in the winter months!
> Now that spring is here
> Once more it blossoms forth.

Naniwa is the old name of Ōsaka; the flower in question is the early-blooming plum blossom. Children in the Heian period were taught the poem for writing practice; accordingly the word *naniwa* (*zu*) was often used as an equivalent of ABC (e.g. in *The Tale of Genji*: 'She still does not know her *naniwazu* properly'); and by extension it could mean 'elementary', 'unformed'.

44. The original poem, which is included in the *Kokin Shū*, was composed by Fujiwara no Yoshifusa while admiring some sprays of cherry blossom in a vase. It was inspired by pleasure at the success of his daughter, Akiko, who had become Emperor Montoku's principal consort, and the flower in his poem refers to the girl. By changing 'flower' to 'lord', Shōnagon makes the poem refer to Emperor Ichijō.

45. See App. 2.

46. Because of its reference to having grown old. Shōnagon had now reached the ripe old age of about thirty and was therefore, by Heian standards, well into her middle years.

47. Imperial Lady: a consort of the Emperor or Crown Prince, ranking below the Second Empress but above the Imperial Concubines.

    Senyō Palace: building in the Imperial Palace compound, used as a residence for Imperial Ladies.

    The woman in question was Fujiwara no Yoshiko, a great favourite of Emperor Murakami's; she was noted both for her poetic talents and for her beauty, especially her long hair.

48. Day of abstinence: one of the frequent inauspicious days determined by the Masters of Divination, when, according to current superstition, it was essential to stay indoors and, as much as possible, to abstain from all activities, including eating, sexual intercourse, and even such seemingly innocuous acts as reading a letter. Particularly strict rules applied to what the Emperor did on these days.

49. *Go*: a fascinating, complicated game, introduced from China in the eighth century. It is played with black and white

stones on a board with 361 intersections (19 × 19). The two players take turns in placing their stones on any suitable intersection. Once a stone has been placed, it cannot be moved to another intersection; stones that have been encircled by the enemy, however, are forfeit unless they are so placed that they themselves enclose at least two independent and viable openings or 'eyes'.

Go stones were frequently used as counters for scoring games and contests.

50. Attendant: the following three ranks of women officials served in the Naishi no Tsukasa (Palace Attendants' Office): (i) two Chief Attendants, (ii) four Assistant Attendants, (iii) four Attendants. Under them came one hundred women. In Shōnagon's time the two top posts were occupied by concubines of the Emperor; in the present passage she refers to the third category of official.

51. High Court Noble: a designation for all gentlemen of the Third Rank and above, as well as for Imperial Advisers of the Fourth Rank, but not usually applied to the Chancellor or the Regent.

52. Gosechi: Court dances performed in the Eleventh Month by young girls of good family (App. 1). Of the four girls who participated in the dances, three were the daughters of High Court Nobles and one (as in the present passage) the daughter of a provincial governor.

53. These nets were designed for catching whitebait during the winter; in spring-time they were useless.

54. Dresses of this colour could be worn only during the Eleventh and Twelfth Months.

55. Scholarly activities, like most other specialized occupations, tended to run in families; and they were not considered suitable for girls (see *W.S.P.*, pp. 220–21).

When reading these lists, we must remember that the word

278

mono can refer to both things and people; *Depressing Things and People* would be a more comprehensive translation of the heading.

56. *Katatagae* (avoidance of an unlucky direction): when a Master of Divination informed one that a certain direction (e.g. north) was 'blocked up' by one of the invisible, moving deities that were central to Heian superstition (*W.S.P.*, p. 138), one might circumvent the danger by first proceeding in a different direction (e.g. west); after stopping on the way at an intermediate place and staying there at least until midnight, one would continue to one's intended destination (e.g. by going north-east). People would also leave their house for a *katatagae* because they wished to obtain release from some future taboo, abstinence, or prohibition, even though they had no particular desire to go anywhere at the time. By performing such a seemingly gratuitous *katatagae*, they were freed in advance from the baleful effect that one of the moving divinities might exert if they remained at home or indulged in some tabooed activity like ground-breaking. Such moves were especially common during the Seasonal Change that followed the onset of the Great Cold in the early part of the year; though this was a festive period, a particularly large number of inauspicious spirits was abroad: 'On the eve of the [Spring] Seasonal Change all sorts of ceremonies took place, and feasts were held to celebrate the occasion. Moreover, it was customary for everyone, including the Emperor, the Retired Emperor, the Empress Dowager, and the Great Ministers, to perform *katatagae*; these were known as the "*katatagae* of the Seasonal Change". *Katatagae* were not limited to occasions on which people wished to travel abroad, but also took place on those inauspicious days when they had to be absent from their homes [because of the unlucky position of one of the moving deities]. At such times they would go and stay in the house of an acquaintance – for a couple of days in the case of a short *katatagae*, for seven or

even forty-nine days in the case of a long one.' (*Kōchū Nihon Bungaku Taikei*, xxv, 211.) Thieves often took advantage of these beliefs to enter their victims' house when they knew that the master and his family would have to be absent because of a *katatagae*.

The traveller who stopped at someone's house during the the performance of any *katatagae* was normally accorded a special welcome and friendly entertainment.

57. Apart from official correspondence the two main types of formal letters were 'knotted' and 'twisted'. Both were folded lengthwise into a narrow strip; but, whereas the knotted kind was knotted in the middle or at one end, sometimes with a sprig of blossoms stuck into the knot, the twisted kind was twisted at both ends and tended to be narrower. A few thick lines of ink were drawn over the knot or fold by way of a seal.

58. The aim of the exorcist was to transfer the evil spirit from the afflicted person to the medium, who was usually a young girl or woman, and to force it to declare itself. He made use of various spells and incantations so that the medium might be possessed by the Guardian Demon of Buddhism. When he was successful, the medium would tremble, scream, have convulsions, faint, or behave as if in a hypnotic trance. The spirit would then declare itself through her mouth. The final step was to drive the spirit out of the medium. See *W.S.P.*, pp. 147–52.

59. One watch was the equivalent of two hours.

60. i.e., appointments to provincial governorships. Despite the low social status of provincial officials, these posts could be extremely lucrative.

61. The messengers cannot bring themselves to announce in so many words that their master has failed to obtain an appointment; instead they answer by giving his existing title, which he had hoped to shed in favour of the new one.

62. When one received a poem, it was *de rigueur* to reply promptly by a 'return' poem in which one would normally ring the changes on some central image. A failure to reply (or at least to have a friend, relation, colleague, etc. make a reply in one's place) was regarded as the height of rudeness. It was socially permissible not to answer love poems, but this of course signified that one was totally uninterested in the sender.

63. On the third, fifth, and seventh days after a child's birth it was customary for the grandparents and other members of the family to send presents of swaddling-clothes.

Presents were also given to people leaving on a journey. Originally it was the custom for the traveller's friends to see him off personally and, just before he left, they would turn his mount's head in the direction for which he was bound. This is the origin of the word used to describe the parting present: 'turning the horse's nose'. Later it became customary to send a messenger with presents of food, etc., rather than to go oneself.

Messengers were originally rewarded by having a gift of clothing (an early form of currency) put on their shoulders; hence 'placed on the shoulders', the name for rewards given to a messenger. In later times other forms of compensation were given (*W.S.P.*, p. 87).

64. Herbal balls: during the Iris Festival in the Fifth Month various kinds of herbs were bound into balls and put into round cotton or silk bags, which were decorated with irises and other plants, as well as with long, five-coloured cords; they were then hung on pillars, curtains, etc. to protect the inhabitants of the house from illness and other misfortunes. They stayed there until the Chrysanthemum Festival in the Ninth Month, when they were changed for balls decorated with chrysanthemum leaves, which were left hanging until the Iris Festival in the following year. A close Western equivalent is the asafoetida bag, worn about the neck to ward off illness.

Hare-sticks: three-inch sticks with long, coloured tassels presented at the New Year to keep away evil spirits. They were hung on pillars in the Palace and in the houses of the nobility on the fourth day of the month, which corresponded to the First Day of the Hare (App. 1). Both the herbal balls and the hare-sticks were of Chinese origin.

65. That is to say, he has still not made his wife pregnant.

66. There was a strong prejudice against taking naps in the day-time (*W.S.P.*, p. 297); the practice was considered especially undignified and unaesthetic for elderly people.

67. Because it interfered with the many New Year's celebrations.

68. Fasting was enjoined by the Buddhist church on the eighth, fourteenth, fifteenth, twenty-third, twenty-ninth, and thirtieth of each month. There were also periods of abstinence in the First, Fifth and Ninth Months; and on certain special occasions, when people wished to expiate serious offences, they would undertake fasts lasting 100 or 1,000 days. The efficacy of the entire fast was sacrificed if one violated the restrictions for a single day.

69. This was the Leaf-turning Month, i.e. the second month of autumn (App. 1). A white under-robe was normally worn only in the summer months. As a rule Shōnagon and her contemporaries strongly disapproved of anything that deviated from the seasonal or diurnal routines. The first three items in the present list belong to the same category.

70. Hunting costume: men's informal outdoor costume, original-ly worn for hunting.

71. *Eboshi* (tall, lacquered hat): black, lacquered head-dress worn by men on the top of the head and secured by a mauve silk cord that was fastened under the chin; two long black pendants hung down from the back of the hat. The *eboshi* was a most conspicuous form of headgear and hardly suited for a clandestine visit.

72. Iyo blind: a rough type of reed blind manufactured in the province of Iyo on the Inland Sea.

Head-blind: a more elegant type of blind whose top and edges were decorated with strips of silk. It also had thin strips of bamboo along the edges and was therefore heavier than ordinary blinds.

73. Sneezing was a bad omen, and it was normal to counteract its effects by reciting some auspicious formula, such as wishing long life to the person who had sneezed (cf. 'Bless you!' in the West).

74. *Owasu* ('good enough to do') and *notamau* ('kindly remarked') designate the actions of a superior; *haberu* (lit. 'to serve') is used to describe one's own or someone else's actions in relation to a superior. See my *Dictionary of Selected Forms in Classical Japanese Literature until* c. *1330*, App. IV. The correct use of honorific, polite, and humble locutions was of course enormously important in a strictly hierarchic society. In the present passage the sentence beginning 'No doubt . . .' is ironic.

75. Etiquette demanded that in the presence of the Emperor or Empress one referred to oneself by one's name rather than by the first person singular. One referred to other people by their real names; if Their Majesties were not present, however, one referred to these people by their offices (e.g. Major Counsellor). On the whole, personal pronouns were avoided and this added to the importance of correct honorific usage.

76. Paper: elegant coloured paper that gentlemen carried in the folds of their clothes. It served for writing notes and was also used like an elegant sort of Kleenex.

77. Takasago: well-known folk-song that starts,

> Ah, the jewel-like camellia
> And the jewel-like willow
> That grow in Takasago
> Upon Saisago Hill. . .

78. Suketada's father, who belonged to the Southern Branch of the Fujiwara family, was Governor of Owari; his mother appears to have come from a humble family in that region. Suketada was adopted by a more influential branch of the Fujiwara family and managed to rise in the hierarchy until he became Governor of Yamato.

79. 'Who can stand next to . . .?': lit. 'He has no one on his left or right.' This has a double meaning: (i) no one is his match (in roughness), (ii) no one wants to be near him (because of his rough manners). Owari, in eastern Japan, was noted for the uncouthness of its inhabitants.

80. The Kamo Festival was also known as the Hollyhock Festival (Aoi Matsuri). During the celebrations (see note 14) hollyhock was attached to the pillars, blinds, etc. and left there until it withered and fell off. Hollyhock was also used to decorate people's hair and head-dresses. 'I am grateful to Professor Cranston for pointing out (*Harvard Journal of Asiatic Studies*, vol. xxix, p. 260) that the *aoi* used in connexion with the Kamo Festival was not *althea rosea* (hollyhock) but *asarum caulescens*, which is a form of snake-weed or bistort with paired, flesh-coloured flowers. A more accurate translation of Aoi Matsuri would therefore be Bistort Festival, but I trust botanists will not be offended if I call it Hollyhock Festival.

81. To find dolls or any of the other things used during the Hiina Asobi (Display of Dolls) would be like coming across a box of old Christmas decorations.

82. Deep violet: another reminder of the Kamo Festival. A piece of material from a costume to be worn at the Festival turns up between the pages of a notebook, where it has been lying for months or perhaps even years.

83. Paper fan: a fan covered with paper on one side of the frame and used in the summer months. When open, it looked like a

bat with spread-out wings. Coming upon this fan, perhaps during the winter, Shōnagon is reminded of something that happened in the summer.

84. In Japan, as in China, the moon traditionally evokes memories of the past.

85. The wickerwork carriage was a lighter, less impressive form of vehicle, covered with a reed or bamboo trellis.

86. Shōnagon refers here to relatively low-ranking members of the Emperor's Private Office. During the six years of their tenure they had access to Seiryō Palace, where they attended the Emperor at his meals and performed similar duties. If at the end of their six years there was no possibility of promotion, they normally retired, or 'went down' as the expression was. It was, in other words, a case of 'up or out'. As a sort of compensation they were elevated from the Sixth to the Fifth Rank; they were, however, no longer allowed to attend the Emperor in the Senior Courtiers' Chamber. Such ex-Chamberlains were known as Fifth Rank Chamberlains. They should not be confused with the Chamberlains of the Fifth Rank, who had obtained the coveted promotion while still in office and who thus had a chance of climbing to the highest rungs of the administrative ladder.

87. Taboo tags: a sign made of willow-wood and hung outside one's house on days of abstinence (note 48) to warn possible visitors. If one was obliged to venture abroad on one of these days, one would wear such a tag on one's head-dress (men) or sleeve (women).

88. This probably refers to women's carriages. Ladies usually remained in their carriages during the service, and the retired Chamberlains are not too pious to have a good look. According to one commentator however, they are actually looking at their own carriages to make sure that they have been placed in a better position than those of the other visitors. In any case their minds are far from religion.

285

89. Eight Lessons: a series of eight services in which the eight volumes of the *Lotus Sutra* were expounded. Two services were held each day, one in the morning and one in the afternoon. The commentary normally took the form of a sort of catechism, in which one priest would ask questions about important sections of the sutra and another would reply.

Dedication of Sutras: refers to the practice of ordering copies of the sutra to be made and dedicated to some person or institution or to the Three Treasures (Sambō), the Buddha, the Law, and the Priesthood. The Chinese characters were usually written in silver or gold on heavy white or dark-blue paper. After the copy was completed, the sutra would be recited in a special service of dedication.

90. 'Jar', costume: costume worn by women for pilgrimages and other journeys; it comprises a long cloak and a large, basket-shaped hat.

91. Eight Lessons for Confirmation: Eight Lessons carried out in order to confirm people in the Buddhist vocation. The ceremony, which lasted from four to five days, included morning and evening services.

92. The service of the Eight Lessons included a scattering of lotus blossoms, and Shōnagon's poem was written on a paper lotus used for this purpose. It contains a pun on *oku* – (i) to settle (of dew), (ii) to depart. I have tried to suggest its effect by the pun on 'leave'.

93. The story of Hsiang Chung is told in *Lieh hsien chuan*, a collection of biographies of Taoist immortals. One day the old man was so absorbed in his study of a Taoist text that he did not realize that the river had flooded and he was surrounded by water: meanwhile his family waited impatiently for him at home.

94. Women normally remained in their carriages during the service; unless they were placed fairly close, they had little chance of hearing.

95. Ministers of the Left and Right: the two highest posts (apart from Prime Minister) in the administrative hierarchy. (App. 2).

96. Michitaka refers to a poem about a man who was always looking for qualities and charms where they could not reasonably be expected:

> The straightest tree
> Grows many a crooked branch:
> Foolish it is to blow the hair
> And so uncover faults.

That is to say, since even the best objects and people in this world have imperfections, there is no point in expecting normal things or people to be ideal; rather we should leave well enough alone. In this particular case Yoshichika has expected too much from the unknown woman in the carriage: by demanding a good poem ('straightening the branches') he has spoiled everything ('broken the tree'). The way in which Michitaka changes the reference to the tree imagery, while retaining the central point of the original verse, is typical of the technique of poetic quotation in Shōnagon's time.

97. Set of robes: set of unlined silk robes worn by women and usually matched to produce a subtle blending of colours. The sleeves of each dress were normally longer than those of the one over it. When travelling in carriages, women often let the sleeves of their various robes hang outside the blinds; this allowed Shōnagon to see exactly what the unknown lady wore.

98. Yoshichika is referring to a passage in the *Lotus Sutra*, the main text of that morning's service, in which the Buddha comments to his disciple, Śāriputra, on the fact that 5,000 people in his congregation have left while he was in the middle of preaching: 'People of such pride do well to depart.' Shōnagon picks up the reference with her usual acumen, and

implies that Yoshichika, by using the Buddha's own words, is no less guilty of pride than the people who left.

99. In the Heian period rooms were not covered with straw mats as became normal in later times; instead mats were spread out when and where they were needed for sleeping, sitting, etc.

100. *Kichō* (curtains of state) were usually classified in terms of the length of the horizontal wooden bar from which the curtains were suspended. A three-foot curtain of state normally had five widths of curtain.

On a hot summer night it was advisable to place one's *kichō* in as cool a part of the room as possible, i.e. near the veranda. Besides, since the main purpose of the *kichō* was to protect women from prying eyes, it would be illogical to place it in the rear of the room where people were unlikely to be looking at one from behind.

101. It was customary in Shōnagon's time to use clothes as bedcovers; also it was normal to sleep fully dressed. The two sets of clothing described in this paragraph are, respectively, the woman's bedclothes and her dress. The present scene evidently takes place in the Imperial Palace; the philandering gentleman is able to peep into the lady's quarters as he walks along the corridor on his way back from his own tryst.

102. Heian women usually let their long, thick hair hang loosely down their backs. The closer it reached the floor, the more beautiful they were considered. For the aesthetic significance of women's hair see *W.S.P.*, p. 215.

103. It was an essential part of Heian etiquette for the man to write a love-letter to the lady with whom he had spent the night; it usually included a poem and was attached to a spray of some appropriate flower. The letter had to be sent as soon as the man returned home or, if he was on duty, as soon as he reached his office. The lady was of course expected

to send a prompt reply. If the man failed to send a letter, it normally meant that he had no desire to continue the liaison.

104. From the poem,

> The sprouts of the cherry-flax
> In the flax fields
> Are heavy now with dew.
> I shall stay with you till dawn
> Though your parents be aware.

The expression 'cherry-flax' is found in a similar poem in the *Manyō Shū* and refers (i) to the fact that flax was sown at the same time that the cherries blossomed, (ii) to the similarity in appearance between cherry blossoms and the leaves of flax.

The gallant declares that he will stay with the girl until daylight, though this probably means that her parents will find out about his visit. His ostensible reason is that it is hard to make his way through the heavy morning dew (a standard euphuism); the real motive, of course, is his reluctance to leave the partner of his night's pleasures. 'Dew on the sprouts' may have a secondary erotic implication such as one frequently finds in early Japanese love poems.

105. i.e., the house of the woman with the long hair and the orange robe.

106. If the man was sensitive to the beauty of the dew, he would want to leave at early dawn before it had disappeared. The real reason for early departures, of course, was fear of discovery; but pretty conceits of this type were common.

107. As a rule a Heian woman of the upper class would not let herself be seen by a man unless she was actually having an affair with him – and not always then. They were usually protected by curtains of state, screens, fans, etc., and above all by the darkness of the rooms.

108. *U no hana*: a shrub with white blossoms, something like the syringa; it blossoms in the Fourth Month (App. 1) at about the time of the Kamo Festival, when *hototogisu* (note 15) were most frequently heard. *Deutzia scabra*, its Linnaean equivalent, brutally conceals the poetic connotations that the plant has in Japan, and I prefer to leave the word in the original.

109. Murasaki [No]: a famous plain north of the capital, named after its gromwell (*murasaki*); it was the site of the Kamo Shrines (see App. 3b).

110. In the Far East animals and plants often have traditional affinities, e.g. in China the tiger and bamboo, the lion and peonies, the phoenix and paulownias. Several early Japanese poems suggest such an affinity between the *hototogisu* and the orange tree. The following *Manyō Shū* verse is an example:

> Ah, my beloved whom I met in the Rice-sprouting Month,
> When the *hototogisu* lurked
> In the mountain's flowering orange tree!

The *hototogisu* is also associated with *u no hana* flowers (note 108); and the *uguisu* has an affinity with plum trees.

111. It was customary to attach flowers or leaves to one's letters; the choice depended on the season, the dominant mood of the letter, the imagery of the poem it contained, and the colour of the paper. See *W.S.P.*, p. 199.

112. 'A spray of pear blossom in spring, covered with drops of rain': reference to 'The Song of Everlasting Regret', a famous poem by the great T'ang writer, Po Chü-i, who was by far the most popular Chinese author in Shōnagon's Japan and, Dr Waley points out (*W.P.B.*, p. 151), the easiest. It tells the story of the tragic love between the Chinese Emperor and his favourite concubine, the beautiful Yang Kuei-fei, who according to one version was hanged from

a pear tree by mutinous troops in 756 owing to her alleged responsibility for the Emperor's neglect of state affairs and to the unpopularity of her scheming family. The grief-stricken Emperor sends a Taoist magician to look for the lost lady; but, though the messenger finds her, he is unable to bring her back. Here Shōnagon refers to the passage in which Yang Kuei-fei comes forth to meet the messenger:

Her face, delicate as jade, is desolate beneath the heavy tears,
Like a spray of pear blossom in spring, veiled in drops of rain.

It appears, however, that Shōnagon had misunderstood the Chinese original, in which Yang Kuei-fei's beauty is compared to that of jade, the pear blossom being introduced only to evoke her pallor. This is one of several instances that have led commentators to question Shōnagon's reputed erudition in the Chinese classics.

113. i.e., the fabulous phoenix, whose appearance presaged the advent of a virtuous Emperor. This splendid, five-coloured bird was said to dwell in paulownia trees.

114. At the time of the Iris Festival. The *Melia japonica* has small, violet flowers.

115. This was one of the Five Festivals; it dated from the early seventh century and was known as Ayame no Sekku or Iris Festival (App. 1). The fifth of the month was regarded as an inauspicious day, and many of the festival observances were aimed at warding off evil spirits. Herbal balls, decorated with irises, were hung on the houses to protect the inhabitants from illness and also attached to the sleeves of people's clothes (see note 64); the eaves were covered with iris leaves and branches of mugwort, which were also believed to have prophylactic virtues. The Emperor, wearing a garland of irises, gave wine, in which iris root had been steeped, to his high officials; the gentlemen of the Court put irises on their head-dresses and the women wore irises in their hair. Irises

were also attached to clothes and to all kinds of objects in daily use – palanquins, swords, pillows, wine-cups, etc. – and placed under the pillow. Abstinence signs were used as a further protection. The officers of the Guards, who were responsible for supplying the various palaces with irises and mugwort for the occasion, brought the festival to an end with a ceremonial twanging of their bow-strings to scare away any evil spirits that might still be hovering in the precincts.

116. Bureau of the Wardrobe: one of the bureaux under the Ministry of Central Affairs (App. 2). Among other things it was responsible for supplying clothes to the Imperial Princesses and noblewomen in the Palace.

Curtain-dais: a platform or dais about two feet high and nine feet square, surrounded by four pillars and by curtains. Curtains of state (*kichō*) were placed on three sides of the dais, and the platform itself was covered with straw mats and cushions. The curtain-dais was used by the master of the house for sleeping and was also the place where he normally sat in the day-time. In the Imperial Palace it served as a sort of throne.

117. Chinese hawthorn, literally 'tree on the side'. The Chinese hawthorn turns red at the beginning of the summer instead of in the autumn; it is therefore very conspicuous.

118. Being dependent on the strength of other trees, the parasite's existence is precarious; hence it is *aware* ('moving', 'pitiful'). For a discussion of *aware* see *W.S.P.*, pp. 207–8.

119. After sunset on the day of the Kamo Festival sacred Shintō dances were performed in the Palace in the presence of the Emperor. The *sakaki* is the sacred tree of the Shintō religion and plays an important part in the dances and other Shintoist observances. The present-day *sakaki* corresponds to the cleyera, but the consensus of scholars is that it was originally an anise tree.

120. Reference to the poem:

> One thousand branches grow
> Upon the camphor tree in Izumi's Shinoda Wood –
> A branch for each sad care that troubles those who love.

121. Lit, 'it is not familiar to people' because it usually grows deep in the hills. Shōnagon refers to the following old song

> Rich indeed has this palace grown.
> To three ridges, four ridges, do its roof extend.

The dew dripping from the leaves of the cypress and the wind blowing through its branches both sound like rain. Shōnagon specifies the Fifth Month since that is the beginning of the rainy season.

122. Large-leaved cypress or *Thuya dalobrata*. Its name literally means 'tomorrow [he will be] a cypress'.

123. Shōnagon refers to the poem,

> Climbing the arduous mountain path,
> I lose my way.
> For the snow from the white oaks
> Has fallen on the craggy slope
> And clad the trail in white.

So far as we know, this has no connexion whatsoever with the Storm God (Susanoo no Mikoto, 'His Impetuous Male Augustness') or with his journey to Izumo in the west of Japan after his expulsion from the Plain of High Heaven. In Shōnagon's time, however, it was evidently believed that Hitomaro wrote this poem to commemorate the hardships that God suffered when he was caught in a snowstorm on his way westward across the steep mountains. The accounts of Susanoo in the chronicles contain no mention of the white oak, but the God is described as having performed dances holding the branches of certain other trees.

124. *Yuzuriha*: the Linnaean equivalent is *Daphniphyllum macropodum*, but I prefer the Japanese word.

In Heian times the Buddhist Festival of the Spirits was celebrated on the last day of the year (App. 1). The spirits of the dead returned to earth at noon on this day and left at six o'clock in the morning of New Year's Day.

Among the many New Year's customs was that of tooth-hardening. This was observed in the Palace on the second day of the year, when the Imperial Table Office prepared certain special dishes, such as melon, radish, rice-cakes, and *ayu* fish, which were supposed to strengthen the teeth. This in fact had the same purpose as many other New Year practices, viz. the promotion of health and longevity. Evidently the tooth-hardening foods were served on *yuzuriha* leaves. This strikes Shōnagon as strange since the same leaves were used to serve the food for the dead.

The poem about the *yuzuriha* that Shōnagon cites in this paragraph is:

> When the leaves of the sheltering *yuzuriha*
> On the plain of Kasuga
> Turn red –
> Not till then shall I forget you.

'Full of promises' refers to this poem. The *yuzuriha* is an evergreen.

125. Lit. 'the god who protects the leaves'. This god was believed to inhabit the Mongolian oak, a tree that the ancient Japanese appear to have regarded with particular awe. Cf. the following poem in *Yamato Monogatari*. The speaker is a man who is paying a secret visit to a married woman and who has mistakenly broken off the twig of an oak to give her; the 'God of Leaves' represents the cuckolded husband:

> Not knowing what I did,
> From the oak where dwells the God of Leaves
> I broke a twig.
> Oh, grant that I be spared
> The punishment for my deed!

It is not clear why the officers of the Middle Palace Guards (Hyōe no Suke Zō) were referred to as 'oaks'. Kamo no Mabuchi suggests that it is because they were held in particular respect, but from what we know of the prestige of the Guards regiments this seems dubious. Kaneko (*Hyōshaku*, p. 242) mentions that in the past an oak had grown outside the Headquarters of the Middle Palace Guards, and this would appear to be a more likely explanation.

126. Objects 'in the Chinese style' were to be found only in the houses and gardens of the aristocracy.

127. Parrots had been imported from Korea in earlier times as tribute, but they appear to have died out by Shōnagon's time and it is unlikely that she had ever actually seen one; hence the vagueness of this sentence.

128. Because it sees itself in the mirror and thinks it is its mate. The copper pheasant is said to have been introduced from China. It was recommended for its beautiful voice, but on arrival at the Palace (so the story goes) it refused to sing. A certain Court lady explained that this was because the pheasant missed its mate. She ordered that a mirror be hung in the cage, and the bird immediately began singing.

129. Shōnagon is thinking of the following poem:

> In Takashima even the herons of Yurugi Wood,
> Where the branches quiver in the wind,
> Refuse to nest alone
> And keenly seek a partner for the night.
> Yet . . . [I, alas, must spend the night alone].

130. Box bird: the bird is mentioned in contemporary poetry and also in *The Tale of Genji*; but its identity is unclear. Its name may be an onomatopoeia derived from a characteristic cry of *hayako-hayako*.

131. Mandarin duck: the traditional symbol of conjugal love in the Far East. Cf. the poem:

> The mandarin ducks, the husband and his mate,
> Brush from each other's wings the frost.
> How sad if one is left to sleep alone!

132. Refers to the poem:

> Autumn is here
> And with it comes the plover's cry –
> The plover who has lost his mate
> On Sao River's misty banks.

133. Refers to:

> In Saitama
> In Osaki Marsh
> The wild duck flaps its wings,
> Striving to sweep away the frost
> That has settled on its tail.

Shōnagon has substituted wing for tail.

134. *Uguisu*: usually translated 'nightingale', but this is misleading since the *uguisu* does not sing at night and is far closer to the Western bush warbler (cf. *hototogisu*, note 15).

135. See note 110.

136. Perhaps Shōnagon is thinking of the following poem,

> Since the morning of this day
> That ushered in the fresh New Year
> I have waited for one sound alone –
> The sound of the *uguisu*'s song.

In the traditional calendar the year began with spring.

137. Ice was stored in ice-chambers and eaten during the summer (for instance in sherbets) or used to preserve perishable food. The stems and leaves of the liana were used for mild sweetening; sugar was not introduced into Japan until the Ashikaga period.

138. *Chi-chi* is the characteristic sound of the basket worm as well as the word for 'milk'. The insect in question is a *psychidae*; it was called 'straw-coat insect' because of the nest in which it is wrapped. This nest is made chiefly of dirt.

139. 'Hateful Things', section 14.

140. In ancient Japan people were often named after animals. Haemaro (in which *hae* means 'fly') was probably given to members of the lower orders because of its unpleasant associations.

141. A rather curious passage, especially in view of Shōnagon's usual fastidiousness. According to Kaneko (*Hyōshaku*, p. 257), it implies, not that she enjoyed the smell of sweat as such, but that she liked familiar clothes to cover herself when sleeping (see note 101); but this seems a quibble.

142. Because such beauty is wasted on *hoi polloi* and inappropriate to their gross nature.

143. Plain waggon: lit. 'carriage without a compartment', i.e. a carriage used to convey goods, not people.

144. Quiver Bearers: another name for the Outer Palace Guards one of the three Guards regiments stationed in the Greater Imperial Palace; it patrolled the grounds and carried out police duties in conjunction with the Imperial Police. As this passage suggests, these guards were regarded with some trepidation. *The Tale of Genji* also refers to the 'terrifying red clothes' of the Quiver Bearers.

145. Imperial Police: established in the ninth century as one of the many departures from the Chinese administrative system. Originally they were responsible for apprehending criminals, but their functions gradually extended into the judicial field, and, as Sansom points out (*History*, i. 208), they 'built up a body of case law of their own'. The hierarchy consisted of a Chief, four Assistant Directors, four

Lieutenants, etc. (App. 2). One of the Lieutenants could hold the additional post of Chamberlain in the Emperor's Private Office; in this capacity he had access to the Senior Courtiers' Chamber and was therefore known as 'Lieutenant of the Courtiers' Chamber'.

Shōnagon obviously resented these parvenu police officers who, despite their low rank, were allowed to swagger about the Palace buildings without proper regard for decorum, and who even had affairs with Court ladies of much higher rank than themselves.

146. Most of the ladies-in-waiting occupied rooms off the long, narrow corridors on both sides of the Palace buildings and in the rear.

147. Incense was normally used to perfume the blinds, screens, and other furnishings in upper-class houses. Often the burner itself was hidden behind a screen or in a neighbouring room so that the visitor could not tell where the smoke was originating.

Indiscreet as it may seem, it was normal for male visitors to hang their trouser-skirts over the curtain of state belonging to the lady they were visiting. Officers of the Outer Palace Guards wore white trouser-skirts of heavy, rough cloth.

148. These weapons were used mainly for ceremonies, processions, and the like.

149. The Controllers were among the most important and busy officials in the government (see App. 2). So that they could move about more freely, they were allowed trains that were considerably shorter than those normally worn by people of their rank.

150. Empress's Office: this building, situated to the north-east of the Imperial Palace, housed several offices of the Ministry

of Central Affairs, the most important of these being the Office of the Empress's Household. The Emperor often lived in the Empress's Office when his own Palace had burnt down; it was also frequently occupied by his consorts, especially by Empress Sadako.

151. Ben no Naishi: one of Empress's Sadako's ladies-in-waiting. From the context it appears that she was a mistress of the Major Controller; hence perhaps the element Ben (Controller) in her name.

152. That business: i.e. Ben no Naishi's relations with the Major Controller.

153. Yukinari refers to a story in Ssu-ma Chien's *Shih chi*. When Yü Jang's lord, the Earl of Chih, had been killed by Viscount Hsiang of Chao, he promised to avenge him; for, as he said, 'A knight dies for one who has shown him friendship. A woman [continues to] yield to one who has taken pleasure in her. Now the Earl of Chih showed me friendship. I will certainly avenge him and die.' Yü Jang, having failed in two attempts to kill Viscount Hsiang, took his own life.

It is interesting that Yukinari should reverse the order of Yü Jang's dictum: in the Heian world the warrior-lord relationship was far less important than a woman's obligation to her lover.

154. The reference is to a poem in the *Manyō Shū*:

> Oh, the willow tree
> On Ado River in Tōtōmi
> Where the hail comes down!
> Oh, the willow on Ado River –
> Though it be felled,
> It grows again, so people say.

155. Her eyes were turned up: i.e. rather than being thin and narrow, which was the mark of the classical Heian beauty. Women plucked their eyebrows, and thick eyebrows were regarded as repulsive. The nose was supposed to be small,

delicate, and up-turned, the chin and neck shapely and well-rounded. See *W.S.P.*, pp. 213–17, for the criteria of feminine beauty in Heian times.

156. Shōnagon deliberately echoes the advice given by Fujiwara no Morosuke to his descendants: 'In all matters, whether it be Court costumes or carriages, take things as they are and use them accordingly. On no account seek out new luxuries.' Shōnagon refers, not to frugality, but to the importance of adapting oneself to circumstances.

157. Reference to the *Analects* of Confucius: 'If you are wrong, do not be afraid to correct yourself.'

158. Despite the sexual licence of the period, adult women normally hid themselves from men behind screens, fans, etc., except at the most intimate moments. This concealment applied even to their fathers and brothers (cf. notes 22, 107, and *W.S.P.*, p. 222).

159. Gentlemen of the Fourth Rank and above wore black over-robes. Noritaka, who belonged to the Sixth Rank, would have worn green, but in the semi-darkness this could easily have been mistaken for black.

160. Fujiwara no Noritaka, the elder brother of Nobutaka (Murasaki Shikibu's husband), was at this time a Chamberlain; later he was promoted to the post of Major Controller of the Left. The reason that the ladies do not mind being seen by Noritaka is that he belongs to the Sixth Rank; Yukinari is of the Fourth Rank and therefore a far more awesome figure.

161. Every night at ten o'clock there was a roll-call of the high-ranking courtiers on duty in Seiryō Palace, followed by a muster of the Imperial Guards of the Emperor's Private Office, who, as they approached, would twang their bow-strings to scare away the evil spirits. When the Officer of the Guards, kneeling on the wide balcony outside the Imperial residence, called out, 'Who is present?' they all

twanged their bow-strings and then announced their names in turn. Since the lattice windows were all closed at night, Shōnagon and her companions could not actually see the roll-call and muster; as a result the impressions in this passage are mainly auditory.

162. Minamoto no Masahiro, a Chamberlain and subsequently governor of Awa Province, appears in *The Pillow Book* as a gauche, ludicrous figure, and Shōnagon obviously enjoys describing his solecisms. Here, instead of listening to the report of the Officer of the Guards and then retiring with silent dignity as was the custom on these occasions, Masahiro feels that he must comment angrily on the absences, even though in the past he went to the opposite extreme of not listening to the report at all. In the following paragraph he commits the appalling gaffe of leaving his shoes on the board where the Imperial meals were served, having presumably mistaken it for a shoe-shelf. Since ancient times the Japanese have regarded shoes as ritually unclean objects, and Masahiro's carelessness therefore calls for purgation.
    For more about Masahiro see section 72.

163. Even Masahiro cannot bring himself to pronounce the name of something so (ritually) unclean as shoes.

164. Because the lower part of their clothes is spattered with mud. For 'shaded material' see note 16.

165. Various grades of attendants were allotted to people according to their rank. A man of the Junior Fifth Rank, for example, received twenty official retainers. This, of course, represented an additional form of income.

166. According to the chronicles, the deity Kamo no Wakii-katsuchi on the eve of his return to the Plain of High Heaven instructed his followers to decorate themselves with holly-hock if they wished to ensure his return to earth.

167. The name of this plant (*itsumadegusa*) has the literal meaning of 'until-when? grass', with the implication that its existence is precarious. It usually grows on old walls, crumbling houses, etc.

168. *Kotonashigusa*: lit. 'nothing-wrong herb'. Commentators have been unable to determine its identity.

169. *Shinobugusa*: a type of fern or moss (*Polypodium lineare*) that grows mainly on rocks, old walls, tree stumps, etc. Its name has the literal sense of 'the grass that endures [hardships]'; this is why Shōnagon considers it pathetic.

170. Shōnagon refers to a well-known Taoist story. One day a woodcutter, Wang Chih, came on two sages playing a game of *go* in a mountain cave. He began watching them and was soon absorbed in their game. They were still playing when he saw to his amazement that the handle of his axe had rotted away. When he returned to his village, he found (in Rip Van Winkle fashion) that everyone he knew had been dead for years. After this disturbing discovery Wang Chih returned to the mountain and in the end joined the ranks of Taoist immortals.

171. The bondage . . . the suffering: Buddhist terms referring, respectively, to the bondage of the flesh and to the suffering inherent in all life. Here, of course, they are used without any religious significance, rather in the way that we might say, 'What a cross to bear!'

172. Being members of the lower orders, they are unaware of good or evil; the words that issue from their mouths are closer to animal grunts than to the rational comments of human beings.

173. Shōnagon is thinking of the poem,

> He who does not speak his love,
> Yet feels its waters seething far below,
> Loves more than he who prates his every thought.

The dismay of the attendants is all the greater for not being expressed in words.

174. They say this in order to encourage their master to end his visit and return home.

175. Fashionable women let the bottom of their many-layered costume protrude outside their curtain of state so that visitors might admire the colour combination. Here the curtain of state has been set up underneath a set of bright green blinds.

176. Shōnagon refers to one of the Special Festivals which had been celebrated since the end of the ninth century. They were held annually in the Eleventh Month at the Kamo Shrines, and in the Third Month at the Iwashimizu no Hachiman Shrine in the district of Tsuzuki south of the capital (App. 9c) and were called 'special' to distinguish them from the Festival (note 14) in the Fourth Month. In the Tenth Month the messengers, envoys, dancers, and singers were chosen, and a series of rehearsals was organized. The festival itself took place in the Eleventh Month, and two days before its opening there was a formal rehearsal of dancing and music in front of Seiryō Palace. During the Kamo and Iwashimizu celebrations the dancers and singers proceeded from the Palace to the respective shrines, where they carried out their performances; they then returned to the Palace and, depending on the occasion (see note 370), performed an encore.

177. Traditional song:

Come, lads, let's pluck the rice-flowers from the freshly-planted fields
And bear them to the Palace for our lord.

178. The approach of a High Court Noble was heralded by prolonged cries of 'Make way!'; the cries for a senior courtier were shorter.

179. 'So on and so forth – and the voice of autumn speaks': the courtiers are reciting a Chinese poem by Minamoto no Hideakira:

> Fresh is the pond,
> Whose waters ban the summer's heat.
> In the wind that sways the towering pines
> The voice of autumn always speaks.

180. Naming of the Buddhas: one of the last of the annual ceremonies, being celebrated in the various palaces towards the end of the Twelfth Month (App. 1). It dated from 774. The ceremony consisted of three services, each directed by a different Leader on three successive nights. It was aimed at expunging the sins one had committed during the course of the year. While the ceremony was being held, painted screens depicting the horrors of hell were set up in Seiryō Palace to remind the participants of the need for penitence.

181. Thirteen-pipe flute: set of reeds comparable with the Pan-pipe; it was used mainly for Court music. According to some of the texts, Yukinari is a mistake for (Taira no) Yukiyoshi, a well-known flautist who at the time of this scene was a Captain in the Middle Palace Guards.

182. 'The music stops, but the player will not speak her name': quotation from Po Chü-i's famous 'Song of the Lute' (*P'i p'a hsing*) describing his exile from the capital. One evening, when he is seeing off a friend whose boat is moored on a river, he hears the sound of the *p'i p'a* (lute) from a neighbouring boat:

> Suddenly we hear the lute's voice on the water.
> At the plucking of its strings.
> The host forgets to go.
> And the guest too lingers on.
> We search the darkness, wondering who the player is.
> The music stops, but the player will not speak her name.

183. Lit. 'my guilt is fearful'. Instead of contemplating the Buddhist paintings of hell, Shōnagon is enthralled by the secular activities in the Empress's apartments.

184. Fujiwara no Tadanobu was a successful official who attained the posts of Chief of the Imperial Police and Major Counsellor. He was one of the 'Four Counsellors' known for their poetic talents. Tadanobu is frequently mentioned as one of Shōnagon's chief lovers, but Waley (*W.P.B.*, pp. 154–5) believes that their affair had already finished by the time she entered the Empress's service and that his position at Court was now too elevated for her to be on terms of easy familiarity with him. The reader can draw his own conclusions from the passages that follow.

185. Black Door: door leading to the gallery at the north of Seiryō Palace, 'Black Door' also referred to the gallery itself.

186. Imperial Abstinence: when the Emperor went into retreat, certain important officials like the Captain First Secretary and the Controller First Secretary secluded themselves in Seiryō Palace with him and observed the rules of abstinence.

187. Game of parts: a popular, upper-class game that consisted in guessing the identity of partially hidden characters in Chinese poems. One of the ladies might, for instance, cover the phonetic part of the character and the other ladies would try to guess it from the radical and from the context.

188. These are the messenger's own words; instead of giving his name or saying who has sent him, he simply refers to himself as 'a certain [person]'.

189. A tale from Ise: proverbial expression referring to stories that were strange or incredible. It apparently derived from the supposed unreliability of the inhabitants of Ise, rather than from any far-fetched quality in the episodes of 'The Tales of Ise' (*Ise Monogatari*), but scholars disagree about the origins of the phrase.

190. Lit. 'during the flower season under the brocade dais'. Tadanobu quotes a line from the third stanza of a poem that Po Chü-i wrote during his exile (note 182) to a friend who was still basking in the delights of the capital:

> With you it is flower time
> Where you sit in the Council Hall
> Beneath a curtain of brocade;
> Here in the mountains of Lu Shan
> The rain pours down all night
> Upon my grass-thatched hut.

Although Shōnagon knows the following line ('Here in the mountains . . .') perfectly well, she prefers to avoid Chinese characters, the so-called 'men's writing'. Instead she uses the phonetic script to write the last two lines (7-7 syllables) of a Japanese poem on the same theme; in her reply she implies that, since Tadanobu is angry with her, she can expect no visitors. To understand why Shōnagon's reply was so successful we must remember that Chinese literature, even the poetry of such a popular writer as Po Chü-i, was supposed to be beyond women's ken. To send a Chinese poem to a woman was most unconventional; that is why Shōnagon was at a complete loss.

191. Grass Hut would be a most inappropriate name for anyone living in the Imperial Palace.

Jade Tower is a further reference to Chinese literature. Here Shōnagon uses it in opposition to 'grass hut', echoing the contrast between the hut and the Council Chamber in Po Chü-i's poem.

192. This was one of the many forms of poetic exchange current in fashionable circles. The standard Japanese poem consists of two main parts: (i) the beginning having three lines of 5-7-5 syllables, (ii) the end having two lines of 7-7. One could send either of these parts, inviting the recipient to provide the other.

193. Office of Palace Repairs: office in charge of building and repair work in the Imperial Palace; (Assistant Master) ranked second among the officials in charge.

Tachibana no Norimitsu: government official who rose to be Governor of Harima and later of Mutsu. He did not obtain his post in the Office of Palace Repairs until 996, one year after the present incident; such anachronisms are common in *The Pillow Book*.

Norimitsu was on such friendly terms with Shōnagon that people referred to him as her 'elder brother', a term often used to describe a husband; he knew nothing of the all-important art of poetry, however, and a few years after the present incident Shōnagon broke with him (see pp. 87–98). The chronicles refer to his physical courage (on one occasion he arrested a bandit single-handed); but this did not count for much among 'good people' of Heian. According to some scholars, Norimitsu was Shōnagon's husband before she entered Court service, but, considering the way in which he is described in her book, this would appear unlikely. It seems more probable that Shōnagon had several lovers, including Norimitsu, but never became a principal wife.

194. It was not obligatory to reply to a reply.

195. Lit. '[Palace of the] Plum-Tree Tub'. It was one of the smaller buildings north of Seiryō Palace, and was usually occupied by Imperial consorts. Many of the Palace buildings, especially those used by women, were named after the flowering shrubs planted in tubs outside.

196. For details about the avoidance of unlucky directions see note 56. In this case the southern direction was 'closed' by the temporary presence of one of the moving divinities and Tadanobu had to stop at some intermediate point southwest of Kurama before returning to the capital. It was essential to reach the intermediate point before sunset, but

one could leave it and proceed to one's destination at any time after 11 p.m. 'Once the Hour of the Boar [i.e. 10–12 p.m.] has passed, one can continue one's journey; there is no need to wait until daybreak' (*Shintei Zōho Konjitsu Sōsho*, xxii, 496). Therefore Tadanobu can reasonably expect to be back in the capital before dawn.

197. Office of the Imperial Wardrobe: housed in Jōgan Palace. Its main duty (overlapping with those of the Bureau of the Wardrobe, note 116) was to provide the robes worn by the Emperor and his wives. The Office was under a Mistress of the Robes, who was often one of the Emperor's secondary consorts. She was in charge of a number of Lady Chamberlains, low-ranking attendants who were responsible for sewing and for miscellaneous duties in the Palace. Here the incumbent is Empress Sadako's sister, the fourth daughter of Fujiwara no Michitaka.

198. Shōnagon was about thirty.
    Aesthetic convention demanded long, straight hair that hung over the shoulders in perfect order.

199. For Michitaka, who had died some ten months earlier.

200. West City: the section of the capital to the left (looking north) of the central north-south avenue (see App. 3c). It fell into an early decline, becoming overgrown with weeds and much frequented by footpads, while the main part of Heian Kyō expanded eastwards.
    Although the temple that Tadanobu had visited lay north of the capital, he was obliged to spend part of the night in a house to the west in order to avoid an unlucky direction (note 196). This is why he reached Shōnagon's house from the West City.

201. Minamoto no Suzushi and Fujiwara no Nakatada were characters in *Utsubo Monogatari* ('The Tale of the Hollow Tree'), a long popular romance of the late tenth century, whose authorship has variously been attributed to the

father of Murasaki Shikibu and to Minamoto no Shitagau.

Nakatada, the handsome hero, was since his early youth noted for his musical gifts, which he displayed on a set of miraculous zithers. He was also distinguished for his filial piety: he looked after his unfortunate mother by feeding her on fish and the fruits of the forest, and even finding her a comfortable shelter in a hollow tree (which had thoughtfully been abandoned by a family of bears who were impressed by the young man's Confucian virtues). In the course of a pilgrimage Nakatada's father eventually discovered his wife and son and brought them back to the capital, where the hero enjoyed a brilliant career.

Suzushi, Nakatada's rival, was also a talented musician. His accomplishments were of course no match for the hero's, though on one occasion when he was playing the zither at dawn he managed to charm a heavenly maiden into descending from the sky for a short time and dancing to his music. It is to this incident that Shōnagon refers in her reply to the Empress, who has evidently been running down Nakatada in favour of Suzushi.

202. Lady Saishō displays her erudition by referring to some nostalgic lines of Po Chü-i's from the poem that describes the desolation of the old palace of Mount Li (to the west of the T'ang capital of Ch'ang An). The poem starts, 'On lofty Mount Li stands a palace' and the lines in question are:

> How many months, how many years, have passed
> Since the Imperial banners last appeared!
> The walls lie silent under moss
> And the tiles are choked with fern.
> His Majesty has been five years on the Throne.
> Why has he not once paid a visit here?
> It is not far from the city's western gate. . .

That is, it does not take long to reach Mount Li from the western gate of the capital, yet during the five years of his reign the Emperor has not once visited the Old Palace. The western gate of the old Chinese capital is of course identified with the desolate West City (note 200) of Heian Kyō.

203. When they were ill and during their *menses* ladies-in-waiting returned to their homes or to some other private dwelling outside the Imperial compound. This was to avoid ritual defilement in the Palace, where Shintō rules of purity were meticulously observed.

204. Seaweed has been part of the Japanese diet since the earliest times; it is usually eaten with rice, fish, etc.

205. Lit. 'a letter from the Outer Palace Guards Left Division'. This was the Guards regiment in which Norimitsu served.

206. Sacred Readings: a half-yearly Buddhist ceremony during which a large group of priests gathered in the Palace and took turns in reading t..e 600 chapters of the Sutra of Great Wisdom (*Mahāprajñāpāramitā Sūtra*). The readings, which took place weekly in the Second and Eighth Months, continued for four days, the last being known as the Day of Conclusion. The eve of this day was an occasion for Imperial Abstinence.

207. Since it was by putting a piece of seaweed in his mouth that he had earlier managed to keep the secret. But Shōnagon's implication ('Continue to hide my whereabouts from Tadanobu!') is completely lost on the blunt-witted Norimitsu.

208. The poem is cryptic and might have confounded a more perceptive reader than Norimitsu.

209. Another brain-twister for the unfortunate Norimitsu. In Shōnagon's poem the river represents the deep, steadfast relationship that has existed between herself and Norimitsu: once it has been broken off, she will no longer be able to recognize him even if they should meet. Because of word-plays the poem can also be understood as follows:

Smoothly runs the river of Yoshino
Between the woman and the one she loves.
Yet, should their bonds be broken off,
No longer would she know that man who used to be so near.

210. Heian women plucked their eyebrows and painted a thick new set about one inch above. See *W.S.P.*, p. 215.

211. Another reference to *Utsubo Monogatari* (note 201). When Minamoto no Suzushi sees that the heavenly maiden, whom he has charmed to earth by his music, is about to leave him, he vents his regret in a poem:

Faintly I saw her by the dawn's pale light,
The heavenly maiden hovering in the air.
Oh, that I could but make her stay a while!

The expedition to the guard-house also took place very early in the morning. In her reply the Empress wonders why Shōnagon should allude to Suzushi's musical talents when previously she had taken the side of his rival, Nakatada.

212. Perpetual Sacred Readings, often abbreviated to 'Perpetual Readings', were held at irregular intervals in the Palace. Readings of the Sutra of Great Wisdom, the Lotus Sutra, and other scriptures would continue day and night; each priest (in a group of twelve) read for about two hours at a time.

This section probably belongs to the Twelfth Month of 998 (see App. 5). The reader should remember that in the Japanese lunar calendar the First Month marked the beginning of spring rather than (as in the Julian calendar) the height of winter: hence the lady's doubts, later in the section, about how long the snow mountain will last.

213. *Hitachi no Suke*: Assistant Governor of Hitachi Province.

214. Mount Otoko, the site of the famous Iwashimizu Shrine south of the capital, was noted for its red autumn foliage. The beggar-nun's song naturally has a double meaning:

just as the colourful leaves have made the mountain famous, so an association with lustful women makes a man notorious.

215. When a courtier or other person of rank received a robe as a reward (this being a common form of payment in Heian times), he would naturally put it over his shoulders and perform a short ceremonial dance of thanks. To Shōnagon and her companions it was shocking that a beggar-woman should ape her superiors in this way.

216. Building snow mountains was a common winter pastime for members of the leisured class. Some of the mountains reached considerable dimensions. The *Taiki* in an entry dated 1146 describes a snow mountain that was about fourteen feet square and over eighteen feet high.

217. Shirayama (White Mountain), situated in the northern prefecture of Kaga in the so-called Snow Country, was dedicated to the worship of the eleven-faced Kannon. The upper part of Shirayama was perpetually covered with snow, and Shōnagon naturally chooses this particular divinity when composing her prayer about the snow mountain.

218. Eastern Palace: refers to the Crown Prince's quarters, which were in the eastern part of the Emperor's own residence, the eastern direction being associated in Chinese geomantic theory with the spring season and thus the idea of growth. The Crown Prince himself was usually called by this name; he was also known as Haru no Miya (Spring Palace). In 998, the date of the present scene, the Crown Prince was Ichijō's cousin, the future Emperor Sanjō (reg. 1011–16).

Koki Palace was the Empress's Residential Palace. (Readers of *The Tale of Genji* will recall that the name of Genji's stepmother, the scheming Empress who helped to have him exiled, was taken from this building.) At this time it was occupied by Ichijō's consort, Fujiwara no Yoshiko.

Kyōgoku Palace was a Provisional Imperial Palace in the

north-east corner of the capital; its present occupant was Michitaka's brother and political successor, Fujiwara no Michinaga.

219. In her poem the first beggar-nun (Hitachi no Suke) reveals her unpleasant character by referring enviously to her crippled colleague, who has been so generously treated by the Empress and her ladies.

220. In aristocratic circles letters were usually attached to sprays or sprigs the colour of whose leaves or flowers matched those of the paper as well as the season and the mood of the poem (see *W.S.P.*, p. 199).

221. The High Priestess of the Kamo Shrines was chosen at the beginning of each reign. Her household was administered by an office under an Intendant. The institution of High Priestess of Kamo was started in 818 (several centuries after that of High Priestess of Ise) and lasted until 1204.

222. i.e., the lattice on the side of the central apartment next to the Empress's bedroom.

223. 'Festive wands' refers to the auspicious hare-wands distributed at the New Year. A confusion of sense impressions (e.g. mistaking the snow for scattering cherry blossoms or vice versa) was a common convention in classical poetry.

224. The plum-blossom colour combination was especially popular at the New Year.

225. Chip-basket: box with curved corners made of strips of wood.

226. Whenever a new minister was appointed to the Great Council of States, the Council officials gave a special entertainment known as the Ministers' Banquet. On the occasion of such an appointment a Chamberlain of the Sixth Rank brought the new official a gift of sweet chestnuts from the Emperor. Lower officials of the Great Council were offered a cup of wine and a special bonus.

227. Doctor of Literature: one of two officials in the Bureau of Education who taught Chinese literature and history and who were also responsible for composing the prayers that the Emperor addressed to the gods on special occasions. Although they belonged to the Fifth Rank, Shōnagon describes them as 'low ranking': scholars in Japan had a considerably lower status than in China and did not usually enjoy the all-important privilege of being admitted to the Senior Courtiers' Chamber.

228. For the purpose of reading the scriptures, the day and night were divided into six periods, each with a special Buddhist designation. Lectors specialized in studying and reciting the Lotus Sutra.

229. A delivery room might seem an incongruous item in this list of 'splendid things'. The delivery of a Heian Empress, however, was attended by a good deal of impressive ceremonial. Religious services took place for several days in the Imperial birth chamber, and the birth itself was witnessed by numerous white-clad courtiers. This was followed by ceremonial bathing, after which a sword and a tiger's head were shaken in front of the infant and rice scattered about the room – all to keep evil spirits at bay.

230. The installation of an Empress was another elaborate ceremony. Shōnagon was probably present when her mistress, Sadako, was installed as Empress in 990. The new Empress would be seated in her curtain-dais, next to which were placed the statues of a leonine creature and of a 'Korean' dog, which were believed to ward off evil influences. (These two animals were actually the same, except that the 'lion' was yellow and had an open mouth, while the dog was white and had a closed mouth; both were originally imported from Korea.) Officials from the Table Office would bring in the Imperial Cauldron, an ancient object which was always taken along when the Court moved from one palace to another. The cauldron represented the god of the hearth,

and the ceremony of setting it before the Empress symbol-
ized that she had assumed a connubial status in which she
and the Emperor would share divine protection (*not*, as
some commentators have suggested, that she was now
assuming responsibility for the Emperor's meals).

231. The little Prince is Atsuyasu. His uncles are Michitaka's
two sons, Korechika and Takaie, who were twenty-five and
twenty-one respectively when the Prince was born.
Shōnagon's optimism about the child's future was mis-
placed: owing to the fall of the Michitaka faction, Atsuyasu
never became Emperor.

232. This was the name of a famous lute that had been kept in the
Palace since ancient times; literally it means 'Nameless'.

233. Rather than spell out the name of the instrument, the
Empress hints at it by saying that it 'does not even have a
name' (cf. note 232).

234. i.e. Fujiwara no Genshi. Her father was Michitaka, who
had died almost exactly one year earlier.

235. Refers to Ryūen, Michitaka's fourth son and the brother of
Empress Sadako and the Lady of the Shigei Sha. He took
orders at an early age, being appointed Provisional Junior
Assistant High Priest (Gon Daisōzu) in 993 when he was
only fourteen. His rapid rise in the ecclesiastical hierarchy
was broken off by a rather early death.

236. Inakaeji was the name of a well-known flute belonging to
the Imperial collection. It is homonymous with the words
meaning, 'No, I will not exchange'; hence the Empress's
pun.

237. Genshō = Above the Mysteries
Mokuma = Horse Pasture
Ide = Sluice
Ikyō = The Bridge of the River Wei
Mumyō = Nameless

Kuchime = Decaying Eye
Shiogama = Salt Kiln
Futanuki = The Two Openings
Suirō = Water Dragon
Kosuirō = Small Water Dragon
Uda no Hōshi = Father (Master of the Buddhist Law) Uda
Kugiuchi = Nail Striker
Hafutatsu = Two Leaves

238. Giyō Palace housed the Imperial treasures.

239. Lit. 'even [she whose face] was half hidden'. Shōnagon refers to a line in Po Chü-i's 'Song of the Lute' (note 182) about a girl whom the poet meets on a boat when he is about to leave on a journey:

> She lifts her lute, and I can see but half her face.

The girl, who has now sunk to the status of professional entertainer, tells the poet that she has known better days. Yet compared to Empress Sadako she is, of course, a 'mere commoner'.

240. Damp weather enhanced the scent of most types of incense.

241. Although the poem was in the standard thirty-one-syllable form, the Empress had not divided it into lines.

The capital was north-east of Hyūga, and when the Empress speaks of facing the sun (the *rising* sun is implied) she means that the nurse will be looking in the direction of the capital.

The two parts of the poem correspond, of course, to the two sides of the fan.

242. Southern Palace: one of the detached palaces (i.e. palaces outside the Imperial Palace compound). Situated in the Third Ward at the south of Tōsanjō In (see App. 3c), it was part of the residence of the Empress's father, Fujiwara no Michitaka, who died there in 995.

243. Archery contests took place on the eighteenth of the First Month as the final event of the New Year celebrations. They were held in the presence of the Emperor. Teams of four men each were chosen from two divisions of the Imperial Guards. Like most events of the kind, the contests were followed by a banquet.

244. Abstinence of the Fifth Month: the Buddhist church enjoined periods of abstinence during the First, Fifth, and Ninth Months. These periods were marked by strict observance of the dietary and other purifying rules that applied during certain days of each month (note 68), and also by the recital of special prayers.

245. The standard measure for rooms, halls, etc. was the distance between two adjacent pillars in the mansion. This was about 3·3 yards, and a 'two-span room' was therefore about twenty feet long.

Fire-proof store-rooms were built in the palaces and patrician houses to keep clothes and other valuables that were not in the outside storehouse.

246. 'Magpie' was the name of the bridge that the Weaver had to cross once a year if she was to meet her Herdsman lover (note 34). The name was 'unpleasant', not because of the sound, but because of its sad legendary association.

247. According to regulations in the *Engi Shiki* (tenth-century civil code), Court ladies were not usually allowed to enter or leave their carriages at this gate; but during the rainy season an exception was made since, if the ladies walked all the way to one of the main gates of the Greater Imperial Palace, they were liable to be caught in the rain and to have their clothes ruined.

248. Four was the normal complement of a Heian carriage.

249. i.e., of the Kamo Festival in the previous month.

250. Takashina no Akinobu was governor of Harima Province and later served as Middle Controller of the Left. He was Empress Sadako's maternal uncle; hence it was natural that he should give hospitality to her ladies.

251. Kaneko (*Hyōshaku*, p. 521) emphasizes the unfamiliarity of the Court ladies with rustic matters like rice plants and threshing machines. 'What I took to be rice plants' ('what I suppose were rice plants'), however, seems almost a deliberate affectation.

252. 'Only rough, country fare': the standard type of self-deprecatory remark that a polite Japanese host makes today just as he would have done a thousand years ago.

253. Shōnagon objects to her host's excessive informality. It was most unconventional for ladies of quality to be served with food in public on a row of tables; usually each of them was given her meal on an individual tray or dish and she would eat in private.

254. Fujiwara no Kiminobu was the first cousin of the Empress and the adopted son of his own brother, Tadanobu. He received several good appointments at Court, including those of Imperial Adviser and Provisional Middle Counsellor.

255. Tsuchi Gate: one of the gates at the east of the Greater Imperial Palace.

256. Carriages were unyoked at the main Palace gates and then pulled by attendants to the veranda of the building where the passengers alighted.

257. For the sake of scansion I have used the conventional translation of *hototogisu* (note 15).

258. A facetious reference to the doctrine of *karma*, according to which all events in this life, even the most trivial, are rigidly predetermined by what has happened in previous incarnations.

259. cf. note 192. People would frequently compose one part of a poem (either the opening 5–7–5 lines or the concluding 7–7 lines) and challenge someone else to write the other part on the spur of the moment. This called for fluency and virtuosity of a type that Shōnagon delighted in displaying. The Empress's lines imply that her ladies were more interested in the food they were served at Akinobu's house than in the poetic song of the *hototogisu*.

260. Shōnagon's father, Motosuke, and her great-grandfather, Fukayabu, were both distinguished poets; many other members of the Kiyowara family were also known for their literary talents.

261. Night of the Monkey: once in every sixty days, when the Sign of the Elder Brother of Metal coincided with the Sign of the Monkey (see App. 1), people were advised to spend the whole night awake in order to protect themselves from the three 'corpse worms', who might otherwise penetrate the sleeper's body and cause him great harm. This belief, which was related to Chinese Taoist superstition, had gained wide acceptance in Heian Japan. Members of the aristocracy spent the inauspicious Kōshin night writing poetry and playing games to keep themselves awake.

262. Reference to a passage in the Lotus Sutra: 'There is but a single vehicle of the Law; there are not two, nor are there three.' Accordingly the Lotus was known as the 'Law of the Single Vehicle'.

263. A rigid rank system applied to the Heian after-life as well as to the present world. There were nine ranks of rebirth in Amida's Western Paradise; the lotus seat obtained after rebirth depended on the weight of sin or merit accumulated in one's former existences. As expounded in the 'Nine Ranks of Rebirth' by the priest, Ryōgen (912–85), these were the Lower, Middle, and Upper Births, each being divided into the Lower, Middle, and Upper Ranks.

Shōnagon makes it clear that she would accept a Lower Birth of Lower Rank. Her Buddhist imagery is of course inspired by the joke about the 'Single Vehicle of the Law' (note 262). She implies that, when it comes to being loved by the Empress, even the lowest rank in her affections would suffice; when less distinguished people are involved, she insists on being first.

264. Fujiwara no Takaie, the Empress's brother, served as Middle Counsellor from 995 to 996. The *Ōkagami* describes him as an 'intractable fellow'.

265. The Japanese use the same word, *hone*, for the frame of a fan and the bone or cartilage of an animal. (The English word 'frame' contains some of the same ambiguity.) Since Takaie claims that his fan has a *hone* which has never been seen, Shōnagon comments that it must be the *hone* of a jelly-fish; for, while everyone knows fan-frames, no one has ever set eyes on the frame of a jelly-fish. Pickled jelly-fish was a popular dish among the Heian aristocracy.

266. i.e. section 63. 'Embarrassing' because it is a case of Shōnagon's blowing her own trumpet. But *The Pillow Book* is full of episodes in which the author shows off her wit and erudition, and it is not clear why she should have felt diffident on this particular occasion.

267. Fujiwara no Nobutsune, a cousin of Murasaki Shikibu's, became Chamberlain in 995 and was appointed Secretary in the Ministry of Ceremonial in 997; later he became Governor of Echigo.

268. It appears that when Nobutsune delivered an Imperial message he usually knelt on the floor next to the cushion as a mark of respect to the Empress, rather than seating himself comfortably on it.

269. *Senzoku* = (i) cushion, (ii) to clean or wipe one's feet. In my translation I have made a lame attempt to suggest the

nature of Shōnagon's joke. The play on words is far more effective in Japanese; also it should be remembered that the Heian tolerance for puns was considerably greater than ours. A closer translation would be: 'Do you suppose this is for the sake of wiping your feet [serving as a cushion]?'

270. Great Empress: Fujiwara no Yasuko, the consort of Emperor Murakami. She enjoyed great influence as Acting Empress Dowager under Emperor Reizei and Acting Great Empress Dowager under Emperor Enyū. The incident that Shōnagon recounts here is at least thirty years old.

Enutagi was the name of one of Empress Yasuko's low-ranking women. According to *Hyōshaku*, p. 535, it had the unfortunate double sense of 'dog's vomit'; but other texts give Enudaki, which means 'holding a dog in one's arms'.

Tokikara, an obscure member of the Fujiwara family, was appointed Governor of Mino in 968 and died *en poste*. His name, which could be taken to mean 'depending on the weather', does not appear in any of the Fujiwara genealogies; some of the texts give it as Tokikashi.

271. Nobutsune suggests that, just as it was he who put the idea of the *senzoku* pun (note 269) into Shōnagon's head, so Tokikara gave Enutagi her opportunity to shine: in both cases the inspiration came from the man. This is hardly a suggestion that would endear him to Shōnagon and it may well have promoted her subsequent attack.

272. Office of Palace Works: an independent government office (i.e. not attached to any of the eight Ministries). Its workshop was in the Imperial Palace compound, and it was responsible for supplying the Palace with furniture, objects of art, etc. Nobutsune became Director of this office in 996.

273. i.e. when she became his consort.

274. A good example of the formality of Court life. See *W.S.P.*, pp. 178–80.

275. i.e. the Chancellor, Fujiwara no Michitaka, the father of the Empress and of the Shigei Sha.

276. Shakuzen Temple: founded by Michitaka in 990; it was situated in Hōkō Palace, his father's old residence in the Second Ward (App. 3c).

277. Members of the aristocracy normally observed a rigid correlation between the seasons and the colour of their clothes. Red plum colour was worn from the Eleventh Month until the beginning of the Second Month. Now the time had come to change to light green or to some similar vernal colour, but the Empress had decided to defy convention.

278. 'Creep out' might seem an odd form of locomotion for an Empress; but it becomes clear when we remember the traditional Japanese seating position, which was a sort of squat. If one was seated and wished to move to a place near by, one would normally go on one's knees, rather than stand up and kneel down again in the new place.

279. She was now twenty years old.

280. Shigei Sha (palace) was connected to Tōka Palace by covered galleries which passed through Senyō and Jōgan Palaces.

281. Demons had straw coats that made them invisible.

282. Michitaka is alluding to the *Kokin Shū* poem:

> Ah, what fond memories she summons forth –
> She whom I dimly glimpsed
> Through the clearing in the mist
> Of mountain cherry blooms!

283. Michitaka is facetiously referring to himself and his wife. As Kaneko points out (*Hyōshaku*, p. 559), the fact that the Empress and her sister were served before their father and mother shows that the State hierarchy (in which members

322

of the Imperial family and their official consorts were ranked above all other people) took precedence over the Confucian hierarchy (where parents came before children).

284. i.e. Korechika and his brother Takaie.

285. Michitaka was head of the main branch of the great Fujiwara clan, and it was only natural that his children should have reached the position they had. His wife, however, came from a relatively undistinguished family of Confucian scholars and for her to be the mother of such impressive offspring must be the result of an unusually auspicious *karma* (note 258).

286. The Empress did not give birth to Prince Atsuyasu until the end of 999. Since the Fujiwaras' position at Court depended to a large extent on whether their daughter bore boy children to the reigning Emperor, Michitaka had good reason to wish that Matsugimi were Sadako's son rather than Korechika's. Emperor Ichijō was now fifteen, which was a normal age to begin siring children.

287. Michitaka, like his brother Michinaga, was known as a heavy drinker but also had the reputation of being able to recover at a moment's notice.

288. The Emperor has been enjoying a long siesta with Empress Sadako; now he gets ready to return to his own palace, Seiryō Den.

289. This was the zenith of Fujiwara no Michitaka's career, and the Emperor's escort appears to have consisted entirely of Michitaka and his sons. With his death shortly afterwards, the preponderant position that he and his sons had enjoyed at Court was taken over by Michinaga and his own numerous progeny.

290. A bridge that had been put up temporarily to span a gap in one of the corridors.

291. Fujiwara no Kintō, the noted poet, literary critic, calligrapher, and musician, had been appointed Imperial Adviser in 992.

292. The idea that snowflakes can be mistaken for scattering blossoms is one of the hoariest conceits in the Japanese poetic vocabulary. We must remember, however, that the use of conventional images was far from being regarded as a weakness among Heian poetasters.

293. Minamoto no Toshikata was appointed Imperial Adviser in 995; in 1018, helped by his family connexion with Michinaga, he reached the apex of his career as Major Counsellor. Toshikata was a distinguished poet (he became one of the 'Four Counsellors' known for their poetic talents), and Shōnagon has good reason to value his opinion.

294. The reference to a one-measure jar is proverbial; but in general Masahiro's remark is as meaningless in Heian Japanese as in the English translation.

295. The popping of peas in a stove was proverbially compared to people who are in a great hurry; but Masahiro's use of the expression is as peculiar as everything else about his speech.

296. 'Five parts' is a Buddhist term (Sanskrit *pañcāṅga*) referring to the knees, elbows, and head; when all are placed on the floor, it implies the utmost respect. It can also refer to the head, hands, and feet, or to the sinews, veins, flesh, bones, and hair. Some elegant courtier has no doubt used this expression to his mistress, instead of the more commonplace 'your whole body'.

297. Little Screen: the screen in Seiryō Palace that divided the Imperial Dining Room from the Imperial Washing Room. It had a cat painted on one side, birds and bamboo on the other.

298. See App. 3a.

299. Water-oats were used for making rush mats.

300. Poem chanted as an accompaniment to a *kagura* dance:

> Ah, what sweet repose
> On this my sheaf of water-oats
> Culled from the waters of Takase Pool!
> To such a pillow I'll entrust my sleep
> And care not if I drift away.

301. In preparation for the Iris Festival two days later. The iris decorations were arranged on the fourth.

302. A typical example of Shōnagon's shorthand style. She says that the young priests were wearing only their sashes. This would be a bizarre costume to find in a Buddhist monastery; what she actually means is that the priests were informally dressed in their under-robes and sashes without their full sacerdotal vestments. High clogs were presumably unfamiliar to a city-dweller; hence 'things called'.

303. Sacred Storehouse, a Sanskrit metaphysical treatise translated into Chinese. For ease of recitation it was divided into verses of four words each; the full text comprised 600 such verses.

304. These were no doubt country folk who wore their clothes inside out to prevent them from being soiled on the way to the temple.

305. Dog barrier: low, latticed screens separating the inner part of the temple from the outer. They were derived from the barriers placed at the foot of the steps leading up to private mansions in order to keep out stray dogs (which were numerous in the capital).

306. Platform of worship: special dais placed in front of a Buddhist statue or image for the use of the priest reading the sutras.
    The petitions were written requests that the priests

addressed to the Buddha on behalf of their patrons; they were based on the 'original vows' to help believers (see note 307).

307. 'Platform', 'altar', had the secondary meaning of 'alms', 'offering'. 'One thousand platforms' signified a generous offering.

Members of the aristocracy frequently dispatched messengers to Hase and other temples carrying letters and offerings. The letters contained petitions that the priests were to convey in their prayers after reciting the appropriate sutras; the offerings consisted of robes, lengths of silk, and other valuables.

308. Normally the ends of the shoulder-sash were knotted in front of the skirt.

309. It appears from the context that the man has been weeping; hence Shōnagon's sympathy.

310. Conch-shells were used in temples to announce the time.

311. Instruction and guidance: the priests direct their prayers at the evil spirits who cause difficult childbirth and illness. They 'instruct' the spirits by preaching the Buddhist Law; they 'guide' them from evil to good.

312. Proud, charming voice: when it came to one's tone in addressing servants there was obviously no contradiction between the two adjectives.

313. Matins lasted from 1 to 4 a.m.

The sutra in question is the *Avalokiteśvara*, dedicated to the eleven-faced Kannon.

314. This was the officer who, seated in a special stand, presided over the archery and wrestling contests held in a garden of the Imperial Palace; he was dressed in full uniform and carried arms – all extremely hot on a summer day.

315. The sex of the second thief is not specified.

As Kaneko observes, the situation was amusing for the thief but shameful for the person whom he catches in the act of pilfering.

Petty theft was a common occurrence in the type of dormitory atmosphere inhabited by Shōnagon and her colleagues.

316. Certain priests were always on duty at night in the Imperial Palace and elsewhere, so that they could be summoned immediately in case of illness or other emergencies. In Empress Sadako's palace the room occupied by the priests on night duty was directly next to that of Shōnagon and the other ladies-in-waiting. Owing to the flimsy nature of Japanese architecture, these priests were all liable to overhear the 'shameful things' spoken by the young ladies, but a light sleeper was particularly defenceless since he would almost certainly be awakened by the sound of their gossip.

317. *Sumō (Sumai)* wrestling tournaments normally took place in the Imperial Palace every year at the end of the Seventh Month, skilled fighters being specially recruited from the provinces. The traditional beginning of these tournaments is recorded in the chronicles in the Seventh Month of the seventh year of Emperor Suinin's reign (probably *c.* A.D. 260): 'Tagima Kehaya and Nomi-no-Sukune, the latter being from Izumo-no-kuni, were summoned to fight each other to see who was the stronger. [... Nomi-no-Sukune won by killing his opponent with terrific kicks.]' (*E.J.H.*, A. 118).

318. i.e. from his visit to Iwashimizu no Hachiman Shrine at Yawata near Yodo River, some ten miles south of the capital. This was one of the three main shrines dedicated to Hachiman, the God of War. Kaneko points out (*Hyōshaku*, pp. 630–31) that this was the first Imperial procession that Ichijō (now aged fifteen) had taken without his mother, the

Empress Dowager; therefore it was an especially moving occasion for everyone concerned.

Gallery: an elaborate sort of grandstand, complete with screens, curtains, etc., built for viewing Imperial processions and the like. Here the spectacle is the return of the Imperial procession to the capital.

319. Second Avenue: one of the nine great avenues (*jō*) that ran at equal distances across the capital from east to west (App. 3c). The Second Avenue, being directly south of the Imperial Palace, was the largest and most impressive of these nine streets; it was almost sixty yards wide.

Because of the Emperor's return the streets through which the procession passed (i.e. Suzaku Ōji and Nijō Ōji) had been specially swept and kept clear of all other traffic.

320. Michitaka refers to himself (cf. note 283).

321. For the special significance of shoes see note 162.

322. i.e. better than being a Chancellor.

323. Michinaga's meteoric rise to undisputed political control started in 995–6 with the death of Michitaka and the disgrace of Korechika. His great days of glory, however, did not come till after Sadako's death in 1000. This passage was obviously written at least six years after the event it describes (see App. 5).

Shōnagon had the reputation of being partial to Michinaga (cf. p. 163); this proved very damaging to her at Empress Sadako's Court, since Michinaga was soon to emerge as his niece's chief political enemy.

324. i.e. for the Festival of Young Herbs in the First Month (note 3).

325. *Miminagusa*, which literally means 'herb without ears', corresponding to our myosotis; both words contain the element 'ear' (*mimi* and *ōtos*). The *miminagusa* is not usually included among the seven herbs.

326. A tissue of double meanings, which the children would certainly not have understood. Shōnagon identifies the children who did not answer when she first spoke to them with the myosotis which 'have no ears'. Yet surely, she says in her last two lines, since there are so many plants / children, there must be some that hear / that are chrysanthemums.

Kaneko observes (*Hyōshaku*, p. 640) that pinching was evidently one of the ways in which children were punished; in the present instance, of course, it is used simply as a figure of speech and to provide an extra pun.

327. Cold, square rice-cakes filled with special vegetables, goose eggs, duck, and other delicacies were presented to the Court Nobles and top-ranking officials on the day after Reken and Kōjō. Shōnagon again uses the phrase 'things known as', suggesting her vagueness about this 'purely male' activity; and later she wishes there were someone there to tell her what she should do when she has received the cakes.

328. Submission: official document submitted by a Bureau or provincial office to some higher authority in the capital.

329. Nari-yuki is a reversal of the two characters in the given name of Shōnagon's friend, Fujiwara no Yukinari, and the note is from him. Mimana is the name of an ancient clan descended from one of the royal families of Mimana in southern Korea. By the time of *The Pillow Book* the Mimana family had come down in the world, its members occupying lowly posts in the Sixth Rank or under. Since submissions normally came from humble officials of this sort, Yukinari playfully assumes the name of such a family.

330. Reference to the legend about Hitokotonushi no Kami, one of the gods of Mount Kazuraki, who, when asked why he was taking so long to build the bridge between his mountain and Mount Kimbu, replied that he was too ugly to show himself during the day and therefore could work only at

night. Hence the bridge was never finished, and as a punishment for his negligence he was bound by a spell in a deep valley.

Having assumed a menial role in his letter, Yukinari now compares himself to the unfortunate god who was treated like a servant.

331. Apart from being a distinguished poet Yukinari was one of the great calligraphers of his day. The Empress takes his letter, no doubt intending to keep it as an example of skilled penmanship.

332. This could be either Ben no Naishi or Ben no Omoto, both ladies-in-waiting to the Empress. Sei Shōnagon refers to herself as Shōnagon.

333. Pun on *heidan* ('cold square cakes') and *reitan* ('cold', 'cool', 'indifferent').

334. Tachibana no Norimitsu was known for his dislike of poetry (see note 193); Nariyasu is unidentified, but he too must have belonged to the small band of poetry-haters. In the present scene they are delighted to hear that Shōnagon has for once turned down an opportunity to answer in verse.

335. In Shōnagon's time this building was greatly dilapidated and parts of the wall had come to pieces. For one reason or another, either because this was the part that had crumbled first, or because of *yinyang* directional theories, it had become traditional to take wood from the framework of the south-east corner of the mud wall in order to make batons for newly appointed Chamberlains of the Sixth Rank.

336. *Hosonaga* (long robe worn by women and children): lit. 'thin and long'.

   Kazami (woman's loose coat, note 24): lit. 'sweat garment'. *Kazami* originally referred to an undergarment that was designed to absorb sweat, but later it was applied to the coats worn by Palace girls.

Shiranaga (robe with a long train worn by boys): lit. 'long train'.

Karaginu (short jacket worn by women): lit. 'Chinese robe'.

Ue no kinu (men's over-robe): lit. 'robe above'.

Ue no hakama (over-trousers, trouser-skirt worn by both men and women together with the over-robes as part of their formal Court costume): lit. 'trouser-skirt above'.

Shitagasane (man's formal under-robe, note 69): lit. 'under-suit'.

Ōguchi (wide, red trouser-skirt worn by men): lit. 'big mouth'.

Hakama (trouser-skirt or divided skirt worn by men and women): lit. 'wear train' (*haki-mo*).

Sashinuki (loose, laced, silk trousers worn by men): lit. 'insertions'.

337. None of these derivations (*kazami*, *hakama*, etc.) is particularly obscure; but the study of etymology was not very advanced in Shōnagon's time.

338. For a description of Shōnagon's relations with Tadanobu earlier in the year see section 51.

339. There is no distinction in Japanese between defining and non-defining relative clauses. It is not clear, therefore, whether Shōnagon's remark about insensitivity to the pathos of things applies to young people in general or whether it is intended to define these particular young people.

340. From a Chinese poem written by Michizane's grandson, Sugawara no Fumitoki, for Fujiwara no Koretada as a prayer in memory of Koretada's father and mother. The quotation is especially appropriate since the present service

is in memory of the Empress's father; note also that the season (autumn) is correct. The poem goes as follows:

This golden valley, this earth,
Whose perfumed flowers make one drunk!
It's spring, and once again the air is heavy with their scent;
Yet he, their master, is no longer here.
He who climbed the southern tower
To gaze with joy upon the moon,
Where is he now
When moon and autumn reappear at the appointed time?
Those deeply loved should deeply bear [these things] in mind,
And those who are most honoured [by the world] should also be most fearful.

As usual in quotations from Chinese, Tadanobu says the words in Japanese.

341. Because Shōnagon was known to be especially fond of Tadanobu.

342. The Japanese *norokeru*, meaning i.e. 'to speak fondly or proudly of one's wife, husband, lover, etc.', has no real equivalent in English. It is always used in a derogatory sense, and in the present passage Shōnagon, though she does not use the word itself, expresses her doubts about people who indulge in this activity. An exaggerated effort to avoid such partiality can make people seem disloyal, and this is the tenor of Tadanobu's final remark. Kaneko suggests (*Hyōshaku*, pp. 657–8) that Shōnagon's argument is a skilful pretext to avoid having an affair with Tadanobu, and he describes his last remark as 'the disappointed voice of a man whose proposal has been rejected'. There is considerable evidence, however, that Tadanobu had already been Shōnagon's lover; perhaps she is now simply trying to avoid resuming a relationship that no longer suits her.

343. i.e. before 2 a.m. (App 1).

344. A conventional euphuism; cf. *W.S.P.*, pp. 240–41.

345. 'Back to front', 'reverse', 'contrary'; by referring to the rooster's crow, the letter gives the impression that he had spent the night with Shōnagon as a lover.

346. T'ien Wen, the Lord of Meng-ch'ang, was the grandson of the King of Ch'i. In 289 B.C. he was invited to the state of Ch'in, where he became a minister. The King of Ch'in grew suspicious of him and had him arrested, but T'ien Wen was able to escape one night and to reach the frontier barrier of Han-ku. This barrier remained closed until dawn; a posse had set out in hot pursuit, and the prince would certainly have been captured had not one of his party, who was skilled at making bird calls, conceived the astute idea of imitating the crow of a rooster. This deluded the barrier keeper into believing that it was dawn, whereupon he opened the gate, permitting the prince and his party to escape and return to Ch'i. Shōnagon playfully suggests that Yukinari's cock-crow is as untrue as the rest of his letter in which he falsely suggests (note 345) that they have shared a night of love.

347. Determined to show that he is familiar with Shōnagon's historical allusion, Yukinari adds a detail that is in fact incorrect. The *Shih chi* mentions that the Lord of Meng-ch'ang had 3,000 followers in his fief at home; it certainly does not suggest that this was the number of men who accompanied him on his escape. We can assume that Shōnagon failed to notice the error; for she would hardly have missed such an opportunity to discomfit Yukinari.

348. Far from being hard to cross as Shōnagon had suggested in her poem, the barrier of the 'slope of meetings' is always wide open to the traveller. Yukinari alludes to Shōnagon's reputation of having many lovers. It is hardly a flattering innuendo, but she takes it in good part. This poem of Shōnagon's ('There may be some who are deceived ...') did a great deal towards confirming her

literary reputation at Court; it is included in the famous *Hyakunin Isshu* anthology.

Her postscript implies that the gate-keeper at Ōsaka is far more prudent than the one who let Prince Meng-ch'ang cross the barrier; it suggests, in other words, that she will not let down her defences so easily.

349. Shōnagon is thinking of the bamboo-loving Wang Hui-chih (d. A.D. 388), who referred to bamboo as 'this gentleman'. The *Chin shu* (chap. 80) has the following passage: 'Hui-chih merely whistled and hummed. Pointing to the bamboo, he said, "How could I be without this gentleman for a single day?"' 'This gentleman' as used by Shōnagon therefore means 'bamboo'. She probably derived this particular piece of erudition from the preface to a Chinese poem by Fujiwara no Atsushige (included in *Wakan Rōei Shū*): 'Wang Tzu-yu planted bamboo and called it "this gentleman". The follower of the heir-apparent of T'ang, Po Lo-t'ien [Po Chü-i]. loved it and considered it "my friend".'

350. The only identifiable member of this party is the 'new Middle Captain'. This must be either Minamoto no Yorisada, who was appointed to the rank in 998, or Fujiwara no Sanenari, who received the appointment in the same year. The 'Middle Captain' may be Minamoto no Tsunefusa. In the Sangenbon texts we find (instead of 'the Middle Captain, the new Middle Captain'): 'the Mina-moto Middle Captain, [son of] Prince [Tamehira], the Minister of Ceremonial'. This can only be Minamoto no Yorisada.

351. Since Heian Japanese, like the modern language, usually makes no distinction between singular and plural, *kono kimi* can mean both 'this gentleman' (i.e. bamboo) and 'these gentlemen' (i.e. the men who came to the Empress's residence). Though Shōnagon knew the first meaning perfectly well, and would have been horrified if anyone had

doubted it, she playfully pretends to Yukinari, and later to the Empress, that she was using the phrase in its second, more conventional, sense.

352. From the prose preface by Atsushige (note 349). Because of their close link with poetry it was customary to refer to the prefaces themselves as poems.

353. Emperor Enyū, who died in 991, was Empress Sadako's father-in-law. This scene takes place when Emperor Ichijō is only twelve years old (App. 5).

354. The poem is by the illustrious cleric Henjō and commemorates the first anniversary of the death of Emperor Nimmyō in 850:

> All, once more, in flowery clothes are decked.
> Oh, that these mossy sleeves of mine might dry!

The poet contrasts the bright clothes of the courtiers, who have now discarded their mourning, with his own dark habits. 'Moss clothes' is a standard epithet for priestly robes. There is the usual sleeves-wet-with-tears imagery.

355. Tōzammi was Morosuke's daughter, Fujiwara no Shigeko, who served as Imperial Nurse to Emperor Ichijō. She was married to Fujiwara no Michikane and, after his death in 995, to Taira no Korenaka. Imperial Nurses were chosen from among Court ladies of the highest birth and rank; hence Tōzammi's familiar behaviour with the Empress later in this section.

356. Account of scrolls: when someone had arranged for incantations, sacred texts, etc. to be read at a temple, he would receive an 'account of scrolls', a long strip of paper attached to a white stick, stating the number of scrolls that had been recited at his request, e.g. 'Sutra of Great Wisdom, 600 scrolls'. Here Tōzammi has arranged for readings to be carried out on behalf of the Emperor, and

she assumes that the missive which arrived on the previous evening is a document of this kind. She washes her hands and kneels down out of respect for what she believes to be a sacred object; hence her annoyance when she finds out that it is a poem.

357. *Shiishiba* was a type of oak used to produce a dark dye for mourning dress. (Dark brown was associated with Buddhist priests, death, etc., and the poem is written on dark-brown paper.) *Shii* also means Fourth Rank and may allude to the fact that Tōzammi, to whom the poem is written, has recently been promoted from Fourth to Third Rank.

358. Archbishop of Niwa: Niwa (usually Ninna) Ji was a Shingon temple a few miles west of the capital (App. 3b). The Archbishop was Kanchō, a son of Prince Atsumi. Note that Henjō, the author of the 'flowery clothes' poem (note 354), was also an archbishop. Henjō's poem has obviously influenced this one.

359. Small wooden cupboard with twin leaves, originally used for storing Sutra scrolls and Buddhist images, but later also used for books and personal effects.

360. The child who brought the poem looked like a basket worm, and the Emperor is alluding to the legend about the insect's demon-father (section 30). It now becomes evident that the first letter originated in his Palace but was made to look as if it came from a priest. Lady Kohyōe was known as something of a wag; she is clearly the prime mover in the practical joke that has been played on Tōzammi with the knowledge of the Emperor and the Empress.

361. Putting starch in laundered clothes was so plebeian an occupation that Shōnagon hesitates even to hint at its existence. She points out, however, that her notes were not intended for other people to see and that she would there-

fore be justified in including so inauspicious an item as parting-fire tongs (below), which were associated with death.

Tongs used for the parting fires: the Festival of the Dead (Urabon), which corresponded in some ways to All Souls' Day in the West, was celebrated from the thirteenth to the sixteenth of the Seventh Month (App. 1). Sticks of peeled hemp were lit on the first day of the festival so that the souls of the dead might find their way to earth; on the last day, parting fires were again lit, this time to speed the ghostly visitors on their way back. On the fifteenth a special Buddhist service was held in intercession for the dead who were suffering in hell, especially for those who were undergoing the ordeal of Headlong Falling.

The wooden tongs used for the parting fires clearly deserved to be included among Things Without Merit. The tongs used for the welcoming fires could be used again at the end of the festival, but afterwards they had to be thrown away because of their inauspicious connotations.

362. Shōnagon is clearly defending herself from some criticism that she has received or expects to receive (e.g. 'Why do you write about such vulgar subjects as starching laundered clothes?'). Her answer is that she originally had no intention of letting anyone read her notes.

363. Housekeeping Office: Government office under the Ministry of the Treasury (App. 2) in charge of furnishings used in the Palace buildings and gardens.

364. Indeed it is. Since the present festival takes place in the spring, and since there was no Sacred Dance of the Return (note 370), it must be the one held at Iwashimizu (not Kamo) Shrine. At the Iwashimizu festival the Imperial envoys faced south towards Iwashimizu; at the Kamo festival (in the Eleventh Month) they faced north towards Kamo. For the importance of directions see note 21; for the Special Festivals and the rehearsal, note 176.

365. It was usual after large Court banquets to let commoners come and help themselves to the left-overs. The custom is typical of the many informal aspects of Palace life.

366. Fire-huts: small, roofless huts built in the Palace gardens to house the bonfires that provided illumination, especially during nocturnal festivals and ceremonies.

367. The musicians ranked so low in the social hierarchy that they were not normally allowed to move about in the Emperor's presence.

368. Udo Beach: folk-song from the eastern provinces. Its racy character is typical of popular songs of the time (cf. p. 100):

> At Udo Beach
> In Suruga,
> Ay, at Udo Beach!
> The wave that beats against the shore
> Is mistress of the seven herbs.
> Oh, how good!
> Oh, how good!
>
> The mistress of the seven herbs –
> Oh, how good!
> But what does she do when she meets her herbs?
> Sleep with them? Oh does she now!
> The mistress of the seven herbs –
> Oh, how good!

For 'seven herbs' see note 3; here they may well have a phallic connotation.

369. Another folk-song from the east:

> Be mindful of the plovers
> That come to play upon the beach!
> Ay, be mindful of the plovers,
> Do not cast your net
> Over the branches of the little pines,
> For that would be a foolish act.

370. Sacred Dance of the Return: a dance performed by the dancers after their return to the Palace. This encore took place when the festival was held at the Kamo shrines, but not when the dancers came from the more distant shrine in Iwashimizu.

371. The director of the dancers and musicians was usually a Guards officer of the Sixth Rank. The singers and dancers included noblemen of the Fourth, Fifth, and Sixth Ranks; in a very rank-conscious society it was of course a particular satisfaction to be obeyed by people who were usually giving the orders.

372. Shōnagon is probably referring to a poem by Fujiwara no Tadafusa:

> Ah, upon this festive day
> When the eight young maidens dance at Kasuga
> Even the Gods must be overwhelmed with joy.

373. This became a precedent and Sacred Dances of the Return were held after the Iwashimizu Festival until the end of the Kamakura period. The reason the ladies did not expect the Emperor to keep to his decision was that the extra performance involved a break with traditional usage and such breaks were not lightly made in the Heian period.

374. 'They lifted their skirts over their heads': in order to avoid being recognized. The ladies had several underskirts, petticoats, etc., beneath their divided skirts and were in no danger of revealing their bodies.

375. For the political background and for Shōnagon's reputation of being partial to the 'enemy' faction see note 323. 'Stir and movement' refers specifically to the Korechika-Takaie disgrace and to Sadako's becoming a nun.

376. Owing to Bedchamber intrigues that Michinaga fostered after his brother's death, Sadako was obliged to leave the Imperial Palace. In 996 (Fourth Month) she moved into

the Smaller Palace of the Second Ward (Ko Nijō In), which had been built as her private residence in 992.

377. i.e. to Michinaga, the leader of the 'Opposition'.

378. From the poem quoted in note 173. The mountain rose points to the same poem, because its yellow colour is designated by a word that is homonymous with 'does not speak'.

379. i.e. with tears. The conceit is based on the following poem:

> Before we even learn
> How sad, how fleeting is this world of ours,
> We know already of the world of tears.
> [*More lit.*, 'The thing that one knows first of all is tears.']

380. Riddles: the game was played by two teams, left and right, who tried to solve each other's riddles and conundrums. Preparations for matches (*awase*) of this kind usually continued for several weeks (*W.S.P.*, pp. 162–3). During the competition two participants, one from each team, would exchange riddles; then another pair would make an exchange, and so forth. Victory went to the team whose members had solved more riddles and received the greater number of winning tokens (note 381) from the judge.

The answer to the present very simple riddle is 'crescent moon', because *hari* means 'drawing', 'stretching', *yumi* 'bow', and *yumi-harizuki* 'crescent moon' (lit. 'bow-draw-moon'). No self-respecting courtier could fail to know the answer, since the same riddle had been asked by Emperor Daigo (reg. 897–930) and recorded in *Utsubo Monogatari*. It is precisely because the answer is so obvious that the player fails to answer and loses the first point for his team.

381. Lit. 'put out a token (counter)'. Tokens were given to each team as it scored a point in a competition. Sometimes valu-

able gold and silver ornaments were used instead of simple counters.

382. His team-mates assume that he did in fact know the answer but refused to give it because it was too obvious.

383. Because he is bending over the board, the upper part of his costume reaches up and covers his face.

384. i.e. before they are properly fledged.

385. The present Japanese custom of a daily bath did not become current, even in aristocratic circles, until a much later period. Thus in his advice to his descendants Fujiwara no Morosuke writes: 'Next choose a[n auspicious] day for your bath; bathe once every five days.'

386. Drawing faces on melons was a common pastime, especially for women and children.

387. Women and children of the leisured class often kept baby sparrows and other little birds as pets. The squeak of a mouse was a *chū-chū* sound used to attract pet birds.

388. i.e. cut at shoulder length. So great was the aesthetic value attached to a woman's hair that nuns were not expected to take the tonsure, but simply cut their hair at about the level of their shoulders.

389. i.e. about 10 a.m. (App. 1).

390. i.e. about 2 p.m. (App. 1).

391. Dining Hall of the High Court Nobles: this was part of the Government Offices of the Great Council of State. It included kitchens and a dining hall used by the High Court Nobles.

392. One of the functions of the Bureau of Divination in the Ministry of Central Affairs was to keep time by means of clepsydrae. This important duty was entrusted to the Time Office, which was staffed by two Doctors of the Clepsydra

assisted by twenty Time Watchers. At the last quarter of each watch (i.e. every two hours, App. 1) the Time Watchers would go to the courtyard outside Seiryō Palace and inscribe the time on a board, which an officer of the Guards then attached to a post (see *W.S.P.*, pp. 144–5; at each new watch a fixed number of strokes was sounded on a gong in the bell-tower of the Bureau of Divination, which was directly to the north of the Government Offices of the Great Council of State; this could be heard throughout the Palace enclosure, but obviously it was louder in a place like the Dining Hall of the High Court Nobles, where Shōnagon was now staying. During the course of each of the night watches an officer would strum his bowstring to keep away evil spirits; then, after naming himself, he would announce the time in a stentorian voice.

393. Shōnagon is thinking of the following poem:

> There in the sky,
> Where the paths of summer and autumn cross,
> A cooling wind will blow from many sides.

We are still at the beginning of the Seventh Month, which corresponds to early autumn in the Western calendar (App. 1). 'From the side' suggests that the autumn winds are only just beginning.

394. i.e. the Weaver and the Herdsman (note 34). The Tanabata Festival was celebrated on the Seventh of the Seventh Month.

395. Lit. 'the Fourth Month of men'. From Po Chü-i's poem:

> The Fourth Month in this world of men
> Is when all flowers have lost their scent.
> But the peach trees by the mountain temple
> Have just put out their clouds of bloom.

In the traditional Far Eastern calendar the last day of the Third Month marked the end of spring (App. 1). This of course called for special recitations of poetry. Tadanobu's quotation is especially appropriate because it also alludes to Michitaka's death ('when all the flowers have lost their scent'), which occurred in the Fourth Month of the preceding year.

396. Lit. 'ladies certainly do not forget such things'. Yet, only four months later, Shōnagon herself forgot a far more famous poem (section 94).

397. Lit. 'they must be the tears of parting of dew'. Tadanobu is quoting from a Chinese poem by Sugawara no Michizane concerning the unhappy love of the Weaver and the Herdsman (note 34):

> The tears she sheds on parting will turn to dew when morning comes . . .
> Those tears, like pearls, that fall in vain. . .

398. See note 330. Because of his appalling ugliness the God of Mount Kazuraki, to whom Tadanobu playfully compares himself, had to hide during the daytime. As Kaneko points out (*Hyōshaku*, p. 766), it is a rather trite joke and hardly worthy of a man of Tadanobu's parts. Possibly he has been thrown off balance by Shōnagon's recent comment and cannot find anything better to offer as a parting shot.

399. The terms are as follows (for the game of *go* see note 49):
'To yield one's hand': to place one's pieces without paying too much attention to one's opponent's strategy; a daring style of play in which one occasionally risks one's own position in the expectation of later successes and in the hope that one's opponent will not be able to take advantage of one's temporary weakness. Thus a man and a woman who are on intimate terms may be prepared to risk 'showing their hands'.
'To fill up the spaces': to fill in the points that neither player can claim as his own territory. These spaces are

known as 'false eyes', and the process of filling them alternately with black and white stones is one of the last stages in a game of *go*. In the same way the physical intimacy of a couple 'tying the true lovers' knot' is the culminating stage in their relationship.

'To keep one's hand': the opposite of 'yielding one's hand'; a cautious style of play in which one is constantly on one's guard, closely observing one's opponent's moves. Here Shōnagon and Tadanobu refer to men and women who handle their partners with circumspection.

'To part the pieces': the final stage in the game is to determine which of the players controls the larger territory, that is, has secured the greater number of viable 'eyes'. In order to facilitate the counting, the players 'break up' the position, re-arranging the pieces in such a way that the territories controlled by the two sides are clearly visible. Just as in *go* 'parting the pieces' is the ultimate stage of the game (after 'filling up the spaces'), so in a love affair 'intolerable familiarity' is the final stage (after physical intimacy).

400. The exchange between Nobukata and Shōnagon is full of double meanings, based on the secret *go* language (note 399). When Nobukata asks whether she will yield her hand, he is in fact suggesting that their relations become more intimate. Next he tells her that he is as good a player (i.e. lover) as Tadanobu. Kaneko (*Hyōshaku*, p. 767) remarks on the unsubtle way in which Nobukata uses the secret language. Not surprisingly, Shōnagon rejects his overtures. 'If I played like that' means 'if I gave myself to every man who asked me'. Then comes an ingenious pun: *sadamenaki* means (i) not fixed, flighty, (ii) lacking a fixed 'eye' (i.e. a secure space as opposed to an insecure 'false eye') in *go*. 'Roving eye' suggests some of the implications, but of course there is nothing in English corresponding to the use of 'eye' in the game of *go*.

401. 'Had not yet reached the term of thirty': i.e. he did not live to be thirty. This is a Chinese poem by Minamoto no Hideakira:

> Yen Hui, the sage of Chou, had not yet reached the term of thirty;
> And P'an Yüeh, great gentleman of Chin,
> Wrote his 'Song of Autumn Thoughts' at an early age.
> Both were some years younger than myself
> Who here observe my first grey hairs.
> So let me now rejoice
> That their sight has been delayed so long.

The poet, whose hair is turning white at the age of thirty-five, consoles himself by recalling two distinguished men of ancient times to whom this (or something worse) happened at even earlier ages. P'an Yüeh became white-haired at thirty-two; Yen Hui died in his twenties.

402. Clerk was the lowest of the four classes of officials in a government department (App. 2). In the Inner Palace Guards he had the rank of Assistant Lieutenant.

403. In his forties Chu Mai-ch'en (d. 116 B.C.) was still an impecunious wood-cutter. When his wife threatened to leave him, Chu admonished her, saying, 'I am already forty, but I shall have riches and honours by the time I am fifty.' Despite these assurances his wife deserted him. Thanks to his tireless studies Chu achieved his ambition and became the governor of a province. His wife then returned to him but was so ashamed by the magnanimous way in which he received her that she hanged herself in remorse. The story appears in the *History of the Former Han Dynasty*.

Nobukata was in fact twenty-seven (or twenty-eight in the Japanese count). According to Kaneko (*Hyōshaku*, p. 768), Shōnagon is teasing him by pretending that he appears much older than he actually is.

404. The original has 'forty-nine', but this is almost certainly a copyist's error for 'over forty'.

405. Else he would hardly have told the Emperor something so unflattering about himself.

406. A pun on the name of his mistress's mother (*uchifusu* = 'to lie down') The reason that Nobukata is ridiculed for his affair with Sakyō and finally breaks it off is probably connected with the humble birth of her mother; Uchifushi appears to have been a lower-class name.

407. Shōnagon may be referring to private celebrations which were carried out near the Palace but which it was impossible, owing to protocol, for her and other members of the Court to attend.

408. Because the temple seems close but in fact takes a long time to reach because of the constant turns in the path.

409. Paradise refers to the Pure Land or Western Paradise, into which the believer who invokes the name of Amida Buddha will be reborn. The following statement is attributed to the great Amidist leader, Genshin (942–1017): 'Though [Paradise] be infinitely distant – separated by seas and mountains and thousands of millions of provinces – yet I tell thee: if only the path of thy spirit be smooth, thou canst reach it overnight.'

410. When boats kept their course, they could travel a great distance in a surprisingly short time, whereas travel by land was slow and uncomfortable.

411. The posts of Senior Secretary (Ministry of Ceremonial), Senior Lieutenant (Outer Palace Guards), and Senior Scribe normally corresponded to the Sixth Rank (App. 2); for such an official to be appointed to the Fifth Rank was an unusual honour.

   When a Chamberlain of the Sixth Rank was promoted, he automatically lost his right of attendance on the Emperor; hence their reluctance.

412. These are marks of ostentation, unwarranted for a man of this rank and clearly condemned by Sei Shōnagon. Readers of *The Tale of Genji* will recall Mura;aki's sarcastic descriptions of the efforts of parvenus like the Governor of Hitachi to decorate their houses in a style to which neither their rank nor their taste entitles them. Such uneducated efforts are bound to result in incongruities. The trees in the garden and the private carriages, for example, make an absurd contrast with the small, shingle-roofed house where the ambitious official lives. The effect is something like that of a Rolls Royce parked in front of a small, semi-detached villa in the suburbs. Shōnagon herself belonged to the provincial (Fifth Rank) class and was particularly sensitive to the pretensions of some of its members.

413. Sage-brush was the standard mark of the dilapidated Heian dwelling. Book 15 of *The Tale of Genji*, which describes the red-nosed Suetsumuhana and her desolate household, is entitled *Yomogiu* (lit. 'land overgrown with sage-brush', i.e. waste land, or (Waley) 'The Palace in the Tangled Woods'). The forlorn dwelling of Lady Toshikage in *Utsubo Monogatari* is similarly surrounded by sage-brush.

It was customary to strew fine white sand on the gardens of Heian houses to protect people and carriages from mud, and also for aesthetic reasons (*W.S.P.*, p. 45).

414. Because she is in her own home. The parents of Court ladies appear to have been quite lax with their daughters.

415. From the poem by Taira no Kanemori:

> Here in my mountain home
> The snow is deep
> And the paths are buried [in white].
> Truly would he move my heart –
> The man who came today.

416. On the arrival of male visitors ladies usually retired behind their curtains of state or blinds, from where they could see but not be seen.

Kaneko (*Hyōshaku*, pp. 796–7) refers admiringly to the endurance of the Heian gentlemen, who can spend an entire winter's night on an unheated veranda for the pleasure of viewing the snow while conversing with Court ladies.

417. He refers to the Chinese poem:

> At dawn I walked into the garden of the King of Liang;
> Snow lay upon the many hills.
> At night I climbed the Tower of the Duke of Yü;
> The moon lit up the country for a thousand miles.

The hills in question had been artificially built in the king's garden. The correct quotation would be 'cluster of hills'; but the courtier, not having the benefit of modern commentaries, simply says 'such-and-such hills'.

418. Lit. 'the time of snow, moon, flowers'. From a poem of Po Chü-i:

> My friends – the zither, poetry and wine –
> Have all three left me;
> It's when I see the moon, the snow, the flowers,
> That I most recall my lord.

419. A web of ingenious puns, whose general flavour I have tried to convey by a few simple word-plays in English. Lady Hyōe's composition is more like a conundrum than a proper poem.

420. Because they were covered by her sleeves. In the winter the long sleeves of Heian robes served as a sort of muff.
     Light-pink hue: lit. 'light plum blossom'. Kaneko (*Hyōshaku*, p. 813) rather prosaically suggests that it was the cold which gave the Empress's hands their attractive colour.

421. Lady in charge of my room: lady-in-waiting in charge of a number of younger maids-of-honour who lived in the same room or set of rooms.

348

422. Shen: region in China that produced a type of aromatic wood imported into Japan and used for making braziers, etc.

423. The Empress and her brother are referring to the poem quoted in note 415.

424. cf. note 73. Sneezing in Heian Japan had many of the same implications as in the West (see *W.S.P.*, p. 142), but in addition it suggested that the last person who had spoken was not telling the truth.

425. The first poem is fairly clear. Shōnagon's reply, however, is most obscure. Kaneko's interpretation is as follows (*Hyōshaku*, p. 811): If I did not really love the Empress, the insincerity of my reply ('How could I possibly not be found of you?') might well be determined by someone's sneezing in the next room; but, since in fact I do love her deeply, it makes me wretched to think that something as trivial as a sneeze should have made her judge me to be dis-. honest. Here is a more literal translation:

> A shallow [feeling can] indeed
> Depend on that.
> [But] it is sad that I too should know
> Wretchedness
> Because of a sneeze (nose).

426. Shiki was the name of a demon invoked by magicians and other practitioners of the occult when they wished to put a curse on someone. Shōnagon implies that the ill-timed sneeze was due to a power of this kind.

427. See note 424. He looks pleased with himself because everyone wishes him good luck (cf. 'God bless you!' in the West). Kaneko (*Hyōshaku*, p. 810) quotes the late Heian poet, Kenshō: 'Sneezing is altogether ominous. If someone sneezes at the New Year, everyone wishes him good luck.' It appears that in Shōnagon's day this custom was not

restricted to any particular time of the year. Cf. p. 47 for Shōnagon's dislike of sneezers.

428. Hidden rhymes: popular game among the aristocracy; one of the players covered a character in some old Chinese poem, and the winner was the player who, from context, rhythm, etc., first guessed the hidden character.

429. See notes 49, 399, 400. Because of the large size of the *go* board and because the stones cannot be moved to a new place once they have been played, the battle in its early stages can be carried out on several independent fronts. A player who decides that he is not making sufficient headway on one part of the board may switch his attention to another sector. In the present instance he is pleasantly surprised to find that his opponent's position in this new sector is weaker than it had appeared to be. The opponent is unable to keep the 'eyes' that determine the viability and value of any position and the greedy player succeeds in capturing a large number of stones. If he had played in a more conservative way and continued to concentrate on the original part of the board, he might have missed the opportunity.

In *go* as in chess a 'greedy' player is one who is more interested in capturing his opponent's stones (pieces) than in slowly building up a strong position.

430. The parvenu governor with his absurd pretensions is a stock figure in Heian literature (cf. note 412).

431. High ranks in the Imperial Guards were as a rule honorary positions reserved for members of the aristocracy. A provincial governor would naturally be more flattered to receive such an appointment than a young nobleman, who would take it for granted.

432. Empresses were usually chosen from the Imperial family itself or from among the daughters of the Chancellor, the

Regent, or one of the Great Ministers. When Shōnagon writes about a High Court Noble's daughter who has been appointed to the rank of Empress, she may be thinking of Fujiwara no Takeko, the daughter of Naritoki, who was appointed First Empress to Emperor Sanjō though her father during his lifetime never advanced beyond the rank of Major Counsellor.

433. Palace Chaplain: one of ten priests in charge of the Palace Oratory, where they carried out readings of the scriptures, made offerings to the Buddhist statues, etc. They were frequently on night duty, and therefore tended to come into contact with the Court ladies.

434. The padded garments were worn in the rainy season and then put aside during the hot summer months. As the summer advanced, the weather became so stifling that even clothes of unlined silk were uncomfortable. Then all of a sudden there was a cool, rainy wind, and people had to throw their padded clothes over their silk ones, making for the kind of incongruous combinations that frequently struck Shōnagon's fancy.

435. The thirteen-pipe flute was a rather formidable instrument, and the player had to puff out his cheeks in order to fill the air chamber.

436. In Heian times people's hair stood on end when they were deeply impressed by something, rather than when they were frightened (cf. p. 229).

437. The Special Festival at Kamo (note 176) took place during the height of winter in the Eleventh Month.
   The flowers that the participants in the Special Festivals wore in their head-dress (wistaria for the Imperial envoys, cherry blossom or yellow roses for the dancers and musicians) were artificial.

438. As a rule the envoys, who followed the dance in the Kamo procession, were chosen from among the Imperial Guards

(note 176), but on this occasion high provincial officials had been selected for the honour. Shōnagon's scorn for these officials is typical of contemporary attitudes (*W.S.P.*, pp. 93–7) and was not mitigated by the fact that her own father belonged to this class.

439.

> The princess pines that grow outside
> All-powerful Kamo Shrine –
> Ten thousand years may pass away
> And yet their colour will not fade.

Himekomatsu is the short pine or *Pinus parriflora*. *Chihaya-buru* ('swift and mighty', 'all-powerful') is a stock epithet (*makura kotoba*) used in poetry before the names of gods and shrines.

An introductory note explains that Toshiyuki's poem was associated with the winter festival at Kamo.

440. Bureau of Imperial Attendants: Bureau under the Ministry of Central Affairs (App. 2). It was in charge of the Imperial Attendants who served the Emperor in the Palace and during Imperial Processions. The Assistant Directors belonged to the Senior Sixth Rank, Lower Grade.

441. cf. p. 69.

442. Lit. 'shoulder palanquin, hand palanquin, etc.'. These were the conveyances used by the High Priestess within the precincts of the Shrine. When she left the Shrine, she travelled by ox-carriage. The porters (in red clothes) are now carrying back the empty palanquins.

443. After the Kamo Festival a special banquet was held in the palace of the High Priestess. The guests of honour were princes of the blood and top-ranking officials like the Chancellor; in addition a number of gentlemen were invited as 'extra guests'.

444. The gentleman refers to the love poem:

> The fleecy clouds that scatter on the peak,
> Blown asunder by the mountain winds –
> Surely your heart is not all cold like them.

445. The original has 'yesterday, the day before yesterday, today'. This type of departure from the normal chronological or numerical order is an idiosyncrasy of Shōnagon's. Cf. p. 21, where she speaks of the crows flying 'in threes and fours and twos'.

446. Shōnagon deviates from conventional standards of male beauty, which prescribed narrow eyes for men as well as for women (*W.S.P.*, p. 156).

447. Large winter cherries were used as toys or dolls.

448. Traffic congestion and altercations of this kind were a normal occurrence at Heian processions and ceremonies. Known as *kuruma-arasoi*, they figure frequently in contemporary literature (see *W.S.P.*, pp 51–2).

The present encounter was a very mild one and Shōnagon obviously enjoyed it.

449. The Empress's message contains the first three lines (seventeen syllables) of a poem. Shōnagon's reply caps it, in linked-verse style, by providing two final lines (fourteen syllables). The exchange is more ingenious than poetic. 'Though innocent of rain' refers to a woman's virtue; but in view of her many love affairs Shōnagon can hardly have expected the Empress to take this protestation too seriously.

450. i.e. Prince Atsuyasu, who was six months old.

451. The flour used for these cakes was made from unripe ('green') wheat.

452. The phrase 'from across the fence' means 'from outside'; it comes from the poem,

Stretching his neck across the fence,
The little colt can scarcely reach the wheat.
So I myself cannot attain
The object of my love.

The link between the poem and the cake (note 451) is the word 'wheat'.

The Empress's poem is rather cryptic. 'To hurry about searching for flowers and butterflies' means 'to be busy with festive activities'. Possibly Sadako implies that on this day of the Iris Festival, when all the other ladies are busy with elaborate preparations for the joyful occasion, only Shōnagon, by presenting her with a simple green-wheat cake 'from across the fence', shows that she has understood her mistress's somewhat melancholy mood. As Kaneko points out (*Hyōshaku*, pp. 890–91), this was a time when things were not going too well for Empress Sadako, owing to the elevation of Akiko to the rank of Chūgū and to the growing hostility of the Michinaga faction (note 323).

453. Narinobu's great acoustic talent (section 131) was to tell *who* was speaking; Masamitsu's lay in distinguishing *what* they said.

454. Black-lacquered boxes and tiled inkstones were inelegant types of writing equipment.

455. Miwa Shrine at the foot of Mount Miwa in Yamato (Shiki) was famous for the cryptomeria that grew at its entrance. A poem of Ki no Tsurayuki has the words,

It is the *sugi* tree
That marks Mount Miwa's heights.

456. This can be taken to mean literally 'prayers that are fully answered'. The basis is a punning poem that starts,

This is indeed a shrine
Where every prayer's been glibly answered [by the God].

('In such an indiscriminate / glib way' has a decidedly disrespectful tone).

354

457. In the collected works of Ki no Tsurayuki we read that one day, when he was riding back to the capital, his horse suddenly became ill. The local inhabitants informed him, 'This is the doing of the God who dwells in these parts. For all these many years he has had no shrine, and there is nothing to mark his presence here. Yet he is a fearful God, and this is how he always lets people know of his existence.' Since Tsurayuki had no suitable offering to present to the irate deity, he simply washed his hands (to acquire ritual purity) and, 'facing the hill, where no sign of the God existed', dedicated the following poem to him:

> How could I have known
> That in this cloudy, unfamiliar sky
> There dwelt the Passage of the Ants?

Thereupon the God, appeased by this belated recognition of his existence, promptly restored the poet's horse to health.

458. The legend of Aridōshi probably dates in its present form from the eighth century, but it is an amalgam of various ancient traditions. Part I of *Samyukta-Ratna-Pitaka Sūtra*, 'The Sutra of the Collection of Varied Jewels', refers to the exile of old people and also describes the puzzles of the piece of wood and of the two snakes. The story of the jewel and the cats occurs in a Chinese Buddhist work, *Tsu t'ing shih yüan*, which was compiled during the Sung period; in this version, however, the jewel has nine, instead of seven, curves. The story in which a king tests the level of intelligence in a foreign state by posing various problems (usually three) is an old one, being told *inter alia* in the thirty-three-chapter Han compilation, *Chan kuo ts'e*, 'Schemes of the Warring States', and in the Japanese chronicle, *Bidatsu Tennō Ki*.

The entire legend is brought up to date and Japanized by the hero's rank of Middle Captain of the Inner Palace Guards. The Captain's filial piety makes him a standard

Confucian-type hero and a striking contrast to the officer described in section 164.

459. i.e. which end of the log grew nearer the trunk of the tree from which it was cut?

460. The god's poem (whose source is unknown) is a typical example of early pseudo-etymology: almost certainly Aridōshi Shrine in Izumi became associated with the legend because of its name, not vice versa.

461. 'The tints that leave at dawn': this is traditionally believed to have come from a poem by Sung Yü (fl. 290–223 B.C.),

> At dawn [they] make the morning clouds.
> At night [they] make the driving rain.

462. cf. p. 109. The name zōshiki (Subordinate Official) means 'various colours' and derived from the fact that, whereas the colours worn by gentlemen of higher rank were stipulated in the legal codes, these lowly officials were free to wear any colour that was not specifically prohibited.

463. These belts were part of the Court uniform, but were not usually worn by gentlemen on night watch.

464. A village about one mile west of the capital; it was the site of Kōryū Ji, a Shingon temple built in 603 on the orders of Shōtoku Taishi.

465. Shōnagon is thinking of a Kokin Shū autumn poem, which contains a typical lament about the rapid passage of time:

> Only yesterday, it seems,
> They were pulling out the sprouts.
> And now already autumn's stolen up,
> And rice leaves rustle in the wind.

In Shōnagon's time, as today, the light-green rice sprouts were pulled from the seed-bed in the spring (at about the time of the Kamo Festival) and planted in the paddy-fields by hand; in the autumn, when the ears were formed, the field was drained and harvesting began.

466. A knife or something of the sort: Shōnagon again shows her unfamiliarity with agricultural matters. She is obviously referring to a scythe.

467. This is almost identical with the last paragraph of section 63; but here Shōnagon is interested not so much in the awkwardness of the situation as in whether or not an unfaithful son-in-law feels sorry for the wife he has deserted.

468. Kite's tail: refers to the end of each of the shafts of an ox-carriage.

469. Even other women: the implication (a rather dubious one) is that women are less critical than men when it comes to judging a girl's appearance.

470. Object match: lit. 'comparison of objects'. See note 380. Among the 'objects' used in these games were flowers, roots, seashells, birds, insects, fans, and paintings.

471. The Empress refers to the *Kokin Shū* poem,

> Inconsolable my heart
> As I gaze upon the moon that shines
> On Sarashina's Mount Obasute.

The Empress implies that Shōnagon manages to comfort herself too easily, and contrasts her with the inconsolable poet who gazed at the moon in Sarashina. The other ladies express the idea that Shōnagon's method of curing her world-weariness is far too cheap; prayers for warding off evil normally involved making expensive gifts to Buddhist priests.

472. Sutra of Longevity: a short sutra frequently recited or copied in order to ward off personal dangers and to secure a long life. The Empress refers to this particular sutra because of (*a*) Shōnagon's feeling that she cannot go on living

for another moment (p. 218), (b) the ladies' comment about a prayer for warding off evil (p. 218). The statement that the paper is of poor quality belongs, of course, to the 'Please step into my filthy hovel' class of modesty.

473. Shōnagon refers to her earlier remark that the sight of some good paper makes her feel she can stay a little longer on earth. The crane is a standard symbol of longevity in the Far East, and numerous Japanese poems refer to his thousand-year life expectancy.

474. *Sōshi* (collection of notes): collection of miscellaneous notes, impressions, anecdotes, etc., of which Shōnagon's *Pillow Book* (*Makura no Sōshi*) is the only extant example from the Heian period. Shōnagon must have received this paper from the Empress well after the notebooks mentioned in section 185 (note 582), and it seems likely that she had already started writing her *Pillow Book* by this time.

475. If the messenger in red had been found, Shōnagon would have asked him whether he came from the Empress; since he has disappeared, she prefers not to let the people in her house know what she is thinking.

476. The action described in this section takes place in 994, the year before Michitaka's death, when he and his immediate family were at the very height of their power and glory (App. 5). For Dedication of the Sutras see note 89. The Full Canon was a compilation of all the sutras containing the statements of Gautama Buddha with commentaries. Originally it consisted of 5,084 volumes, but later it reached the grand total of 8,534. The copying and recitation of this vast collection was, of course, a major event in the capital. Shakuzen Temple had been founded by Michitaka himself in his father's Hōkō Palace four years earlier (see note 276). Only a very small proportion of this section (the longest single section in *The Pillow Book*) deals

with the religious ceremony itself; Shōnagon's real interest lay elsewhere.

477. Palace of the Second Ward: this was the building in which Empress Sadako frequently resided when she left the Imperial Palace enclosure; it was situated quite near Shakuzen Temple (App. 3c) and was therefore convenient for attending the present services.

478. The cherry trees usually came into bloom in the Second Month of the lunar calendar; the plum blossoms appeared about one month earlier. The vile custom of decorating trees with artificial paper blossoms was already well established in Shōnagon's time; despite her usual fastidiousness, she does not object to it in the slightest.

479. From an anonymous separation poem:

Sadly I behold them,
The cherry blossoms moistened by the dew,
Like tearful lovers
Forced to say farewell.

480. Minamoto no Kanezumi was a poet and provincial governor. The present line does not appear among his extant works. There is, however, a poem by the priest, Sosei, that does contain the words in question:

Let him tell me what he will,
The mountain warden of these parts!
I'll pick a spray of cherry blooms
On Takasago's Mount Onoe,
And wear them as a chaplet on my head.

Either Shōnagon has confused the authors, or there is a non-extant poem by Kanezumi that may be similar to Sosei's.

481. i.e. his idea that the ruined paper blossoms should be removed while it was still dark.

482. Possibly an allusion to the poem by Hitomaro which contains the syllepsis, 'both the rain and my tears come

359

pouring down'. But the Empress's phrase is a fairly standard one, and she may not be referring to any particular poem. Whether or not this is a quotation, the Empress is subtly indicating that she understands her father's motive in ordering the rain-drenched blossoms to be removed.

483. This is a pun on *asagao* = (i) morning face, i.e. one's dishevelled appearance on getting up in the morning, (ii) 'morning face', i.e. the althea flower. Now that the sun has risen it is 'unseasonal' for Shōnagon to look as if she has just woken up; the Second Month is unseasonal for the althea.

484. In the tenth century the suggestion that someone was telling a falsehood had far less damaging implications in Japan than in the West and was usually more in the nature of a joke than of an accusation.

485. The Empress alludes to Tsurayuki's poem,

> The time has come
> To till the rice fields in the hills,
> Oh, do not blame the wind
> For scattering the blossoms [far and wide below]!

Quoting, with a few changes, from the first two lines of the poem, Empress Sadako suggests that Shōnagon should not blame the wind for removing the blossoms when she knows perfectly well who the real culprit is.

486. 'Simple remark' normally referred to a conversational statement that did not include any quotation from Chinese or Japanese.

487. The Empress is quoting from Po Chü-i:

> In the Ninth Month the west wind quickens;
> [Under] the cold moon, flowers of frost have formed.
> When I think upon my lord, the spring day seems long.
> My soul, nine times, rises towards him in one night.

In the Second Month the east wind comes,
Tearing at the plants till the flowers lay bare their hearts.
When I think upon my lord, the spring day passes slowly.
My heart, nine times, leaps up to him in one night.

Sadako is asking Shōnagon whether she misses her lord (i.e. herself); Shōnagon replies that she does miss her ('I feel my heart rising nine times towards you in the night') and implies that she will soon return. The phrase 'my heart ... leaps up' refers to the painful uncertainties of love.

488. The following scene is a 'flashback' describing what happened during and immediately after the move mentioned on p. 220; if the narrative were in normal time sequence, this scene would of course come *before* the story of the cherry blossoms.

489. cf. p. 198.

490. 'Ill-natured' might seem a strong word to describe Shōnagon's suggestion that the serving-women should be seated before herself and her companions; but, in view of Heian class attitudes, the idea that the normal order of procedure might be reversed was nothing short of indecent.

491. Normally carriages were lit at night by pine-torches; but this one was intended for servants and therefore left suitably murky.

492. Four passengers were the normal complement of a carriage (*W.S.P.*, p. 52).

493. About 4 a.m. See App. 1.

494. Fujiwara no Korechika and his younger brother, Takaie.

495. Doctor attached to the Bureau of Medicine; this Bureau, which was under the Ministry of the Imperial Household (App. 2), was in charge of curing people of the Fifth Rank and above (see *W.S.P.*, p. 146).

496. 'Forbidden colours' were those, like dark purple, that could be worn only by members of the Imperial family or High Court Nobles. Light purple and grape colour were not included among the forbidden colours. Yamanoi's remark, in which he refers to a Palace Girl by a man's name, is entirely facetious.

497. Onion-flower decoration: onion-shaped metal finial on the roof of an Imperial palanquin. The onion was regarded as an auspicious decoration because of its long-lived flowers.

498. This refers to ceremonial Court music of the *gagaku* type, which had been imported from the Continent and which was preserved in Japan long after it disappeared in its country of origin.

499. In order to keep their long hair in place, ladies often tucked it under their jackets, especially when travelling; but the shaking of the carriage was apt to disarrange it.

500. There appears to have been a young Fujiwara gentleman of this name. Possibly he was reputed to have an eye for women; this would explain the need to get Shōnagon and her companions out of their carriages secretly.

501. Elephant-eye silk: Chinese silk decorated with delicate gold and silver designs.

502. Master of the Household: i.e. Master of the Office of the Empress's Household (App. 2); refers here to Fujiwara no Michinaga, who later became Empress Sadako's greatest political enemy. See *W.S.P.*, pp. 76–7.

503. This passage provides a good illustration of the type of jealousy that prevailed among the ladies at Court. All of them vied for the favours of the Empress and therefore tended to resent her particular affection for Shōnagon. (Murasaki Shikibu's diary suggests that she suffered from

similar jealousy at Empress Akiko's Court.) When the Empress tells Saishō to go and see what is happening in the gentlemen's hall, the lady realizes that her mistress intends to put Shōnagon in her place on the straw mat. She replies rather bluntly that there is room for three people on the mat (i.e. herself, Lady Chūnagon, and Shōnagon). Sadako's 'Very well then' is a shorthand way of saying, 'Well, if you feel so strongly about it, you may as well stay where you are.' She then invites Shōnagon to sit near her on the mat. This irks some of the other ladies-in-waiting who are seated on a lower level, where they cannot observe the ceremony so well, and they vent their annoyance by denigrating Shōnagon, whose social position is of course inferior to that of Ladies Saishō and Chūnagon. First, one of them compares her to a page-boy, who is not normally allowed into the Imperial presence even though he may be favoured on special occasions. Another jealous lady compares her to a mounted escort, implying that, despite the Empress's partiality, Shōnagon's social relationship to Lady Saishō is like that of an inferior attendant to his master. There is a reference here to the fact that Saisho's father, Atsusuke, was Director of the Bureau of Horses, Right Division (Uma Ryō no Kami). Shōnagon wisely refuses to allow this backbiting to spoil her pleasure.

504. Military paraphernalia might seem inappropriate for a Buddhist ceremony; but the function of the Guards was almost entirely ceremonial and it was the elegance of the uniform that counted.

505. This is one of the great days in Michitaka's life and he does not want its memory to be spoiled by subsequent complaints that the women were uncomfortable in their formal costumes.

506. They wept for joy. For a discussion of male weeping see *W.S.P.*, pp. 157–8.

507. Michitaka refers facetiously to the fact that Buddhist priests wear robes of the same red colour as Shōnagon's jacket.

508. The names of Buddhist priests were read in the Sino-Japanese pronunciation; *Sei*, which is the Sino-Japanese reading of the first element of what is generally believed to be the author's family name (*Kiyowara*), lends itself to Korechika's witticism in a way that would be impossible with pure Japanese names like Ono, Izumi, and Murasaki.

509. The numerous stone images of Jizō in Japan represent him as a Buddhist priest with shaven head, clad in bonze's vestments and carrying a rosary. Ryūen was the Empress's brother (note 235); hence his presence among the ladies-in-waiting. Despite his high ecclesiastical rank, he was only fifteen years old.

510. The flowers were artificial (cf. note 478).

511. Prayer for Salvation: comprises sixteen characters from the *Amitāyur Buddha Dhyāna Sūtra*. Anesaki gives the following translation:

> His light pervades the world in all the ten directions,
> His grace never forsakes anyone who invokes his name.
> Masahara Anesaki, *History of Japanese Religion*, p. 178.

512. Reference to an old love poem:

> Though close at hand
> The Chika kilns
> In Michinoku's land,
> People can still not meet their salty taste.

Lit. 'the saltiness does not meet people', i.e. even though the salt-kilns are close, their salty flavour does not reach people in the vicinity. There is a play of words on Chika = (i) place name, (ii) close. The poem applies to a situation in which, although two people happen to be near each other (like Empress Sadako and the Empress Dowager during the present ceremony), they are still unable to meet.

513. Such a reduction in retinue was normal on the return from ceremonies, festivals, etc.

514. *Karma*: if it had rained on the previous day, much of the ceremony would have been ruined. Michitaka attributes his good luck with the weather to an accumulation of merit in previous incarnations (cf. note 285).

515. About midnight.

516. Emperor Ichijō was a keen flautist (*W.S.P.*, p. 60). For music at night see *W.S.P.*, pp. 162, 200.

517. Minamoto no Kanesuke, the Governor of Iyo, descended from a brother of Emperor Seiwa (reg. 858–76), the main ancestor of the Minamoto clan. His daughter was originally one of Fujiwara no Takaie's wives and she had at least two children by him; after her husband's disgrace she transferred her affections to the handsome young Narinobu, only to be abandoned by him a few years later.

518. *Hyōbu* = Military Affairs. No doubt she had a father, brother, or other close relative in the Ministry of Military Affairs. The lady's full last name was therefore something like Taira no Hyōbu, but the other ladies teased her by using her original family name, which was presumably a rather humble one.

519. This was unusual. The names of most of the Court ladies consisted of the offices, ranks, provinces, etc. with which their close relations were associated (e.g. Shikibu, Uma, Sammi, Naishi, Izumi, Sagami, Ise), or pseudonyms like Murasaki and Sei, or personal names like Yoshiko and Akiko.

520. Shōnagon is offended by the idea that Narinobu, who had come to visit her, should so easily have been put off by her pretence at being asleep and that he should have been satisfied to spend the night with such an inferior creature as

Hyōbu. Her reaction, in other words, is what men often describe as 'feminine'.

521. Shōnagon is coyly referring to herself.

522. cf. note 84.

523. The episode of the old fan (about which we know nothing since *Komano no Monogatari* is not extant) seems to have made a particular impression on Shōnagon.

524. From the poem,

> The evening now is dark,
> The path has disappeared from sight,
> As I go towards my native town.
> Yet I ride without a care –
> My horse has come this way before.

525. Shōnagon refers to *Ochikubo Monogatari*, 'The Tale of Room Below', a romance in four scrolls written towards the end of the tenth century (authorship unknown) and telling the story of an unfortunate young lady who is mistreated by her stepmother but eventually rescued by the hero, Sakon no Shōshō. Captain Katano (Katano no Shōshō) figures as an unsuccessful rival for the heroine's hand, but the extant version of *Ochikubo Monogatari* contains no reference to his being criticized by the hero. 'Captain Ochikubo' is clearly Ukon no Shōshō, and the extant version does in fact contain a scene in which he pays the heroine a 'third-night visit' (*W.S.P.*, p. 227) in the rain and has to wash the muck off his feet.

526. Possibly an allusion to the poem

> Until my life becomes extinct,
> How can she vanish from my thoughts –
> She whom I cherish more each day?

The quoted line means 'Can I (*or* he) forget?'

366

527. Short green robe: worn by men of the Sixth Rank. For its derogatory connotations see *W.S.P.*, p. 81. As a rule Shōnagon would not have welcomed a gentleman visitor below the Fifth Rank.

528. Even by Heian standards (*W.S.P.*, p. 194) this is a rather laconic communication. Its implication, however, would instantly be grasped by any perceptive member of Court society: 'There is nothing special for me to say, except to ask how you are enjoying this moonlight.'

529. Reference to the opening lines of the poem:

> When dawn appears,
> The ceaseless cry of the cicadas
> [Greets my ears] . . .

530. This is obviously a quotation, but the source is unknown. According to some of the early commentaries, the gentleman is referring to a *Kokin Shū* poem in which the writer compares his growing love to Yodo River, whose waters swell in the rain.

531. Because the tip of the writing-brush was frozen; but, as Kaneko remarks (*Hyōshaku*, p. 1022), this is surely an exaggeration. It is also hard to understand how Shōnagon could have observed the delicate indentations and other details of the letter from where she was standing.

532. Thunder Guard: another name for the Inner Palace Guards, derived from the fact that, when there were violent thunderstorms, members of the Inner Palace Headquarters would arm themselves with bows and arrows and post themselves in Seiryō and Shishin Palaces to protect the distinguished inhabitants from harm.

533. i.e. 'Proceed to the Imperial Palace' or 'Return to barracks'.

534. 'How is the snow on Hsiang-lu peak?': the Empress refers to some famous lines of Po Chü-i:

> The sun has risen in the sky, but I idly lie in bed;
> In my small tower-room the layers of quilts protect me from the cold;
> Leaning on my pillow, I wait to hear I-ai's temple bell;
> Pushing aside the blind, I gaze upon the snow of Hsiang-lu peak . . .

The poem was well known in Heian Kyō. It had been imitated by Sugawara no Michizane; and, as Shōnagon points out, it was often rendered in Japanese form. Once again, it is not Shōnagon's erudition that distinguishes her from the other ladies but her ability to rise instantly to the occasion.

535. Shōnagon compares the leaves of the unsightly willow tree to human eyebrows (*mayu*); the eyebrow image leads directly to the word 'face' in 'lose face'. *Mayu* also has the sense of cocoon, and there is a further implicit comparison between cocoons and the downy buds of the willow. Like so many of Shōnagon's verses, the present one is more ingenious than poetic.

536. It has been hard enough for the Empress to get through the past two days (lit. 'yesterday and today'). How, she wonders, can she have managed to exist during the long period before Shōnagon came into service? The exchange of this type of romantic poetry between ladies at Court was entirely conventional and should not be taken as evidence of Lesbian attachments (see *W.S.P.*, p. 233 n.).

537. An allusion to the poem,

> Evening comes
> And still I pine away;
> Truly the time seems long,
> Long as the pine tree's life:
> I feel as though I'd waited for a thousand years.

There is the usual pun on *matsu* = (i) to wait (pine), (ii) pine tree.

538. 'One who lives above the clouds' refers, of course, to the Empress. High members of Court society were commonly known as 'people above the clouds'.

539. This is probably a reference to Fukakusa no Shōshō. He fell in love with the famous ninth-century poetess and beauty, Ono no Komachi, but she said that she would trust and accept him only after he had spent every night outside her house for one hundred nights. Captain Fukakusa almost managed to pass the test; but he succumbed on the ninety-ninth night and accordingly failed to win Komachi. His un-appeased spirit returns to torment her in *Kayoi Komachi*, a famous Nō play.

In a type of insincere hyperbole that was common in Court circles Shōnagon suggests that she too may be un-able to survive her last night away from the object of her devotion (i.e. the Empress).

540. Because, says Kaneko (*Hyōshaku*, p. 1031), Shōnagon's reply poem was more concerned with her own unhappy feelings than with those of the Empress.

541. The 'mountain' (which is really more of a hill) is Otowa Yama; Kiyomizu Temple is situated about half-way up the slope.

542. The lotus petal is artificial, like those on p. 233. Pos-sibly Shōnagon selected it from among the petals that had been used in the Buddhist rite of scattering flowers. Both red and purple were associated with sunset and there-fore appropriate for evening poems (note the Empress's reference to vespers). The fact that Shōnagon does not quote her reply suggests she was not particularly proud of it.

369

543. This is from a ninth-century Chinese poem by Kung Ch'eng-i:

> [The moon,] piercing cold,
> Spreads like ice over the thousand leagues of the realm of Ch'in,
> And lucently adorns the thirty-six palaces of Han with silver grains.

544. Presumably during the friend's absence at Court; but the passage is somewhat obscure.

545. The image is not as original as it might seem: Japanese children make toy boats out of bamboo leaves.

546. Reference to a poem by the early eighth-century priest, Mansei:

> This world of ours –
> To what shall I compare it?
> To the white waves behind a boat
> That disappear without a trace
> As it rows away at dawn.

547. Since ancient times the Japanese have used women divers, partly because they can hold their breath longer than men, partly because they are more resistant to the cold.

548. For being old and ugly, according to Kaneko (*Hyōshaku*, p. 1045); but perhaps the real reason was that they were embarrassingly provincial (*W.S.P.*, p. 96).

549. Dōmei, the eldest son of Fujiwara no Michitsuna, was noted for the beauty of his sutra-chanting and for his skill at poetry. In the present poem there may be a play on the word *bon* = (i) the Festival of the Dead, (ii) the splash that the old couple made on hitting the water. The poem may also suggest the irony of the fact that, after pushing his parents into the sea, the lieutenant attended a service that was particularly concerned with interceding with those who

were undergoing the Ordeal of Headlong Falling (*Tōken no Ku*) in Hell (note 361).

For the Confucian significance of this anecdote see *W.S.P.*, p. 110.

550. The fourth quarter of the Hour of the Ox began at 3.30 a.m.

551. From a poem by Miyako no Yoshika (d. 879):

> When the cock-man cries the advent of the day,
> The prudent monarch rises from his sleep.
> When in the night the bell of Fu rings out,
> Its sound pervades the darkness of the sky.

The 'cock-man' was an official in charge of delivering fowls for sacrifice; his head-dress was decorated with a cock's comb. For all official ceremonies he announced the daybreak and the hour when the ceremony was to start. The bell of Fu was named after a family that in the ancient times of Chou had been responsible for casting bells.

The top lines refer to the conscientious Emperor who, as soon as dawn had been announced, would get up and busy himself with affairs of state instead of idling away his time in bed.

552. From a poem by Chia Tao (fl. 793–865),

> At dawn when bells of Wei begin to ring,
> The lovely girl adorns herself with care.
> When cocks crow at the barrier of Han Ku,
> The traveller journeys by the dying moon's faint light.

Wei was the name of a palace (Wei Kung); for the barrier of Han Ku see note 346.

553. For Mistress of the Robes see note 197. The bishop is Empress Sadako's brother, Ryūen. Mama was a name commonly given to nurses in the Heian period; a woman with this mammalian name also appears in *The Tale of Genji*.

554. Lit. 'thrusting my buttocks into other people's houses', i.e. imposing myself on people's hospitality. The phrase has a crude ring and emphasizes the low social status of the speaker.

555. Shōnagon's poem is riddled with puns and would be quite incomprehensible to anyone unaware of the double meanings involved. The unfortunate recipient of the poem would have had little chance of understanding it even if he had been able to read the words.

Using a second set of meanings, we get the following translation, which is of course immediately relevant to the situation:

> If the spring-time is strong enough
> To make the fodder burn,
> Even the bedroom of a house like yours
> Could still survive its heat.

556. Record-slip: narrow strip of paper or tag used among other things for noting the amount of rice or other alms to be given to people. By Shōnagon's time decorated record-slips were also being used in Court circles for writing poems. The poor man in the present section obviously believes that Shōnagon has written down the amount of rice he will receive as charity; instead all he gets is a callous, mocking poem, which he cannot even understand. For 'good' people's attitude to the lower orders, of which this is a peculiarly unattractive example, see *W.S.P.*, p. 99.

557. Like many sections in *The Pillow Book* this reads like a character sketch for a possible story or novel. On the other hand, Shōnagon may be describing some real person.

The wicked stepmother theme was common in Heian fiction, but the unfortunate stepchild was usually a girl (e.g. note 525).

558. When travelling by carriage, people would frequently wear asymmetrical robes, which had very wide, low-

hanging sleeves on one side and sleeves of ordinary width on the other; they would then let the wide sleeves trail conspicuously outside the carriage.

The reader should remember that even ordinary Court robes had very wide, heavy sleeves; the extra-wide sleeves to which Shōnagon refers in this section must have been exceedingly cumbersome.

559. These were all the standard attributes of feminine beauty in the Heian period (*W.S.P.*, p. 213).

560. As a rule the voluminous hair of Heian women hung loosely over their shoulders (*W.S.P.*, p. 213), but this was inconvenient for someone who was ill in bed.

561. The river is the Hasegawa, which flows near the foot of the hill on which Hase Temple was built.

562. Normally the soup and vegetables were eaten together with the rice; to finish each of the dishes separately and with such speed was unspeakably ill-mannered (*W.S.P.*, p. 100).

563. cf. p. 49.

564. From the poem by Hitomaro:

> If you but came and lingered by my side,
> Like the moon that lingers in the dawning sky
> During the Long-Night Month,
> What need for me to languish as I do?

The Long-Night Month (Nagatsuki) is the Ninth. Hitomaro's poem ends with a combination of particles that gives it the form of a rhetorical question expecting a negative reply.

565. See *W.S.P.*, pp. 244–5. This is one of the many passages in *The Pillow Book* where Shōnagon gives her idea of the perfect lover (cf. pp. 49–50).

566. This section describes a summer evening in the women's quarters of an elegant mansion. The woman behind the

curtain of state is the mistress of the house, the visitor is presumably her lover.

567. For the nuances of olfactory impressions see *W.S.P.*, pp. 202–5.

568. See note 552.

569. Magic Incantation of the Thousand Hands: one section of the Thousand Hand Sutra, which was especially associated with Shingon. I. was recited to ward off illnesses, discord, slander, and other evils.

570. Lit. 'a person suffering painfully from an evil spirit'. For a discussion of Heian beliefs about evil spirits as a cause of illness, and about the method of curing such illness by exorcism, see *W.S.P.*, pp. 147–52. Heian exorcist practices were closely associated with Shingon and were frequently of Indian origin.

571. Wand: a type of mace, particularly connected with Shingon and used by priests, exorcists, etc., who brandished it in all directions while reciting their prayers and magic formulae.

572. The groans and wails come from the evil spirit, which has temporarily been transferred to the medium and is now being painfully subdued by the priest's incantations.

573. 4 p.m. (App. 1).

574. Kaneko (*Hyōshaku*, p. 1089) remarks on the similarity between the priest's well-chosen, rather pompous words and those of many fashionable doctors in modern times.

575. cf. p. 192.

576. High clogs were a rough, rustic form of footwear and looked incongruous with a *hakama* trouser-skirt. The same type of incongruity can be found in modern Japan, where students sometimes wear *geta* (clogs) at the same time as a *hakama*.

577. Even if they were in a hurry, well-bred people walked in a slow, dignified manner.

578. Many *yin-yang* beliefs and practices became associated in Japan with Shintō (*W.S.P.*, pp. 136 ff.), and conversely many Shintō services, such as purification, were performed by the *yin-yang* practitioners known as Masters of Divination. Such was the complexity of Heian eclecticism, however, that Buddhist priests also performed services like purification which had no connexion whatsoever with their own religion.

The paper head-dress to which Shōnagon refers was a triangular hat fixed to the front of the head and tied in the back. It was worn by Shintō priests, exorcists, and others, but not normally by Buddhist priests, whose heads were completely shaven. When performing an essentially non-Buddhist service like purification, however, Buddhist priests frequently did wear these triangular hats. This produced an ugly, incongruous effect, much as if a Roman Catholic priest were to don a magician's cap in order to perform a primitive type of service.

579. cf. note 66 for the prejudice against daytime naps.

580. Shōnagon obviously found it more unpleasant to see ugly people when they were lying down than when they were up and about.

581. Because the scarlet colour hides their dark skin. For the importance of white skin see *W.S.P.*, p. 213.

582. It appears that Korechika also presented Emperor Ichijō with a quantity of paper (good paper being in short supply even at Court) and that the Emperor had decided to use his allotment for making a copy of the huge Chinese historical work, *Shih chi*.

583. 'Make them into a pillow': i.e. a pillow book. Here we have one likely explanation of the title of Shōnagon's book

(for a detailed discussion of the title and its possible origins see Ikeda–Kishigami, pp. 6–7, where about a dozen distinct theories are suggested). *Majura no sōshi* ('pillow book') referred to a notebook or collection of notebooks kept in some accessible but relatively private place, and in which the author would from time to time record impressions, daily events, poems, letters, stories, ideas, descriptions of people, etc. (For *sōshi* see note 474.) The phrase *makura no sōshi* does not appear to have been original with Sei Shōnagon; but her work is the only extant one of its type with that title as well as being by far the oldest surviving book of the typically Japanese genre known as *zuihitsu*.

In later times the name *makura no sōshi* came to designate books of erotic illustrations depicting the standard forms of sexual intercourse; such books were frequently included in a bride's trousseau as a remedy for her supposed innocence in these matters.

584. Since Shōnagon's judgement tended to be the exact opposite of other people's, it was only natural that they should praise a book (her own) which she considered to be deficient in so many respects.

The traditional Japanese calendar was a great deal more complicated than anything we have known in the West. Also, because of *yin-yang* and related ideas, it was far more important in people's everyday lives than even the medieval European calendar with its plethora of Saints' Days, movable feasts, and other observances.

In order to explain as clearly as possible the calendar that dominated Heian activities, ranging from the appointment of high government officials to trivia like cutting one's toe-nails, it is best to start with the Chinese Zodiac, which was the basis of dates, time, and directions. This diagram drawn by Mrs Nanae Momiyama, gives the following information from outside to inside: (i) the compass directions, (ii) the hours of day and night (midnight at the top, noon at the bottom),

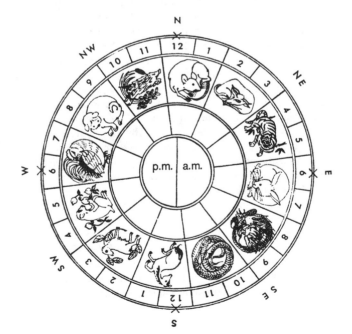

(iii) drawings of the twelve 'branches', each corresponding to one watch or two Western hours.

In order to designate a date the Japanese normally used a combination of two series, which produced a cycle of sixty days or sixty years, sixty of course being the first number divisible by both ten and twelve. The first series consisted of the twelve signs of the Zodiac as shown in the diagram. These signs, known as 'branches', were as follows: (i) rat, (ii) ox, (iii) tiger, (iv) hare, (v) dragon, (vi) snake, (vii) horse, (viii) sheep, (ix) monkey, (x) bird, (xi) dog, (xii) boar. They referred to (a) time (e.g. Hour of the Snake – 10 a.m. to midnight), (b) direction (e.g. Dragon–Snake – south-east), (c) day of the month (e.g. First Day of the Snake), (d) year (e.g. Year of the Snake – sixth year of any sexagenary cycle). At present the only frequent use of the Zodiac is to designate years: 1969 is the Year of the Bird, 1970 the Year of the Dog, and so on.

The second series consisted of ten 'celestial stems' which were produced by dividing each of the five elements into two parts, the 'elder brother' and 'younger brother'. The 'branches' and 'celestial stems' were combined to produce the basic cycle of sixty (see opposite).

If, for example, a month started on the fifteenth day of the sexagenary cycle the third day of that month would be designated as: (i) the (first) Day of the Dragon, (ii) the (first) Day of the Elder Brother of Metal, (iii) a combination of (i) and (ii). In any given month there was a maximum of three days named after each of the twelve 'branches' and three days named after each of the ten 'celestial stems'. These days could be identified by the prefixes 'upper', 'middle', and 'lower' for the first, second, and third respectively.

Years could also be designated in terms of year-periods, which were regularly decided by the Japanese Government from the beginning of the eighth century. This was an involved system of dating, because year-periods could begin in the middle of a calendar year and were often changed several times in the course of a single imperial reign; a further complication for the Westerner is that the latter part of the Japanese lunar calendar falls in the first part of the following year according to our solar calendar. Later Japanese historians made the year-periods retroactive to the first day of the first lunar month of the year in which it was adopted, but this in fact only served to complicate matters further.

THE SEXAGENERAY CYCLE

	Rat	Ox	Tiger	Hare	Dragon	Snake	Horse	Sheep	Monkey	Bird	Dog	Boar
1. Elder brother of wood	1	:	51	:	41	:	31	:	21	:	11	:
2. Younger brother of wood	:	2	:	52	:	42	:	32	:	22	:	12
3. Elder brother of fire	13	:	3	:	53	:	43	:	33	:	23	:
4. Younger brother of fire	:	14	:	4	:	54	:	44	:	34	:	24
5. Elder brother of earth	25	:	15	:	5	:	55	:	45	:	35	:
6. Younger brother of earth	:	26	:	16	:	6	:	56	:	46	:	36
7. Elder brother of metal	37	:	27	:	17	:	7	:	57	:	47	:
8. Younger brother of metal	:	38	:	28	:	18	:	8	:	58	:	48
9. Elder brother of water	49	:	39	:	29	:	19	:	9	:	59	:
10. Younger brother of water	:	50	:	40	:	30	:	20	:	10	:	60

The names of the months in pre-Heian Japan were far more evocative than our dull Januarys and Februarys. This is their literal translation:

1. Sprouting Month
2. Clothes-lining Month
3. Ever-growing Month
4. U no hana Month (the *u no hana* was a pretty white shrub)
5. Rice-sprouting Month
6. Watery Month
7. Poem-composing Month
8. Leaf Month (i.e. the month when the leaves turn)
9. Long Month (i.e. the month with long nights)
10. Gods-absent Month
11. Frost Month
12. End of the year.

Charming though many of these names are, I have avoided them in my translation for fear that they might produce a false exoticism of the 'Honourable Lady Plum Blossom' variety. Instead I have designated them by the numbers (First Month, Second Month, etc.) that are used in all the early texts of *The Pillow Book*. It should be understood that, though Tenth Month, for instance, was normally written with the characters for 'ten' and 'month', it was pronounced Kaminazuki, which means 'Gods-absent Month', and that it could also be written with the phonetic symbols representing *ka*, *mi*, *na*, *zu*, and *ki*. Months were either twenty-nine or thirty days long, with an intercalary month added about once every three years.

Days, as we have seen, were designated in terms of the sexagenary cycle. They could also be defined by their order in the month, e.g. Third Day of the Rice-sprouting (Fifth) Month. When reading premodern literature we should remember that there was a discrepancy, varying from seventeen to forty-five days, between the Japanese (lunar) calendar and the Western (Julian) calendar, the Japanese calendar being on an average about one month in advance of the Western. For example, the twentieth day of the Twelfth Month in 989 (the date when Fujiwara no Kaneie became Prime Minister) corresponded to 19 January 990 in the West; and the thirteenth day of the Sixth Month in 1011 (the date of Emperor Ichijō's death) corresponded to 25 July. Accordingly the most important day of the year, New Year's

Day, came at some time between 21 January and 19 February in our calendar.

The dates of the four seasons were rigidly respected. To wear clothes of an unseasonal colour was an appalling solecism in Sei Shōnagon's society; a white under-robe in the Eighth Month figures among 'depressing things'. Spring started on New Year's Day; all the associations of New Year's Day were therefore vernal, rather than wintry as in the West. Summer, autumn, and winter started on the first day of the Fourth, Seventh, and Tenth Months respectively.

The Heian calendar was crammed with annual observances of all kinds. The five main festivals were New Year's Day (first day of the First Month), the Peach Festival (third day of the Third Month), the Iris Festival (fifth day of the Fifth Month), the Weaver Festival (seventh day of the Seventh Month), and the Chrysanthemum Festival (ninth day of the Ninth Month). Other observances described in *The Pillow Book* were as follows:

Spring

First Month	2nd day	Tooth-hardening (note 124)
	7th day	Festival of Young Herbs (note 3)
		Festival of the Blue Horses (note 5)
	15th day	Full-Moon Gruel (note 9)
Second Month	during four days	Seasonal Sacred Readings (note 206)
Third Month	2nd day of the Horse	Special Festival at Iwashimizu Shrine (note 176)

Summer

Fourth Month	2nd day of the Bird	Kamo Festival (note 14)

Autumn

Seventh Month	13th to 16th days	Festival of the Dead (note 361)
Eighth Month	during four days	Seasonal Sacred Readings (note 206)

Winter

Eleventh Month	2nd day of the Ox	Dais Rehearsal
	2nd day of the Tiger	Banquet with songs and dances

	2nd day of the Hare	{ Attendants' Dance / Festival of the First Fruits
	2nd day of the Dragon	Gosechi Dances
	last day of the Bird	Special Festival at Kamo Shrine (note 176)
Twelfth Month	19th–22nd days	Naming of the Buddhas (note 180)
	last day	Festival of the Spirits (note 124)

Finally, the Heian day was divided into twelve watches, each two hours in length and divided into four quarters. Time was specified by the Zodiacal signs. The watch of the Horse, for instance, started at noon and continued until two o'clock in the afternoon; the fourth quarter of the Horse therefore corresponded to the thirty minutes between half past one and two o'clock in the afternoon.

I shall conclude with a single complete example. The fourth quarter of the watch of the Tiger on the fifteenth day of the Sprouting (First) Month in the Fourth Year of the Chōtoku year-period, in which the Elder Brother of the Earth coincided with the sign of the Dog, corresponded to about 6 a.m. on 15 February A.D. 998. And it was at this moment in history that a maid announced to Sei Shōnagon (p. 107) that her precious snow-mountain had disappeared.

Appendix 2: THE GOVERNMENT

In the seventh century the leaders of Japan instituted a Great Reform which, at least on paper, affected every aspect of national life. Their main aim was to weaken the ancient clan-family system that had dominated Japanese society since the beginning of history and to substitute a modern Chinese style of government. As in the corresponding great change some twelve centuries later when Japan renovated herself on Western models, the reform movement of the seventh century was spread over several decades; the final codes incorporating the changes were not promulgated until the eighth century. Though few of the specific changes were to be permanent, and though the structure collapsed almost entirely with the advent of feudalism, the new modes of provincial and central administration were still the theoretical basis of government in Sei Shōnagon's time, and some of the innovations have lasted in form until modern times.

A primary motive of the reformers was centralization. In the provinces all local officials were subordinated to a Governor who was appointed every six years by the central government. The central government itself was reorganized in pyramidal form with the emperor at the apex. Theoretically all authority in the land derived ultimately from him; but, as it turned out, few emperors in Japanese history had any real secular power, and by Shōnagon's period the divine sovereign was in fact an impotent young puppet manipulated by the Fujiwara family.

Under the emperor came the two divisions of government, one religious and the other secular. The secular branch was headed by the Great Council of State, whose hierarchy included a Prime Minister and the Great Ministers of the Left, Right, and Centre. Since the first and last of these posts were usually unfilled, the highest officials were the Ministers of the Left and Right, who from the middle of the ninth century were usually leading members of the Fujiwara family.

By Shōnagon's time, however, the real ruler of the country was neither the emperor nor any of these Great Ministers but the Chancellor, who was always the head of 'northern' branch of the Fujiwaras. This post was extra-legal in the sense that it was not part of the system officially adopted in the seventh century. Though the Chinese hierarchy was never repudiated, no one in Shōnagon's period would have dreamt of challenging the hegemony of the Fujiwara Chancellor. A similar dichotomy between theory and reality applied to many of the lower strata of the hierarchy. Almost all the multifarious government departments and officials established as part of the Great Reform were preserved; but more and more frequently their actual functions were usurped by private or extra-legal organs of government. As a result, many of the impressive titles mentioned in *The Pillow Book* and *The Tale of Genji* were almost entirely formal, and the corresponding posts had become mere sinecures; real work and power had moved elsewhere, often to the Administrative Councils of the vast and prepotent Fujiwara family. This distinction should be kept in mind when examining the following account of the hierarchy under the Great Council of State.

Next in rank to the Great Ministers were the Major, Middle, and Minor Counsellors and the eight Imperial Advisers, who were all members of the Great Council. The Major Counsellors, of whom there were usually three, retained a good deal of real administrative influence long after other parts of the structure had lapsed into desuetude.

Under the Great Council came the Controllers. They were responsible for the two Controlling Boards, which like almost every part of the hierarchy were divided into Left and Right in imitation of the formal arrangement of officials in the Chinese Court. The Controlling Board of the Left was in charge of four Ministeries, including the Ministry of Central Affairs and the Ministry of Ceremonial; the Board of the Right controlled the Ministries of the Imperial Household and of the Treasury among others. The Ministry of Central Affairs, whose responsibilities included Palace ceremonial, the promulgation of edicts, the supervision of officials, the study of astronomy and divination, and the compilation of official histories, was by far the most important; the least respected was, quite rightly, the Ministry of War.

Each of the eight Ministries was headed by a Minister and composed of a varying number of Offices and Bureaux. The following are mentioned in *The Pillow Book*:

1. *Ministry of Central Affairs*: Bureau of Divination, Bureau of Imperial Attendants, Bureau of the Wardrobe, Imperial Storehouse, Office of the Empress's Household.

2. *Ministry of Ceremonial*: Bureau of Education.

3. *Ministry of the Imperial Household*: Bureau of Carpentry, Bureau of Medicine, Office of Grounds, Table Office.

4. *Ministry of the Treasury*: Housekeeping Office.

To keep things in proper perspective we should remember that most of this elaborate governmental machinery, of which the above is only a minute fraction, was concerned with the affairs of a select aristocracy who comprised about ten thousand people out of a population of some four million.

Of vital importance for this aristocracy was the complex rank system, which was an integral part of the Great Reform. In Shōnagon's time the system included four grades for Imperial Princes and thirty ranks for other mortals. Each rank was divided into Senior and Junior, and below the Third Rank each was further sub-divided into Upper and Lower grades. Every courtier and official had some sort of rank, ranging from the Senior First Rank for the Prime Minister to the Lesser Initial Rank, Lower Grade, for a Clerk in the Division of Carpentry and Metal Work. As we know from section 8 of *The Pillow Book*, even a cat could receive Court rank: indeed Emperor Ichijō's pet cat belonged to at least as high a rank as the Governor of the largest province in Japan. The joys of rank were also extended to troublesome ghosts and even to inanimate objects like ships.

Rank was closely correlated with governmental office. By combining the aristocracy with the civil service in such a way that a person was usually first given rank and then a suitable office to fit that rank, and by making it impossible for anyone to enter the rank hierarchy by merit, the Japanese made their system diverge in fundamental and very damaging ways from the Chinese model. Not only were holders of rank automatically appointed to government posts, but many of them received large allotments of tax-free rice land as well as other privileges like exemption from military service and the rights to have certain types of clothes and carriages, to send their sons to the University, and ultimately to rest under burial mounds of specified degrees of magnificence.

For people of Shōnagon's circle almost every aspect of material life was dictated by position in the rank system. It is small wonder that many of them became obsessed with matters of appointment and promotion and that members of the provincial governor class should sometimes have chafed at their lowly status in the rank system. It was provincial notables and the despised military who were largely instrumental in undermining the entire structure during the century that followed Sei Shōnagon's death.

Appendix 3: PLACES

3A. HOME PROVINCES (KINAI = YAMASHIRO, YAMATO,
IZUMI, KAWASHI, SETTSU) AND NEIGHBOURING PROVINCES

Alphabetical Listing		*Geographical Listing*
Biwa Ko	2	1. Hieizan
Hasedera	6	2. Biwa Ko
Heian Kyō	3	3. Heian Kyō
Hieizan	1	4. Yodogawa
Kōya San	9	5. Nara
Kumano	10	6. Hasedera
Mitake	8	7. Yoshino
Nara	5	8. Mitake
Yodogawa	4	9. Kōya San
Yoshino	7	10. Kumano

3B. THE SURROUNDINGS OF THE CAPITAL*

Alphabetical Listing		*Geographical Listing*
Chisoku In	4	1. Kuramadera
Inari no Jinja	8	2. Kamo no Jinja
Iwashimizu no Hachiman Gū	10	3. Murasaki No
Kamo no Jinja	2	4. Chisoku In
Kuramadera	1	5. Ninna Ji
Murasaki No	3	6. Uzumasa
Ninna Ji	5	7. Ōsaka no Seki
Ōsaka no Seki	7	8. Inari no Jinja
Otoko Yama	9	9. Otoko Yama
Uzumasa	6	10. Iwashimizu no Hachiman Gū

* The maps in Appendices 3b and 3c are adapted from R. K. Reischauer's
Early Japanese History, Volume B, published in 1937 by Princeton University
Press, with whose permission they are reproduced.

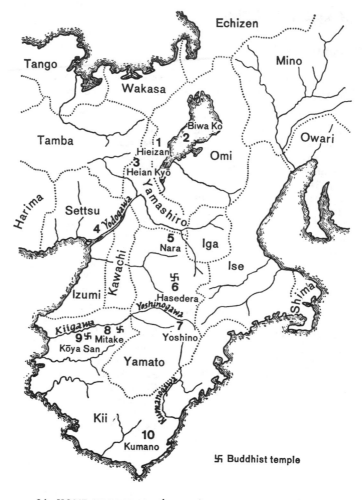

Echizen

Tango

Mino

Wakasa

Tamba

Biwa Ko

Owari

1
Hieizan

2

Omi

3
Heian Kyō

Yamashiro

Harima

Settsu

4 Yodogawa

Nara

Iga

Ise

Kawachi

5

Izumi

卍
6
Hasedera

Shima

Yoshinogawa

Kiigawa

卍 **8** 卍

9 卍 Mitake
Kōya San

7
Yoshino

Yamato

Kumanogawa

Kii

10
Kumano

卍 Buddhist temple

3A. HOME PROVINCES (KINAI) AND NEIGHBOURING PROVINCES

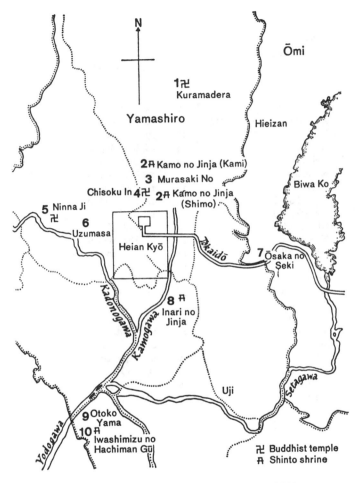

N

Ōmi

1卍
Kuramadera

Yamashiro

Hieizan

2A Kamo no Jinja (Kami)
3 Murasaki No

Chisoku In **4**卍 **2**A Kamo no Jinja
(Shimo)

Biwa Ko

5 Ninna Ji
卍 **6**
Uzumasa

Heian Kyō

Tōkaidō

7 Ōsaka no
Seki

8 A
Inari no
Jinja

Uji

9 Otoko
Yama
10 A
Iwashimizu no
Hachiman Gū

卍 Buddhist temple
A Shinto shrine

3B. THE SURROUNDINGS OF THE CAPITAL

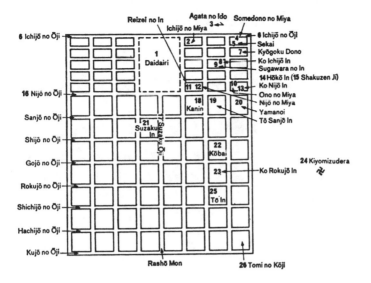

3C. THE CAPITAL

In = Temple   Miya = Palace   Ōji = Avenue

Appendix 4: CLOTHES, HOUSES, ETC.

4A. CLOTHES
MEN'S CLOTHES

ORDINARY COURT COSTUME

head dress
over robe
baton
ribbon attached to sword belt
trouser skirt
shoes

FULL COURT COSTUME

head dress
fan
court cloak
loose-laced trousers

head dress
hunting cloak
fan

HUNTING COSTUME

WOMEN'S CLOTHES

back view
unlined dress
chinese jacket
skirt with long train

front view

hair ornament
fan
matched set of unlined dresses
skirt with long train
chinese jacket
robe
trouser skirt   unlined dress

FULL COURT COSTUME

4B. HOUSES

Outside: Reconstruction of a *shinden* mansion and its garden by Mr Mori Osamu (N.B. this reconstruction of Higashi Sanjō Dono is taken from *Nihon Emakimono Zenshū*, vol xii).

1. Main building   2. Wing   3. Corridor   4. Gate

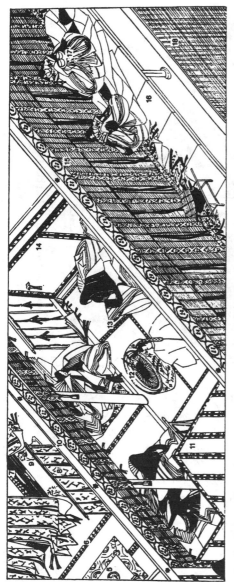

Inside: Schematic redrawing by Mrs Nanae Momiyama of the section from *Makura no Sōshi Emaki* that illustrated the Shigei Sha's visit to her sister (section 70).

5. Cushion
6. Straw mat with floral design
7. Curtain-dais
8. Curtain of state
9. Lion
10. Beam
11. Screen
12. Brazier
13. Straw mat with white and black design
14. Sliding-door
15. Blinds
16. Open veranda
17. Tray
18. Garden fence

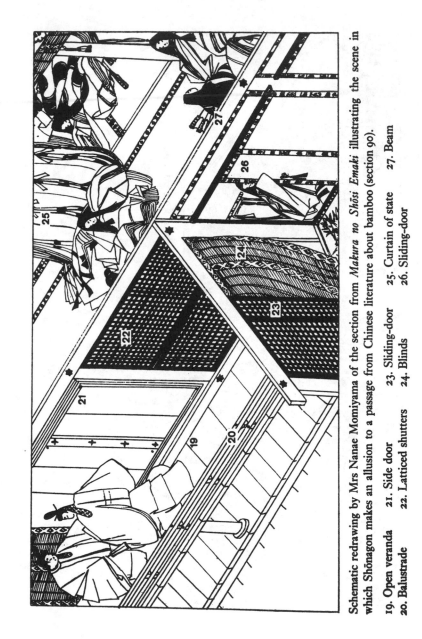

Schematic redrawing by Mrs Nanae Momiyama of the section from *Makura no Shōsi Emaki* illustrating the scene in which Shōnagon makes an allusion to a passage from Chinese literature about bamboo (section 90).

19. Open veranda
20. Balustrade

21. Side door
22. Latticed shutters

23. Sliding-door
24. Blinds

25. Curtain of state
26. Sliding-door

27. Beam

Imperial palanquin with onion decoration

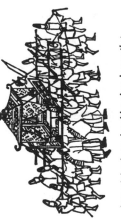

Palm-leaf carriage

Wickerwork carriage

Style of letting one's sleeves hang
outside the carriage in which one is travelling

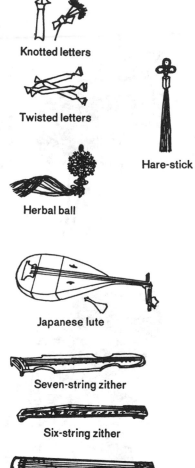

Knotted letters

Twisted letters

Herbal ball

Hare-stick

Go

Backgammon

Japanese lute

Seven-string zither

Six-string zither

Thirteen-string zither

Thirteen-pipe flute

Appendix 5: CHRONOLOGY

Dates are given according to the lunar calendar; '23.6', for example, means the twenty-third day of the sixth lunar month. Italicized entries are from *The Pillow Book*; datable sections are listed at the end of the Chronology.

986

23.6   Emperor Kazan secretly visited Kazan Temple and took holy orders.
        Emperor Ichijō acceded to the Throne (aged six).
24.6   Fujiwara no Kaneie, the father of Michitaka, was appointed Regent and became Head of the (Fujiwara) Clan.
6th Month   *Shōnagon heard the Eight Lessons at Ko Shirakawa (section 23).*
5.7   Emperor Ichijō's mother, Fujiwara no Senshi, became Empress Dowager.
22.7   The enthronement ceremony of Emperor Ichijō took place.

987

7.1 (?)   *Shōnagon visited the Imperial Palace to view the Ceremony of the Blue Horses (section 2).*
14.10   Emperor Ichijō visited the residence of the Regent, Fujiwara no Kaneie.
15.12   Emperor Ichijō made a pilgrimage to Kamo Shrine.

988

25.3   Emperor Ichijō celebrated the sixtieth birthday of the Regent, Fujiwara no Kaneie.
16.9   Fujiwara no Kaneie held a banquet at his new residence in Nijō.
27.10   The Priestly Retired Emperor, Enyū, visited Fujiwara no Kaneie in Nijō.

399

16.2   Emperor Ichijō made a pilgrimage to Enyū Temple.
22.3   Emperor Ichijō made his first pilgrimage to Kasuga Shrine.
20.12   Fujiwara no Kaneie was appointed Prime Minister.

990

5.1   Emperor Ichijō, aged ten, celebrated his coming-of-age ceremony.
25.1   Fujiwara no Sadako, Michitaka's daughter, became an Imperial consort at the age of fourteen.
11.2   Fujiwara no Sadako was appointed Imperial Lady (Nyōgo).
?   *Shōnagon probably entered Court service during this year as Empress Sadako's lady-in-waiting (section 116).*
5.5   Fujiwara no Kaneie was appointed Chancellor.
8.5   Fujiwara no Kaneie took holy orders, and Fujiwara no Michitaka succeeded him as Chancellor.
13.5   Fujiwara no Michitaka became Head of the (Fujiwara) Clan.
26.5   Fujiwara no Michitaka was appointed Regent.
6th Month Kiyowara no Motosuke, Shōnagon's father, died in Higo at the age of eighty-two.
2.7   Fujiwara no Kaneie died at the age of sixty-one.
5.10   Fujiwara no Sadako was appointed Second Empress; Fujiwara no Nobuko became First Empress.

991

1st Month Emperor Ichijō visited his father, the Priestly Retired Emperor, Enyū, in Enyū Temple where he lay ill.
3.2   The Priestly Retired Emperor, Enyū, died at the age of thirty-two.
7.9   Fujiwara no Tamemitsu was appointed Prime Minister.
16.9   Fujiwara no Senshi, the widow of Emperor Enyū, being in ill health, took holy orders and received the name Higashi Sanjō no In.
3.11   Higashi Sanjō no In moved into the residence of her brother, Fujiwara no Michinaga.

6.2 The one-year period of mourning for Emperor Enyū came to an end; *Shōnagon described this as 'a most moving time'; a practical joke was played on Tōzammi* (section 91).

3rd Month (?) *Shōnagon visited her friend's house to perform abstinence* (section 159).

6th Month Fujiwara no Tamemitsu, the Prime Minister, died at the age of fifty.

8th Month (?) *At some time between 992 (8th Month) and 994 (8th Month) Fujiwara no Korechika visited the Palace and Emperor Ichijō was awakened by a rooster* (section 167).

12th Month *Empress Sadako, residing at the Southern Palace, ordered a dress to be sewn in a hurry* (section 62).

7.12 Empress Sadako returned to the Imperial Palace from the Southern Palace.

993

3.1 Emperor Ichijō made his annual New Year visit to his mother, Higashi Sanjō no In.

22.1 There was an Imperial banquet attended by Higashi Sanjō no In and Empress Sadako.

22.4 Fujiwara no Michitaka was appointed Chancellor and resigned as Regent.

Summer There was an epidemic of smallpox and an amnesty was proclaimed.

Intercalary 20.10 Sugawara no Michizane was posthumously appointed Prime Minister.

(Early spring or early winter Shōnagon entered Court service, according to Ikeda Kikan, Kishigami Shinji, etc.)

Between 993 (4th Month) and 994 (8th Month) *Fujiwara no Michitaka came out through the Black Door and his brother, Michinaga, did obeisance to him* (section 83).

15.11 (?) *Empress Sadako sent Gosechi dancers to the Palace.*

27.11 Emperor Ichijō made his first pilgrimage to Ōhara No.

22.12 *A screen depicting the horrors of hell was taken to Empress Sadako's Palace; Korechika recited a Chinese poem* (section 50).

994

23.1   Fujiwara no Michitaka held a great banquet.

17.2   Fires broke out in Koki Palace and other palaces.

2nd Month   *Shōnagon attended services at Shakuzen Temple* (section 150).

3rd Month   *Emperor Ichijō ordered Empress Sadako's ladies to write poems* (section 11).

3rd Month (?)   *Empress Sadako played the lute* (section 59).

9.5   Lady Jōshi, the Crown Prince's consort, gave birth to a son, the future Prince Atsuakira.

5th Month   *Fujiwara no Tadanobu visited the Empress's apartments in Seiryō Palace and impressed her ladies with his scent* (section 60).

7.8   Fujiwara no Michitaka organized a wrestling tournament.

28.8   Fujiwara no Korechika was appointed Minister of the Centre.

After 8th Month   *Fujiwara no Korechika presented some notebooks to Empress Sadako, who gave them to Shōnagon 'to make into a pillow'* (section 185).

Autumn (?)   Shōnagon may have started writing *The Pillow Book* about this time.

13.11   Fujiwara no Michitaka fell ill.

12th Month   There was a solar eclipse, robberies occurred in the provinces, and a great epidemic broke out.

995

2.1   Owing to illness, Fujiwara no Michitaka was unable to appear at Court.

9.1   Several residences on Nijō no Ōji were destroyed by fire, including those of Fujiwara no Michitaka and Fujiwara no Korechika.

19.1   Fujiwara no Michitaka's second daughter, the Shigei Sha, became a consort of the Crown Prince.

3.2   The palace attendants of Higashi Sanjō no In fought with those of Empress Sadako.

5.2   Fujiwara no Michitaka resigned as Chancellor.

12.2 (?)   *Fujiwara no Yukinari sent rice cakes to Shōnagon* (section 86).

18.2   *The Shigei Sha visited Empress Sadako, her sister* (section 70).

26.2   Fujiwara no Michitaka confirmed his resignation as Chancellor.

End of the 2nd Month *Fujiwara no Tadanobu and Shōnagon exchanged messages and he put her to the test* (section 51).

9.3   Owing to his father's illness, Fujiwara no Korechika assumed the duties of Imperial Examiner (Nairan).

6.4   Fujiwara no Michitaka took holy orders.

10.4   Fujiwara no Michitaka died at the age of forty-two.

27.4   Fujiwara no Michikane was appointed Chancellor.

28.4   Fujiwara no Michikane became Head of the (Fujiwara) Clan.

Between 995 (4th Month) and 996 (4th Month) *Fujiwara no Takaie presented a fan to his sister, Empress Sadako* (section 68).

8.5   Fujiwara no Michikane died at the age of thirty-four.

4th and 5th Months There was a great epidemic, in which many high officials died.

11.5   Fujiwara no Michinaga was appointed Imperial Examiner (Nairan).

5th Month (?) *Shōnagon and her companions went to hear the* hototogisu *and failed to produce any poems* (section 65).

11.6   Fujiwara no Michiyori, Empress Sadako's brother, died at the age of twenty-five.

19.6   Fujiwara no Michinaga was appointed Minister of the Right and became Head of the (Fujiwara) Clan.

28.6   Empress Sadako moved into the Empress's Office.

6th Month *Shōnagon and the other ladies-in-waiting moved with the Empress into the Dining Hall of the High Court Nobles and visited the Time Office* (section 105).

8.7   Empress Sadako returned to the Palace.

24.7   There was a dispute between Fujiwara no Michinaga and his nephew, Fujiwara no Korechika.

27.7   There was a fight between the attendants of Fujiwara no Michinaga and those of Fujiwara no Korechika's brother, Takaie.

10.9   *Empress Sadako held a memorial service for her father, Fujiwara no Michitaka, in the Empress's Office; after the service Fujiwara no Tadanobu quoted a Chinese poem, deeply impressing the Empress and Shōnagon* (section 88).

21.10   Emperor Ichijō made a pilgrimage to Iwashimizu Hachiman Shrine at Yawata.

22.10   *Emperor Ichijō visited his mother, Higashi Sanjō no In, on his return from Yawata* (section 82).

10.10 Fujiwara no Korechika, who had secretly returned to the capital, was ordered to be expelled from the city and sent to his post.

10th Month   Empress Sadako's mother, the widow of Fujiwara no Michitaka, died.

1.11   Fujiwara no Michinaga made a pilgrimage to Kasuga Shrine

2.12   Fujiwara no Motoko became an Imperial Concubine.

16.12   Empress Sadako gave birth to her first child, Princess Osako.

All year   There were rice shortages and famines.

During the year (?)   *Minamoto no Masahiro behaved strangely when serving as Chamberlain on duty during the roll-call* (section 36).

997

25.3   Owing to the illness of Higashi Sanjō no In, a general amnesty was proclaimed.

5.4   Thanks to the amnesty, Fujiwara no Korechika and Fujiwara no Takaie were recalled to the capital.

21.4   Fujiwara no Takaie returned to the capital.

22.6   Emperor Ichijō visited Higashi Sanjō no In because of her illness.

22.6   Empress Sadako moved to the Empress's Office with Princess Osako.

6th or 7th Month   *Shōnagon and her companions amused themselves in the garden of the Empress's Office and visited the guard-house of the Left Guards* (section 49).

8th Month (?)   *Lady Ukon played the lute in the Empress's Office* (section 66).

Autumn   *Shōnagon received a message from Empress Sakado recalling the visit to the guard-house and asking her to return to the Palace* (section 55).

Between 997 (1st Month) and 998 (1st Month)   *Fujiwara no Nobutsune came to the Empress's Palace and was ridiculed by Shōnagon* (section 69).

2.11   The Government Headquarters in Kyūshū reported the repulsion of the southern barbarians.

12th Month   Fujiwara no Korechika returned to the capital.

2nd Month *Empress Sadako moved to the Empress's Office. Minamoto no Nobukata had a liaison with Lady Sakyō, but broke
with her after being teased by Shōnagon* (section 108).

2nd or 3rd Month *Fujiwara no Yukinari and Shōnagon exchanged
poems about Ōsaka Barrier* (section 89).

3rd Month *Fujiwara no Yukinari saw Shōnagon in her bedroom*
(section 35).

5.7 Empress Sadako was ill.

18.7 Emperor Ichijō was ill.

20.7 Owing to Emperor Ichijō's illness, a general amnesty was
proclaimed.

After 10th Month *Fujiwara no Masamitsu overheard Shōnagon
making an objectionable remark* (section 132).

10.12 *There was a heavy fall of snow; snow mountains were built outside the Palace, and Shōnagon predicted that the one outside the
Empress's Office would last until the 15th day of the New Year*
(section 56).

After 10th Month *Shōnagon was impressed by Minamoto no Narinobu's ability to recognize people's voices* (section 131).

3.1 Empress Sadako returned to the Palace, but without the usual
ceremonial.

9.2 Fujiwara no Akiko, Michinaga's daughter, celebrated her
coming-of-age ceremony at the age of eleven and was appointed to the 3rd Rank.

Last day of 2nd Month *Shōnagon was challenged by a poem from
Fujiwara no Kintō and other gentlemen* (section 71).

End of 2nd Month (?) *Shōnagon stayed at home secretly and Fujiwara no Tadanobu tried to discover where she was* (section 53).

5th Month *Shōnagon astonished some courtiers by recognizing a
Chinese reference* (section 90).

14.6 The Imperial Palace burnt down.

16.6 Emperor Ichijō moved to the Palace of the First Ward.

6th Month (?) *Shōnagon wrote that she had been serving for ten years
in the Palace* (section 28).

9.8   Owing to her pregnancy, Empress Sadako moved from the Empress's Office to the house of Taira no Narimasa.

9.8   *Shōnagon accompanied Empress Sadako to the house of Taira no Narimasa and found many occasions to tease their host* (section 7).

1.11   Fujiwara no Akiko entered the Palace.

7.11   Empress Sadako gave birth to Prince Atsuyasu at the house of Taira no Narimasa.

7.11   Fujiwara no Akiko was appointed Imperial Concubine.

1.12   The Great Empress Dowager died at the age of fifty-five.

1000

12.2   Empress Sadako moved to the Palace of the First Ward.

20.2   *Emperor Ichijō was given a music lesson by Fujiwara no Takatō* (section 15).

25.2   Empress Sadako was appointed First Empress, Fujiwara no Akiko became Second Empress, and Fujiwara no Nobuko became Great Empress Dowager.

3rd Month   *The dog, Okinamaro, was punished for attacking the Emperor's cat* (section 8).

27.3   Empress Sadako returned to Taira no Narimasa's house.

5.5   *Herbal balls were presented to Empress Sadako and Empress Akiko; Shōnagon exchanged poems with Empress Sadako* (section 130).

8.8   Empress Sadako returned to the Imperial Palace.

8th Month (?)   *Minamoto no Narinobu visited Shōnagon on a rainy night, but she pretended to be asleep* (section 152).

27.8   Empress Sadako returned to the house of Taira no Narimasa.

11.10   Emperor Ichijō moved into the rebuilt Palace.

15.12   Empress Sadako gave birth to a second princess.

16.12   Empress Sadako died from childbirth at the age of twenty-four.

27.12   Empress Sadako was buried in Rokuhara.

Section	Date
86	995 (2nd Month) (?)
88	995 (9th Month)
89	998 (2nd or 3rd Month)
90	999 (5th Month)
91	992 (2nd Month)
94	996 (about 7th Month)
105	995 (6th Month)
106	996 (3rd Month)
108	998 (2nd Month)
116	990 (?)
130	1000 (5th Month)
131	998 (after 10th Month)
132	998 (after 10th Month)
149	996 (4th or 5th Month)
150	994 (2nd Month)
152	1000 (8th Month) (?)
159	992 (3rd Month) (?)
167	992 (8th Month) (?)
184	Between 995 (12th Month) and 996 (12th Month)
185	994 (after 8th Month)

FURTHER READING

Beaujard, André, *Les Notes de chevet de Séi Shōnagon*', Paris, 1934.
Séi Shōnagon' : *son temps et son oeuvre*, Paris, 1934.
Brower, Robert, and Miner, Earl, *Japanese Court Poetry*, Stanford, 1961.
Cranston, Edwin, *The Izumi Shikibu Diary*, Cambridge (U.S.A.), 1969.
de Bary, William Theodore, et al., ed., *Sources of the Japanese Tradition*, New York, 1958.
Eliot, Sir Charles, *Japanese Buddhism*, London, 1959.
Frank, Bernard, *Kata-imi et kata-tagae : étude sur les interdits de direction à l'époque Heian*, Tokyo, 1958.
Keene, Donald, *Anthology of Japanese Literature*, New York, 1955.
Japanese Literature, London, 1953.
McCullough, Helen Craig, *Tales of Ise*, Stanford, 1968.
Morris, Ivan, *The World of the Shining Prince : Court Life in Ancient Japan*, Penguin Books edition, 1969.
Dictionary of Selected Forms in Classical Japanese Literature, New York and London, 1966.
Nippon Gakujutsu Shinkokai, *The Manyōshū*, Tokyo, 1940.
Omori, Annie, and Kochi Doi, *Diaries of Court Ladies of Old Japan*, Boston, 1935.
Purcell, Dr. T. A., and Aston, William, *A Literary Lady of Old Japan*, Transactions of the Asiatic Society of Japan, XVI. 3, Tokyo, 1888.
Reischauer, Edwin, and Fairbank, John, *East Asia : The Great Tradition*, Boston, 1958.
Reischauer, Edwin, *Enin's Travels in T'ang China*, New York, 1955.
Reischauer, R. K., *Early Japanese History*, Princeton, 1937.
Revon, Michel, *Anthologie de la littérature japonaise, des origines au XXe siècle*, Paris, 1928.
Sansom, G. B., *A History of Japan* (Vol. I: to 1334), London, 1958.
A Short Cultural History of Japan, London, 1931.
Seidensticker, Edward, *The Kagero Nikki : Journal of a 10th Century Noblewoman*, Tokyo, 1955.
Waley, Arthur, *The Pillow-Book of Sei Shōnagon*, London, 1928.
Japanese Poetry, London, 1919.
The Tale of Genji (originally published in 6 volumes, London, 1925–33).

Other Works in the Columbia Asian Studies Series

TRANSLATIONS FROM THE ASIAN CLASSICS

STUDIES IN ASIAN CULTURE

COMPANIONS TO ASIAN STUDIES

INTRODUCTION TO ASIAN CIVILIZATIONS
Wm. Theodore de Bary, Editor

NEO-CONFUCIAN STUDIES

Instructions for Practical Living and Other Neo-Confucian Writings by Wang Yang-ming, tr. Wing-tsit China   1963

Reflections on Things at Hand: The Neo-Confucian Anthology, comp. Chu Hsi and Lü Tsu-ch'ien, tr. Wing-tsit Chan   1967

Self and Society in Ming Thought, by Wm. Theodore de Bary and the Conference on Ming Thought. Also in paperback ed.   1970

The Unfolding of Neo-Confucianism, by Wm. Theodore de Bary and the Conference on Seventeenth-Century Chinese Thought. Also in paperback ed.   1975

Principle and Practicality: Essays in Neo-Confucianism and Practical Learning, ed. Wm. Theodore de Bary and Irene Bloom. Also in paperback ed.   1979

The Syncretic Religion of Lin Chao-en, by Judith A. Berling   1980

The Renewal of Buddhism in China: Chu-hung and the Late Ming Synthesis, by Chün-fang Yü   1981

Neo-Confucian Orthodoxy and the Learning of the Mind-and-Heart, by Wm. Theodore de Bary   1981

Yüan Thought: Chinese Thought and Religion Under the Mongols, ed. Hok-lam Chan and Wm. Theodore de Bary   1982

The Liberal Tradition in China, by Wm. Theodore de Bary   1983

The Development and Decline of Chinese Cosmology, by John B. Henderson   1984

The Rise of Neo-Confucianism in Korea, by Wm. Theodore de Bary and JaHyun Kim Haboush   1985

Chiao Hung and the Restructuring of Neo-Confucianism in Late Ming, by Edward T. Ch'ien   1985

Neo-Confucian Terms Explained: Pei-hsi tzu-i, by Ch'en Ch'un, ed. and trans. Wing-tsit Chan   1986

Knowledge Painfully Acquired: K'un-chih chi, by Lo Ch'in-shun, ed. and trans. Irene Bloom   1987

To Become a Sage: The Ten Diagrams on Sage Learning, by Yi T'oegye, ed. and trans. Michael C. Kalton   1988

The Message of the Mind in Neo-Confucian Thought, by Wm. Theodore de Bary   1989

MODERN ASIAN LITERATURE SERIES

Modern Japanese Drama: An Anthology, ed. and tr. Ted Takaya. Also in paperback ed.   1979